Ultimate React Testing with Jest

Build Reliable Web Applications Using React Testing Library, Modern Testing Patterns, Async Flows, and CI/CD Integration

Sreejith Salgunan

www.orangeava.com

First Published: January 2026

Published By: Orange Education Pvt Ltd, AVA®

Address: 9, Daryaganj, Delhi, 110002, India

275 New North Road Islington Suite 1314 London,

N1 7AA, United Kingdom

ISBN (PBK): 978-93-49887-25-1

ISBN (E-BOOK): 978-93-49887-30-5

Preface

Which cloud gives itself
to become a single raindrop,
opening a bud into fruit?

Which bare thread
takes form as the cloth
that touches millions?

Quality is this–
seeing the whole path,
where nothing becomes everything,
from first seed to final harvest.

The book, ***Mastering Quality Engineering for SAP S/4HANA*** is a journey from blueprint to real-world impact, with success measured not just by delivery, but by sustained business value. This book reflects the accumulated lessons of iterative SAP landscapes, complex enterprise architectures, and rigorous testing frameworks. Each chapter integrates technical precision and strategic clarity, with a focus on how robust testing empowers scalable and reliable SAP deployments. The aim is to equip practitioners, leaders and technical contributors to see the full lifecycle, and that is how foundational landscape decisions inform process optimization, where testing strategy drives efficiency, and how continuous improvement defines enduring quality. So, let us go through the summaries of different chapters incorporated in the book.

Chapter 1: This establishes the context for SAP's ecosystem, including core modules, integration patterns, and the architecture underpinning enterprise transformation. It provides foundational knowledge for strategic system design and process alignment.

Chapter 2: This chapter dissects SAP's layered architecture - applications, middleware, data management, and assesses how various SAP S/4HANA choices shape scalability, security, and business continuity for global deployments.

Chapter 3: This analyzes essential SAP characteristics such as: Change management, key data structures, customization capabilities, and project implementation frameworks.

Chapter 4: This chapter explores where threads weave into fabric, that is understand the core SAP business process flows, and how they express and automate organizational value from source to outcome.

Chapter 5: This chapter lays the groundwork for quality such as: Grasp key testing concepts, mindsets, and the essential vocabulary defining the quality journey from initial builds to stable deployments.

Chapter 6: This explores strategies for embedding quality early, and maintaining it throughout every phase of SAP project life cycle.

Chapter 7: This chapter explores the variety of testing types such as unit, integration, regression, UAT, and beyond.

Chapter 8: This surveys the evolving landscape of automation, cloud platforms, and analytics. Discover how tools become the rain that nourishes the scalable and reliable SAP testing.

Chapter 9: This goes deeper into test data management. Learn SAP data models, and its best practices for test data management processes which ensure that the fruit of each process is robust.

Chapter 10: This chapter uncovers the art and science of strategy. Know how to build scalable test programs for SAP projects, balancing speed, coverage, and change resilience for lasting harvests.

Chapter 11: This chapter embraces continuous delivery, that is see how testing becomes an ongoing source of quality in evolving SAP landscapes, unlocking sustainable automation and speed.

Chapter 12: This distills experience into principles, such as access to hard-earned insights, mistakes to avoid, and step-by-step wisdom for reliable SAP testing journeys.

Chapter 13: This chapter navigates complexity such as learning how to shape operating models that thrive at scale, enabling teams to deliver real-time SAP test programs with confidence and adaptability.

Chapter 14: This chapter sees the path from blueprint to delivery. Read tales and business strategies from major SAP transformation initiatives, revealing what works, and why on the journey from seed to harvest.

Chapter 15: This chapter looks toward tomorrow, that is, discovers the intersections of SAP and AI, and how innovation will shape the next generation of quality assurance, process automation, and business success.

Get a Free eBook

We hope you are enjoying your recently purchased book! Your feedback is incredibly valuable to us, and to all other readers looking for great books.

If you found this book helpful or enjoyable, we would truly appreciate it, if you could take a moment to leave a short review with a 5 star rating on Amazon. It helps us grow, and lets other readers discover our books.

As a thank you, we would love to send you a free digital copy of this book, and a **30%** discount code on your next cart value on our official websites:

www.orangeava.com

www.orangeava.in (For Indian Subcontinent)

☑ **Here's how:**

Leave a review for the book on Amazon.

Take a screenshot of your review, and send an email to **info@orangeava.com** (it can be just the confirmation screen).

Once, we receive your screenshot, we will send you the digital file, within 24 hours.

Thank you so much for your support – it means a lot to us!

Downloading the code bundles and colored images

Please follow the links or scan the QR codes to download the ***Code Bundles and Images*** of the book:

https://github.com/ava-orange-education/Mastering-Quality-Engineering-for-SAP-S-4HANA

The code bundles and images of the book are also hosted on ***https://rebrand.ly/4448ab***

In case there's an update to the code, it will be updated on the existing GitHub repository.

Errata

We take immense pride in our work at **Orange Education Pvt Ltd,** and follow best practices to ensure the accuracy of our content to provide an indulging reading experience to our subscribers. Our readers are our mirrors, and we use their inputs to reflect and improve upon human errors, if any, that may have occurred during the publishing processes involved. To let us maintain the quality and help us reach out to any readers who might be having difficulties due to any unforeseen errors, please write to us at :

errata@orangeava.com

Your support, suggestions, and feedback are highly appreciated.

DID YOU KNOW

Did you know that Orange Education Pvt Ltd offers eBook versions of every book published, with PDF and ePub files available? You can upgrade to the eBook version at **www.orangeava.com** and as a print book customer, you are entitled to a discount on the eBook copy. Get in touch with us at: **info@orangeava.com** for more details.

At **www.orangeava.com**, you can also read a collection of free technical articles, sign up for a range of free newsletters, and receive exclusive discounts and offers on Print Books and eBooks.

PIRACY

If you come across any illegal copies of our works in any form on the internet, we would be grateful if you would provide us with the location address or website name. Please contact us at **info@orangeava.com** with a link to the material.

ARE YOU INTERESTED IN AUTHORING WITH US?

If there is a topic that you have expertise in, and you are interested in either writing or contributing to a book, please write to us at **business@orangeava.com**. We are on a journey to help developers and tech professionals to gain insights on the present technological advancements and innovations happening across the globe and build a community that believes Knowledge is best acquired by sharing and learning with others. Please reach out to us to learn what our audience demands and how you can be part of this educational reform. We also welcome ideas from tech experts and help them build learning and development content for their domains.

REVIEWS

Please leave a review. Once you have read and used this book, why not leave a review on the site that you purchased it from? Potential readers can then see and use your unbiased opinion to make purchase decisions. We at Orange Education would love to know what you think about our products, and our authors can learn from your feedback. Thank you!

For more information about Orange Education, please visit **www.orangeava.com**.

Table of Contents

Chapter 1
Getting Started with SAP

Introduction

SAP is not just a software - it is the digital backbone of global commerce. Around 77% of the world's transaction revenue flows through an SAP system. This translates to over $16 trillion in daily consumer purchases. If you are working with SAP, you are not just dealing with enterprise IT; you are operating the critical infrastructure that powers the world's largest companies.

When you log into an SAP environment, you are accessing the same platform trusted by 98 of the top 100 global brands. SAP serves more than 269 million users across 425,000+ organizations. These aren't casual users - they're running core business processes across finance, supply chain, manufacturing, HR, and customer engagement. This scale and impact demand more than functional knowledge - it requires precision, engineering discipline, and system-wide awareness.

Any seasoned SAP professional will tell you: these systems are inherently complex. A typical SAP landscape spans far more than a single application. It's an integrated web of systems—SAP S/4HANA or SAP ECC backends, BW/HANA for analytics, CRM and SRM platforms, Fiori launchpads, Solution Manager, and countless custom interfaces, APIs, and legacy connections. Diagnosing a seemingly simple issue - such as a failed sales order - can involve deep-diving into the SD (Sales and Distribution), MM (Materials Management), and FICO (Financial Accounting and Controlling) modules, validating IDocs and RFCs, and debugging ABAP logic, all while staying aligned with business rules and compliance requirements.

This complexity makes systems testing in SAP fundamentally different from traditional QA. Testing in this environment is not about executing test cases in isolation. It is about validating business processes end-to-end, across interconnected modules and dynamic data flows. You cannot test Procurement without considering downstream impacts in Inventory, Finance, and Vendor Management. You cannot test Order-to-Cash without understanding pricing, delivery scheduling, billing, and revenue recognition. A fragmented approach leads to false confidence - and undetected failures.

That is why SAP quality engineering demands more than functional test scripts. It requires a thorough understanding of the architectural view of the system, a deep appreciation of how modules interact, and the ability to think like both a technologist and a business process owner. This book is not a traditional technical manual. It is designed to bridge that gap - to show how data, processes, interfaces, and users come together in a real SAP ecosystem. With this understanding, you can design test plans that reveal hidden risks, communicate issues clearly to both developers and business stakeholders, and elevate your role from tester to trusted advisor.

Structure

This chapter aims to provide you with a holistic overview of SAP landscape with the following topics:

- Overview of SAP
- Evolution of SAP Technology from Core Functional System to an ERP Platform
- Overview of SAP S/4HANA
- Understanding Enterprise Technology Ecosystem
- Understanding SAP UI Technology
- Understanding SAP Functional Areas
- Understanding SAP Roles and Responsibilities
- Understanding SAP Data Management
- SAP Change and Release Management
- Essential SAP Terminologies

Overview of SAP

When people hear "SAP," they often think of a complex, enterprise-grade software system—and they are not wrong. But from a technology perspective, SAP is much more than a software product. It is a platform, a development environment, a data processing engine, and a deeply integrated business process framework used by some of the most demanding environments in the world.

SAP stands for *Systems, Applications, and Products in Data Processing*. At its core, SAP is an integrated suite of software applications designed to help organizations manage their business operations end-to-end—from procurement to production, from finance to HR, from customer orders to shipping and billing.

Technically, SAP is built as a modular, layered system. Each module handles a specific business function (like finance or logistics), but all modules operate on a shared platform and data model. This unified design enables seamless integration of business processes across departments and geographies.

Core Architecture

An SAP system follows a three-tier architecture, and it ensures scalability, modularity, and separation of concerns between UI, processing, and storage.

- **Presentation Layer:** This is the user interface–where business users interact with the system. Traditionally accessed through the SAP GUI, modern interfaces now include SAP Fiori apps that run in a web browser.
- **Application Layer:** This is where business logic is processed. It interprets user requests, performs computations, manages transactions, and connects to the database. This layer runs on one or more application servers and is typically developed in ABAP (Advanced Business Application Programming) or Java, depending on the SAP solution.
- **Database Layer:** This stores all business data, configuration, and metadata. Earlier systems used databases such as Oracle or IBM DB2, but today SAP systems (especially SAP S/4HANA) run on SAP's in-memory database called HANA.

Key SAP Systems and Solutions

There are multiple types of SAP systems, each designed for a specific purpose:

- **SAP ECC (ERP Central Component):** The classic version of SAP's ERP platform. ECC has been widely used for over two decades and is still in use today, though it is gradually being replaced by S/4HANA.
- **SAP S/4HANA:** The next-generation ERP platform, built to leverage the HANA in-memory database. It simplifies data models and accelerates performance. Designed with Fiori UI and real-time analytics. If ECC is the traditional business engine, S/4HANA is the modern electric vehicle with a digital dashboard and real-time sensors.
- **SAP BW/4HANA:** This system is designed specifically for reporting and analytics. It gathers data from SAP and non-SAP systems, organizes it, and allows companies to run reports and dashboards. While S/4HANA focuses on daily operations (such as making sales or paying suppliers), BW/4HANA helps managers and analysts understand performance, trends, and forecasts by looking at the bigger picture.
- **SAP CRM (Customer Relationship Management):** SAP CRM is used by companies to manage customer interactions - from sales calls and marketing campaigns to customer service requests. It keeps track of leads, sales opportunities, and customer communication history.

- **SAP SRM (Supplier Relationship Management):** Like CRM but focused on suppliers instead of customers, SRM helps businesses manage their procurement and vendor relationships. It streamlines activities such as sourcing, contract management, and supplier performance monitoring.
- **SAP SCM (Supply Chain Management):** This system helps companies plan and manage their supply chain operations–including demand forecasting, production planning, and logistics. It supports collaboration between internal departments and external partners to ensure that products are delivered on time and in the right quantities.
- **SAP Fiori:** SAP Fiori is not a system, but a user experience (UX) technology. It provides a modern, web-based interface that replaces the older, more technical SAP GUI.

Evolution of SAP

SAP has evolved significantly since its founding in 1972 by five former IBM employees in Walldorf, Germany. The evolution of SAP's architecture reflects broader trends in computing technology:

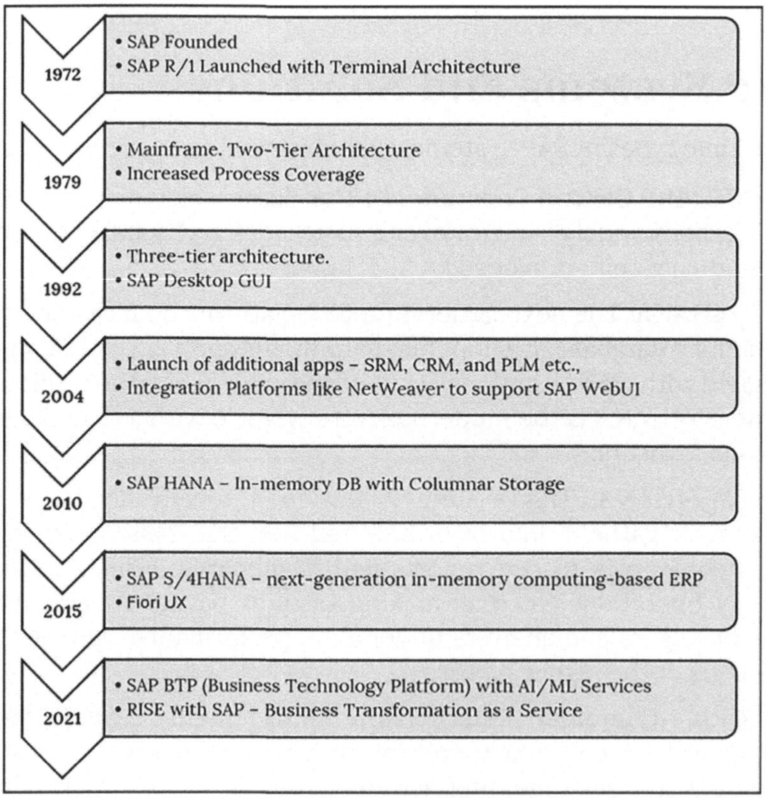

Figure 1.1: *Evolution of SAP*

SAP R/1 (1972)

This was the first version of SAP software, a financial accounting system that ran on a mainframe.

SAP R/2 (1979)

SAP introduced a more advanced version that supported multiple languages and currencies. This release expanded the range of modules beyond finance to cover other business functions. The switch from R/1 to R/2 was a more subtle evolution from a technical perspective with increases in the core functionality as SAP started to increase their customer base.

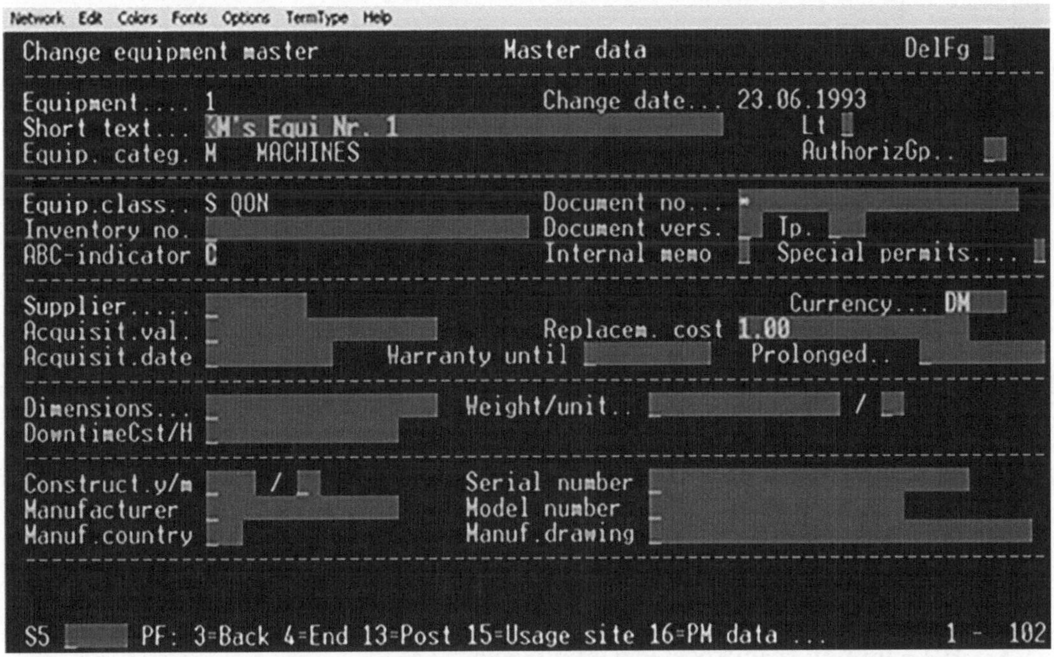

Figure 1.2: SAP R/2 UI

SAP R/3 (1992)

This version became highly successful and established SAP as a leading provider of enterprise software. R/1 and R/2 are classified as mainframe systems and R/3 as a client-server system.

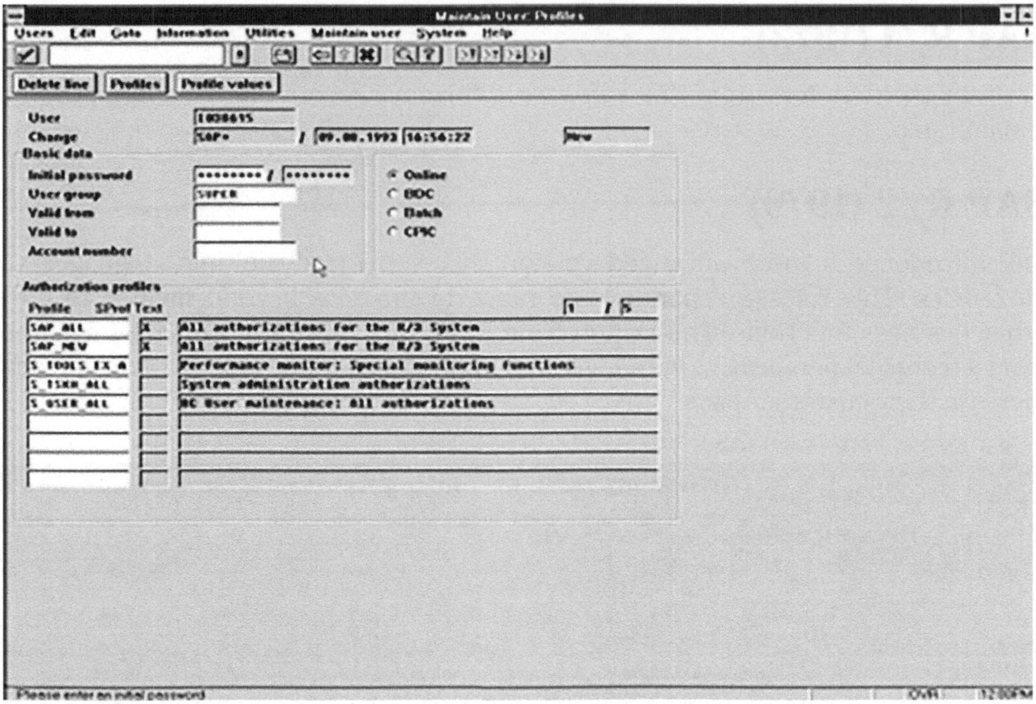

Figure 1.3: SAP R/3 UI

In R/3, business processes were modularized and integrated for end-to-end business operations. Here are some simple examples:

- **FI – finance**: Record periodic accruals.
- **CO – controlling**: Record/view expenditure against a department.
- **SD – sales and distribution**: Record a sales order for a sale to a client.
- **PP – production planning**: Plan a production schedule.
- **HR – human resources**: Pay employees.

mySAP ERP (2004)

Here, SAP rebranded its product line as mySAP ERP, emphasizing the integration of e-business capabilities and internet technologies into its ERP suite. The key focus here is:

- Need to connect with the emerging web technologies to extend the integrations with B2B or B2C channels.
- Enable Add-on products integration for data analytics. R/2 and R/3 are technically optimized as systems to record data. They are not optimized to analyze data. The late 90s saw the release of the first business warehouse

system (BW). This system is technically designed to analyze data. Organizations would use ERP to record data, and carry out simple real-time reporting and then send data in daily batches to BW for more complex analysis.

- Address the need for integration with various acquisitions and niche competitor solutions.

SAP ERP 6.0 (2005)

This version focused on enhancing user experience, introducing a more intuitive interface, and improving integration with other SAP and non-SAP systems.

Prior to the launch of HANA, it is important to reflect on where the SAP portfolio was:

- The core of ERP had been developed over decades with a continuing increase in the volume and complexity of processes covered.
- Multiple industry-specific solutions were also available.
- There was a split between applications for recording transactions (OLTP) and carrying out simple reporting and applications for information analysis (OLAP). Real-time integration was not present across the entire range of applications.
- The product portfolio became huge, in part due to multiple new products being developed by SAP and in part by many acquisitions.
- Major advancements in the standards and approach to integration and web technologies over the years.

Altogether the complexity of business systems landscapes has been massively increasing since the mainframe days. This sets the scene for what is to come with HANA and brings us to the 2010s where part of the focus from SAP is on reducing the complexity of the core product, while also continuing to advance in new technologies. HANA plays a significant role in reducing complexity and bringing real-time back to include analytics capabilities.

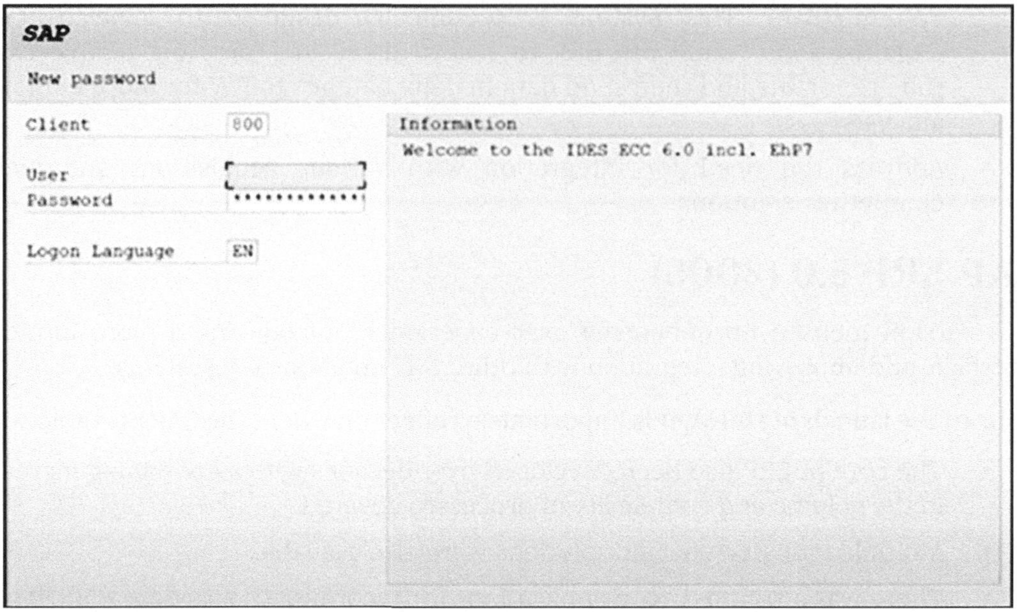

Figure 1.4: SAP ECC 6.0 GUI

SAP Business Suite

During the 2000s, the number of processes covered by the R/3 or ERP continuously increased, in addition to that, a number of additional applications were launched to provide more advanced capabilities in certain areas. SAP started to package a number of these together in the late 90s under the name, "*business suite*". The main components of business suite are:

- **Enterprise Resource Planning (ERP)**: The core including FI, HCM, Operations, and Services
- **Customer Relationship Management (CRM)**: Sales, Marketing, and Service
- **Supply Chain Management (SCM)**: Procurement, Distribution, Planning, and execution of supply operations
- **Product Life Cycle Management (PLM)**: Product ideation to production
- **Supplier Relationship Management (SRM)**: Procurement of materials, goods and services

SAP HANA (2010)

SAP HANA, introduced in 2010, was SAP's answer to several long-standing challenges in enterprise systems. Traditional databases were often slow, especially when handling large volumes of data or running complex reports, which created performance bottlenecks for business users. Data was typically stored in separate layers for transactions and analytics, making real-time insights difficult. SAP HANA changed that by combining in-memory computing, columnar storage, and real-time processing in one platform.

SAP S/4HANA (2015)

SAP S/4HANA stands for SAP *Business Suite* 4 SAP HANA. It's not just a new version of SAP - it's a major transformation in how businesses run their core operations. What makes S/4HANA unique is that it blends both technical advancements and functional changes, which is why it cannot be described as just a simple upgrade. At its core, S/4HANA runs on the high-speed, in-memory SAP HANA database, enabling real-time processing and faster analytics. It also introduces a simplified data model, removes unnecessary data tables, and modernizes how users interact with the system through a cleaner, more intuitive interface. Companies moving to S/4HANA need to decide what changes they want to adopt, it's not one-size-fits-all. Whether deployed on-premises or in the cloud, S/4HANA gives organizations a flexible, future-ready platform for running finance, supply chain, sales, and other core business processes more efficiently.

SAP Business Technology Platform and RISE with SAP (2021)

SAP BTP serves as the technical foundation for the entire SAP ecosystem, providing a unified platform for data management, analytics, application development, integration, and AI capabilities. RISE with SAP packages this technology with S/4HANA Cloud, methodology frameworks, and hyperscaler infrastructure into a comprehensive "*Business Transformation as a Service*" offering.

This combined approach aims to solve several key problems for businesses: reducing technical complexity, accelerating project cycles, minimizing upfront infrastructure investments, standardizing business processes, and enabling cloud migration at a customer's own pace while maintaining a "*clean core*" system.

Understanding Building Blocks of SAP S/4HANA

SAP S/4HANA's architecture is built on four foundational components that work together to create a comprehensive enterprise solution.

At the top tier, the Fiori UI delivers a modern, responsive user experience with role-based access, personalized applications, and interactive analytics dashboards that adapt seamlessly across devices. The Business Suite forms the functional core, integrating essential processes across finance, supply chain, sales, and HR into a unified system with simplified data models and enhanced reporting capabilities. Powering this ecosystem is the HANA Platform, an in-memory database that enables real-time processing through column-based storage and advanced analytics, eliminating traditional batch processing delays. The SAP Business Technology Platform (BTP) completes the architecture as an extension and innovation layer, offering five key pillars: database and data management, analytics, application development, integration and automation, and intelligent technologies.

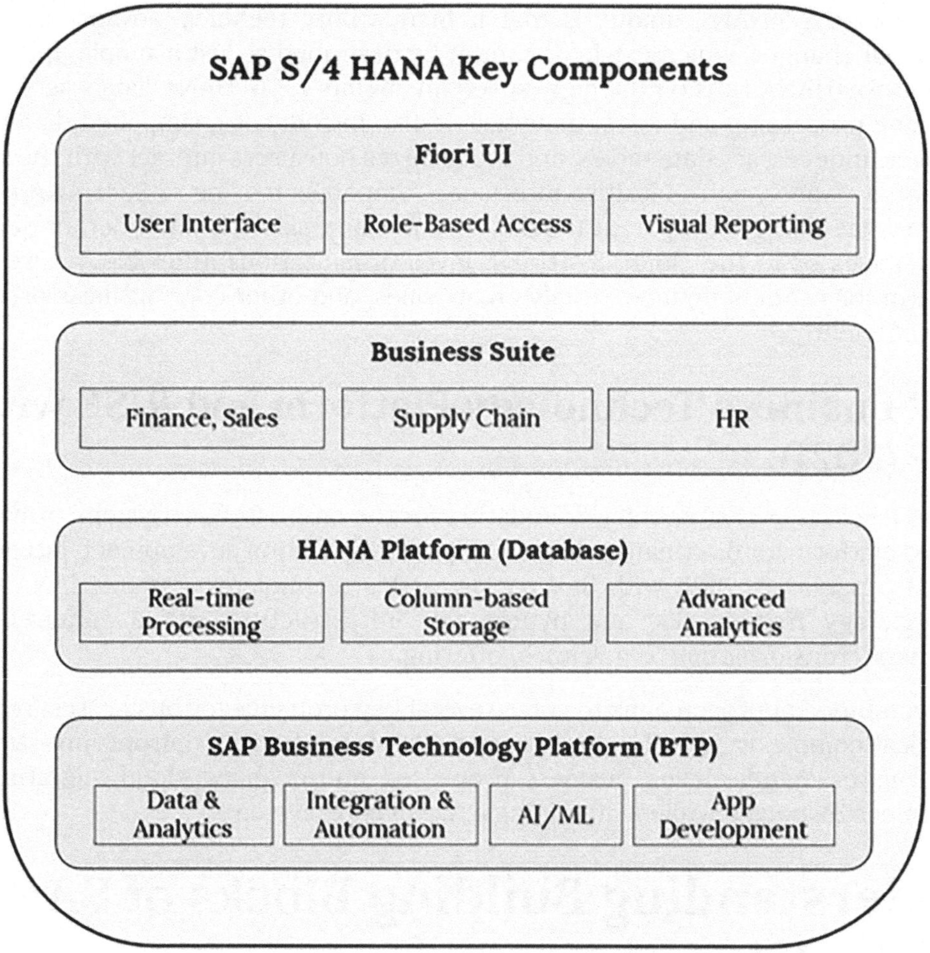

Figure 1.5: *Key Building Blocks of SAP S/4HANA*

Enterprise Technology Ecosystem

SAP provides a reliable infrastructure for enterprise-level business process management. However, it does not offer a full coverage of technological solutions for every enterprise requirement. Many enterprises rely on a vast range of applications and technologies to cater to their specific business needs. This might include customer relationship management systems, e-commerce platforms, advanced analytics, or even custom-built solutions specific to their industry.

While SAP is a leader in Enterprise Resource Planning (ERP), an enterprise might also need other tools to fully meet its needs. For example, Salesforce might be used for managing customer relationships or Tableau for data visualization. This range of applications and systems yields a diverse, yet connected, ecosystem wherein SAP must integrate seamlessly with non-SAP applications. This ensures end-to-end process efficiency, real-time data flow, and operational flexibility.

Quality Engineering (QE) plays a crucial role in this integrated ecosystem. It keeps these intricate, connected systems operating smoothly, ensuring their continued reliability and integrity. In a technological environment, where multiple applications and solutions are interconnected, a single point of failure could potentially impact the entire business. QE ensures the functionality of all integrations and conformity to business and regulatory standards through comprehensive testing. Essentially, QE acts as the connecting gum, ensuring that all interconnected systems function efficiently together and keeping risks at bay.

Now, it is important to understand how SAP integration has evolved over time to facilitate this interconnected enterprise ecosystem. The diagram here provides you a brief overview.

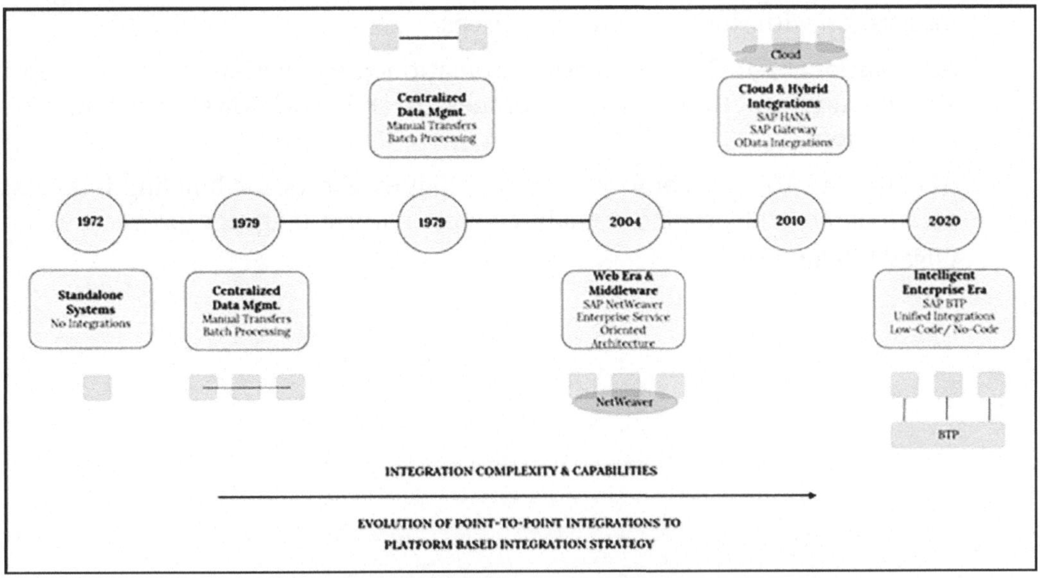

Figure 1.6: *Evolution of SAP Integrations*

In contemporary businesses, enterprise integration platforms such as SAP Business Technology Platform (BTP) can enable a unified digital ecosystem by harnessing the strengths of both SAP and non-SAP solutions.

In the following section and subsequent chapters, we will delve deeper into SAP BTP and advanced concepts related to the enterprise technology ecosystem.

Overview of SAP Business Technology Platform (BTP)

SAP BTP is a unified, comprehensive cloud platform that serves as the technical foundation of the entire SAP ecosystem. Introduced in January 2021, BTP consolidates SAP's cloud technologies into a single platform, enabling businesses to integrate, extend, and build applications while leveraging advanced technologies such as AI, analytics, and automation.

Here are the core building blocks of BTP:

- **Application Development and Integration:** Enables in building custom applications and connecting various SAP systems using Low Code capabilities.
- **Analytics:** Tools such as SAP Analytics Cloud within BTP offer insightful dashboards, predictive analytics, and planning features, to help in making data-driven decisions.
- **Database and Data Management:** To handle vast amounts of structured and unstructured data. BTP includes tools such as SAP HANA Cloud for in-memory data processing, SAP Data Warehouse Cloud for real-time reporting, and integration with third-party data sources.
- **Automation:** SAP Build Process Automation (BPA) within BTP can help in streamlining repetitive business processes and workflows with Low Code automation.
- **AI/ML:** SAP BTP's in-built AI/ML capabilities allows for building intelligent solutions around predictive maintenance, natural language processing, and image recognition.

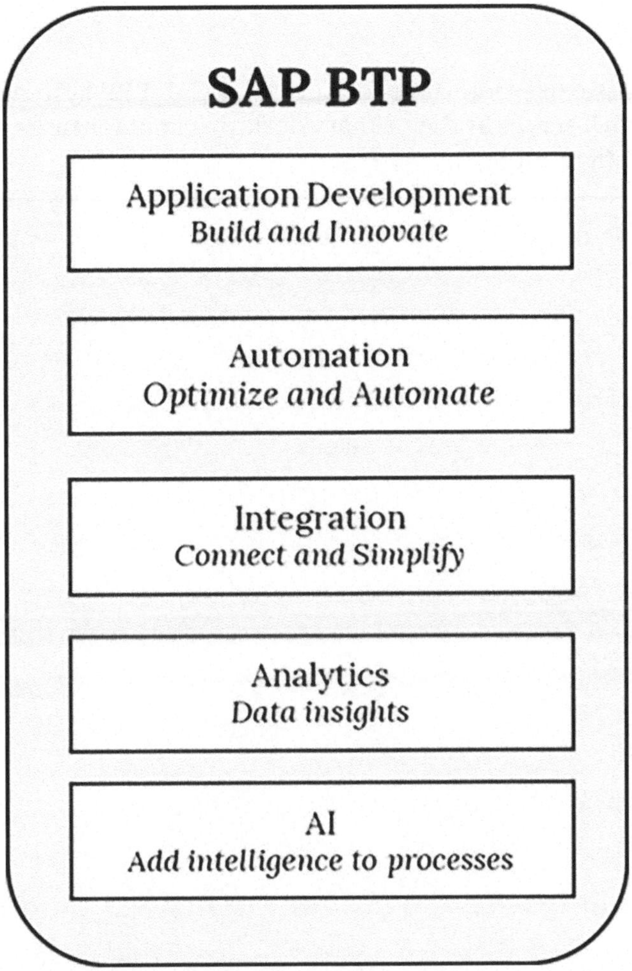

Figure 1.7: *Building Blocks of SAP BTP*

Understanding SAP User Interfaces

SAP UI technology has undergone significant evolution over the years, transitioning from function-heavy, technical interfaces to modern, and user-centric designs. The journey began with SAP GUI, introduced in the early days of SAP ERP systems, offering a consistent interface for desktop-based enterprise applications. However, over time, it has proved to acquire its complexity and steep learning curve, catering more to technical users than business users. Hence, the need for more modern SAP Fiori UI for SAP S/4HANA applications.

SAP GUI

SAP GUI is the classic user interface for accessing SAP ERP systems, first introduced in the 1990s. SAP GUI serves as the primary desktop client for tasks such as data entry, reporting, and configuration.

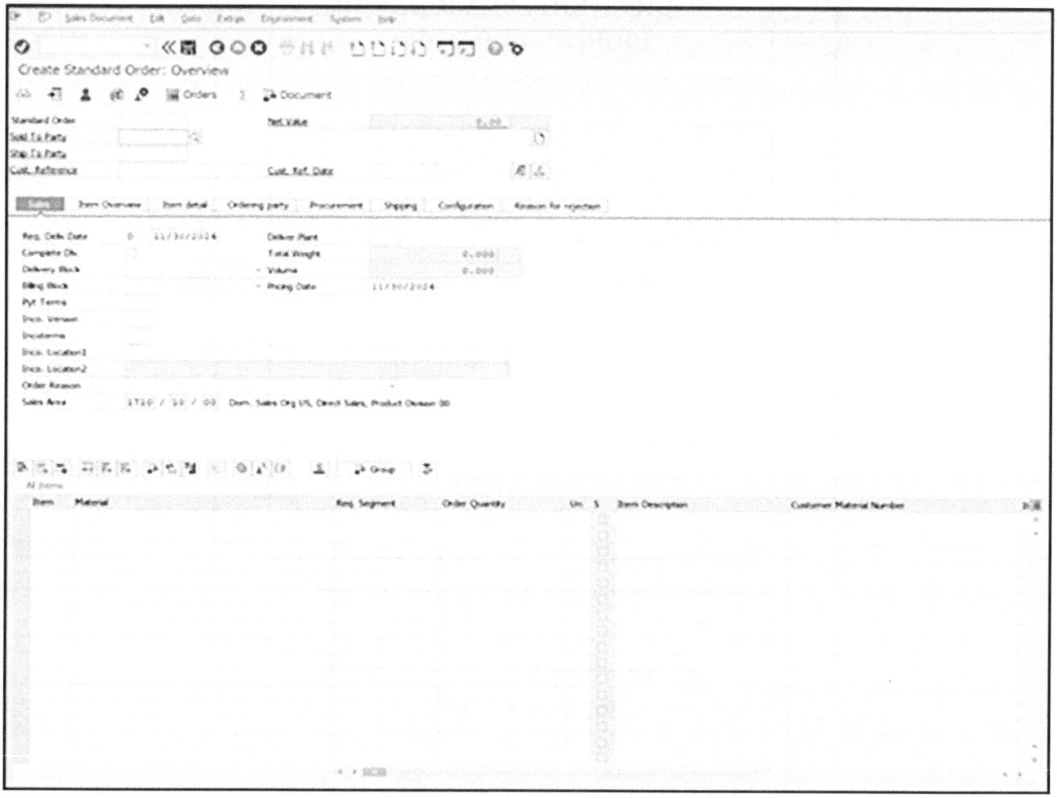

Figure 1.8: *Classic SAP GUI*

SAP Web-Based UI Frameworks

There are two key UI frameworks found in SAP Web UI-based applications.

SAP Web UI is largely HTML-based, whereas SAP NetWeaver UI supports broader frameworks, including Web Dynpro and SAP Portal. SAP Web UI is primarily used in SAP CRM and other applications for browser-based access to business processes. The following figure depicts an example of SAP Web UI based application:

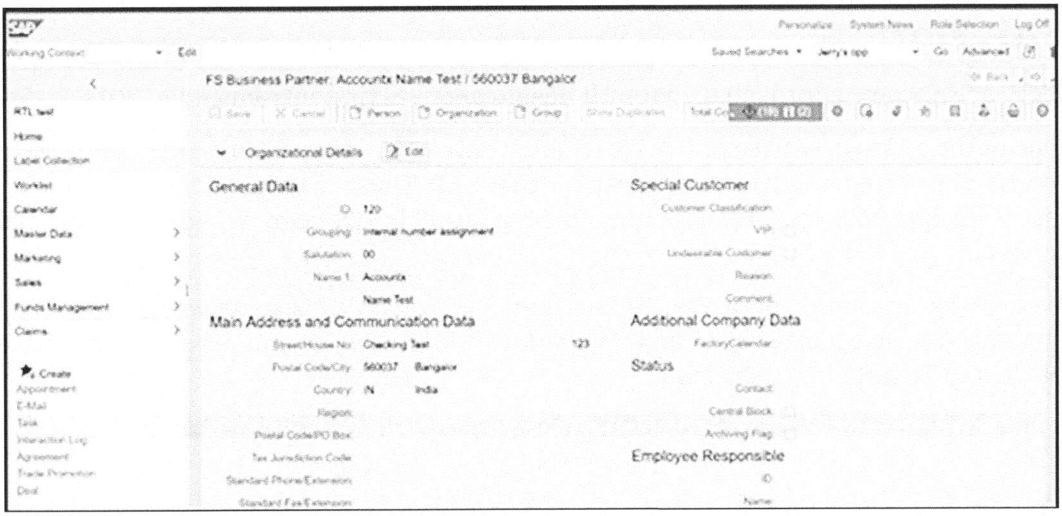

Figure 1.9: SAP Web UI-based UI

Here is an example of SAP NetWeaver-based application:

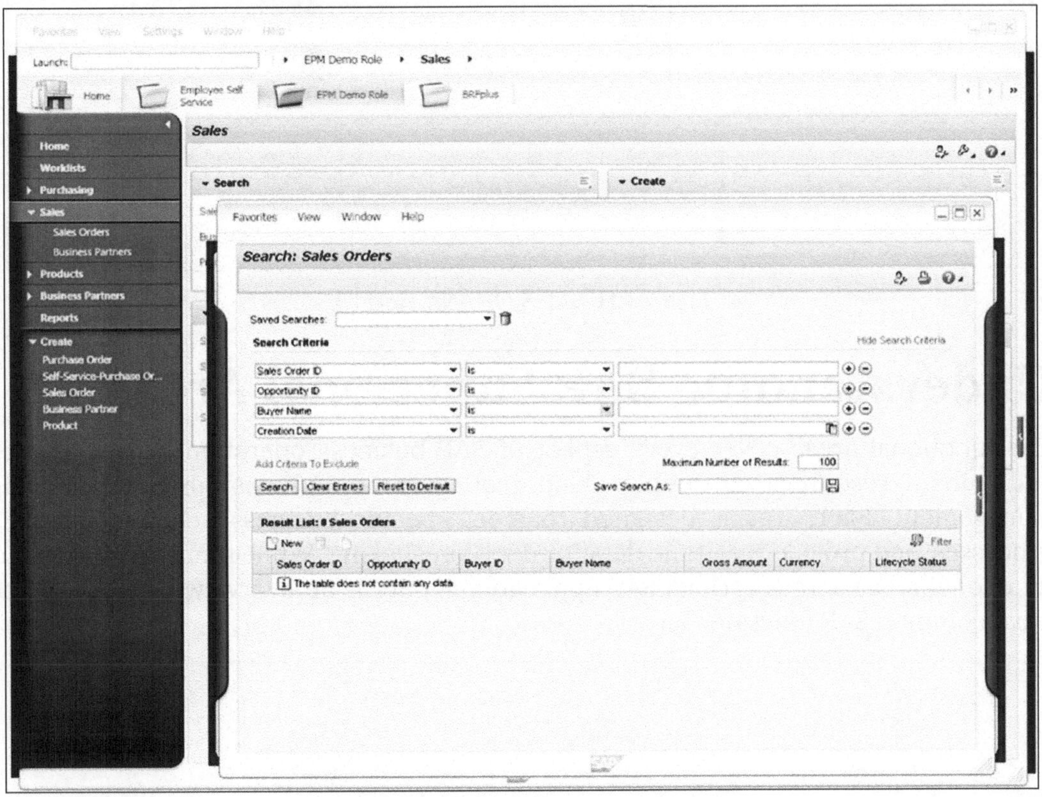

Figure 1.10: SAP Netweaver-powered UI

SAP Fiori

Fiori is SAP's new approach for Web UI design and was first introduced in 2013.

One of the main objectives of Fiori is to allow developers to quickly create '`apps`' as an interface for specific activities or tasks within SAP. These apps can feature improved visual design, role-specific actions and be adaptable between desktop, tablet, and mobile.

We will discuss more about Firori's functional and technical aspects in the upcoming chapters because it plays quite an important role in the design and development phase of Quality Engineering projects.

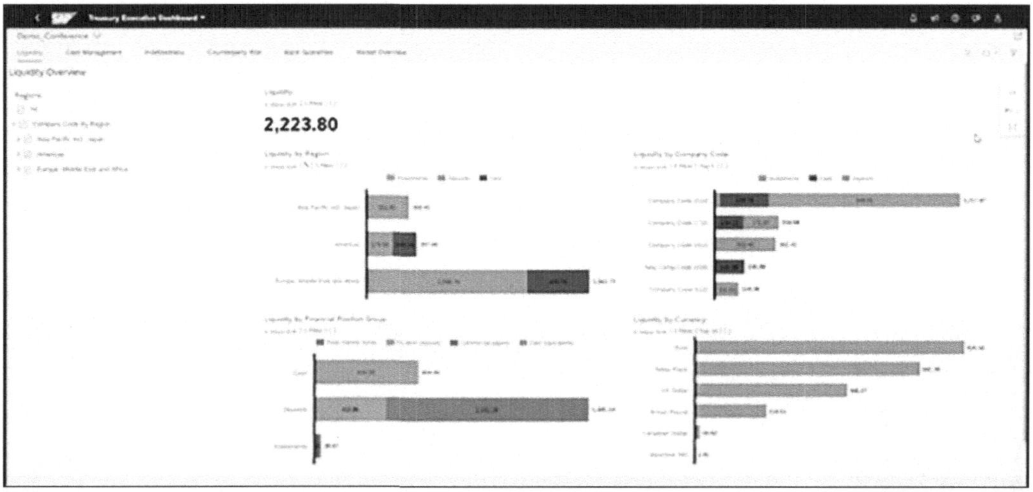

Figure 1.11: SAP S/4HANA *Fiori* UI

Understanding SAP Functional Areas

The functional areas cover every aspect of SAP business operations, from finance and human resources to supply chain management and customer relationship management. Each area is designed to meet specific business needs, streamline processes, and provide real-time data for decision-making. While there are numerous functional areas across various SAP applications, here is an overview of some of the most common SAP functional areas:

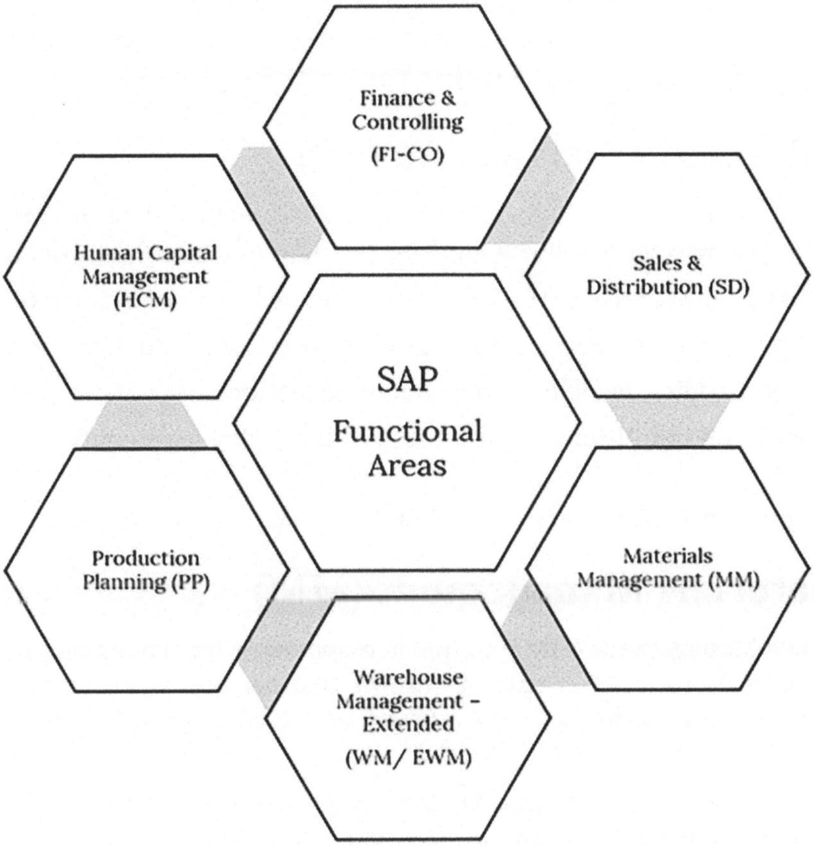

Figure 1.12: *Common Functional Areas in SAP*

SAP Financial Accounting and Controlling (FI-CO)

The Financial Accounting and Controlling (FI-CO) module is at the core of SAP's ERP system and manages all financial transactions as well as cost management within an organization. Key functions of the FI module include:

- **General Ledger (G/L)**: Tracks and records all financial transactions.
- **Accounts Payable (AP)**: Manages vendor invoices and payments.
- **Accounts Receivable (AR)**: Handles customer invoices and payments.
- **Asset Accounting (AA)**: Manages fixed assets and their depreciation.
- **Cost Center Accounting (CCA)**: Tracks costs incurred within specific areas of the business.
- **Profit Center Accounting (PCA)**: Analyzes profitability across different parts of the business.

- **Internal Orders**: Monitors costs for specific projects or internal tasks.
- **Product Costing**: Calculates costs associated with the production of goods.
- **Integration Touchpoints:** MM | SD | PP

SAP Sales and Distribution (SD)

The Sales and Distribution (SD) module manages all aspects of the sales process, from order creation to delivery and invoicing. The key functions of SD include:

- **Sales Order Management**: Tracks customer orders from creation to fulfilment.
- **Shipping and Delivery**: Manages product shipments and delivery processes.
- **Billing**: Handles invoicing and payment collection.
- **Pricing and Conditions**: Determines product pricing, discounts, and payment terms.
- **Integration Touchpoints:** FI | MM | PP

SAP Materials Management (MM)

The **Materials Management (MM)** module is responsible for managing procurement, inventory, and material master data. It ensures that organizations maintain efficient supply chain operations, manage stock levels, and control procurement costs. Key functions of MM include:

- **Procurement (Purchasing)**: Manages the purchasing process, from vendor selection to order creation.
- **Inventory Management**: Tracks the movement of materials and monitors stock levels.
- **Invoice Verification**: Matches supplier invoices with goods receipts to ensure payment accuracy.
- **Material Requirements Planning (MRP)**: Calculates the materials needed to meet production demands.
- **Integration Touchpoints:** FI | SD | PP

SAP Warehouse Management (WM/EWM)

SAP Warehouse Management (WM) and Extended Warehouse Management (EWM) are responsible for streamlining warehouse operations such as managing inventory, storage, and movement. The key functions of Warehouse Management include:

- **Warehouse Structure Management**: Create and manage storage types, storage bins.

- **Inventory Management Tasks**: Stock Overview, Counting, Reconciliation, and more.
- **Goods Receipt and Goods Issue**: Movement of incoming/outgoing stocks.
- **Picking/Packing**: Order picking based on FIFO/LIFO/ Custom strategies.
- **Integration with Production Planning and Quality Management**: Staging raw materials for production orders, storing finished goods for quality inspections, and more.
- **Integration Touchpoints:** MM | SD | TM, along with PP | QM

SAP Production Planning (PP)

SAP Production Planning (PP) facilitates the planning, execution, and control of manufacturing processes. Key functions of PP include:

- **Production Scheduling**: The creation of production schedules based on demand and available resources.
- **Work Centers**: A work center is a physical or logical unit within the production environment where specific operations or tasks are performed.
- **Capacity Planning**: Capacity planning is used to ensure that there is enough resource availability to meet production demands.
- **Shop Floor Control**: SAP PP enables real-time tracking of production activities, providing insights into production status, material availability, and equipment performance.
- **Routing**: Routing defines the steps involved in the production process, including the machines, labor, and materials needed for each operation.
- **Integration Touchpoints:** MM | SD | CO

SAP Plant Maintenance (PM)

SAP Plant Maintenance (PM) is another essential module in SAP that focuses on maintaining plant equipment and ensuring that machinery operates efficiently throughout its lifecycle. The key functions of PP include:

- **Work Order Management**: Work orders are used to manage maintenance tasks, whether preventive, corrective, or emergency repairs.
- **Preventive Maintenance**: Preventive maintenance is essential to avoid unexpected breakdowns.
- **Corrective Maintenance**: Corrective maintenance occurs when equipment fails unexpectedly.
- **Integration Touchpoints:** MM | PP | SD | CO

SAP Human Capital Management (HCM or simply HR)

The Human Resources (HR) module, also known as SuccessFactors in newer cloud-based versions, is designed to manage the entire employee lifecycle. This includes everything from recruitment and onboarding to payroll and employee development. The key features of HR include:

- **Personnel Administration**: Manages employee records and personal information.
- **Organizational Management**: Tracks company structure, job positions, and reporting relationships.
- **Payroll**: Manages employee salaries, deductions, and tax calculations.
- **Time Management**: Tracks employee work hours, attendance, and leaves.
- **Talent Management**: Facilitates employee training, performance evaluations, and career development.
- **Integration Touchpoints:** FICO (Finance and Controlling)

In summary, while SAP can be logically divided into various functional areas, it is important to recognize that these areas are deeply interconnected to streamline end-to-end business processes. Although different functional teams often focus on their specific domains, most of the activities within these areas impact and share data with other functional areas to complete the broader business workflows. This interconnected nature underscores the critical role of Quality Engineering teams in ensuring not just the quality within individual functional areas but also the seamless integration between them.

Understanding SAP User Roles and Responsibilities

SAP systems require clearly defined user roles and permissions to function effectively in organizations. These roles determine who can access specific functions and data, ensuring system security and operational efficiency. This overview explains how SAP user roles are typically structured to support business processes, and maintain appropriate access controls.

- **SAP End Users:** End users are the most common SAP users who directly interact with the system. They perform tasks such as data entry, reporting, and transaction processing based on their department's requirements.
- **SAP Super Users:** Super users are typically experienced end users who have a broader understanding of SAP functionalities, and can assist others with system-related issues. They serve as a bridge between the business process owners and IT support teams.

- **SAP Business Process Owners (BPOs):** Business Process Owners (BPOs) are responsible for the oversight of specific business processes within the SAP system.
- **SAP Functional Consultants:** Functional consultants are responsible for configuring SAP modules to meet specific business needs. They focus on understanding the requirements of different business units and configuring the SAP system to meet those needs.
- **SAP Technical Consultants:** Technical consultants are responsible for the technical aspects of the SAP system, including system performance, customization, and integrations with other enterprise systems.
- **SAP Security and Authorization Roles:** Security and authorization roles define who has access to which data and functionality within the SAP system. Proper access control is essential for maintaining data privacy and ensuring compliance with regulatory standards.
- **SAP System Administrators:** System administrators are responsible for the overall health and maintenance of the SAP system, ensuring that it runs efficiently and that all technical aspects, such as servers and databases, are well-maintained.
- **SAP Project Managers:** Project Managers oversee the implementation and upgrading of SAP systems. They coordinate the efforts of various teams, manage timelines, and ensure that the project aligns with the business objectives.

Understanding SAP Data Management

SAP's evolution in data management has gone from a siloed, transactional approach to a more unified, real-time, and analytics-driven model, leveraging advanced technologies such as in-memory computing, AI, and cloud-based solutions. Here is a quick overview of data structures in typical SAP systems.

- **SAP R/3 Systems (Pre-S/4HANA):** SAP R/3 used traditional relational databases such as Oracle, DB2, and SQL Server. Here, data was stored in traditional table-based data models where entities like customer orders, financial records, and inventory were stored in discrete tables. Data management was more siloed and required heavy customization to handle different types of data.

  SAP wanted to focus on integrating data across different modules (for example, Materials Management, Sales and Distribution) but did not have an advanced, unified Master Data Management (MDM) strategy due to technical constraints. This led to fragmented master data that could exist in multiple systems.

- **SAP NetWeaver and SAP BW (SAP Business Warehouse):** The NetWeaver platform introduced a more flexible approach for handling diverse data sources, including non-SAP systems, using tools such as SAP PI (Process Integration) and SAP BW (Business Warehouse). SAP BW emerged as a dedicated tool for managing large volumes of historical and transactional data. It allowed organizations to store and analyze data in a central repository, providing better reporting and business intelligence capabilities.

  However, these approaches, with time, become a constraint for SAP and its customers mainly due to the time-intensive ETL (Extract-Transform-Load) functions and data integrity concerns.

- **SAP HANA and Real-Time Data Processing:** SAP significantly re-architected their data models with their in-house Database system called SAP HANA, especially for organizations with large amounts of data. With this initiative, SAP brought in-memory computing capabilities that allow for real-time processing of massive data volumes. This also eliminated the need for traditional ETL processes and drastically improved data access speeds.
- **SAP S/HANA for Further Simplification of Data Models:** With S/4HANA, SAP introduced simplified data models by removing redundant tables, indexes, and aggregate layers. The result was reduced complexity, faster processing times, and improved data management efficiency. SAP also introduced advanced data governance through tools like SAP Data Hub and SAP Master Data Governance.

The following figure summarizes the evolution of data management within SAP environments:

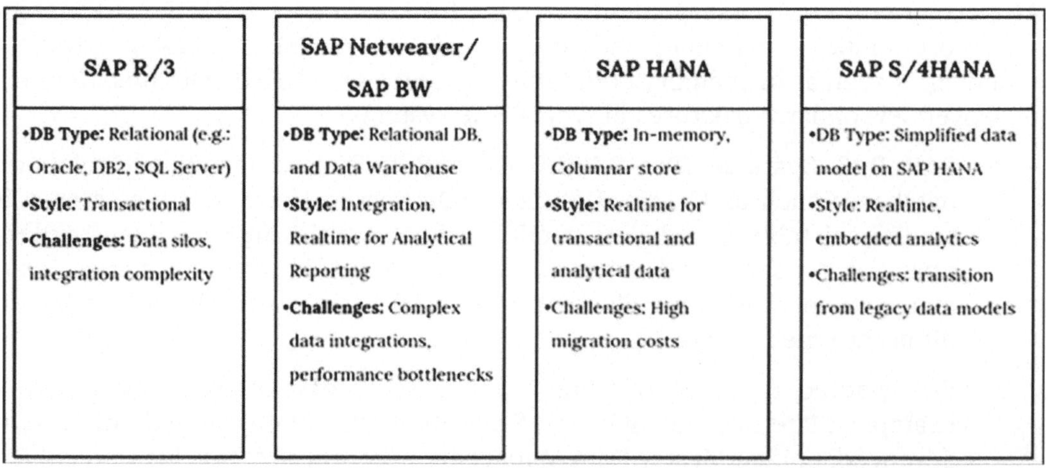

Figure 1.13: *SAP Data Management Evolution*

Recent Innovations (2022-Present)

SAP has further evolved its data architecture through:

- Integration with cloud data platforms (SAP Data Intelligence)
- AI-powered data quality and governance capabilities
- API-first approach to data access and integration
- Hybrid transactional/analytical processing (HTAP) optimization

Understanding Change Management in SAP

SAP Change Management is a structured framework that allows organizations to implement changes to their SAP systems safely and efficiently. It enables businesses to incorporate both SAP's innovations and their own custom requirements while maintaining system stability and integrity.

Evolution of SAP Change Management

- **Early Days (R/1 and R/2)**: Rigid processes prioritizing stability through manual updates.
- **Middle Era**: Introduction of tools like Solution Manager as complexity grew.
- **Modern Approach**: Emphasis on flexibility and automation with DevOps practices, CI/CD pipelines, and CloudALM for better coordination.

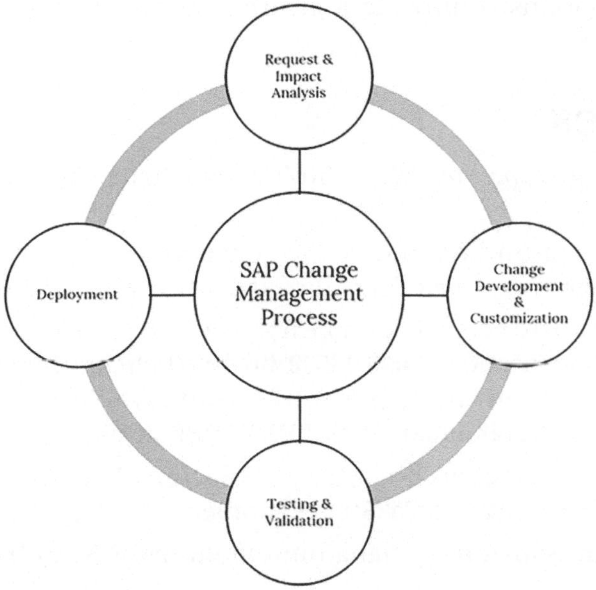

Figure 1.14: *Change Management Process in SAP Systems*

Figure 1.14 highlights how a custom development in SAP systems is built and deployed.

Common Customization Methods

- **Configurations:** A configuration change involves adjusting system settings using SAP's built-in tools, such as changing field layouts, setting up organizational structures, or defining custom workflows, all without coding.
- **Development:** For more complex needs, custom development is used, where developers create custom programs, reports, or enhancements using tools like ABAP (Advanced Business Application Programming) or modern frameworks like SAPUI5 for user interfaces.
- **Enhancements:** SAP also supports customizations through Enhancement Frameworks, BAdIs (Business Add-Ins), and user exits, which allow changes without directly modifying standard code, ensuring easier upgrades and maintenance. Properly managing customizations helps strike a balance between meeting business needs and maintaining system stability.

Conclusion

This chapter covered how SAP has evolved from a basic ERP system into a modern digital platform focused on cloud technology, enterprise integration, and AI/ML. It highlighted the transition from early mainframe-based systems such as R/1, R/2, and R/3 to the advanced, in-memory computing platform SAP S/4HANA.

The next chapter will dive deeper into SAP system architecture, data models, and deployment options to provide a clearer understanding of these enterprise systems.

References

- https://blogs.sap.com/2020/06/04/sap-hana-and-s-4-hana-a-simple-guide/
- https://community.sap.com/t5/crm-and-cx-blogs-by-sap/direct-navigation-in-crm-webui-crm-fiori-and-c4c/ba-p/13321618
- https://support.sap.com/en/release-upgrade-maintenance.html?anchorId=section_1464013573 https://help.sap.com/docs/SLTOOLSET/5f1948a3e0c94f3babd9ebb6f3c55d47/67bca55286b9ac44e10000000a44176d.html?version=CURRENT_VERSION
- https://help.sap.com/docs/SAP_Solution_Manager/c3c5ec585ee248228ddb6c3f08073ea9/ccf7a2802be041bf9ec9bd5734ce0921.html
- https://fioriappslibrary.hana.ondemand.com/sap/fix/externalViewer/#wizard
- https://inui.io/sap-facts-statistics/

CHAPTER 2

SAP Applications and Architecture

Introduction

An IDC study highlights that 55% of SAP S/4HANA project failures are traced back to inadequate understanding of underlying technical architecture, underscoring the critical need for QA teams to master these concepts early in project lifecycles. This knowledge is foundational, not optional. Because it reveals how key components such as data structures, project frameworks, and integrations interconnect and operate within SAP landscapes. Without this insight, testing efforts risk missing vital dependencies and critical issues that could disrupt business operations.

In this chapter, we will explore the technical architecture of SAP systems, data models, deployment models, and integrations.

Structure

This chapter is designed to provide a solid understanding of the key SAP applications and frameworks that Quality Engineering (QE) teams commonly use - either directly or indirectly during SAP testing and validation projects. We will cover the following topics:

- Enterprise Landscape with SAP Systems
- SAP S/4HANA Architecture
- SAP HANA Architecture
- SAP Data Models
- SAP S/4HANA Deployment Models
- SAP Application Lifecycle Management
- SAP Activate
- SAP BTP

- SAP Solution Manager
- SAP Cloud ALM

Enterprise Landscape with SAP Systems

SAP systems form the backbone of enterprise landscapes, offering comprehensive technical solutions to manage and integrate core business processes. From finance and supply chain management to human resources and customer experience, SAP provides an extensive suite of tools that ensure seamless data flow, real-time insights, and operational efficiency. These tools include SAP S/4HANA, SAP SuccessFactors, SAP Ariba, SAP Customer Experience (CX), and many others.

The following figure illustrates a typical enterprise landscape of SAP ERP, Line of Businesses (LOBs), and Enterprise connectivity solutions:

Figure 2.1: *Overview of an Enterprise with SAP Systems*

In an enterprise landscape with SAP, key components would include:

- **SAP S/4HANA or SAP ECC serves as the digital core**: It connects multiple functions such as finance, manufacturing, logistics, and sales, ensuring unified and streamlined operations. For enterprises still transitioning to SAP S/4HANA, legacy systems such as SAP ECC also play this role.
- **Line-of-Business (LoB) Solutions**: Beyond the core, specialized Line-of-Business (LoB) solutions extend SAP's reach across specific domains. These solutions connect to the core system, enabling cross-functional integration that aligns departmental processes with enterprise goals. For example,
    - **SAP SuccessFactors** for human capital management (HCM) offers capabilities such as talent management and employee experience.
    - **SAP Ariba** facilitates procurement and supplier collaboration with automated workflows and supplier networks.
    - **SAP Customer Experience (CX)** integrates CRM, e-commerce, and marketing functions for enhanced customer engagement.
- **SAP Business Technology Platform (BTP)**: It acts as the glue binding the ecosystem together, providing a unified framework for data integration, application development, process automation, and advanced analytics, ensuring connectivity across systems and third-party applications.

SAP S/4HANA Architecture

SAP S/4HANA is built with a streamlined three-layer architecture to address the complex, interconnected, and dynamic needs of modern enterprises. This architecture includes:

- **Database Layer**: Powered by the in-memory SAP HANA database, it ensures high-speed processing and real-time data access.
- **Application Layer**: The core where all business logic, processes, and rules are executed, managing tasks including finance, procurement, and logistics.
- **Presentation Layer**: Delivered through SAP Fiori, it provides a user-friendly interface for seamless interaction across devices.

Let us take a high-level look at the technical architecture of SAP S/4HANA by examining its core components - data structures, application engines, and user interface frameworks:

- **SAP HANA:** Serving as the foundation, SAP HANA is an in-memory database platform that powers S/4HANA. It enables high-speed processing for both transactional and analytical data, reducing the need for separate systems.

- **SAP S/4HANA ABAP Layer:** This is the development environment where custom business logic is built using ABAP (Advanced Business Application Programming). In S/4HANA, ABAP has evolved to support modern development practices and in-memory optimization. A key feature here is Core Data Services (CDS), which provide a powerful way to define semantic data models directly on top of the HANA database for real-time access and reuse.
- **SAP Fiori Layer:** SAP Fiori delivers a modern, role-based user experience across devices. It provides intuitive, responsive apps that replace traditional SAP GUI transactions, making the system easier to use.
- **End-User Access:** Users can interact with SAP S/4HANA through web browsers, mobile apps, or desktop clients, offering flexible and seamless access to business applications from anywhere.

The following figure highlights how the core components of SAP systems connected across enterprise architecture layers:

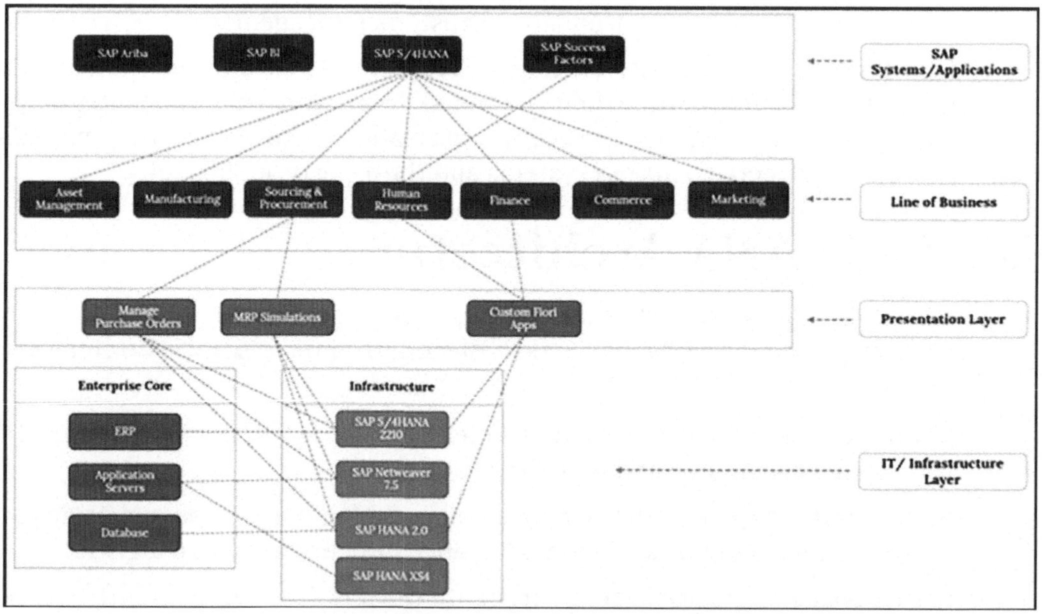

Figure 2.2: *SAP S/4HANA Architecture Model*

The following figure highlights the technical architecture covering the key aspects we briefly covered so far:

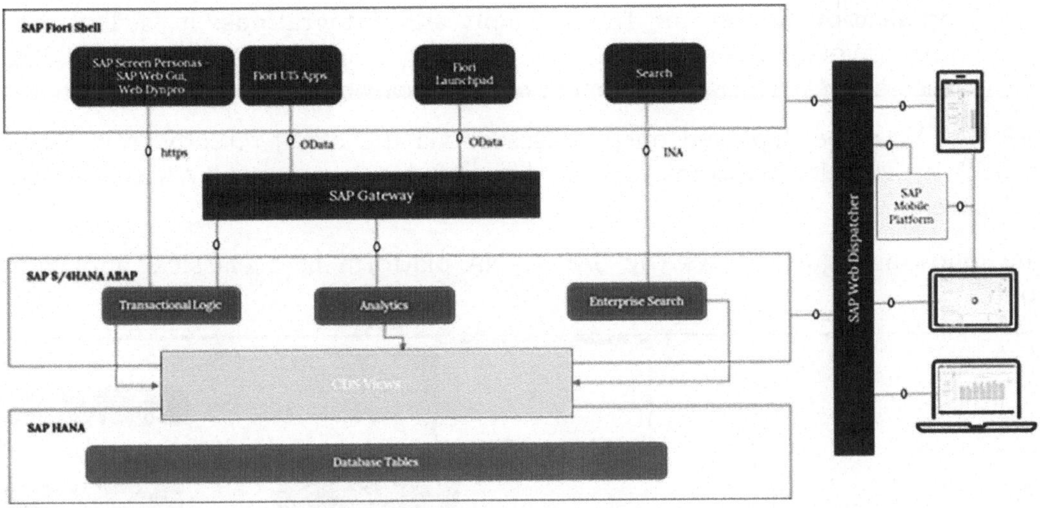

Figure 2.3: *High-Level Architecture Stack of SAP S/4HANA*

SAP HANA Architecture

Often, SAP HANA is thought of as just the database, but it is much more than that.

"*Why does* SAP HANA's *in-memory approach matter*?" Imagine a traditional database as a large warehouse where you have to search through every shelf to find a specific item. SAP HANA's columnar storage is like having everything sorted by type, allowing for lightning-fast retrieval.

Here is an overview of core components and concepts:

- **Columnar Storage**: SAP HANA uses columnar storage, which organizes data by columns instead of rows. For example, "*reading only the relevant pages in a book instead of every page*". This approach is a key feature of SAP HANA's in-memory database. With columnar storage, the system can quickly access and process large amounts of data, improving the performance of queries and analytics by focusing only on the relevant columns. This architecture helps businesses run complex reports and transactions much faster than traditional row-based databases.
- **Index Server**: This is the central server responsible for processing SQL/MDX queries, managing data storage, and providing transaction management, session handling, and data consistency.
- **Preprocessors and Additional Services**: Handle tasks such as text analysis and extraction.
- **Name Server:** Manages the distributed system landscape and keeps track of topology, such as information about where data resides in the cluster.

- **Application Server for Development and Integrations**: It facilitates the creation of data-centric applications by providing web-based tools and direct access to SAP HANA's in-memory database capabilities.

SAP HANA can be deployed on-premises or via the cloud directly from SAP or through hyperscaler platforms such as Microsoft Azure, Amazon AWS, Google GCP, and more.

The following figure shows the SAP HANA platform in a classical application context:

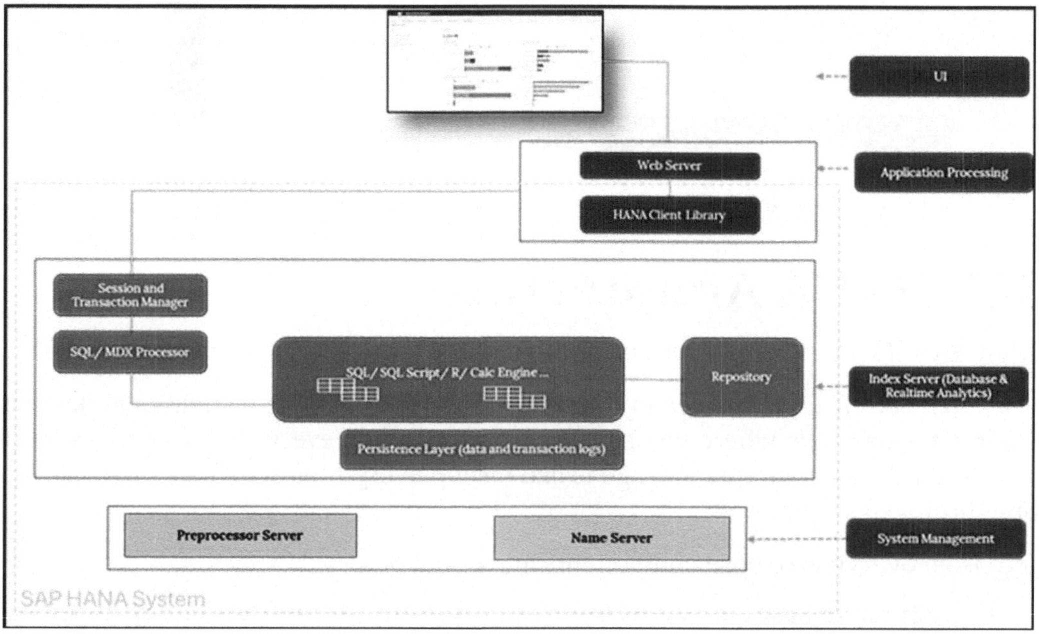

Figure 2.4: SAP HANA *Architecture Model*

Let us try to understand how SAP HANA communicates with the UIs in comparison to traditional methods. Traditional database applications use interfaces such as ODBC and JDBC with SQL to manage and query their data. The following figure shows the common architecture with such applications:

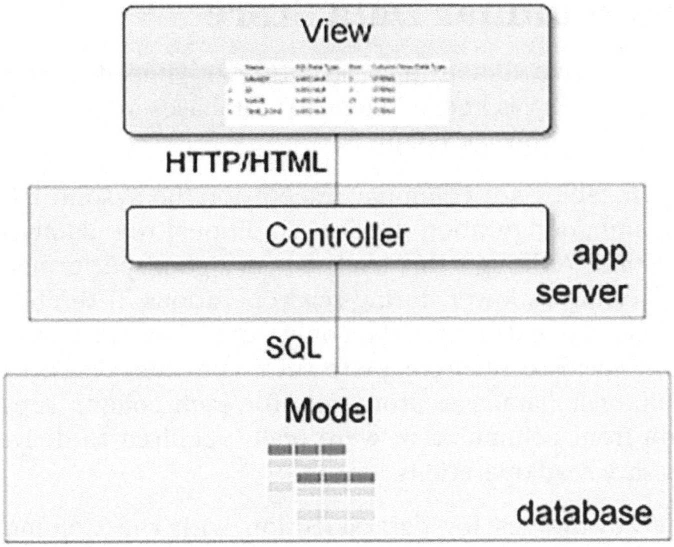

Figure 2.5: *Traditional Communication with ODBC/ JDBC (from help.sap.com)*

SAP HANA greatly extends the traditional database server role. SAP HANA functions as a comprehensive platform for the development and execution of native data-intensive applications that run efficiently in SAP HANA. By restructuring the application architecture in this way, not only do you gain from the increased performance due to the integration with the data source, but you can also eliminate the overhead of the middle-tier between the user-interface (the view) and the data-intensive control logic, as shown in the following figure.

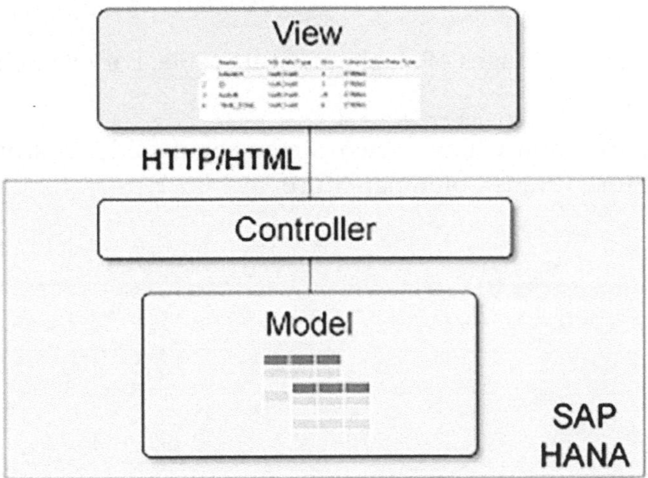

Figure 2.6: SAP HANA System Communication *(from help.sap.com)*

SAP HANA Columnar Data Store

A database table is a two-dimensional structure organized in rows and columns, whereas computer memory is linear. Relational databases organize data in tables that can store data records in rows or columns.

In SAP HANA, most tables are columnar, except for the system tables (a table that stores meta data and configuration details). Traditional row databases store data in a row as one "*bundle*". Although this leads to very good performance during write operations, its efficiency is lower during read operations. If the table has too many columns, and you need to extract the data only from some of those columns, classical row databases still need to read complete rows and then discard the unnecessary data. Because columnar databases store data for each column separately, they can retrieve only data from columns that were really required to deliver the response, avoiding unnecessary read operations.

In summary, the advantages for data selection with the Columnar store are as follows:

- Only the relevant columns are accessed when running a query, reducing unnecessary reads.
- Since columns are stored separately, projections (queries on a subset of columns) are faster.
- Any column can act as an index, eliminating the need for single-column indices persisted on disk. Multi-column indices, however, persisted but do not require manual maintenance.
- In many cases, columnar storage eliminates the need for additional index structures altogether.

There are certain disadvantages of a column-store table. For example, insert-updates are not easy.

The following figure shows how a two-dimensional table is stored in computer memory in Row-Store versus Columnar-Store:

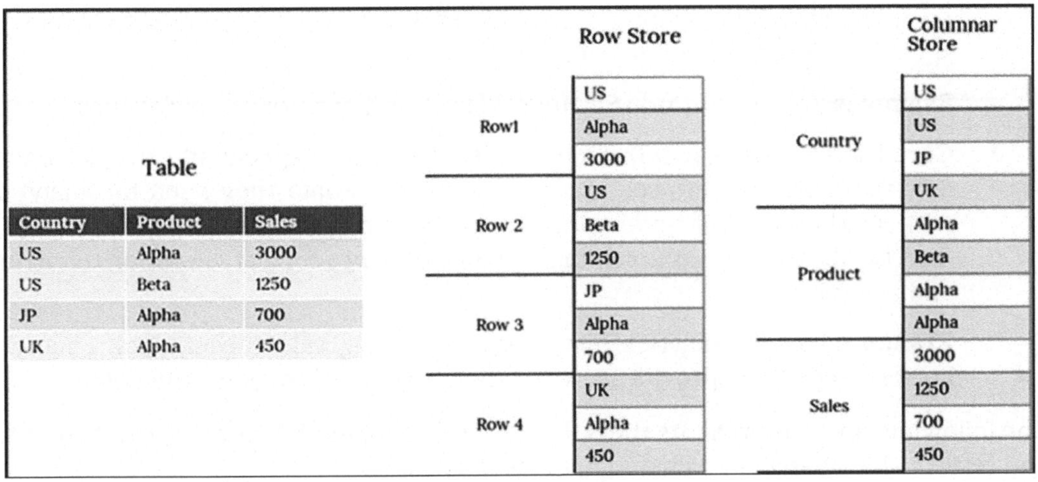

Figure 2.7: *Row Store versus Columnar Store Illustration*

SAP Data Models

In the world of SAP ERP, understanding the underlying data models is crucial. Because, these data models form the backbone of the system, structuring how business-critical information is organized, stored, and accessed. Both SAP ERP (ECC) and SAP S/4HANA have robust data models, designed to handle complex business processes across industries. However, SAP S/4HANA introduces transformative changes, modernizing the data model to align with enterprise scalability needs.

Data models in SAP are organized into three data structures:

- **Master Data**: It represents the core entities or objects essential for business operations. Master Data ensures consistency and integration between SAP functional areas such as FI (Finance), MM (Materials Management), and SD (Sales and Distribution).

  Examples: Customer Master, Vendor Master, Material Master

- **Transactional Data**: It refers to the dynamic, time-sensitive data generated during business operations. It records day-to-day activities including sales, purchases, or financial postings. This data directly influences reporting, analytics, and operational workflows.

  Examples: Sales Orders, Purchase Orders, Financial Postings, Logistics information

- **Customizing Data**: It represents configuration settings in SAP that define how the system behaves to meet specific business requirements. It tailors SAP functionality to fit an organization's processes. Customizing data ensures flexibility in SAP implementation, making the software adaptable to industry-specific and regional requirements.

Examples: Company Code Settings, Plant Configurations, Tax Settings

- **Core Data Services (CDS):** Think of CDS views as a special filter on a camera lens that helps testers see exactly the business data they need for analytics without the noise of underlying table structures. It simplifies access to SAP data by abstracting complex table structures into logical views for reporting and analytics.

  Examples: Sales Analytics View for aggregating sales order data; Financial Performance View provides a real-time overview of revenue and costs.

The following figure represents the SAP ERP (ECC) data model covering the structure, and relationships between data and database tables.

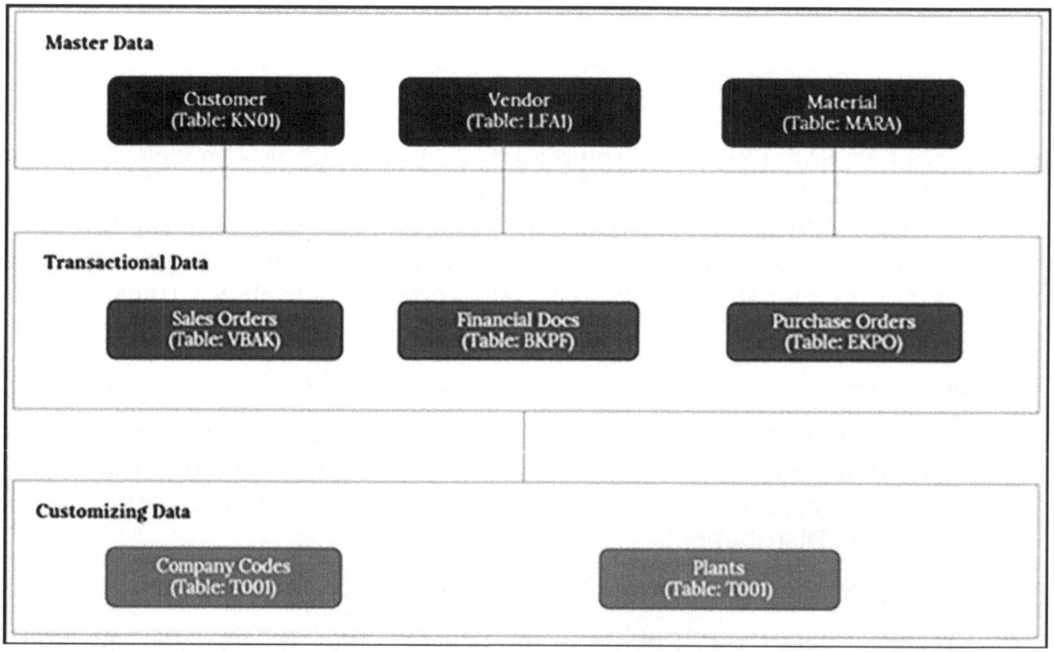

Figure 2.8: *SAP ERP (ECC) Data Model*

Pro Tip: *When working with SAP S/4HANA simplified data models, prioritize validating the Universal Journal (ACDOCA) for all financial line-item updates, as it consolidates multiple legacy tables and represents a single source of truth.*

One of the key innovations in SAP S/4HANA is the **simplified data model**, which reduces complexity and improves performance compared to SAP ECC. Here are some high-level enhancements:

- **Elimination of Redundant Tables**: Traditional aggregate and index tables such as BSIS and BSAS used for line-item reporting in Finance were removed. Instead, real-time reporting is enabled directly on transactional data, eliminating the need for data replication and batch processing.

- **Introduction of the Universal Journal (ACDOCA)**: This single line-item table combines data from Financial Accounting (FI) and Controlling (CO), removing the need for reconciliation between modules. It serves as the foundation for unified financial reporting.
- **Integrated User and Analytics Experience**: SAP S/4HANA tightly integrates **SAP Fiori apps** with the embedded analytics layer, allowing users to access real-time insights within their workflows. This supports faster, smarter decision-making with a modern, intuitive user interface.

The following figure shows the SAP S/4HANA data model covering the structure, and relationships.

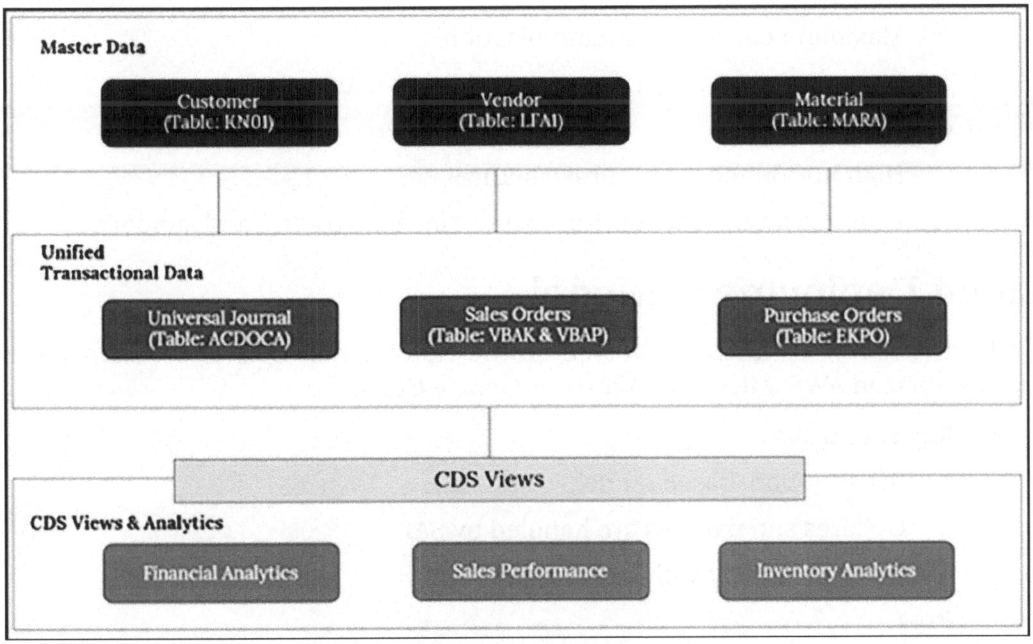

Figure 2.9: *SAP S/4HANA Data Model*

SAP S/4HANA Deployment Models

SAP S/4HANA, launched in 2015, is SAP's next-generation ERP platform built to run exclusively on the high-performance, in-memory SAP HANA database. It also comes with a modern user interface (SAP Fiori) that enhances user experience. With support for SAP ECC ending in 2027, many organizations are planning or already undergoing the migration to S/4HANA.

One of the key decisions in this journey is selecting the **right deployment model**–how and where the S/4HANA system will be hosted. Broadly, SAP S/4HANA can be deployed in three ways:

On-Premises Model

In this traditional setup, all the hardware, software, and data remain within the company's own IT environment.

- **Key Features**
  - Hosted in your data center.
  - Full control over system, data, security, and compliance.
  - Suitable for regulated industries (for example, pharma, defense).
- **Pros**
  - Maximum control and customization.
  - Meets strict regulatory or data residency needs.
- **Cons**
  - High upfront cost for infrastructure.
  - Requires internal teams for maintenance, upgrades, and support.

Cloud Deployment Model

In this model, SAP S/4HANA is hosted on the cloud, either by SAP or a hyperscaler such as Amazon AWS, Microsoft Azure, or Google Cloud.

- **Key Features**
  - Subscription-based model.
  - Updates and patches are handled by SAP.
  - Quick to deploy and scale.
- **Pros**
  - Faster go-live timelines.
  - Lower infrastructure and maintenance costs.
  - Access to the latest features with regular updates
- **Cons**
  - Limited customizations in some editions (especially public cloud).
  - Rely on internet connectivity and cloud SLAs (Service Level Agreements).

Hybrid Deployment Model

This approach combines both cloud and on-premises systems. Businesses keep some processes in-house (example, financial core), while others (example, customer engagement apps) run in the cloud.

- **Key Features**
  - Flexibility to modernize in phases.
  - Can integrate SAP and non-SAP systems.
  - Ideal for complex enterprise landscapes.
- **Pros**
  - Balance of control and innovation.
  - Smooth transition from legacy systems.
- **Cons**
  - Integration complexity.
  - Requires clear governance to avoid data silos or inconsistent processes.

Here is a brief comparison of these deployment models:

Aspect	**On-Premises**	**Cloud**	**Hybrid**
Hosting Location	Company's own data center	SAP Cloud or Hyperscaler (AWS, Azure, and more)	Mix of on-premises and cloud
Control and Customization	Full control, highly customizable	Limited (especially in public cloud)	Selective control based on process
Cost Structure	High upfront Costs	Pay-as-you-go	Depends on mix
Scalability	Limited by hardware	Highly scalable	Moderate - depends on design
Update Management	Managed by internal IT	Handled by SAP or provider	Shared responsibility
Use Case Fit	Regulated industries, legacy integration	Fast innovation, less regulated industries	Gradual transformation, large/global enterprises

Table 2.1: *SAP S/4HANA Deployment Models Comparison*

SAP Application Lifecycle Management

Application Lifecycle Management (ALM) in SAP refers to the processes, tools, and methodologies used to manage the entire lifecycle of an SAP application, from initial concept and development through to deployment, operations, maintenance, and continuous improvement. It ensures that SAP teams are aligned effectively, and project tasks are delivered efficiently while maintaining the health and performance of the system post-go-live.

In SAP S/4HANA projects, ALM plays a key role in ensuring that implementations, upgrades, and operations are aligned with business processes and best practices.

Key Phases of ALM in SAP

- **Requirements Management:** During SAP S/4HANA projects, requirements are gathered through Fit-to-Standard workshops or stakeholder discussions. Applications such as SAP Solution Manager, SAP Cloud ALM, or third-party tools like Jira are used to document and manage these requirements. SAP Central Business Configuration (CBC) streamlines and centralizes the configuration of SAP S/4HANA Cloud, enabling faster, guided, and consistent setup across business processes and landscapes.
- **Design:** In the Design phase, the focus is on understanding the business needs and defining how SAP should be set up to support them. Teams work together to map out processes, gather requirements, and create solution designs. Tools such as SAP Signavio help visualize and improve business processes, while SAP Enable Now can be used to create training content and documentation early, so users are ready when the system goes live.
- **Build:** Once the design is clear, the Build phase begins. This is where the actual system configuration and development happen–setting up SAP, building reports, workflows, interfaces, and custom code if needed. To manage all these changes efficiently and safely, SAP ChaRM (Change Request Management) comes into play. It helps control how changes are made in the system, tracks approvals, and ensures everything moves smoothly from development to testing and production.

  Together, the Design and Build phases set the foundation for a successful SAP project by aligning business goals with technical setup, all while ensuring quality and readiness for the next steps.
- **Testing:** The Testing phase in SAP Application Lifecycle Management is essential for ensuring system stability and minimizing go-live risks in SAP S/4HANA projects. It includes various testing types such as unit testing, system testing, integration testing, user acceptance testing (UAT), end-to-end testing, business process testing, and regression testing. These tests help validate both technical functionality and business process readiness. Tools such as SAP Solution Manager and SAP Cloud ALM are commonly used to plan, manage,

and track testing activities. To improve speed and efficiency, organizations often adopt test automation using various open source and commercial tools such as Selenium, Tricentis, UiPath, Worksoft, and Microfocus. Additionally, SAP Focused Run supports real-time monitoring during testing, while SAP Landscape Management (LaMa) helps manage system copies and test environment readiness. Together, these practices and tools ensure a high-quality, reliable SAP system before it is moved to production.

- **Deployment:** The Deployment phase in SAP Application Lifecycle Management is the process of moving the finalized solution from development and testing environments into the live production environment. This step must be carefully managed to avoid disrupting business operations. Change and Release Management processes are used to control what changes go live and when, ensuring everything is properly tested and approved. Tools like SAP Solution Manager (for managing transports and changes) and SAP Cloud ALM help coordinate and track the deployment process. Additionally, SAP Business Technology Platform (SAP BTP) supports smooth integration between SAP systems and third-party applications, making sure everything works well together in the live system.
- **Operations and Monitoring:** The Operations and Monitoring phase in SAP Application Lifecycle Management focuses on keeping the system stable, available, and performing well after go-live. It involves proactive monitoring of system health, business processes, and integrations to quickly detect and resolve issues before they impact users. Tools like SAP Solution Manager and SAP Cloud ALM provide real-time insights into performance, errors, and system usage. Additionally, IT Service Management (ITSM) tools are used to handle incidents, manage problems, and process change requests—ensuring smooth day-to-day operations and ongoing business continuity.

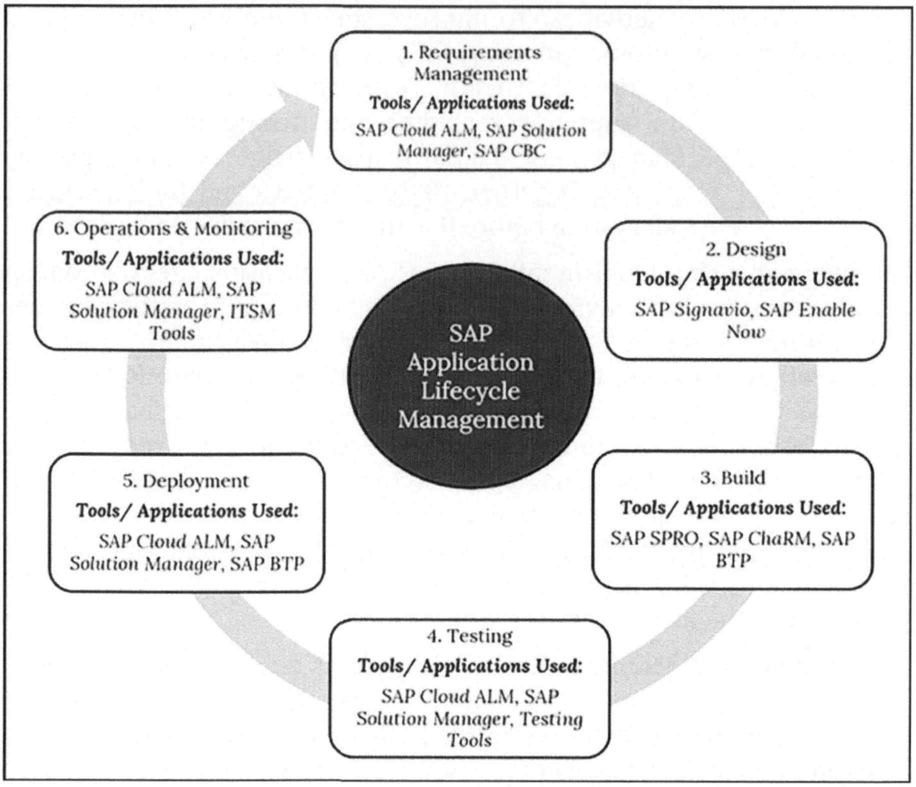

Figure 2.10: *SAP Application Lifecycle Management*

SAP Activate

SAP Activate is a comprehensive framework designed by SAP to guide organizations in implementing and managing SAP systems, including SAP S/4HANA. It combines best practices, guided configurations, and a structured methodology to streamline the journey from planning to go-live and beyond. SAP *Activate is tailored for different project scenarios, including greenfield, brownfield, and hybrid approaches, making it a versatile tool for diverse business needs.*

According to a Gartner Report (2024), organizations adopting SAP Activate methodology experience up to a 25% reduction in project deployment timelines and a 30% decrease in change-related defects during SAP S/4HANA implementations.

The methodology emphasizes agility, enabling organizations to adapt quickly to changing business requirements. It consists of six core phases:

- **Discover:** Define the project vision and objectives.
- **Prepare:** Plan the project and assemble the team.
- **Explore:** Conduct workshops to align on requirements and identify gaps.

- **Realize:** Configure, build, and test the solution iteratively.
- **Deploy:** Transition the solution to production.
- **Run:** Optimize and continuously improve the solution post-go-live.

Key Components of SAP Activate

- **Best Practices:** Predefined business processes and templates designed to accelerate deployment and reduce risks. These cover various industries and functions, ensuring alignment with standard practices.
- **Guided Configuration:** A set of tools within SAP S/4HANA that simplifies system setup and configuration. It provides a user-friendly interface for customizing processes.
- **Methodology:** A structured approach that includes templates, accelerators, and checklists to guide project teams through each phase.
- **Tools:** Project management and collaboration tools, such as SAP Cloud ALM and SAP Solution Manager, to ensure seamless project execution. Enterprise Architecture tools like SAP LeanIX, and process modelling tools like Signavio, and various test automation tools can be utilized in a streamlined manner to ensure effective outcomes with SAP transformation projects.

The following figure highlights the SAP Activate framework and typical project activities performed across the six phases:

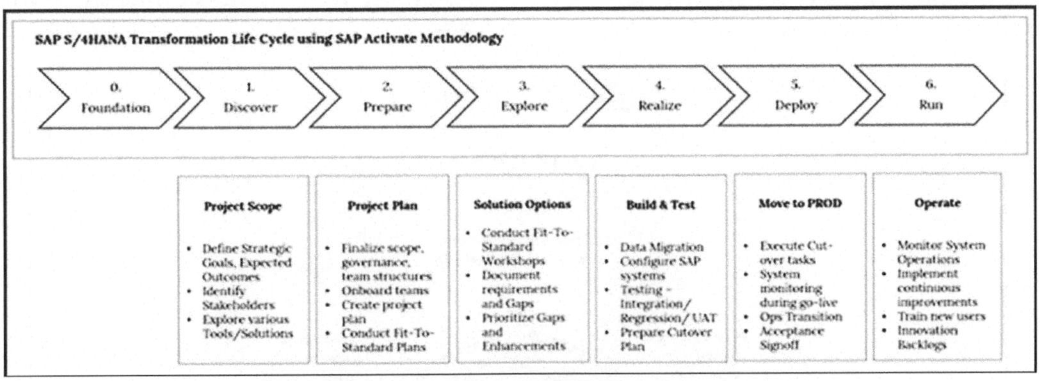

Figure 2.11: *SAP Activate Framework*

Let us look at how a global manufacturing company modernized its ERP system using the SAP Activate methodology while moving to SAP S/4HANA–a move aimed at supporting business growth and boosting operational efficiency (Reference: www.sap.com)

Using SAP Activate, the project followed a structured, step-by-step approach:

1. **Discover:** Business goals and project scope were defined through early workshops.

2. **Prepare:** A detailed plan was created, and teams were onboarded.
3. **Explore:** Fit-to-standard workshops identified where existing processes matched or needed improvement.
4. **Realize:** Configuration, development, and testing were executed in agile sprints.
5. **Deploy:** The system went live smoothly with minimal disruption to operations.
6. **Run:** Post-go-live, the focus shifted to ongoing monitoring and performance optimization.

This example highlights how SAP Activate provides a clear roadmap for successful ERP transformation, reducing risk, accelerating timelines, and keeping the business at the center of every phase.

SAP Business Technology Platform (BTP)

Modern businesses use multiple software systems - some from SAP, others from different vendors. SAP Business Technology Platform (BTP) is SAP's cloud-based platform that helps businesses connect their systems, build applications, and make smarter decisions using data and AI. Think of it as a digital hub that brings together all your business tools and data in one place.

The following figure shows the high-level model of SAP BTP and its connectivity with enterprise landscapes.

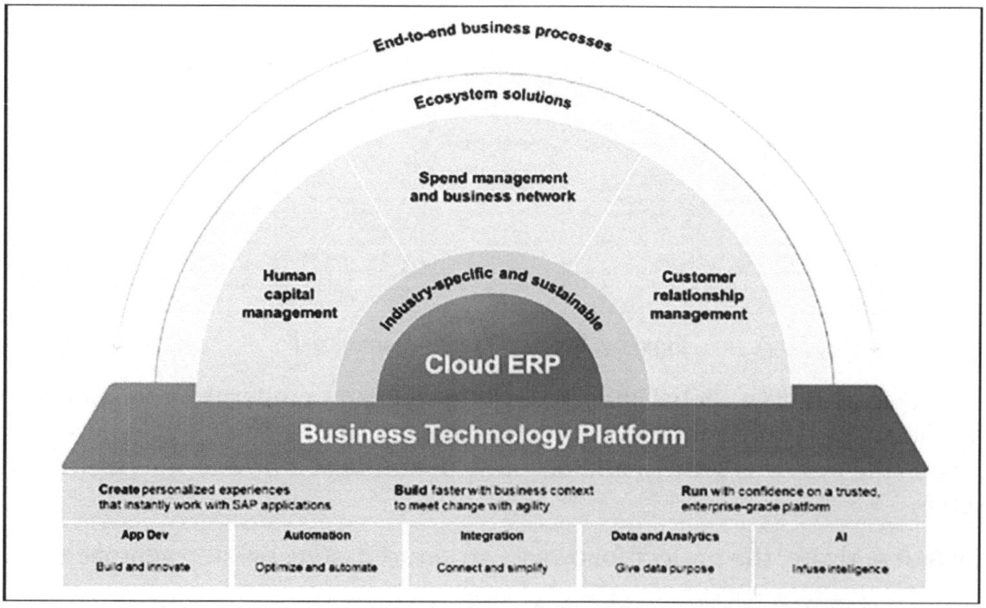

Figure 2.12: SAP BTP Overview (from https://help.sap.com/docs/btp)

The Five Core Capabilities

- **App Development:** Build custom applications quickly using low-code/no-code tools like SAP Build. Perfect for creating mobile apps or extending existing SAP functionality without extensive programming knowledge.
- **Integration:** Connect SAP systems with third-party applications (such as Salesforce or Microsoft) through pre-built connectors and APIs. No more manual data entry between systems.
- **Data and Analytics:** Transform raw data into actionable insights using SAP HANA Cloud for real-time processing and SAP Analytics Cloud for visualization and reporting.
- **Automation:** Streamline repetitive tasks using robotic process automation (RPA) and Agentic workflows. Let bots handle routine work while employees focus on strategic activities.
- **Artificial Intelligence:** Leverage pre-built AI services for document processing, sentiment analysis, and predictive insights – no need to build AI models from scratch.

To fully appreciate what **SAP BTP** offers today, let us understand how SAP's technology has evolved - from rigid systems to a flexible, cloud-native platform that supports modern business needs.

- **1990–2005: ERP Add-ons – Big but Inflexible:** Back then, SAP focused on its Business Suite, which included systems such as ERP (Enterprise Resource Planning), SRM (Supplier Relationship Management), PLM (Product Lifecycle Management), and CRM (Customer Relationship Management). These were tightly integrated but lacked flexibility and scalability for evolving business demands.
- **2005–2015: Composite Applications (SOA) – Modular Thinking Begins:** With the rise of Service-Oriented Architecture (SOA), SAP introduced composite applications that leveraged enterprise service repositories. This approach aimed to enhance modularity, enabling services to be reused across applications. It laid the groundwork for broader integration and flexibility.
- **2015–Present: Cloud Applications and SAP BTP – Built for Agility:** SAP transitioned to a cloud-first strategy, culminating in the SAP Business Technology Platform (formerly SAP HANA Cloud Platform). SAP BTP acts as a unified environment for connecting SAP and non-SAP systems (for example, Salesforce, Ariba). It supports innovations such as mobile apps, SaaS, and IoT while integrating core systems like S/4HANA with external applications through APIs and pre-built connectors.

Case Study

A global utility company faced a common challenge - their IT landscape was complex, with disconnected systems and siloed data that made reporting slow and decision-making difficult.

- **Challenge:**
  - Core business ran on older ERP systems like SAP ECC and R/3.
  - Custom features were deeply embedded, making upgrades hard.
  - Data was moved through complex manual processes.
  - Reporting was delayed and mostly based on outdated data.
- **SAP BTP Transformation:**

  With SAP Business Technology Platform (BTP), the company modernized its systems:
  - SAP S/4HANA became the new digital core—modular, flexible, and easier to manage.
  - Real-time data flow was enabled using event-driven architecture.
  - Extensions and custom apps were built outside the core system using SAP Business Application Studio, reducing upgrade risks.
  - SAP Data Intelligence connected and orchestrated data across systems.
  - SAP Analytics Cloud provided live dashboards and AI-powered insights.
  - Integration Suite made it easier to connect SAP and non-SAP systems.
  - Lightweight microservices allowed rapid innovation.
  - Intelligent Robotic Process Automation (RPA) for automating workflows.

SAP Solution Manager

SAP Solution Manager, first introduced in the early 2000s, has evolved into a comprehensive application lifecycle management platform that serves as the backbone for managing SAP and non-SAP environments. What began as a simple desktop tool has transformed into an integrated platform that centralizes the management of complex IT landscapes.

Currently on release 7.2 (launched in 2016), SAP Solution Manager is part of every SAP installation and continues to be the only release supported by SAP. However, the landscape is shifting as organizations increasingly embrace cloud-first strategies.

Core Capabilities

SAP Solution Manager serves as a unified hub for application lifecycle management, consolidating critical IT functions under one roof:

- **Change Request Management (ChaRM)** streamlines change processes through automated workflows, ensuring efficient testing and approval cycles. Organizations typically see deployment time reductions of up to 30% through these standardized processes.
- **Integrated Test Management** transforms manual testing efforts into automated, accurate processes. Companies leveraging these tools often reduce manual testing by 40% while significantly improving accuracy and consistency.
- **Real-time System Monitoring** enables proactive issue identification and resolution before business operations are impacted. This capability has proven instrumental in reducing system downtimes across enterprise environments.
- **Business Process Management** provides comprehensive tools for documenting, analyzing, and optimizing processes, leading to measurable improvements in cycle times and operational efficiency.

Solution Manager communicates with other systems using remote function call (RFC) technology and via Web Services. The following figure illustrates the system landscape of the SAP Solution Manager:

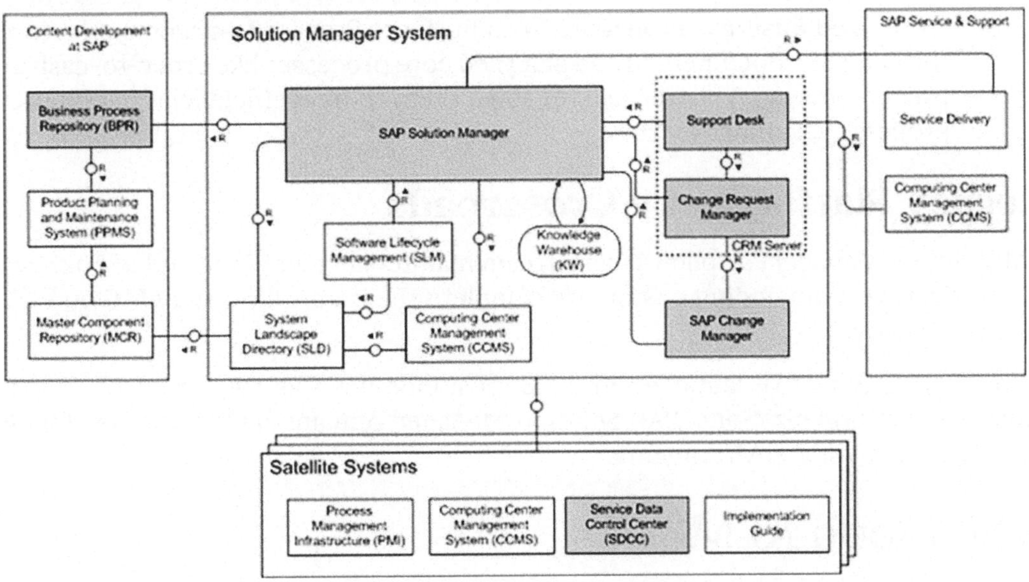

Figure 2.13: *SAP Solution Manager Architecture (from https://help.sap.com)*

Case Study

A global manufacturing company was struggling with managing its complex SAP ERP environment. Frequent system downtimes, slow testing cycles, and inefficient change management processes were delaying projects and affecting business performance.

To overcome these challenges, the company adopted **SAP Solution Manager** - an integrated platform designed to support the full lifecycle of SAP applications.

The following are the key highlights of the solution:

- **Smarter Change Management with ChaRM:** By implementing Change Request Management (ChaRM), the company automated and streamlined its change processes. This ensured that all changes were properly tested and approved, reducing deployment times by 30% and improving overall release quality.
- **Efficient Testing with Built-In Tools:** Using Solution Manager's Test Suite, the team automated key test scenarios. This cut down manual testing efforts by 40%, reduced errors, and accelerated validation for both customizations and standard updates.
- **Proactive System Monitoring:** Real-time monitoring capabilities helped IT teams detect issues before they escalated. As a result, system downtimes were minimized, and business operations became more stable and predictable.
- **Optimized Business Processes:** With Business Process Management features, the company documented and analyzed core processes like order-to-cash and procure-to-pay. This visibility enabled them to fix inefficiencies and improve process cycle times by 20%.

Legacy Platform at a Crossroads

SAP Solution Manager 7.2 follows mainstream maintenance until the end of 2027, with SAP actively recommending customers complete their transition to SAP Cloud ALM before this date.

While SAP Cloud ALM, launched in 2020, positions itself as the future of ALM for cloud-centric organizations, SAP Solution Manager remains highly relevant for on-premises and hybrid environments.

SAP Cloud ALM

SAP Cloud ALM (Cloud Application Lifecycle Management) is an essential tool to optimize and streamline the lifecycle management of SAP implementations or operations projects. Tailored for cloud environments, SAP Cloud ALM enables customers to manage their applications efficiently through improved project execution, operational excellence, and enhanced visibility into system performance.

SAP Cloud ALM is a cloud-native solution, hosted on the SAP Business Technology Platform (BTP). Its architecture leverages modern cloud technologies to ensure scalability, reliability, and seamless integration.

SAP Cloud ALM is typically designed to address the following types of SAP projects:

- **SAP S/4HANA Implementation Projects:** It supports the customers in the implementation of cloud-centric solution landscapes with a preconfigured, out-of-the-box, cloud native solution.
- **SAP S/4HANA Operations Projects:** It provides full stack monitoring and alerting covering business processes, integration, users, applications, and the health of cloud services and systems

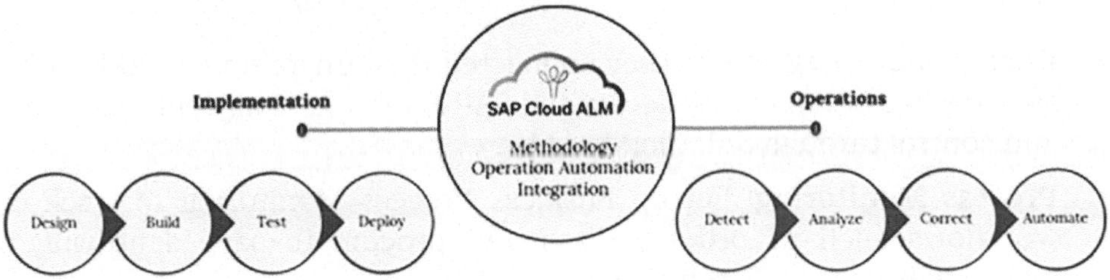

***Figure 2.14:** SAP Cloud ALM for SAP Projects*

Key Elements

- **Core Infrastructure:**
    - **SAP BTP Integration:** SAP Cloud ALM is tightly integrated with BTP services, leveraging its connectivity, analytics, and AI capabilities.
    - **Multi-Tenant Architecture:** The platform supports multi-tenant architecture, ensuring data isolation and customization for each customer.
    - **API-First Design:** RESTful APIs and OData services are used for integration with SAP and non-SAP systems.
- **Key Services:**
    - **Automation Service:** Orchestrates testing, deployment, and operations tasks, minimizing manual effort.
    - **Integration Framework:** Ensures seamless data exchange between on-premises and cloud systems using SAP Cloud Connector.
    - **Monitoring and Alerting Service:** Collects telemetry data from SAP solutions and third-party applications for performance analysis.

- **User Experience**:
  - **SAP Fiori Interface:** A role-based, intuitive UI provides dashboards and actionable insights for different stakeholders.
  - **Mobile Access:** Cloud ALM supports mobile access, ensuring that users can monitor and manage operations on the go.

Case Study

A global manufacturing company struggled to manage a hybrid SAP landscape, with systems both on-premises and in the cloud. Frequent downtime and slow project execution were hurting operations and customer satisfaction. To solve this, the company adopted SAP Cloud ALM to help monitor, manage, and optimize SAP applications across their lifecycle.

Key highlights of the solution:

- **Deployment Integration:** They connected their on-prem SAP ERP with cloud systems like SAP SuccessFactors and SAP Ariba, enabling centralized visibility and control through SAP Cloud ALM.
- **Process Monitoring:** Set up Business Process Monitoring to track critical workflows such as order-to-cash and procure-to-pay, identifying issues before they caused disruptions.
- **Automation and Alerts:** Introduced test automation, cutting regression testing time by 50%, and set up real-time alerts to catch problems early and respond faster.
- **User Training:** Ran hands-on workshops to help teams get comfortable with the SAP Fiori interface and analytics dashboards, boosting adoption and productivity.

SAP Solution Manager versus SAP Cloud ALM

Let us look at the high-level differences between SAP Cloud ALM and Solution Manager:

Aspect	**Solution Manager**	**Cloud ALM**
Objective	Enable Application Life Cycle Management for On-Premises or Hybrid SAP Landscapes	Enable Application Life Cycle Management for SAP Cloud Landscapes
Launch Date	Approximately 2005	2020
Use cases	Used in Companies where several SAP systems exist and often operated on-premises	Used for Cloud based systems
Extensibility	Integrations require complex development effort	Using Open APIs

Ease of Use	Complex with several navigations	Simplified
Ease of Setup	Complex process with several prerequisites	Quick. Only accessible as SaaS application
Test Data Management	Complex due to the Test Data Container management	Simple due to cloud-native approaches
Cost	Higher due to on-premises setup	Lower due to SaaS model

***Table 2.2:** Differences between SAP Cloud ALM and Solution Manager*

Conclusion

This chapter introduced the key SAP applications, tools, and frameworks that are commonly used by QA teams across SAP Landscapes. We explored them not individually, but through architectural insights and practical examples to help you build a broader understanding of how these elements work together in real-world scenarios.

In the next chapter, we will dive into the key aspects of SAP S/4HANA landscapes – such as change management, data management, project blueprints, and document models. This will provide a clear view of how SAP S/4HANA transformations evolve from initial ideation to full scale realization.

References

- https://docs-eam.leanix.net/docs/modeling-sap-s4hana
- http://www.sapevents.edgesuite.net/TechEd/TechEd_Vegas2015/pdfs/TEC206.pdf
- https://www.redwood.com/resource/sap-s-4hana-architecture-guide/
- https://ktern.com/article/sap-s-4hana-architecture-key-differences-benefits-and-components/
- https://help.sap.com/doc/e95f6750b0fd10148ea5c6be75016694/2.0.03/en-US/SAP_HANA_Master_Guide_en.pdf
- https://help.sap.com/doc/e95f6750b0fd10148ea5c6be75016694/1.0.12/en-US/SAP_HANA_Master_Guide_en.pdf
- https://help.sap.com/doc/c979ce316d754200a805c876e19a6177/2.0_SPS00/en-US/SAP_HANA_EIM_Master_Guide_en.pdf
- https://help.sap.com/docs/SAP_HANA_PLATFORM/52715f71adba4aaeb480d946c742d1f6/d8d14ef53e244f6cabd10dd3f5e8c11e.html

- https://www.linkedin.com/pulse/understanding-key-data-structures-kds-sap-s4hana-must-know-koneti-jrwxc/?trackingId=JBmf97SIqyb3lJqJdDTiTw%3D%3D
- https://help.sap.com/docs/SAP_HANA_PLATFORM/52715f71adba4aaeb480d946c742d1f6/8c1fb4ff2f9640ee90e2dccea49c1739.html
- (Book) SAP S/4HANA – An introduction
- https://help.sap.com/doc/819cdef021e44d7aad27b31c8bb1ebfc/2023/en-US/START_OP2023.pdf
- https://docs-eam.leanix.net/docs/welcome-to-the-user-documentation-for-leanix-eam
- https://support.sap.com/en/alm/sap-cloud-alm/learning.html
- https://support.sap.com/content/dam/support/en_us/library/ssp/alm/sap-cloud-alm/Welcome_to_SAP_Cloud_ALM.pdf
- https://help.sap.com/docs/signavio-process-transformation-suite
- https://support.sap.com/en/alm/sap-cloud-alm/implementation.html?anchorId=section_111831259
- https://help.sap.com/docs/SAP_PROFITABILITY_AND_COST_MANAGEMENT/f1a6aa8ade38419692d0cf7186b6c585/fa9968dd6faf1014878bae8cb0e91070.html

CHAPTER 3
Key Aspects of SAP

Introduction

Understanding the fundamental reasons behind every process, architectural choice, and decision in SAP S/4HANA is not just beneficial, it is indispensable for successful SAP testing initiatives. Without deep insight into these core aspects, the management, planning, and execution of rigorous testing strategies become fragmented, reactive, and prone to costly oversights.

For quality engineering professionals, grasping these key concepts is the gateway to designing robust test frameworks that mitigate risks, ensure seamless upgrades, and accelerate innovation. This chapter lays the groundwork for your SAP S/4HANA journey, exploring the essential architecture, deployment choices, and project methodologies. Armed with this knowledge, testing leaders can transform complexity into clarity, driving confidence and success in any SAP initiative.

Structure

This chapter lays the groundwork for your SAP S/4HANA journey by covering:

- SAP in an Enterprise Landscape
- SAP Migration Approaches (Green Field, Brown Field, and Blue Field)
- SAP S/4HANA Deployment Options
- SAP S/4HANA Release Planner
- SAP Clean Core
- SAP Project Implementation Frameworks
- SAP User Interfaces (Fiori)
- SAP Custom Developments
- Transport Management
- WRICEFA - Understanding Changes
- Key Data Structures
- Understanding the Consequences of SAP Migration Failures

SAP in an Enterprise Landscape

Acknowledging the end-to-end enterprise perspective with SAP S/4HANA as the digital core is the first starting point. S/4HANA connects with other SAP systems like Ariba for procurement, SuccessFactors for HR, as well as third-party CRMs and legacy systems, creating a unified enterprise ecosystem. This ensures consistent data, real-time insights, and automation across key areas including finance, supply chain, and customer experience.

The following figure illustrates a typical enterprise landscape with S/4HANA at the center, integrated with various critical SAP and non-SAP applications:

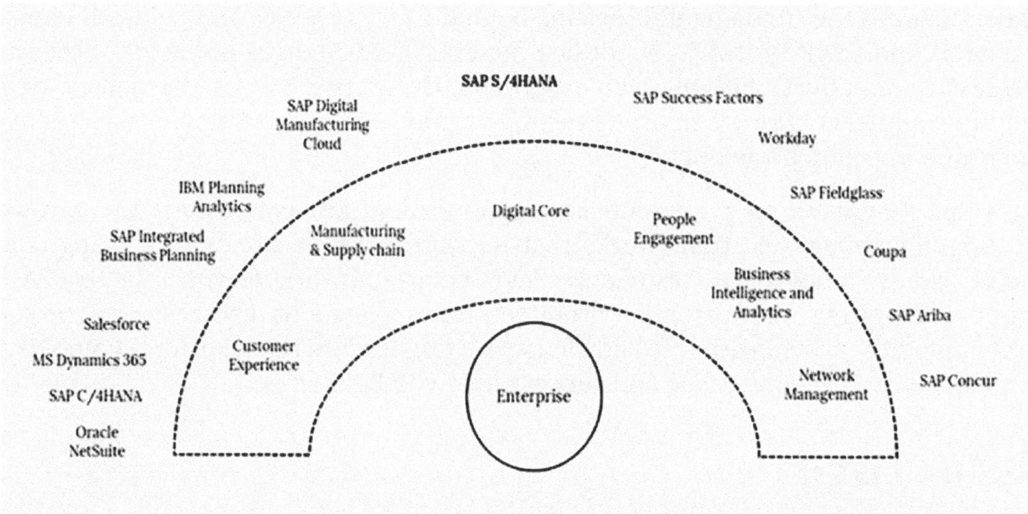

Figure 3.1: *Overview of Enterprise Landscape with SAP S/4HANA as Digital Core*

Pro Tip: *Imagine a test case verifying Purchase Order workflows created in SAP S/4HANA correctly update supplier data in SAP Ariba and trigger expense entries in SAP Concur. Testing teams must engineer the quality to validate API data consistency, retry logic, and error handling across these integrations to ensure smooth end-to-end processing.*

Let us explore the typical enterprise applications that form part of the enterprise technology stack, designed to digitize end-to-end business processes and their integration landscapes with SAP S/4HANA.

Oracle NetSuite:

- **Description**: A cloud-based ERP solution for mid-sized businesses, offering financials, CRM, and e-commerce capabilities.
- **Integration**: Typically integrates with SAP S/4HANA using APIs, middleware like SAP Integration Suite (on SAP BTP), or third-party tools. Data

synchronization covers areas such as finance, order management, and inventory.

SAP C/4 HANA:

- **Description**: A suite of customer experience solutions covering marketing, sales, and service management.
- **Integration**: Native integration with SAP S/4HANA through pre-built scenarios on SAP Cloud Integration (SAP BTP), leveraging OData APIs and IDocs for bi-directional data exchange.

Microsoft Dynamics 365:

- **Description**: A CRM and ERP platform providing customer engagement and financial operations capabilities.
- **Integration**: Integration is achieved using RESTful APIs or middleware like SAP Integration Suite, enabling synchronization of customer, sales, and finance data between systems.

SAP IBP (Integrated Business Planning):

- **Description**: A cloud-based supply chain planning tool enabling demand planning, inventory optimization, and S&OP (sales and operating) processes.
- **Integration**: Native integration with SAP S/4HANA using CPI-DS (Cloud Platform Integration Data Services) or SAP Integration Suite for real-time demand and inventory data exchange.

IBM Planning Analytics:

- **Description**: A performance management solution powered by IBM TM1, used for budgeting, forecasting, and financial planning.
- **Integration**: Integrated with SAP S/4HANA using custom connectors or middleware, such as SAP Integration Suite, with REST APIs and flat file data exchange for financial data.

SAP Digital Manufacturing Cloud (DMC):

- **Description**: A cloud-based manufacturing execution system for shop floor data and production analytics.
- **Integration**: Direct integration with SAP S/4HANA Production Planning using pre-configured APIs and SAP BTP for real-time data exchange.

SAP SuccessFactors:

- **Description**: A cloud-based Human Capital Management (HCM) solution for core HR and talent management.

- **Integration**: Pre-built integration with SAP S/4HANA via SAP Cloud Connector and OData APIs for employee, payroll, and organizational data synchronization.

Workday:

- **Description**: A cloud-based HCM and financial management solution.
- **Integration**: Connects with SAP S/4HANA using RESTful APIs or middleware for HR data exchange, ensuring seamless workforce data flow.

SAP Fieldglass:

- **Description**: A cloud-based vendor management system for contingent workforce and services procurement.
- **Integration**: Native integration with SAP S/4HANA through APIs and SAP Integration Suite to streamline vendor and procurement data flow.

SAP Ariba:

- **Description**: A cloud-based procurement and supply chain collaboration solution.
- **Integration**: Native integration with SAP S/4HANA through Ariba Network, leveraging APIs, SAP Cloud Connector, and pre-configured adapters for seamless procurement processes.

SAP Concur:

- **Description**: A cloud-based travel and expense management solution.
- **Integration**: Connects with SAP S/4HANA through pre-built connectors using APIs on SAP BTP, automating expense posting and reimbursement processes

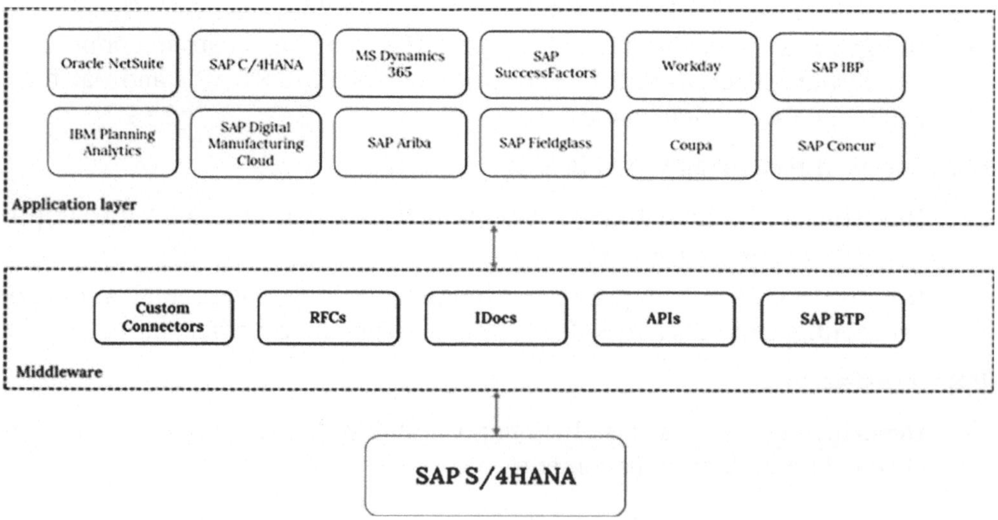

***Figure 3.2:** Enterprise Landscape with SAP Integrations*

SAP Migration Approaches

SAP migration refers to the process of transitioning from a legacy SAP system, such as SAP ECC, or a non-SAP system to SAP S/4HANA, SAP's next-generation intelligent ERP suite. This migration is a critical step for organizations seeking to leverage the advanced capabilities of SAP S/4HANA, including real-time analytics, simplified processes, and enhanced performance. The migration journey is not merely a technical upgrade but a transformational process that touches on multiple aspects of the business and IT landscape.

There are three migration scenarios possible to implement SAP S/4HANA, listed as follows:

- **Green Field (New Implementation):** The Green Field scenario involves starting fresh with a new SAP S/4HANA system, redesigning processes, and adopting best practices.
- **Brown Field (System Conversion):** In the Brown Field scenario, an existing system is converted to SAP S/4HANA. The Brownfield approach involves converting an existing SAP ECC system to SAP S/4HANA while retaining historical data and existing configurations. The system conversion approach is typically used for on-premises systems and cannot be used to migrate to the S/4HANA cloud.
- **Blue Field (Landscape Transformation or Selective Data Transition):** In the Landscape Transformation or selective data transition scenario, a new implementation or system conversion is combined with a consolidation of several SAP or non-SAP systems. The Bluefield approach is often positioned as a hybrid of the Greenfield and Brownfield approaches, combining the best of both worlds – Green Field and Brown Field.

The following figure highlights the three migration approaches with SAP S/4HANA projects:

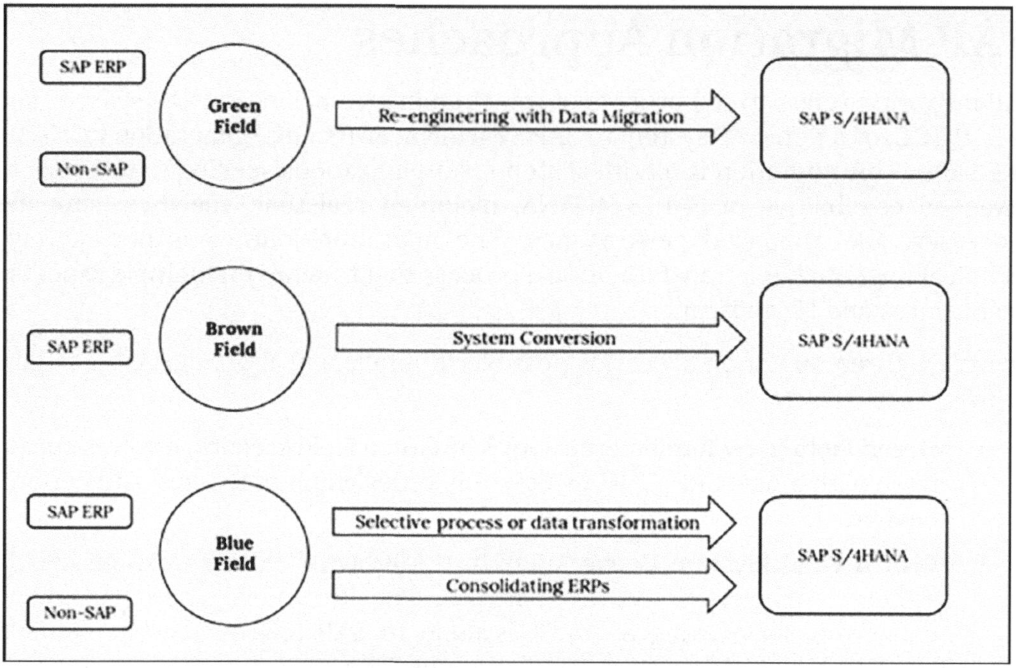

Figure 3.3: *Migration Approaches for* SAP S/4HANA

Here are a few real-world customer examples for the Greenfield, Brownfield, and Bluefield approaches, highlighting their unique scenarios:

Case Study #1: Retail Giant's Digital Transformation

- **Scenario:** A large retail company operating on legacy non-SAP systems aimed to modernize its operations and adopt industry-standard best practices.
- **Goal:** Eliminate redundant processes, achieve real-time inventory visibility, and enable omnichannel customer experiences.
- **Why Greenfield?**
  - The company wanted a complete process overhaul rather than adapting legacy processes.
  - This allowed them to embrace SAP's out-of-the-box capabilities, such as real-time analytics and AI-driven supply chain optimizations.

Case Study #2: Global Manufacturing Company's SAP S/4HANA Migration

- **Scenario:** A global manufacturing company using SAP ECC 6.0 wanted to leverage SAP S/4HANA without disrupting its ongoing operations.
- **Goal:** Minimize downtime, preserve historical data, and gradually adopt new features.
- **Why Brownfield?**

- The company needed to retain its heavily customized processes and historical data for compliance.
- To avoid retraining employees on entirely new processes by maintaining familiarity.

Case Study #3: Conglomerate's ERP Consolidation

- **Scenario:** A multinational conglomerate with various ERP systems, both SAP and non-SAP, aimed to unify them into a single SAP S/4HANA system.
- **Goal:** Streamline operations, reduce IT costs, and adopt harmonized business processes while retaining critical data.
- **Why Bluefield?**
  - Allowed selective migration of clean, relevant data from multiple systems while redesigning outdated processes.
  - Enabled gradual adoption of SAP S/4HANA's advanced features in phases.

Here is a high-level summary covering key aspects of the three approaches:

Aspect	**Greenfield**	**Brownfield**	**Bluefield**
Scope	New system, new processes	Retain the existing system	Hybrid; select and redesign
Use case	Process redesign	Cost-effective upgrade	ERP Consolidation
Disruption	High	Low	Moderate
Customization	Low (Standard SAP)	High	Balanced
Data Retention	Limited	Full	Selective

Table 3.1: *Greenfield versus Brownfield versus Bluefield*

SAP S/4HANA Deployment Options

SAP S/4HANA is primarily deployed in two ways: **SAP S/4HANA On-Premises and SAP S/4HANA Cloud**. Typically, the term "SAP S/4HANA" refers to the on-premises edition by default.

SAP S/4HANA (SAP S/4HANA On-Premises)

This edition gives companies complete control over their hardware, software, and system management. Key highlights include:

- **Flexibility**: Offers full customization and seamless integration with both SAP and non-SAP systems.

- **Responsibility**: The company manages system availability, disaster recovery, security, and upgrades.
- **Pace of Change**: Organizations can decide when to introduce upgrades, aligning with their business needs.

SAP S/4HANA Cloud

This is a **software-as-a-service (SaaS)** model with two options, as mentioned here:

- **Essentials Edition (ES):**
    - Multi-tenant, shared environment.
    - Automatic upgrades four times a year.
    - Cost-effective and streamlined for a lower total cost of ownership (TCO).
    - Best for standardized, less complex needs.
- **Extended Edition (EX):**
    - Single-tenant, offering more flexibility.
    - Upgrades planned with the customer, not automatic.
    - Allows for some customization, but less than on-premises.
    - Ideal for companies requiring more control than essentials but less than on-premises.

Private Cloud Option (IaaS)

This model combines the best of both worlds:

- Hosted in SAP-managed private data centers.
- Fully managed by SAP, providing reduced administrative effort for the customer.
- Offers more flexibility compared to SAP S/4HANA Cloud editions.

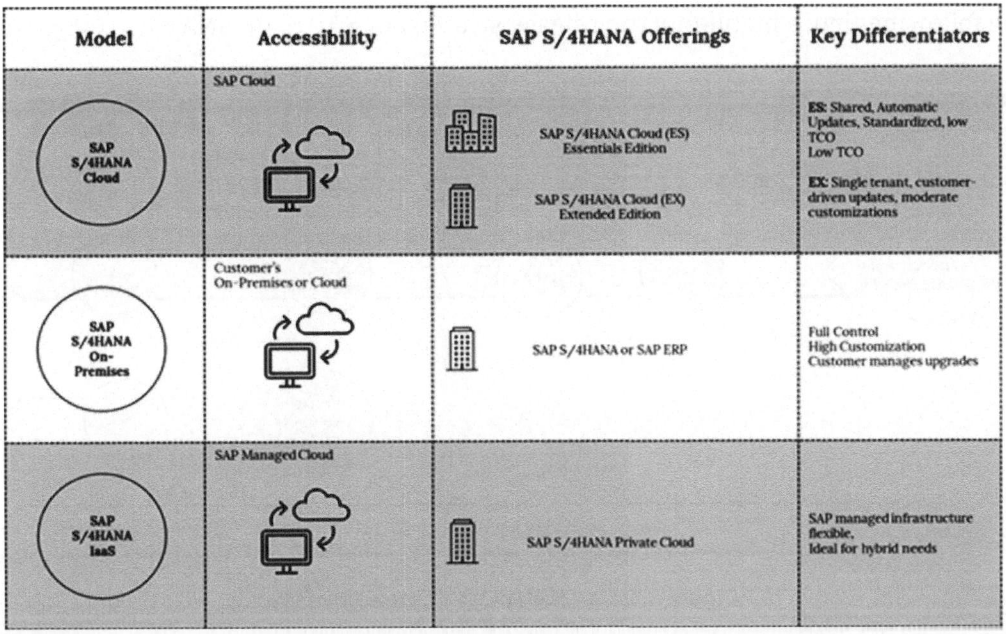

Figure 3.4: *Deployment Options for SAP S/4HANA*

Pro Tip: *Testing cloud editions requires validating upgrade automations and scheduled maintenance windows, ensuring continuous transactional availability. However, on-premises systems provide the test teams some control on the upgrade timing.*

SAP S/4HANA Release Planner

In an ideal world, software would never fail, but reality tells a different story. While SAP strives to deliver complex functionalities with exceptional quality, regular updates are essential to address issues and introduce innovations. These updates come in the form of Support Package Stacks (SPS), Enhancement Packages (EHP), and Feature Package Stacks (FPS).

The SAP S/4HANA On-Premises edition receives an annual upgrade, typically released in September, along with quarterly Feature Package Stacks (FPS) that provide new features and fixes. Meanwhile, the SAP S/4HANA cloud edition is automatically updated for all customers every quarter.

Given these continuous release cycles, quality engineering emerges as a strategic necessity to mitigate the risks of functional and operational failures. In Parts 2 and 3 of this book, we will delve deeper into the methodologies that underpin effective quality engineering.

The following figure highlights the release strategy of SAP S/4HANA:

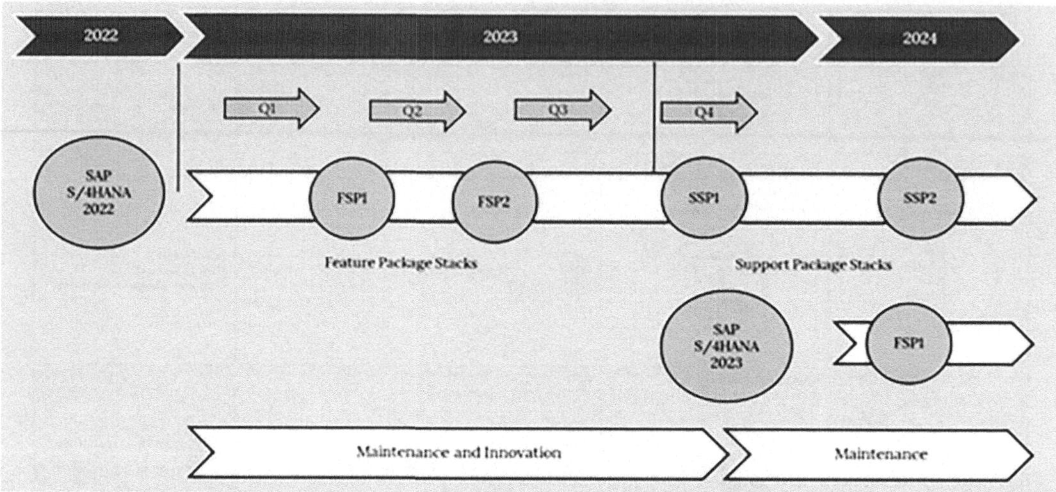

Figure 3.5: SAP S/4HANA *Release Strategy*

The following figure highlights the differences between Feature Package Stack and Support Package Stack:

Aspect	Release	Feature Package Stack (FPS)	Support Package Stack (SPS)
Example	SAP S/4HANA 2023	SAP S/4HANA 2023 FPS01	SAP S/4HANA 2023 SPS04
Number and frequency	Once every two years	Three per release (FPS01, FPS02, and FPS03)	Starting from SPS04, shipped 1-2 times per year
Content	Larger changes, enhancements, and replacements	Smaller changes and enhancements, including legal changes and software corrections	Mainly software corrections and legal changes
Testing required	Thorough testing required	Regression testing of existing business processes and functional testing of new features required	Regression testing recommended
End user training required	End user training usually required	Some end user training may be required	End user training usually not required

Figure 3.6: SAP S/4HANA *Release – Key Release versus FPS versus SPS*

SAP Clean Core

SAP Clean Core is technical strategy and a business enabler for ERP system management that minimizes custom code and modifications within the standard

SAP S/4HANA environment. Instead of altering the core system, businesses leverage extensibility frameworks and external platforms, such as the SAP BTP to build and manage custom functionalities.

Importance of SAP Clean Core

- **Seamless Upgrades**: A clean core ensures the SAP S/4HANA quarterly updates can be adopted without disruptions or extensive rework of custom code.
- **Agility for Innovation**: Businesses can quickly deploy new features or integrate emerging technologies such as AI, IoT, or blockchain without being bogged down by legacy customizations.
- **Cost Efficiency**: Over-customization inflates maintenance costs and complicates system operations. Clean core practices significantly reduce the total cost of ownership (TCO).
- **Regulatory Compliance**: Clean systems are easier to audit and adapt to evolving regulatory standards, reducing risks and ensuring operational continuity.

Tools and Technologies Supporting Clean Core:

- **SAP Business Technology Platform (BTP)**: Enables side-by-side extensions that interact with S/4HANA through APIs, leaving the core untouched.
- **SAP Cloud ALM and SAP Solution Manager**: Provides tools for managing and monitoring custom code, ensuring compliance with clean core principles.
- **ABAP Test Cockpit (ATC)**: Analyzes custom code for performance, security, and compatibility, supporting clean core objectives.
- **Change Impact Analysis Tools**: Predict the impact of customizations and ensure changes do not disrupt core functionalities.

Customer Case Study

A global manufacturing company recently transitioned to SAP S/4HANA, embracing a clean core strategy to streamline operations. By leveraging SAP BTP for custom developments and implementing a robust continuous testing framework, they ensured that all extensions and updates were rigorously validated before deployment. This approach not only reduced system downtime during upgrades by 70% but also minimized the risk of disruptions to core functionalities.

SAP S/4HANA Project Implementation Framework

The SAP S/4HANA project implementation framework offers a structured methodology to effectively plan, execute, and deliver SAP S/4HANA migration projects. While SAP advocates using the SAP Activate framework for all SAP S/4HANA implementations, some customers adopt alternative approaches, including standard Agile, fit-to-standard, and hybrid frameworks. In this section, we will delve into these methodologies and their applications.

SAP Activate

The SAP Activate methodology is a comprehensive framework designed specifically for SAP S/4HANA projects. It combines best practices, guided configuration, and agile principles to streamline implementations.

- **Key Features:**
  - Incorporates Agile delivery methods for flexibility.
  - Offers pre-built accelerators and templates for faster implementation.
  - Supports both Greenfield and Brownfield approaches.
- **Best Fit:**
  - A comprehensive framework can be established to streamline all project phases.
  - Can be used across diverse scenarios such as Greenfield, Brownfield, and Bluefield.
  - Customers want to use and reuse SAP standard tools, templates, best practices to streamline implementations.
  - Teams to ensure iterative testing and stakeholder engagement for continued focus.

Agile Methodology

An iterative, flexible approach that focuses on delivering incremental value throughout the SAP project lifecycle.

- **Key Features:**
  - Continuous collaboration with stakeholders.
  - Divides work into short sprints to deliver functional features regularly.
  - Emphasizes adaptability to changing requirements.
- **Best Fit:**
  - Projects with dynamic requirements.
  - Teams familiar with iterative development practices.

Hybrid Approach (Agile + Waterfall)

It combines the structured planning of Waterfall with the iterative delivery of Agile.

- **Key Features:**
  - Initial project scoping and planning follow Waterfall.
  - Development and testing phases adopt Agile principles.
  - Allows flexibility while maintaining oversight for critical milestones.
- **Best Fit:**
  - Complex projects requiring both detailed planning and iterative adjustments.

Fit-to-Standard Analysis

It is used primarily in Greenfield implementations; this methodology emphasizes aligning business processes with SAP's standard best practices instead of customizing them.

- **Key Features:**
  - Workshops to compare existing processes with SAP standards.
  - Minimal customizations to leverage SAP S/4HANA's out-of-the-box capabilities.
  - Accelerated implementations with pre-configured templates.

SAP User Interface (Fiori)

SAP's User Interface (UI) journey spans over five decades, reflecting the technological advancements and changing user expectations of each era. From the command-line interfaces of SAP R/2 in the 1970s to today's intelligent, user-centric designs, the evolution has been transformative.

In the 1970s, SAP R/2 relied on alphanumeric transaction codes executed in a mainframe environment. These command-line interfaces were functional but lacked usability, demanding extensive training from users. The 1990s introduced SAP R/3, which marked a significant leap with its graphical user interface (GUI). This client-server architecture enhanced accessibility and efficiency but retained a complex and tabular structure. The 2000s saw SAP adapt to the web era with solutions such as the SAP Enterprise Portal and NetWeaver Business Client. These web-based UIs introduced role-based access and centralized integration, offering a glimpse of the personalization capabilities that would later define modern interfaces.

The launch of SAP Fiori in 2013 was a turning point in SAP UI evolution. Moving away from monolithic and cumbersome designs, Fiori adopted a modern, mobile-first approach, focusing on simplicity, responsiveness, and task-specific functionality. Built on the SAPUI5 framework and HTML5 technology, Fiori introduced a set of lightweight, role-based apps to streamline user tasks. Over time, Fiori evolved into the default UI for SAP S/4HANA, with Fiori 3 delivering a unified design language across the SAP ecosystem. Fiori 3 also integrated advanced features including conversational UI, artificial intelligence, and machine learning, aligning with SAP's vision of the intelligent enterprise.

Technical Architecture of SAP Fiori

Understanding the technical underpinnings of SAP Fiori is crucial for Quality Assurance teams, as it directly influences testing strategies and automation.

SAP Fiori Frontend Server in SAP S/4HANA includes:

- **SAP Fiori for SAP S/4HANA Component**: Contains SAP Fiori applications tailored for specific business processes.
- **SAP_UI Component**: Hosts the SAPUI5 libraries, which underpin Fiori's modern, responsive design. Regular updates to this component bring new functionalities, performance improvements, and bug fixes.
- **SAP Fiori Component (UIBAS)**: Provides base user interface libraries essential for common functionalities, such as the "My Inbox" app.
- **SAP_GWFND Component**: Embedded in the core ABAP platform since release 1809, it contains the development tools for creating OData services, which power the communication between the frontend and backend.

Integration and Extensibility:

- Fiori leverages OData protocols to fetch real-time data from the SAP backend, ensuring seamless integration across devices.
- It supports extensibility through SAP's Business Technology Platform (BTP), allowing organizations to adapt apps to their unique workflows without disrupting core processes.

SAP Fiori Deployment Options

There are several deployment options when it comes to SAP Fiori. SAP Fiori consists of frontend components, which provide the UI. These components connect to the backend, and the backend components provide the data. The frontend and backend components are delivered as separate products or add-ons. SAP Fiori can be deployed in several ways as follows:

- **Hub Deployment**: The frontend components are deployed on a gateway system installed for this purpose. The advantage of the hub deployment is that the gateway system can be used as a single point of access for all mobile applications.

- **Embedded Deployment**: Frontend and backend components are deployed in the same system. This avoids the need to install an extra system, reduces TCO, and simplified system administration.
- **Cloud Deployment**: SAP Fiori Cloud is a ready-to-use system in the SAP Cloud Platform. The connection to the backend systems is realized via the SAP Cloud Platform Connectivity.

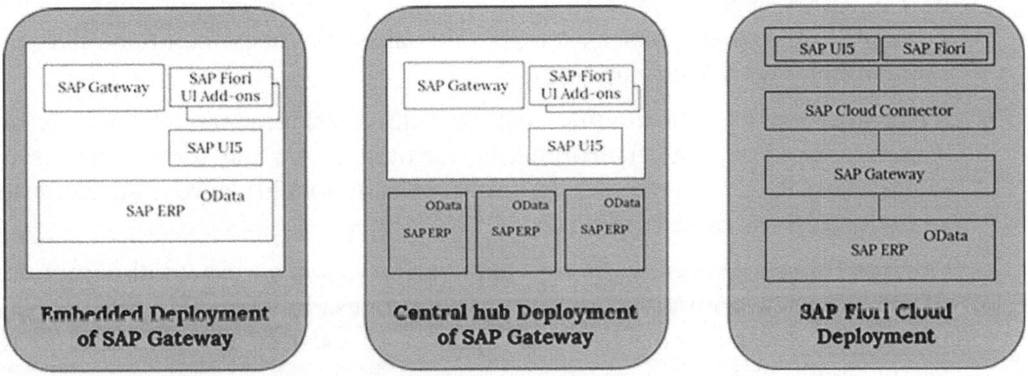

Figure 3.7: *SAP Fiori Deployment Options*

The Fiori Apps Library available at https://fioriappslibrary.hana.ondemand.com/ is especially useful for businesses and developers to identify suitable apps for their SAP environment and understand how to implement them.

SAP Custom Developments

SAP S/4HANA comes with ready-to-use business processes, but every company is different. To meet specific needs - like unique rules or staying ahead of competitors - many businesses add custom features. These customizations help make SAP S/4HANA fit each business better.

While custom developments are essential, over-customization can lead to increased costs, prolonged implementation timelines, and higher maintenance efforts.

Ensuring Custom Developments Do Not Impact Existing Functionality

One of the greatest challenges with custom developments is ensuring they coexist seamlessly with standard SAP functionality. Key strategies to achieve this include:

- **Follow the Clean Core Principle:** SAP emphasizes maintaining a clean core system by minimizing custom code within the core application. Instead, businesses should leverage the SAP Business Technology Platform (BTP) to develop side-by-side extensions that interact with SAP S/4HANA via APIs.

- **Leverage SAP's Extensibility Framework:** Utilize SAP's extensibility options, such as in-app extensions for simple UI or workflow modifications and side-by-side extensions for more complex logic. These frameworks are designed to keep customizations isolated from the core system, reducing upgrade risks.
- **Adopt Standard Development Tools:** Use SAP's recommended tools, such as the ABAP Development Tools (ADT) in Eclipse, to ensure adherence to coding standards and best practices. This also enhances maintainability and compatibility with future upgrades.
- **Rigorous Testing:** Thoroughly test custom developments in sandbox and quality assurance (QA) environments. Automated testing tools, such as the UiPath Test Suite or Tricentis, can validate functionality across all scenarios, reducing the risk of disruptions.
- **Change Impact Analysis:** Change impact analysis is an essential component of managing custom developments. This process helps assess the potential impact of new customizations or updates to existing ones on the overall system landscape.

The next sections will cover the key aspects of the customizations in the SAP systems.

Transport Management

Transport management in an SAP landscape refers to the structured process of moving configuration or development changes from one SAP environment to another. It ensures changes are systematically captured, reviewed, and deployed across different system landscapes without errors or inconsistencies. This process is pivotal to maintaining system integrity and supporting business continuity during system updates.

This section explores the concept, types of transports, processes, and an example process journey for SAP S/4HANA transport management, complete with an architecture diagram.

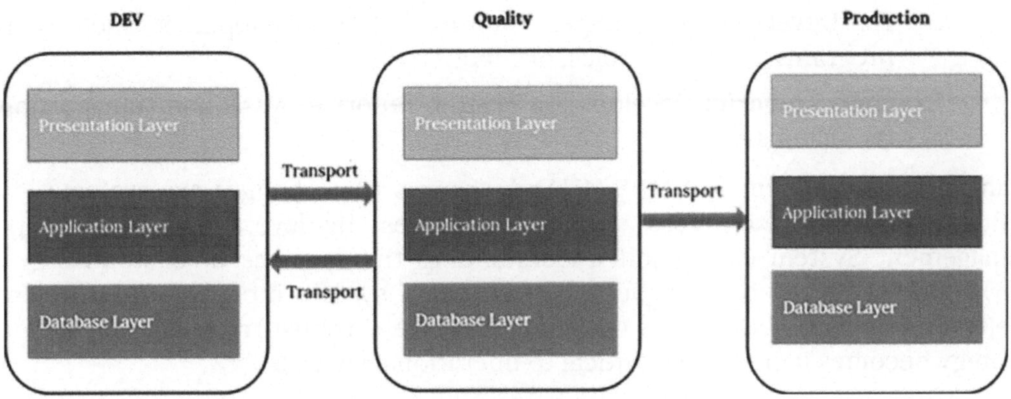

Figure 3.8: *Typical 3-Tier SAP Landscape*

Different Types of Transports

In SAP S/4HANA Transport Management, two primary types of requests are central to moving changes across systems: **Customizing Requests** and **Workbench Requests**.

- **Customizing Requests**

  Purpose: Customizing requests transport client-specific configuration settings, such as changes in the enterprise structure, financial settings, or other client-dependent customizations.

  - **Key Characteristics**:
    - **Client-Specific**: Changes affect only the client where the configuration is done.
    - **Involves Client-Dependent Tables**: These requests are linked to tables whose entries are specific to a client.
    - **Common in Implementation Projects**: Often used during implementation or configuration phases to adjust system settings.
  - **Example Scenario**: Configuring a test client for financial reporting changes and transporting those adjustments to a production client.

- **Workbench Requests**

  Purpose: Workbench requests transport cross-client development objects such as custom ABAP code, system-wide configuration changes, or dictionary objects.

- **Key Characteristics**:
  - **Cross-Client**: Changes affect all clients in the SAP system.
  - **Involves Cross-Client Tables**: Often includes tables or data applicable to the entire system.

    - **For Development Changes**: Captures ABAP development, such as new programs, database tables, or function modules.
- **Example Scenario**: Developing a custom report in ABAP and transporting it across systems.

Transport management in SAP S/4HANA ensures that changes are systematically and efficiently moved across system landscapes. By leveraging the Transport Management System (TMS) and understanding the nuances of customizing and workbench requests, organizations can maintain system integrity and accelerate project timelines. As businesses continue to evolve, a robust transport management strategy becomes increasingly critical to operational success.

WRICEFA – Understanding Change Objects

WRICEFA, an acronym representing Workflows, Reports, Interfaces, Conversions, Enhancements, Forms, and Automations, defines the backbone of custom developments in SAP S/4HANA projects. It encompasses distinct categories of development objects tailored to meet specific business needs that standard SAP functionality does not address. Understanding WRICEFA requires thorough knowledge of its components, their roles in business processes, and how to test them effectively to ensure smooth system operations.

The following figure highlights examples of various change object types across WRICEFA objects:

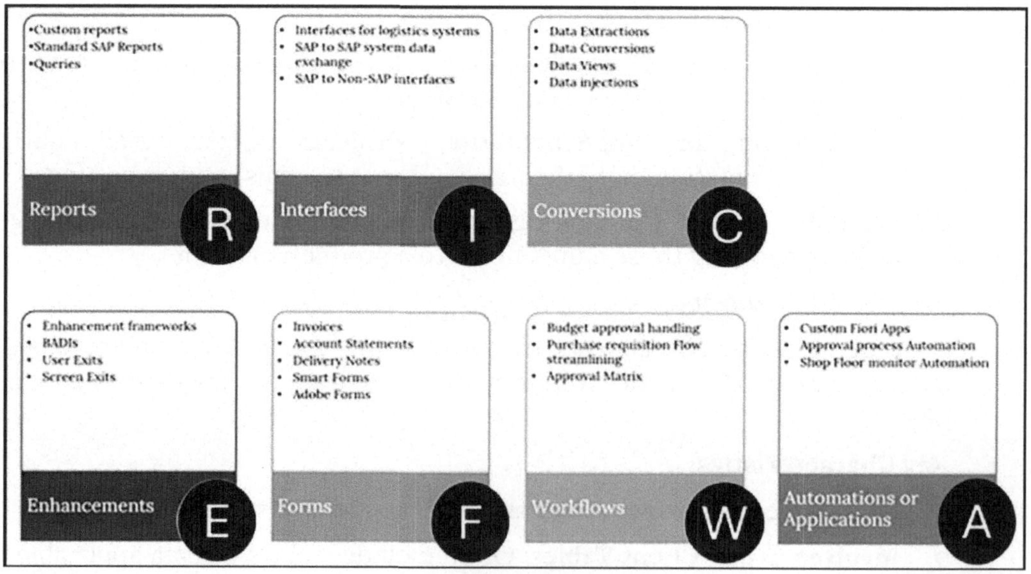

Figure 3.9: WRICEFWA *Overview*

Components of WRICEFA:

- **Reports (R):** Custom-designed reports that retrieve and display data to fulfil business requirements. Examples include sales performance dashboards or inventory analysis.
- **Interfaces (I):** Enables data exchange between SAP and external systems, such as transferring customer order data from an e-commerce platform to SAP.
- **Conversions (C):** Data migration scripts or programs that transform legacy system data into SAP-compatible formats during system implementation.
- **Enhancements (E):** Customizations of standard SAP functionality without modifying core code, achieved via user exits, BAdIs (Business Add-Ins), or enhancement points.
- **Forms (F):** Custom forms for output documents such as invoices, purchase orders, or shipping labels, often built using tools like SAP script, Smart Forms, or Adobe Forms.
- **Workflows (W):** Automated sequences for task approvals or notifications, such as purchase requisition approvals.
- **Automations or Applications (A):** Custom standalone applications or automated workflows built on SAP platforms, such as Fiori apps or intelligent automated processes.

Pro Tip: *Add targeted testing techniques for each WRICEFA object type. For example, interface testing with data validation for Interfaces, conversion validation scripts for Conversions, and workflow simulation for Workflows.*

Key Data Structures (KDS)

Imagine building a skyscraper without understanding its foundation. Wouldn't it be risky to construct something so intricate without knowing the elements that hold it together? In the world of SAP, the underlying data structures are that foundation. They direct how data is stored, accessed, and processed, impacting the entire system's efficiency and reliability. Whether you are designing automation workflows, streamlining operations, or troubleshooting processes, these structures are the hidden framework that drives success.

Let us explore the key data structures from two perspectives - functional and technical.

Key Data Structures from a Functional Perspective

From a functional perspective, key data structures represent the foundational elements of business processes within SAP S/4HANA. Here are some of the most important ones:

- **Universal Journal:** The Universal Journal, also known by its table name ACDOCA, is a central data structure in SAP S/4HANA that consolidates financial and managerial accounting data into a single table. The Universal Journal simplifies operations by using a single table for both transactions and analytics, thanks to SAP S/4HANA's in-memory technology. This eliminates the need for reconciling totals tables or replicating data to separate analytics systems, enabling finance teams to quickly address inquiries about business decisions' financial impact.

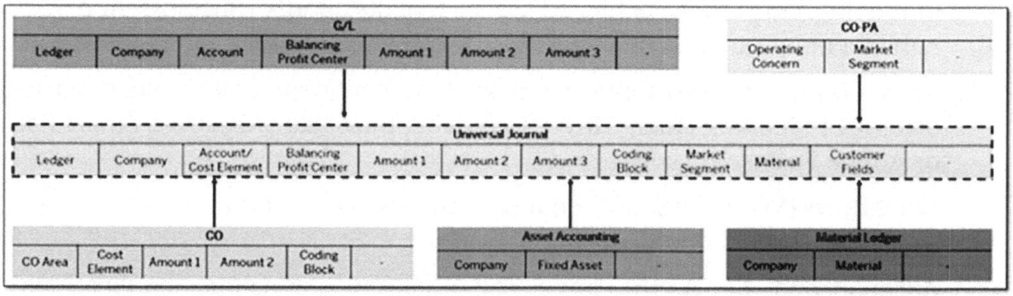

***Figure 3.10**: Universal Journal and Its Relationships in SAP S/4HANA (from help.sap.com)*

- **Material Master:** The Material Master contains information about all materials that an organization procures, produces, stores, and sells. It includes details such as material descriptions, dimensions, units of measure, and procurement data. Automation teams often interact with Material Master data to streamline inventory management and production workflows.

  Common T-Codes for managing Material Master: MM01, MM02, MM03, MM60, CT04, CL01, CL02, CL03, CL2B, CLMM

- **Business Partner:** In SAP S/4HANA, the Business Partner concept replaces the traditional Customer and Vendor master records with a single data structure. This unified structure centralizes information about entities such as customers, vendors, and employees, making it easier to manage relationships and streamline processes.

  Common T-Codes for Business Partner: BP, BUA1, BUA2, BUA3, FLBPD1, FLBPD2

- **Product Master:** The Product Master contains detailed information about products or services that an organization offers. It includes attributes such as product descriptions, categorizations, pricing, and sales data. This data structure is integral to supply chain automation and customer order management.

- **Organizational Units:** Organizational Units define the enterprise structure within SAP, including company codes, plants, storage locations, and sales organizations. They provide the framework for conducting business transactions and managing data efficiently.

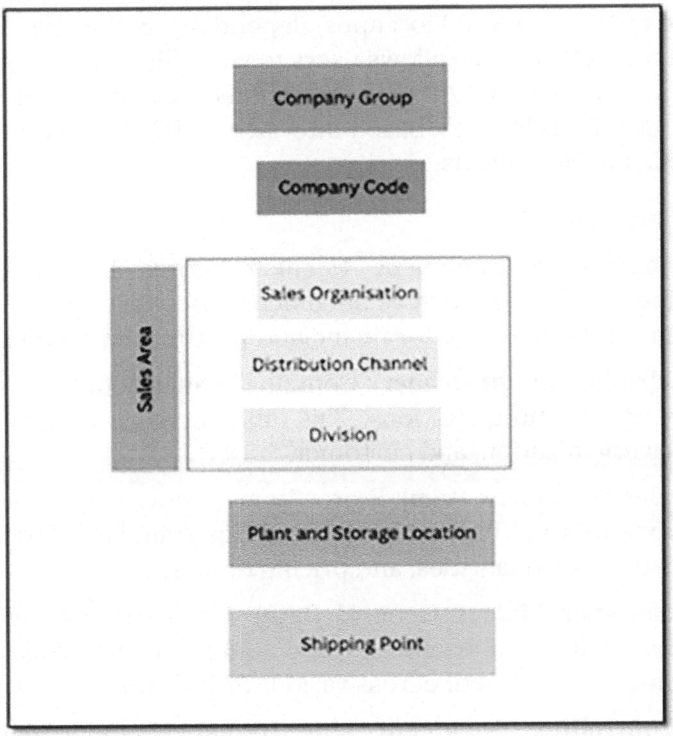

Figure 3.11: *Business Organizational Units (from community.sap.com)*

- **Configuration Data:** Configuration Data encompasses various settings and parameters that define how the system behaves and processes data. Examples include fiscal year variants, document types, and payment terms. The Quality Engineering or Automation teams must consider configuration data to ensure their scripts and workflows align with system settings.

Key Data Structures from a Technical Perspective

From a technical perspective, data structures in SAP S/4HANA dictate how data is stored, accessed, and manipulated. Understanding these structures enables the Quality Assurance teams to design solutions that are both robust and efficient.

Transparent Tables

Transparent tables are the most commonly used type of table in SAP S/4HANA, serving as the foundation for storing application data. Each transparent table in the

ABAP Dictionary directly corresponds to a physical table in the underlying database, with a structure that mirrors the database schema. These tables play a critical role in supporting business processes by housing transactional and master data.

To access and analyze data in these tables, users can utilize tools such as the **SE16N** transaction code or modern SAP Fiori apps, depending on the specific table and use case. The SE16N transaction code allows users to view, filter, and extract data directly from the tables in a traditional SAP GUI environment. On the other hand, Fiori apps provide a more user-friendly, web-based interface to interact with table data, often tailored to specific business needs.

Key transparent tables include:

- **BKPF (Accounting Document Header):** Stores header information for accounting documents, such as document type, posting date, and fiscal year. Data from this table is vital for financial reporting and reconciliation.
- **VBAK (Sales Document Header):** Contains header details for sales documents like sales orders and quotations. This table includes data such as document type, sales organization, and customer.
- **VBAP (Sales Document Item):** Stores item-level details for sales documents. It complements the VBAK table by providing granular information, including material numbers, quantities, and pricing details.
- **KNA1 (Customer Master General Data):** Holds general information about customers, such as name, address, and contact details. This table is essential for customer management across various SAP modules.
- **COEP (Controlling Document Line Items):** Contains detailed line-item information for controlling (CO) documents, including cost allocations and internal orders. This table is crucial for cost management and performance analysis.

Cluster Tables

Cluster tables in SAP S/4HANA are specialized tables that consolidate multiple logical tables into a single physical table at the database level. This unique structure helps reduce the number of database objects, thereby optimizing storage and improving performance for specific operations, particularly when dealing with large volumes of closely related data. While the use of cluster tables has decreased in SAP S/4HANA due to the shift toward simpler table structures and the HANA database's capabilities, they remain important in certain legacy scenarios and processes.

Cluster tables are primarily used to manage and store data that is logically related but rarely accessed individually. Instead, these tables focus on scenarios where the grouped data is processed together, ensuring efficient read and write operations.

Examples of cluster tables include:

- **BSEC (Accounting: Secondary Index for Customers):** Stores customer line-item data used in accounting. It often complements data in the BKPF and other accounting-related tables, allowing efficient access to customer-related financial transactions.
- **BSED (Accounting: Secondary Index for Vendors):** Like BSEC, but for vendor transactions. It holds detailed information about vendor invoices, payments, and adjustments, facilitating financial reporting and auditing.
- **AUAB (Distribution Document Partially Processed):** Contains records of distribution documents that have been partially processed. This table is crucial in scenarios involving distributed systems or multi-entity financial transactions.

Pooled Tables

Pooled tables are similar to cluster tables but are typically used to store control data (organizational data maintained by BASIS teams) rather than application data.

Examples: M_MTVMA, M_MTVMB, M_MTVMC, M_MTVMD, M_MTVME

Views (Database, Projection, and CDS)

Views are virtual tables that provide a specific perspective on data from one or more tables. SAP S/4HANA supports several types of views, including database views, projection views, and Core Data Services (CDS) views. CDS views are particularly powerful for complex data models and real-time data processing.

Examples: ISLOWNOMOMATC

HANA-Specific Data Structures

SAP S/4HANA introduces several unique data structures, such as column-store tables, calculation views, and HANA-specific indexes. These are designed for high-performance data processing and real-time analytics. For example, column-store tables enable faster data retrieval, and calculation views can pre-aggregate data for automated reporting.

ABAP Data Dictionary (DDIC)

The ABAP Data Dictionary (DDIC) is a critical component of the SAP S/4HANA system, serving as the centralized repository where all data structures and their relationships are defined, maintained, and managed. It provides a framework for defining, storing, and accessing metadata, which is used across the entire SAP system.

Developers and administrators can access the Data Dictionary using the SE11 transaction code. This intuitive interface allows users to create, modify, and manage various database objects, such as:

- Transparent tables
- Cluster and pooled tables
- Views (database, projection, and help views)
- Indexes and search helps
- Data elements and domains

Understanding the Consequences of SAP Migration Failures

SAP S/4HANA migrations are complex endeavors that demand careful planning and precise execution. Following are real-world examples of failures that shed light on critical missteps, their consequences, and the valuable lessons they offer.

Case 1: The Retail Chain's €500 Million Disaster

A major retail chain attempted to migrate to SAP S/4HANA but insisted on customizing the system to match legacy processes. Over seven years, the project consumed massive resources, only to be abandoned due to shifting requirements and misaligned expectations.

Key learnings:

- Avoid over-customizing ERP solutions; adapt business processes to standard functionalities instead.
- Secure consistent executive sponsorship to navigate challenges over extended project timelines.
- Invest in comprehensive change management for organizational alignment.

Case 2: Supply Chain Disruption Due to Poor Planning

A confectionery company faced a disrupted supply chain when its migration to S/4HANA lacked a robust blueprint. Insufficient testing and an unclear understanding of business needs resulted in system failures that affected operations.

Key learnings:

- Develop a well-defined transformation blueprint aligned with business goals.

- Allocate sufficient time for User Acceptance Testing (UAT) to validate functionality.
- Engage stakeholders early to ensure alignment between technical and business requirements.

Case 3: Data Inaccuracy Crippling Operations

An international retailer faced severe inventory and customer service issues following its ERP migration. Inaccurate data migration and insufficient employee training led to widespread operational failures.

Key learnings:

- Prioritize data cleansing and accuracy before migration.
- Conduct end-to-end testing of core business processes to ensure seamless operations.
- Provide thorough training to employees to mitigate post-go-live disruptions.

Case 4: Misalignment of Strategy and Execution

A global fleet management firm attempted to consolidate dozens of systems into a single SAP instance while simultaneously undergoing organizational restructuring. The project failed to align with corporate strategy, leading to termination.

Key learnings:

- Ensure that digital transformation strategies align with overarching corporate goals.
- Avoid combining complex system consolidations with major organizational changes.
- Plan incremental migrations to manage complexity effectively.

Case 5: Cost Overruns and Lack of Expertise

A chemical company experienced significant cost overruns and eventual cancellation of its SAP S/4HANA project. The implementation team lacked expertise, and the scope spiraled out of control.

Key learnings:

- Build a skilled implementation team with up-to-date ERP experience.
- Regularly reassess project scope and budget to prevent overruns.
- Maintain strong executive oversight and support throughout the project lifecycle.

Common themes of learning across Failures

- **Data Management**: Poor data migration and cleansing processes often lead to system failures.
- **Testing**: Inadequate testing is a recurring issue that amplifies post-go-live disruptions.
- **Change Management**: Resistance to adapting business processes to standard ERP functionalities causes significant delays and cost overruns.
- **Leadership**: A lack of executive sponsorship and oversight hinders project alignment and execution.

Pro Tip: *Emphasize the importance of end-to-end integration tests that simulate real business processes crossing SAP and non-SAP boundaries, using mock services or staging environments to uncover latent defects.*

Conclusion

This chapter has delved into the multifaceted SAP S/4HANA landscape, exploring deployment models, enterprise technology landscapes, SAP UI architecture, SAP project simulation, WRICEFA elements, and extensibility methodologies. These foundational concepts provide a strong base for understanding how SAP S/4HANA enables organizations to tailor their systems to meet evolving business needs.

Building on the foundation so far, the next chapter will focus on the business processes layer within SAP S/4HANA landscapes. We will examine these processes from technical, business, and integration perspectives, uncovering how they drive operational efficiency, ensure compliance, and elevate quality engineering programs.

References

- https://www.henricodolfing.com/2020/05/case-study-lidl-sap-debacle.html
- https://onfinity.io/blog/technologies/top-5-sap-s-4-hana-failures-and-lessons-learned/
- https://community.sap.com/t5/enterprise-resource-planning-blogs-by-sap/moving-to-the-universal-journal-how-does-the-new-g-l-fit-in/ba-p/13330388
- https://help.sap.com/docs/SAP_S4HANA_ON-PREMISE/e296651f454c4284ade361292c633d69/df4ef977909a47e293b3762935ec44d8.html?&version=1909.000
- https://help.sap.com/doc/819cdef021e44d7aad27b31c8bb1ebfc/2023/en-US/START_OP2023.pdf

- https://community.sap.com/t5/enterprise-resource-planning-blogs-by-sap/sap-s-4hana-extensibility-simplified-guide-for-beginners/ba-p/13548988
- https://community.sap.com/t5/enterprise-resource-planning-blogs-by-members/sap-s-4hana-cloud-side-by-side-extensibility/ba-p/13381659
- https://www.linkedin.com/posts/alokkumar4_top-20-sap-migration-failures-activity-7278243206373285888-39H0/
- https://www.linkedin.com/pulse/mastering-software-test-automation-strategies-sap-activate-koneti-i0xje/
- https://www.linkedin.com/pulse/understanding-key-data-structures-kds-sap-s4hana-must-know-koneti-jrwxc/

CHAPTER 4
Business Processes

Introduction

Imagine running a relay race where each participant must hand off a baton to the next runner seamlessly. If one falters, the entire team's performance suffers. Business processes work similarly in organizations. They are the tasks or activities arranged in a sequence to achieve a specific goal at the end. These processes ensure every "*runner*" in your business, whether a person or a system, works in harmony to deliver results.

For example, in a manufacturing company, the process starts with receiving a customer order, followed by production planning, procurement of materials, manufacturing, and finally shipping the product. If procurement delays materials, the entire process slows down, affecting customer satisfaction and revenue flow.

But what makes business processes so essential, why are they seen as cornerstone in SAP S/4HANA projects, and how can they be understood in simple yet impactful ways?

Let us dive in.

Structure

This chapter aims to provide a foundational understanding of Business Processes, covering the following topics:

- Overview of a Business Process
- Evolution of Business Processes
- Exploring Core Business Processes with Examples
- SAP S/4HANA Integration Architecture

Overview of a Business Process

Think of an organization as a large city with various neighborhoods (departments) connected by highways (processes). Each highway ensures the smooth flow of vehicles (tasks, resources, or information) between neighborhoods. When highways are clear and well-maintained, the city thrives.

- **Departments as neighborhoods:** Sales, Marketing, IT, HR, and more.
- **Tasks as vehicles:** Cars, trucks, or motorcycles carrying "**resources**."
- **Processes as highways:** Roads connecting all neighborhoods.
- **Bottlenecks as traffic jams:** Areas where inefficiencies occur.

Figure 4.1: *Understanding a Business Process*

Pro Tip: *Map out key business processes such as the city map analogy, identifying critical 'highways' (integration points) and potential 'traffic jams' (bottlenecks) through impact analysis. This helps prioritize testing efforts on processes with the most business impact.*

Evolution of Business Processes

Business processes have evolved from manual, paper-based workflows to highly automated digital frameworks. This transition enables organizations to scale operations, enhance accuracy, and reduce turnaround times.

This journey can be divided into distinct phases:

- **1970s: Manual Workflows**
  - Processes were largely manual, relying on physical documents and face-to-face interactions.

  - Limited scalability and high susceptibility to errors.
- **1980s: Early Computerization**
  - Adoption of basic software applications for data entry and record keeping.
  - Silos persisted, as systems were not integrated.
- **1990s: ERP Systems and Automation**
  - Introduction of Enterprise Resource Planning (ERP) systems, such as SAP R/3.
  - Processes became standardized, and integration across departments improved significantly.
- **2000s: Cloud and SaaS**
  - Emergence of cloud computing and Software as a Service (SaaS) solution.
  - Organizations gained flexibility and scalability in their processes.
- **2010s: Hyperautomation**
  - Integration of advanced technologies such as IoT, and RPA.
  - Processes became faster and adaptive.
- **2020s and Beyond: Digital Transformation**
  - Leveraging AI and machine learning to achieve end-to-end process automation.
  - Real-time analytics and predictive insights drive continuous optimization.

Every organization operates through interconnected business processes and sub-processes to create seamless experiences.

Exploring Core Business Processes

In this section, we will explore industry-standard business processes and the solution patterns that enable organizations to operate efficiently.

Order-to-Cash (O2C) Process

The Order-to-Cash (O2C) process is the backbone of revenue generation in any organization. It encompasses the entire customer journey - from order placement to payment collection - serving as a critical driver for revenue generation and customer satisfaction. This process integrates multiple functions, including sales, logistics, finance, and customer service, to ensure seamless fulfilment and optimal cash flow.

Key Steps in the O2C Process

- **Order Placement:** Receiving customer orders through various channels such as e-commerce platforms, CRM systems, or direct sales.
- **Order Fulfilment:** Picking, packing, and shipping the products or delivering the services as per the order.
- **Shipping:** Plan for shipment and coordinate logistics providers.
- **Invoicing:** Generating and sending invoices to customers.
- **Payment Collection:** Receiving payments and reconciling them with outstanding invoices.
- **Post-Sales Service:** Handling customer queries, returns, or warranty claims if applicable.
- **Reporting:** Analyzing the transactional and performance indicators of the entire process.

Anatomy of the O2C Process

The following figure highlights the anatomy of a standard Order-to-Cash process with its key components: Inputs, Activities, Outputs, Stakeholders, and Controls:

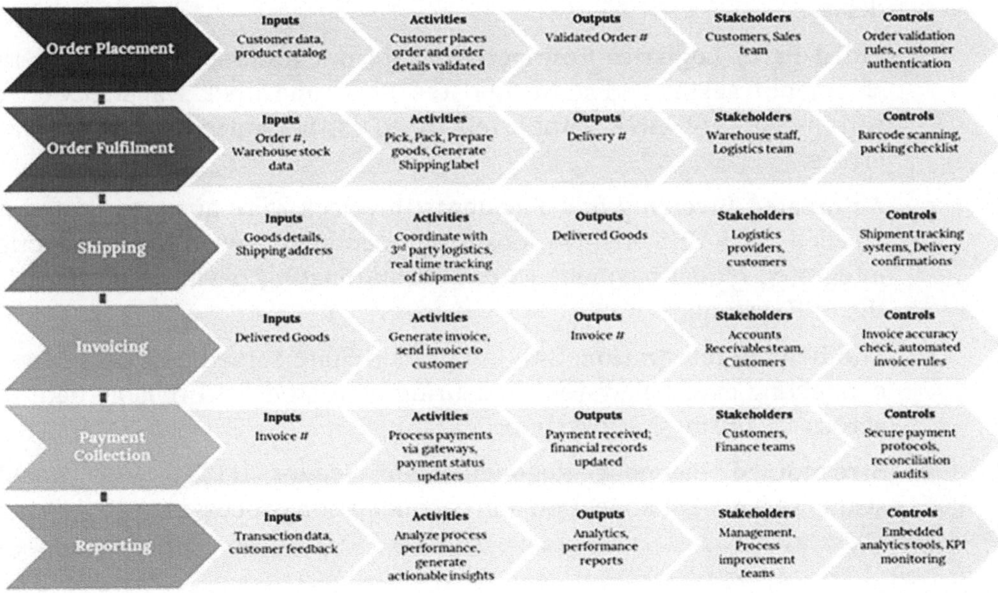

Figure 4.2: *Anatomy of a Standard O2C Process*

Real-World Example: Streamlining O2C with SAP S/4HANA

A leading global manufacturer of industrial equipment, operating across 25 countries, sought to modernize its O2C process to enhance efficiency and integration.

- **Limitations of the existing O2C process:**
    - Disconnected SAP ECC and legacy systems
    - Manual order processing in CRM and invoicing
    - Limited integration with third-party logistics and payment systems
    - Time-consuming reconciliation and reporting tasks
- **The Solution based on SAP S/4HANA:** The company migrated to SAP S/4HANA and reimagined its O2C process to streamline operations and improve integration with non-SAP systems. Key improvements included:
    - **Unified ERP Platform (SAP S/4HANA):** Integrated sales, materials management, and finance ensured seamless workflows.
    - **Enhanced CRM Integration with Salesforce:** Replaced the legacy CRM for real-time order management. Orders captured in Salesforce synced with SAP S/4HANA via REST APIs, automating order processing and reducing delays.
    - **Third-Party Logistics Connectivity:** API integrations enabled real-time shipment tracking and status updates. Real-time stock availability checks within SAP S/4HANA, supported by RFCs, minimized order fulfilment errors.
    - **Automated Invoicing and Payments:** Invoices were auto-generated and emailed via SAP S/4HANA, ensuring accuracy. Secure API connections integrated global payment gateways, automating payment updates into the ERP system.
    - **Middleware Integration:** SAP Integration Suite served as a backbone for connecting external systems, ensuring consistent and reliable data flow across the business ecosystem.
    - **Streamlined Payment Reconciliation:** Secure HTTPS APIs enabled seamless payment collection and reconciliation processes.

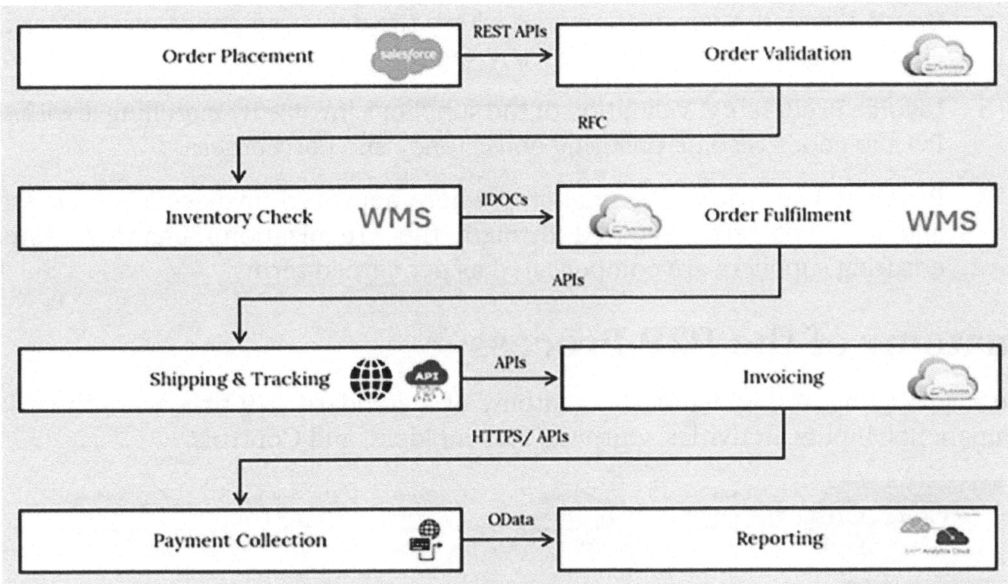

Figure 4.3: O2C Process Architecture

Pro Tip: *Emphasize early integration testing between* SAP S/4HANA SD, *external* CRM, *and logistics providers to catch interface mismatches before production. Use mocking or service virtualization to simulate unavailable third-party systems during testing phases.*

Procure-to-Pay (P2P) Process

The Procure-to-Pay (P2P) process is a vital component of organizational efficiency, enabling seamless procurement and payment operations. It encompasses the entire journey of acquiring goods or services, starting from requisition to payment. P2P ensures that organizations maintain control over expenditures, optimize supplier relationships, and meet compliance standards.

Key Steps in the P2P Process

1. **Purchase Requisition:** A formal request initiated by a department requiring goods or services, detailing the requirements for procurement.
2. **Vendor Selection:** The process of evaluating and choosing a supplier based on predefined criteria such as cost, quality, delivery timelines, and compliance.
3. **Purchase Order (PO) Creation:** Generation of an official document that specifies the order details, including quantities, pricing, and terms, and is shared with the supplier.

4. **Goods Receipt:** A verification step where the delivered goods or services are checked against the PO for accuracy, quality, and quantity.
5. **Invoice Processing:** Validation of the supplier's invoice by matching it with the PO and goods receipt, ensuring consistency and correctness.
6. **Payment Execution:** The final step where approved invoices are processed, and payments are executed through the organization's financial system, ensuring suppliers are compensated as per agreed terms.

Anatomy of the P2P Process

The following figure highlights the anatomy of a standard P2P process with its key components: Inputs, Activities, Outputs, Stakeholders, and Controls.

Figure 4.4: *Anatomy of a Standard P2P Process*

Real-World Example: A Manufacturing Customer's P2P Process Architecture

A global manufacturing company implemented an integrated P2P solution leveraging several interconnected systems. The details are as follows:

- **Purchase Requisition:** Managed in SAP S/4HANA's procurement module to initiate the process.
- **Vendor Selection:** Conducted in SAP S/4HANA using supplier scoring tools and integration with external supplier databases.

- **Purchase Order Creation:** Automated in SAP S/4HANA and shared with suppliers through the Supplier Portal.
- **Goods Receipt:** Updated in a legacy inventory management system integrated via middleware to SAP S/4HANA.
- **Invoice Processing:** Performed in SAP S/4HANA's accounts payable module with automated three-way matching.
- **Payment Execution:** Processed in SAP S/4HANA's financials module with integration into the organization's banking systems.
- **Applications:**
  - **SAP S/4HANA**: Centralized procurement and finance operations.
  - **Non-SAP Systems**: Legacy systems handling inventory and logistics.
  - **Middleware Integration**: Ensured seamless data exchange between systems.

The following figure highlights the technologies and communication channels used for enabling this P2P process.

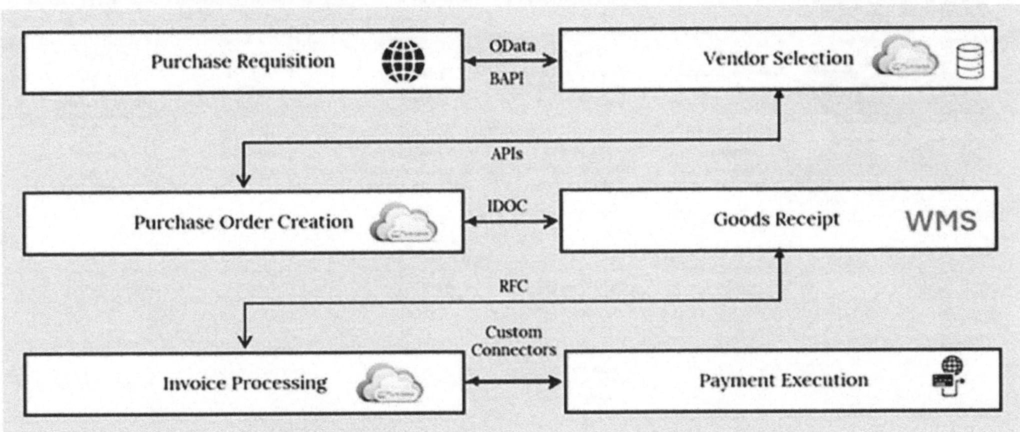

Figure 4.5: *Real-World Example of a P2P Process*

Pro Tip: *Three-way match testing should cover validating the PO, goods receipt, and invoice consistency. Regression testing after enhancement releases is critical given frequent changes in supplier portals and compliance rules.*

Record-to-Report (R2R) Process

Record-to-Report (R2R) is a critical business process within financial management that involves collecting, processing, and delivering financial data to generate actionable insights. For SAP-centric organizations, R2R benefits from SAP's powerful ERP capabilities, enabling automation, real-time insights, and strong compliance.

Anatomy of the R2R Process Flow

A typical R2R process includes:

1. **Data Capture**: Collecting financial and transactional data from various sources to record business activities.
2. **Ledger Maintenance**: Posting transactions to the general ledger and sub-ledgers to maintain accurate financial records.
3. **Reconciliation**: Comparing and reconciling general ledger balances with sub-ledgers to identify and resolve discrepancies.
4. **Financial Reporting**: Generating financial statements such as balance sheets, income statements, and cash flow reports for stakeholders.
5. **Analytics and Decision Support**: Analyzing financial data to derive insights that guide strategic and operational decisions.

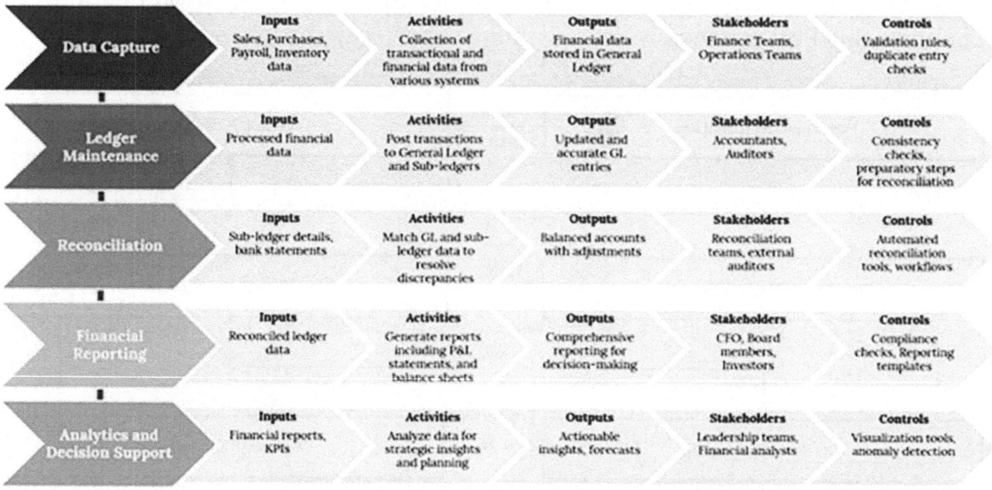

Figure 4.6: *Anatomy of a Standard R2R Process*

Real-World Example: A Global FMCG Company's R2R Process's Architecture

A global FMCG company with operations across 50+ countries streamlined its Record-to-Report process using SAP S/4HANA as the core ERP. The company's existing financial processes were fragmented across SAP and non-SAP systems, leading to inefficiencies and inaccuracies in financial reporting.

To streamline R2R, the company implemented SAP S/4HANA as the core ERP, integrating it with SAP BW/4HANA for analytics and multiple non-SAP systems for payroll, procurement, and inventory.

A high-level technology stack used to digitize their R2R process includes:

- **Core ERP**: SAP S/4HANA
- **Analytics**: SAP BW/4HANA
- **Non-SAP Systems**: Legacy HR systems, third-party procurement platforms
- **Middleware**: SAP Process Orchestration (PO) for integration
- **Cloud Integration**: SAP Cloud Platform Integration (CPI) for connecting cloud applications

The following figure provides a high-level solution architecture diagram:

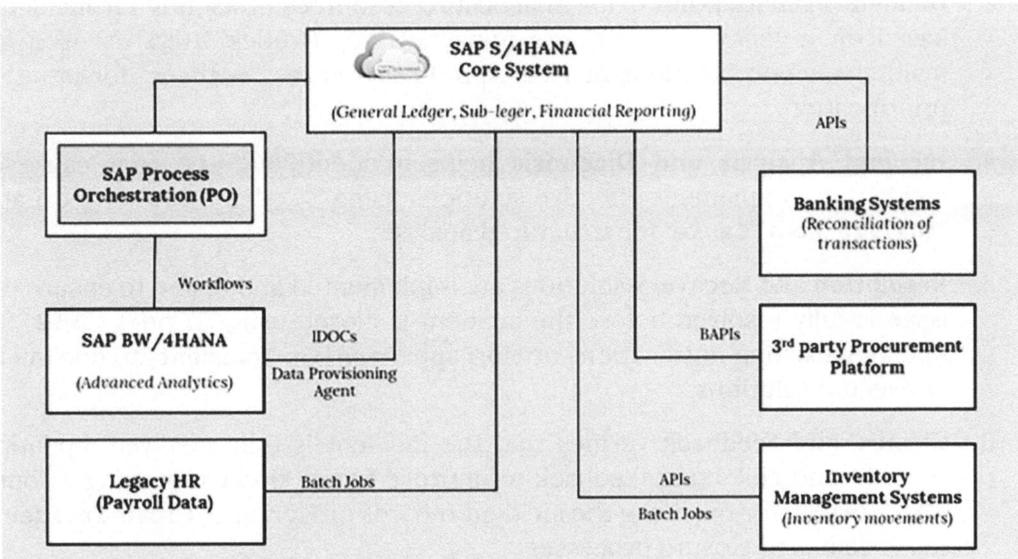

***Figure 4.7**: Solution Architecture of R2R Process*

Incident-to-Resolution (I2R) Process

The Incident-to-Resolution (I2R) process is a critical business function within SAP-centric organizations, ensuring the smooth resolution of operational disruptions. The universality of the I2R process stems from its relevance across industries and its alignment with ITIL (Information Technology Infrastructure Library) best practices. Organizations leveraging SAP S/4HANA integrate the I2R process into their core operations, benefiting from centralized management, enhanced tracking, and improved collaboration between IT and business teams.

Anatomy of the I2R Process

A typical I2R process involves the following stages:

1. **Incident Reporting** is the initial step where end-users or automated systems log issues that disrupt normal operations. This step ensures that every problem is documented for resolution using TCodes "`CRM_UI`" or "`Fiori App Create Incident`".

2. **Incident Categorization** involves organizing the reported incidents into predefined categories to streamline subsequent resolution activities. It uses TCodes "`IQS1`" for Quality Notifications or Fiori app "`Classify Incidents`" to assign categories.

3. **Incident Prioritization** helps in allocating resources efficiently for incidents based on urgency and business impact. Here, TCodes "`IW51`" is used for maintenance notifications or Fiori App "`Prioritize Incident`" for intuitive prioritization.

4. **Incident Analysis and Diagnosis** helps in identifying the root cause of incidents to implement effective solutions using TCodes "`SE80`" or Fiori app "`Analyze Root Cause`" for structured analysis.

5. **Resolution and Recovery** solutions are implemented and tested to ensure the issue is fully resolved before the incident is closed using TCodes "`IW52`" for updating existing notifications or Fiori app "`Resolve Incident`" to document or execute solutions.

6. **Closure and Feedback** verifies that the incident is fully resolved, updating records, and collecting feedback to improve future processes using TCodes "`CRMD_ORDER`" for finalizing the incident records or Fiori app "`Close Incident`" for streamlined closure processes.

Figure 4.8: *Anatomy of a Standard I2R Process*

Real-World Example: A Global Manufacturing Company's I2R Process Architecture

A global manufacturing company implemented an integrated Incident-to-Resolution (I2R) process, seamlessly connecting SAP S/4HANA with non-SAP systems. SAP Integration Suite was used to connect the SAP S/4HANA with the MES and IoT platforms. The solution enabled the centralized incident reporting through a unified service portal, automated alerts from the IoT devices, and collaborative workflows between IT, production teams, and third-party vendors via SAP Workflow Management. With root cause analysis powered by SAP Solution Manager, the system ensures streamlined and efficient end-to-end execution.

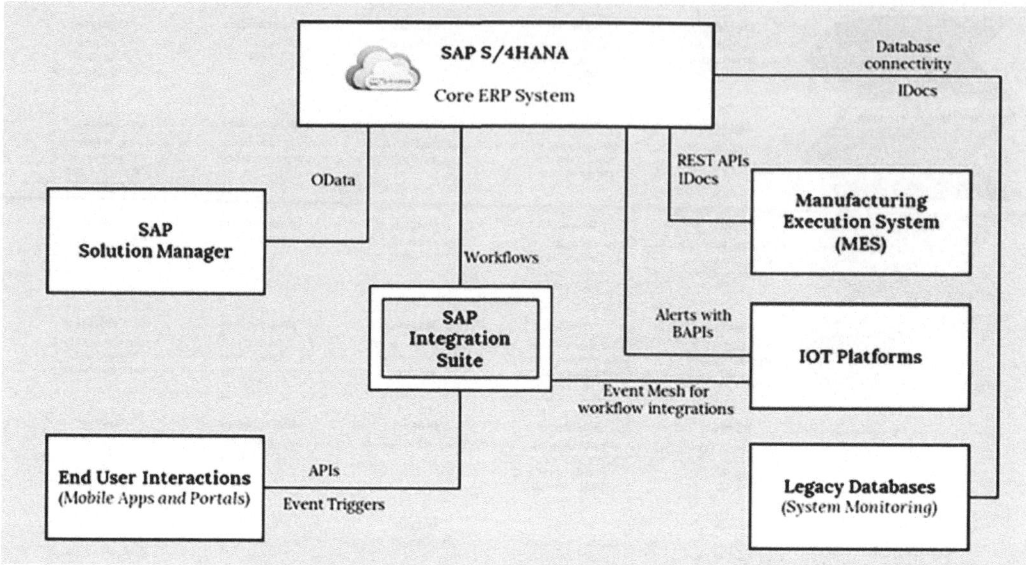

Figure 4.9: *Solution Architecture of I2R Process*

Hire-to-Retire (H2R) Process

The Hire-to-Retire (H2R) process covers the entire journey of an employee within an organization, from recruitment to retirement. It forms the backbone of workforce management by aligning people with business objectives.

H2R ensures that HR operations are standardized, employees have seamless experience throughout their career, and the organization remains compliant with local and global regulations. By streamlining processes such as hiring, onboarding, payroll, performance management, learning, and offboarding, it helps businesses maintain operational efficiency while fostering employee satisfaction and engagement.

Anatomy of the H2R Process

The following activities are covered in a standard H2R Process:

1. **Recruitment and Hiring:** Attracting, assessing, and selecting the right talent to meet organizational needs.
2. **Onboarding:** Integrating new employees smoothly into the organization through effective orientation and documentation processes.
3. **Core HR Operations:** Managing employee records, benefits, organizational structures, and personal information efficiently.

4. **Payroll and Time Management:** Ensuring accurate compensation, benefits administration, and time tracking for compliance and satisfaction.
5. **Performance Management:** Setting clear goals, assessing performance, and enabling continuous feedback to drive growth.
6. **Learning and Development:** Identifying skill gaps, providing training, and fostering professional development to build future capabilities.
7. **Offboarding and Retirement:** Managing employee exits and retirements with proper documentation, knowledge transfer, and final settlements to ensure compliance and smooth transitions.

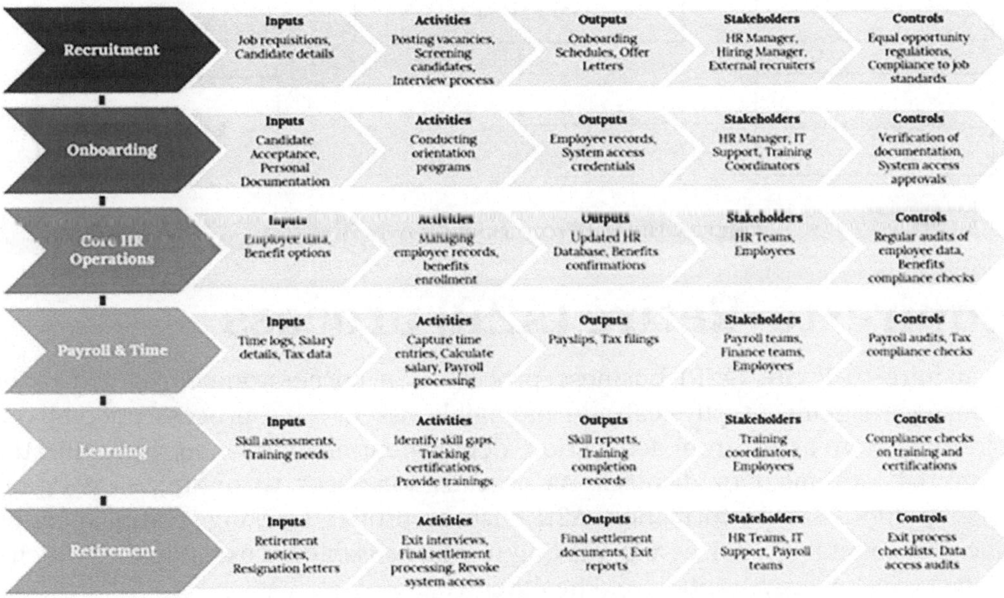

Figure 4.10: *Anatomy of a Standard H2R Process*

Real-World Example: A Manufacturing Company's H2R Process Architecture

The company implemented an integrated H2R process to streamline the workforce management for their 25,000 employees across countries.

- **SAP S/4HANA** for core HR and payroll operations.
- **SAP SuccessFactors** for recruitment, onboarding, and performance management.
- **SAP Analytics Cloud** for HR reporting and insights.

- **Non-SAP systems** for niche requirements such as e-learning platforms and local tax compliance tools.

The following figure illustrates the solution architecture and integrations:

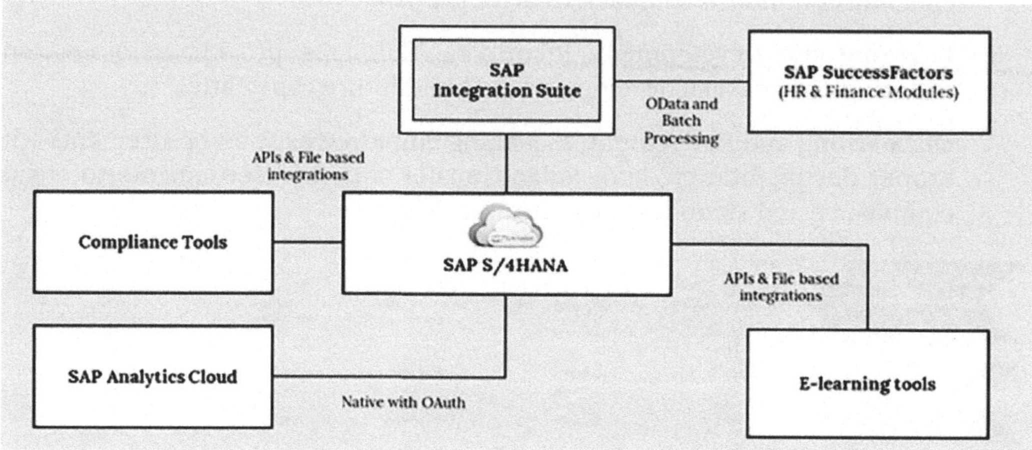

Figure 4.11: *H2R Process Solution Architecture*

Acquire-to-Retire (A2R) process

The Acquire-to-Retire (A2R) business process is a cornerstone for organizations that manage significant physical and intangible assets. This process encompasses the journey of an asset–from acquisition, deployment, maintenance, and utilization, to eventual retirement or disposal. As organizations seek to optimize operational efficiency and asset performance, A2R ensures proper tracking, compliance, and financial accountability for assets, making it indispensable across industries such as manufacturing, energy, utilities, and healthcare.

Anatomy of the A2R Process

The following typical activities are covered in a standard A2R Process:

1. **Planning and Budgeting**: Identifying asset needs based on strategic goals, forecasting requirements, and securing necessary financial approvals.
2. **Procurement**: Selecting suitable suppliers, negotiating contracts, and placing purchase orders to acquire assets at optimal value and quality.
3. **Acquisition and Installation**: Receiving, inspecting, and installing assets to ensure they are fit for purpose and ready for operational use.
4. **Operation and Maintenance**: Managing the effective utilization of assets and scheduling regular maintenance to extend their lifespan and maintain operational reliability.

5. **Depreciation and Financial Management**: Tracking the financial value of assets over time through depreciation and maintaining accurate asset records for reporting and compliance.

6. **Retirement and Disposal**: Evaluating asset condition, determining end-of-life strategies, and managing disposal or retirement in alignment with environmental, financial, and regulatory considerations.

The following figure shows the anatomy of A2R process from its key components including Inputs, Activities, Outputs, Stakeholders, and Controls:

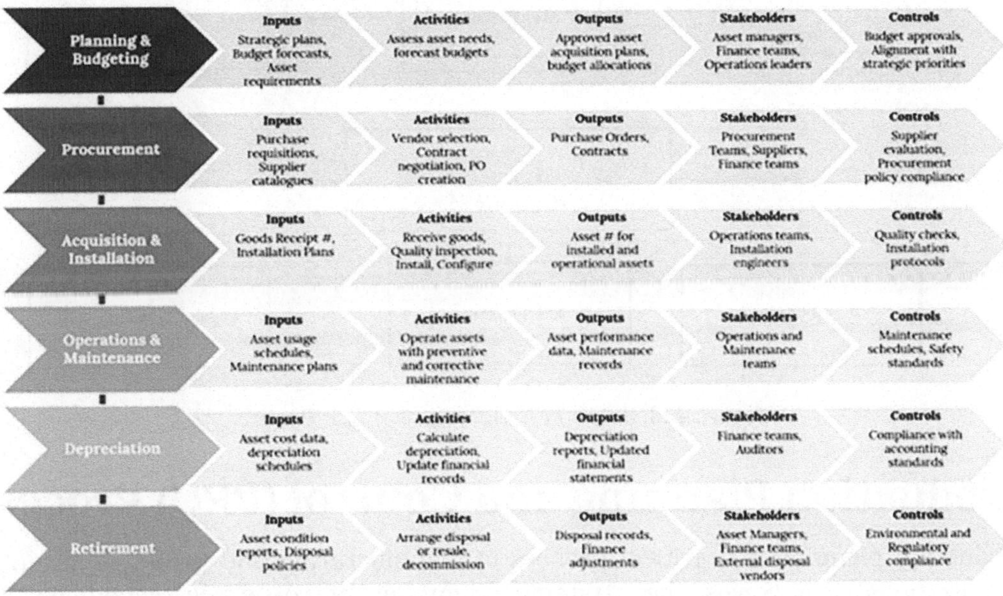

Figure 4.12: *Anatomy of a Standard A2R Process*

Real-World Example: A Global Energy Company's A2R Process Architecture

A leading global energy provider streamlined its asset management process across multiple geographies by leveraging SAP S/4HANA as its core ERP system, integrating it with several non-SAP systems to implement a comprehensive A2R solution. The solution architecture includes the following applications and technologies:

1. **SAP S/4HANA**: Core system managing financials, asset master data, and depreciation.

2. **SAP Asset Manager**: Mobile-enabled tool for operations and maintenance tasks.

3. **SAP Ariba**: Procurement platform for asset acquisition.
4. **IoT Platform**: Non-SAP system for real-time asset performance monitoring.
5. **Custom Integration Layer**: Middleware to connect SAP S/4HANA with external systems, such as Geographic Information System (GIS) and a legacy asset management tool.

The following diagram illustrates the high-level solution architecture.

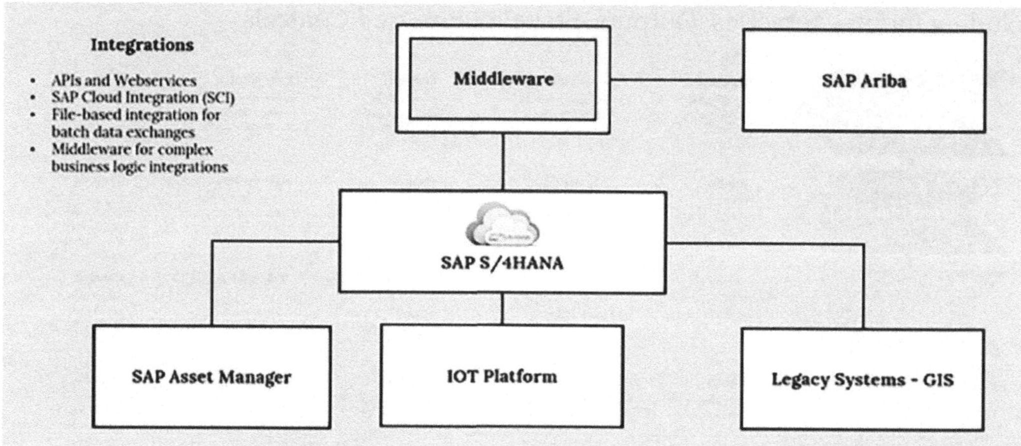

Figure 4.13: *Solution Architecture of A2R Process*

Production Planning and Control (PPC) Process

Production planning is a critical process in manufacturing and production-centric organizations. It involves the strategic alignment of resources, schedules, and processes to meet production goals efficiently. PPC process ensures that the right materials are available when needed, resources are allocated optimally, and customer demands are fulfilled on time.

In every organization, understanding the production planning is vital for:

- Synchronizing supply chain activities to maintain a seamless flow of goods and services.
- Minimizing production costs by reducing waste and optimizing resource usage.
- Enhancing customer satisfaction through timely deliveries.

Anatomy of the PPC Process

A typical PPC process includes the following activities:

1. **Demand Management** is the first step where sales forecasts and customer orders are consolidated to create demand plans.
2. **Material Requirements Planning (MRP)** comes next, calculating the necessary materials and generating procurement proposals.
3. **Capacity Planning** evaluates production capacity against workload to balance resources and avoid bottlenecks.
4. **Shop Floor Control** ensures that production orders are managed and monitored during execution.
5. **Production Execution** involves executing manufacturing tasks and recording actual production data.
6. **Production Monitoring and Reporting** analyzes production performance to identify gaps, improve processes, and ensure plans are met.

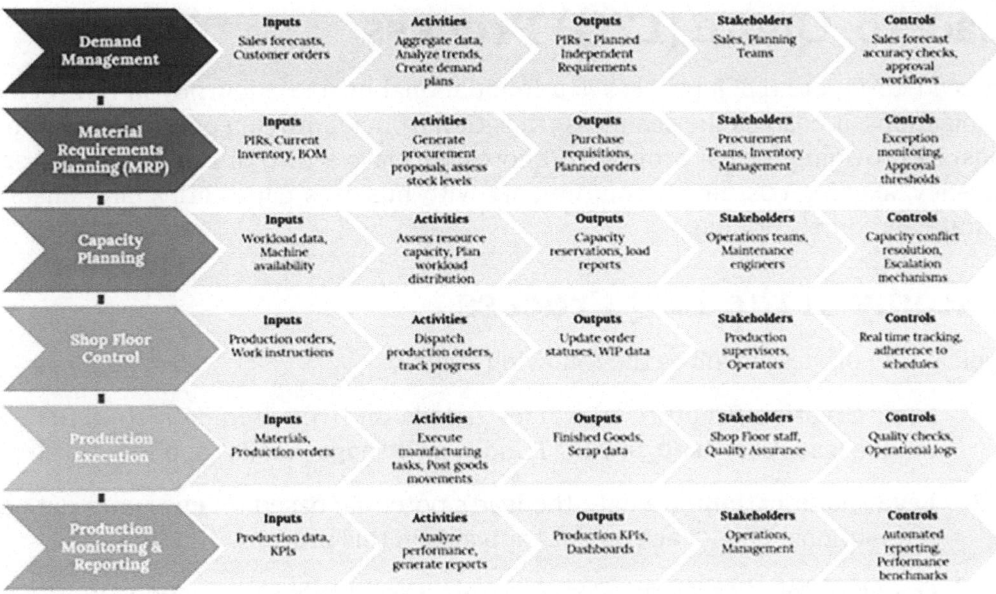

Figure 4.14: *Anatomy of a Standard PPC Process*

Real-World Example: A Global Automotive Company's PPC Process Architecture

A global automotive manufacturer implemented the PPC process with SAP S/4HANA as core ERP and integrated it with SAP PP, Manufacturing Execution System (MES), and non-SAP systems like a custom demand planning tool and third-party logistics (3PL) software.

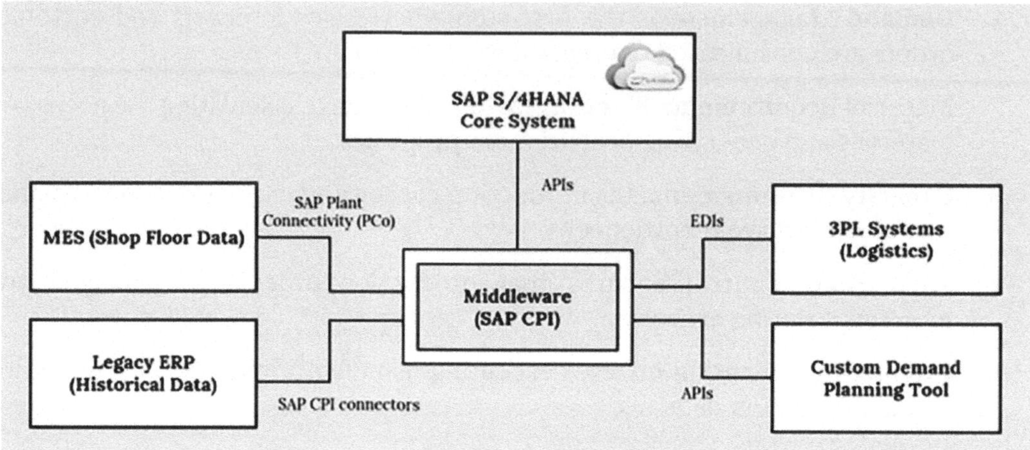

Figure 4.15: *Solution Architecture of PPC Process*

Lead-to-Quote (L2Q) Process

The Lead-to-Quote (L2Q) process is a foundational business journey in SAP-centric organizations. It enables the seamless transition from identifying potential customers (leads) to providing formal proposals (quotes). It plays a pivotal role in driving sales efficiency, aligning customer requirements with business capabilities, and ensuring accurate and timely pricing.

Anatomy of the L2Q Process

A typical L2Q process involves the following stages:

1. **Lead Creation:** Capture customer details and requirements to generate a unique lead. Use "**`CRMD_ORDER`**" TCodes or "**`Manage Leads`**" app for this step.

2. **Lead Qualification:** Evaluate the lead's potential based on customer data and interactions. The "**`Check Leads`**" app aids in this process.

3. **Opportunity Creation:** Convert qualified leads into opportunities by defining sales stages and linking relevant data. Use **`CRMD_ORDER`** or "**`Manage Opportunities`**" app.

4. **Quotation Preparation:** Create a formal quotation with accurate pricing and terms using "**`VA21`**" TCodes or "**`Create Sales Quotation`**" app.

5. **Quotation Review and Approval:** Review and approve the prepared quotation through automated workflows. Leverage the "`My Inbox for Approvals`" app.
6. **Quote Submission:** Deliver the approved quote to the customer using the "`Send Quotation`" app, ensuring proper tracking and acknowledgment.

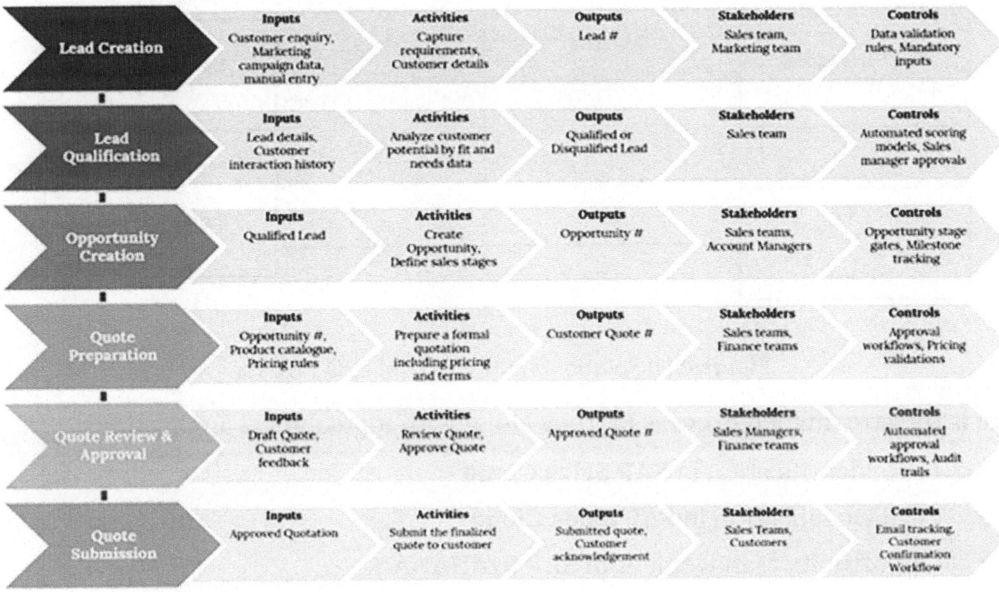

Figure 4.16: *Anatomy of a Standard L2Q Process*

Real-World Example: A Manufacturing Company's L2Q Process's Architecture

A global equipment manufacturing company streamlined their L2Q process with lead management, opportunity tracking, and quotation preparation for faster customer response times, and data consistency across the functions.

The solution architecture includes interconnected systems:

- SAP S/4HANA as ERP Core
- SAP Sales Cloud for lead and opportunity management.
- SAP CPQ for dynamic pricing and quote generation.
- Non-SAP CRM for customer interaction data.
- Third-party Email Services for quote submission.

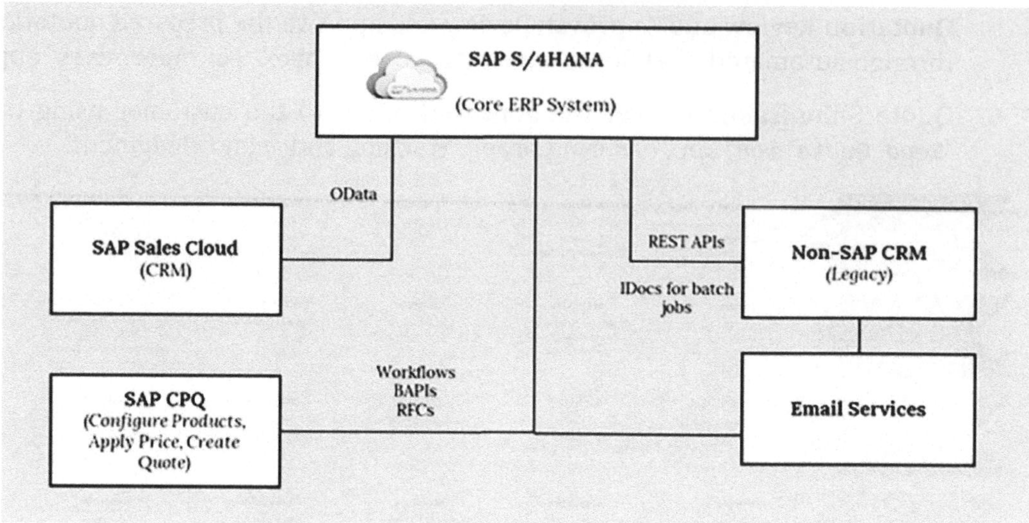

Figure 4.17: *Solution Architecture of L2Q Process*

Here is the streamlined process journey along with its technical applications:

- Lead Identification in **SAP Sales Cloud**
- Lead Qualification in **SAP Sales Cloud**
- Opportunity Management in **SAP S/4HANA**
- Quotation Generation in **SAP CPQ**
- Approval Workflow in **SAP S/4HANA**
- Quote Submission to **Non-SAP CRM**

SAP S/4HANA Integration Architecture

In SAP centric organizations, application integration architecture plays a critical role in enabling seamless interactions with SAP and non-SAP systems. It enables seamless data flow and process execution across the organization.

For QA teams, understanding the integration architecture is essential to:

- **Design Relevant Test Cases**: Knowing which systems interact helps create meaningful integration and regression tests that cover real business scenarios.
- **Ensure Test Coverage:** Testing only SAP without validating integration touchpoints can leave critical gaps.
- **Validate Data Accuracy:** Integration tests confirm that data flows correctly between systems without loss, duplication, or errors.
- **Assess Business Process Continuity:** Integration failures often impact end-to-end processes. Testing them ensures seamless operations.

- **Improve Issue Diagnosis:** Knowledge of integration flows enables faster root cause analysis when defects arise.

Key Components

SAP S/4HANA provides a robust framework to connect with other applications. Some of its key integration components include:

- **SAP Integration Suite**: A cloud-based middleware that facilitates integration using APIs, events, and pre-built connectors, enabling faster time-to-value.
- **IDocs (Intermediate Documents)**: Used for asynchronous data exchange between SAP and external systems.
- **OData Services**: RESTful APIs for lightweight, real-time communication.
- **RFC (Remote Function Calls)**: For synchronous communication with SAP applications.
- **SAP Event Mesh**: Supports event-driven architecture with a publish/subscribe model for real-time communication.
- **Third-party integration platforms**: Tools such as MuleSoft, Dell Boomi, and Informatica are often used to connect SAP S/4HANA with non-SAP applications.

Common Integration Flows in SAP S/4HANA Projects

Here are some typical integration scenarios seen in SAP S/4HANA programs:

- **Financial Data Synchronization**

  Use Case: Synchronization of financial transactions between SAP S/4HANA and Oracle NetSuite or Microsoft Dynamics 365.

  Integration Tools: SAP Integration Suite, MuleSoft connectors.

  Flow: Financial entries created in SAP S/4HANA, such as journal entries or payment runs, are shared with NetSuite/Dynamics for consolidated financial reporting and audit.

- **Customer Data Exchange**

  Use Case: Real-time synchronization of customer profiles between SAP S/4HANA and SAP C/4HANA.

  Integration Tools: OData services, SAP Event Mesh.

  Flow: Updates in customer data (for example, contact details, order history) in SAP C/4HANA are reflected in S/4HANA to support accurate order processing and customer service.

- **Procurement Integration**

  Use Case: Seamless procurement lifecycle management with systems such as SAP Ariba, Coupa, and SAP Fieldglass.

  Integration Tools: Pre-built connectors, APIs.

  Flow: Purchase requisitions created in S/4HANA are sent to SAP Ariba for supplier collaboration, while Coupa/Fieldglass handles external workforce procurement.

- **HR Data Flow**

  Use Case: Synchronization of employee and payroll data between SAP S/4HANA, SAP SuccessFactors, and Workday.

  Integration Tools: OData APIs, IDocs.

  Flow: Employee master data and payroll details flow seamlessly from SuccessFactors to S/4HANA for accurate financial postings.

- **Manufacturing Data Integration**

  Use Case: Real-time integration with shop floor systems via SAP Digital Manufacturing Cloud.

  Integration Tools: Event-driven architecture.

  Flow: Production orders and shop floor data updates (for example, machine status, production output) are synchronized with SAP S/4HANA to ensure end-to-end visibility.

- **Manufacturing Data with Non-SAP Applications**

  Use Case: Integration with non-SAP manufacturing systems such as Siemens MES, Rockwell Automation, and GE Digital's Predix.

  Integration Tools: Third-party middleware (for example, MuleSoft), custom APIs.

  Flow: Shop floor systems such as Siemens MES send production and quality data to SAP S/4HANA for analysis and order tracking, while Rockwell Automation systems provide real-time machine performance data for operational insights. GE Predix can relay IoT data to S/4HANA for predictive maintenance and analytics.

Pro Tip: *For SAP integration testing, adopt end-to-end scenario tests covering both synchronous (RFC) and asynchronous (IDoc, Event Mesh) communications. These test cases can help you detect delayed or failed message flows early.*

Conclusion

Understanding business processes in SAP is foundational for effective quality engineering in SAP landscapes. This chapter explored the intricate interplay of these processes and underscores why grasping their nuances is essential for creating robust test plans and strategies.

In the following chapters, we will translate these foundational insights into actionable test plans and strategies, empowering SAP landscapes to perform at their highest potential.

References

- https://learning.sap.com/learning-journeys/explore-integrated-business-processes-in-sap-s-4hana-
- https://help.sap.com/docs/SAP_S4HANA_CLOUD/1cbcff7ccd35405ab445b223c1ab1588/2f610a5f08cb4142ac188c3e6a127b4e.html
- https://help.sap.com/docs/SAP_PLANT_CONNECTIVITY/c90214be0d934ebdb6f3bce29c63c0ff/46a00344d44852b7e10000000a155369.html
- https://help.sap.com/docs/sap-digital-manufacturing/integration-guide/integration-with-sap-s-4hana-or-sap-erp
- https://help.sap.com/docs/plm-system-integration-for-s4hana/configuration/integration-patterns

CHAPTER 5
Fundamentals of Testing

Introduction

According to a 2022 report by the Consortium for Information and Software Quality (CISQ), poor software quality costs the US economy an estimated $2.41 trillion annually, driven by operational failures, software defects, and legacy system shortcomings. Operational software failures alone account for $1.56 trillion of this loss. Organizations that fail to adopt robust testing practices risk escalating error rates, costly rework, and degraded user trust, all of which undermine business outcomes and competitiveness.

In today's fast-paced digital environment, software testing is the cornerstone of delivering reliable, secure, and high-performing SAP applications. For enterprises, effective testing is not optional - it is essential to mitigate risks such as system downtime, data integrity issues, and business process disruptions.

This chapter delivers a comprehensive overview of software testing fundamentals grounded in SAP best practices. It articulates the core purpose and objectives of testing, highlights foundational principles, and walks through the structured testing process covering key activities, roles, and deliverables essential for success.

Structure

This chapter aims to provide comprehensive coverage on the fundamentals of testing:

- Understanding Software Testing
- Necessity of Testing
- Tester's Mindset
- Principles of Testing
- Test Process
- Risks and Testing
- Typical Operating Models of Testing

Understanding Software Testing

Software testing is the process of evaluating a software application to ensure it meets specified requirements and functions as expected by the Business.

Testing is More Than Running Tests

A common misunderstanding about testing is that it only involves executing tests. Some believe testing is simply following a sequence of steps, providing inputs, and checking the outputs. While this is an important part of testing, it is just one piece of the puzzle.

Testing also includes:

- **Planning:** Deciding the scope, approach, and schedule of tests.
- **Analysis:** Understanding requirements to identify testable scenarios. Prioritizing what features/requirements to start first and why so.
- **Design and Implementation:** Creating effective test cases and scripts.
- **Reporting:** Sharing test progress, results, and defect findings.

Remember, testing activities occur both before and after running tests, such as preparing test cases and analyzing results.

According to the International Software Testing Qualifications Board (ISTQB), software testing encompasses both **static** and **dynamic** testing.

Static testing involves evaluating software or related work products, such as requirements specifications, design documents, or user stories *without actually executing the code.* It includes activities such as reviews, inspections, and walkthroughs to identify defects early.

Dynamic testing, on the other hand, involves evaluating the software *by executing it* to check its behavior, functionality, and performance against expected outcomes.

Understanding both static and dynamic testing is essential, as together they provide a comprehensive approach to ensuring software quality.

Pro Tip: *Static testing uncovers missing authorizations in* SAP Fiori *apps during design review, preventing compliance failures later.*

Testing is More Than Verification

A common misconception is that testing only involves ensuring the system meets requirements, user stories, or specifications. This aspect of testing is called **Verification**, which focuses on answering the question: "*Have we built the system correctly*?" The emphasis here is on meeting the "**specified requirements**."

However, testing goes beyond verification. To truly ensure software quality, we must also validate whether the system meets the needs of its users and stakeholders in a real-world operational context. Often it is the tester who becomes the advocate for the end-user in this kind of testing. This is known as **Validation**, where we ask: "*Have we built the correct system?*" The focus here is on "**intended use**."

In every software development lifecycle, testing is divided into verification and validation:

- **Verification:**
  - Ensures the product, component, or system is built according to specifications.
  - Answers the question: "*Is the deliverable aligned with the design and requirements?*"
- **Validation:**
  - Confirms the deliverable meets user needs and solves the intended problem.
  - Answers the question: "*Is the deliverable fit for purpose?*"

Figure 5.1: *Verification versus Validation in Testing*

Pro Tip: *Conduct "day-in-the-life" user validation sessions to understand the real SAP business processes, not just the documented requirements.*

Testing is not Debugging

Dynamic testing often reveals failures caused by underlying defects, while static testing identifies the defects themselves. However, it is crucial to note that testing does not resolve these defects. Fixing defects is the responsibility of debugging, a development activity where team members analyze and address the root cause of failures.

Once debugging is complete, an additional testing activity called **Confirmation Testing** is performed. This step ensures the applied fix has successfully resolved the original failure.

In terms of roles:

- **Dynamic testing** is primarily a testing responsibility.
- **Debugging** falls under the development team.
- **Confirmation testing** is once again a testing responsibility.

In Agile teams, however, these roles often overlap. Testers may actively participate in debugging and even component-level testing, blurring the traditional boundaries between testing and development. This collaborative approach enhances efficiency and promotes better integration of quality throughout the development lifecycle.

Pro Tip: *Always prepare "confirmation test cases" for defect closure, especially for critical business processes.*

Typical Objectives of Testing

The following are some of the key objectives documented in the ISTQB Foundation curriculum:

- **Evaluate Work Products:** Use static testing techniques such as reviews to assess requirements, user stories, design, and code.
- **Verify Requirements Fulfilment:** Confirm that all specified requirements have been satisfied.
- **Validate Completeness and Usability:** Ensure the test object works as expected by users and stakeholders, often through collaboration with these groups.
- **Build Confidence in Quality:** Achieve trust in the software by passing high-risk tests and addressing any acceptable failures observed in other tests.

- **Prevent Defects:** Identify and fix issues in early test activities, such as requirement specifications, to prevent downstream defects in design, code, or business logic. Activities such as reviews and test design act as verification and validation for foundational documents, reducing issues during later project phases.
- **Identify Failures and Defects:** Discover issues during testing; this remains a key focus of software testing.
- **Inform Stakeholders:** Provide clear, sufficient information to stakeholders for decision-making regarding software quality. For example, reporting on the satisfaction of entry or exit criteria.
- **Reduce Risk:** Minimize risks associated with poor software quality by addressing failures that could arise during operation.
- **Ensure Compliance:** Verify adherence to contractual, legal, or regulatory standards and confirm the test object meets these compliance requirements.

Keep in mind that objectives can vary. Different perspectives, testing levels, and stakeholders may have their own goals.

Pro Tip: *When verifying requirement fulfillment in SAP, use traceability matrices to link each test case with a business scenario and compliance standard.*

Necessity of Testing

Whether you are implementing, upgrading, or maintaining an SAP system, uncertainties can disrupt timelines, inflate budgets, and jeopardize business outcomes. Testing is not just a safety net against potential failures – it is a strategic enabler that equips you to move forward with confidence, ensuring your system is robust, reliable, and ready for success.

Testing is about Mitigating Risks for SAP Projects

In SAP projects, risks are inevitable. But testing offers the best defense against these risks and equips you to move forward with confidence. Here is how testing minimizes risks in SAP environments:

- **Early Defect Detection:** Testing from the start - during requirements and design - helps catch defects early when they are easier and cheaper to fix. This is especially important in SAP systems, where errors in one module can ripple across others.
- **Safeguarding Customizations and Integrations:** SAP systems often involve significant custom developments and integration with other systems. Testing

ensures these changes do not break existing functionality, keeping business operations running smoothly.

- **Ensuring Compliance:** Industries such as finance or healthcare, life sciences, operate under stringent regulations. Testing helps verify that your SAP system meets all compliance requirements, reducing the risk of penalties or reputational damage.
- **Validate Integrations:** SAP systems integrate with multiple SAP and non-SAP systems. Testing confirms these connections work seamlessly to maintain end-to-end business processes.
- **Optimizing Performance:** Performance and load testing identify potential bottlenecks, ensuring the system remains stable during peak usage periods.
- **Smooth Go-Lives:** Testing before go-live validates all configurations, migrations, and custom developments, ensuring a seamless transition with minimal disruption.

Understanding Errors, Defects, and Failures in SAP Testing: A Cost Perspective

In software testing, particularly in SAP systems, understanding the nuances of errors, defects, and failures is crucial for ensuring the quality and reliability of the system.

- An **error** refers to a human mistake made during the development process, such as a misinterpretation of requirements, a design oversight, or incorrect coding logic.

  Example: A developer misunderstands a requirement and writes incorrect ABAP code for a custom transaction.

- A **defect** (or bug) is a flaw in the software caused by an error. It occurs when the actual behavior of the system does not align with the expected behavior defined in the requirements.

  Example: A custom report in SAP does not calculate tax correctly due to a coding error in the calculation logic.

- A **failure** is the manifestation of a defect when the software is executed. It happens when a defect leads to incorrect results or system malfunctions during runtime.

  Example: During UAT, a business user notices that the custom report displays incorrect tax values, impacting business decisions.

The Rising Cost of Defects

Industry studies consistently show that the cost of fixing a defect rises exponentially the later it is detected in the Software Development Life Cycle (SDLC). Research quantifies this escalation, indicating that the cost of remediation can increase by a factor of **10x or more** as defects progress through successive phases of the SDLC.

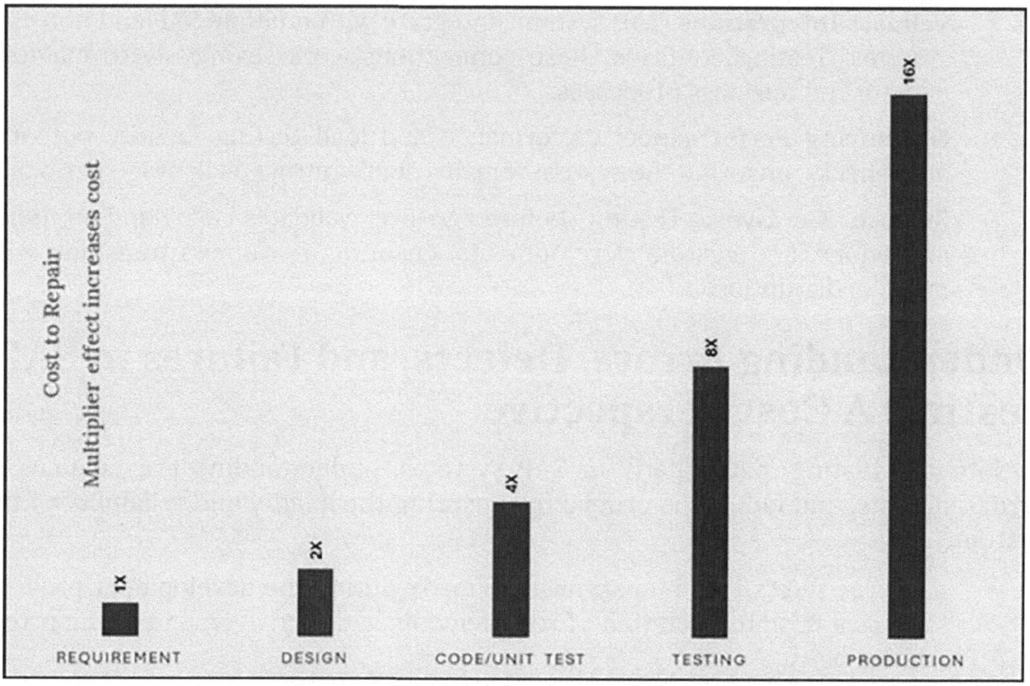

Figure 5.2: *Multiplier Effect on the Cost of Fixing a Defect*

In SAP projects, the multiplier effect is often even higher due to the complexity of integrations, customizations, and cross functional dependencies. Late-stage fixes can also require extensive regression testing to ensure that changes do not inadvertently impact other functionalities.

Pro Tip: *For SAP projects, prioritize integration points and custom code early, as 60-80% of defects cluster there.*

Tester's Mindset

"Testing is like detective work - except your suspects are bugs, and they confess in code and configurations!"

Testers thrive on asking the tough questions: "*What if it fails? What's missing here? What edge case hasn't been considered?*" They look at an SAP requirement and think, "*What could go wrong?*" Developers, in contrast, think, "*How can I implement this?*"

It's a dynamic akin to assembling IKEA furniture—one builds with optimism, the other inspects with skepticism, asking, *"Are we sure this shelf won't collapse under the weight of reality?"*

In SAP's vast landscape—where even minor bugs can ripple through business-critical processes—a tester's mindset is essential. Their independence helps counteract confirmation bias, spotting the issues developers might overlook.

A tester's mindset is illustrated in the following figure, followed by the key patterns of his or her typical thought processes.

Figure 5.3: *A Tester's Mindset at Work*

Curiosity: The Sherlock Holmes of Systems

Great testers have an insatiable curiosity about how systems behave and why they behave that way. When faced with unexpected behavior—say, an SAP Finance report summoning 2025 data in 2024—they instinctively dig deeper. They isolate failures, connect the dots, and often unearth systemic flaws. Their curiosity is fueled by an itch to understand *everything*, leaving no stone—or table, in SAP terms, unturned.

Pro Tip: *Ask the what-if questions - what if the SAP batch job fails? What if data inputs are outside the expected range?*

Professional Pessimism: Hope for the Best, Test for the Worst

A good tester expects to find defects—not because they're negative, but because they understand the fallibility of software. They don't assume a smooth transaction in SAP S/4HANA's procurement flow; instead, they ask, *what happens if the purchase order fails to sync with inventory?*

A Critical Eye: Doubting for the Greater Good

Professional pessimism pairs perfectly with a critical eye. Great testers live by the mantra: "*If in doubt, it's a bug.*" Whether it's a mismatched font size in SAP Fiori or an integration issue in SAP Activate, they question correctness at every step. Their skepticism is not cynicism—it is craftsmanship.

Attention to Detail: A Blessing and a Curse

From subtle UI glitches to warning signs of catastrophic failure, good testers see *everything*. That typo in the SAP workflow message? Spotted. The inconsistent formatting in a transport log? Flagged. Unfortunately, this trait extends beyond work; they're the ones pointing out spelling errors in menus and inconsistencies in movie subtitles. Their friends sometimes wish they came with an off switch.

Experience: The Bug Whisperer

Seasoned testers know defects not just by sight but by instinct. Having faced a parade of bugs—ranging from the trivial to the terrifying—they leverage their experience during exploratory, integration, and regression testing. For instance, they know that in a complex SAP rollout, integration points between modules are fertile ground for hidden defects.

Communication Skills: Speaking Truth Without Bruising Egos

All the technical prowess in the world is futile if a tester can't effectively communicate findings. Imagine telling a developer their code turned an SAP payroll run into a nightmare. Good testers deliver such news with tact, humor, and a collaborative spirit—bridging gaps rather than widening them.

Enterprise Architecture Thinking: Beyond the Silos

The best testers think beyond components or individual applications. They zoom out to evaluate processes, integrations, and end-to-end workflows. In SAP environments, this would mean testing not just a single approval workflow but the entire Procure-to-Pay process, ensuring it operates seamlessly across modules.

Principles of Testing

In this section, we will explore fundamental testing principles refined over the past 40+ years and documented by software quality experts and ISTQB. These principles, though sometimes overlooked or misunderstood, are at play in nearly every project. Understanding how to recognize and apply them will elevate your skills and make you a more effective tester. In this section, we try not only to understand these principles from testing in general but also reflect them on the SAP landscape to gain critical SAP perspectives as well.

Principle 1: Testing Shows the Presence of Defects, not Their Absence

Testing can show that defects are present but cannot prove that there are no defects. The goal is to find as many defects as possible to improve the system quality.

In SAP projects, especially during transports or S/4HANA system upgrades, testing often uncovers functional, integration, or performance issues that might not have been apparent during development. For example, custom Fiori apps may function in a standalone system but fail in a multi-system landscape due to misconfigured communication settings or data inconsistencies. This principle reminds us to focus on uncovering critical issues rather than chasing perfection.

Pro Tip: *In an SAP S/4HANA upgrade, use exploratory testing to uncover integration defects not anticipated in standard scripts.*

Principle 2: Exhaustive Testing is Impossible

Testing every possible input, condition, and scenario in an application is infeasible due to time, cost, and resource constraints.

The complexity of SAP landscapes, with their vast integration points (for example, SAP Ariba, SuccessFactors, and third-party systems), makes exhaustive testing impossible.

Instead, testing should prioritize key business processes like Order-to-Cash (O2C) or Procure-to-Pay (P2P) using risk-based and coverage-oriented approaches. Test Automation tools are usually employed to optimize test coverage.

Principle 3: Early Testing Saves Time and Money

Defects are cheaper and easier to fix when discovered early in the project lifecycle, such as during requirement validation or solution feasibility validation.

Early testing in SAP projects includes validating configurations during the realization phase and leveraging automated testing mindset right from the beginning. For example, catching an incorrectly configured tax procedure during the configuration phase avoids significant downstream rework when testing finance processes.

Further, since much of the cost in SAP projects is associated with human effort, and since the size of a project team is relatively inflexible once the project is underway, reduced cost of defect also means reduced duration of the project.

Pro Tip: *Start test automation and business process validation from blueprint phase. Organizations report up to 40% project savings with early prep.*

Principle 4: Defects Cluster Together

Defects often concentrate in a few modules or areas of the system due to code complexity, frequent upgrades, or dependencies.

In SAP S/4HANA projects, heavily customized modules (for example, SD, MM, or Finance) or areas undergoing frequent changes (for example, integrations or user interfaces) are more likely to harbor defects. This principle highlights the importance of applying focused testing efforts in these high-risk areas, such as regression testing for business-critical processes including payroll or financial reconciliation.

Pro Tip: *Focus testing on custom SD/MM processes or frequent change areas for higher defect detection.*

Principle 5: Beware of the Pesticide Paradox

Repeated execution of the same set of tests eventually makes them ineffective at finding new defects.

In SAP projects, automated regression test suites need continuous updates to account for new functionalities, integrations, or process changes. For example, if you are testing SAP Fiori apps, static test scripts may miss usability or performance issues unless updated regularly. Introducing exploratory testing or varying test data helps mitigate this paradox.

Pro Tip: *Regularly update SAP regression packs and include new business scenarios.*

Principle 6: Testing is Context Dependent

The approach to testing varies depending on the system, project, or industry requirements.

Testing a greenfield S/4HANA implementation requires extensive functional, integration, and UAT testing, while a brownfield migration focuses on data validation and regression testing. For example, a pharmaceutical company may prioritize GxP compliance testing, whereas a retailer may emphasize performance testing during peak sales periods.

Principle 7: Absence-of-Errors is A Fallacy

A system with no reported defects may not necessarily meet user needs or business requirements.

An SAP solution might pass all functional tests but still fail to satisfy end users due to poor performance (for example, slow Fiori app load times) or suboptimal usability (for example, complex navigation). This principle emphasizes the need for holistic quality assurance, including performance, usability, and user acceptance testing.

Principle 8: Test Data Drive Test Accuracy

Accurate and representative test data is critical for meaningful results.

Test data in SAP projects must reflect real-world scenarios, such as customer master data, vendor accounts, and transactional records. Poor test data quality may lead to false positives or missed defects, particularly in end-to-end scenarios such as Supply Chain Management.

Principle 9: Continuous Testing Ensures Quality in Agile Delivery

Frequent and iterative testing is essential in agile or DevOps environments.

As SAP customers adopt SAP Activate or agile methodologies, continuous testing is necessary to validate frequent changes. Automating test cases for sprints, including APIs and interfaces like IDocs, accelerates testing and improves delivery timelines.

Principle 10: Collaboration Enhances Testing Outcomes

Testing cannot succeed in isolation; collaboration with business users, developers, and stakeholders is vital.

In SAP projects, testers must collaborate with functional configuration consultants, developers, and end users to ensure alignment between requirements, configurations, and test cases. For example, close collaboration with business users during UAT ensures that test scenarios reflect real-world business processes.

Pro Tip: *Integrate testers in business workshops and sprint reviews for deeper process understanding.*

Test Process

The test process is a structured approach to ensuring the quality of a software product. In the context of SAP S/4HANA projects, this process plays an important role due to the complexity and scale of implementations. However, the test process is not uniform across all SAP projects; it varies significantly depending on the project type, such as greenfield implementations, brownfield migrations, or hybrid projects. Let us explore how the test process aligns with these variations and examine its key components.

Project in Context

Understanding the context of the project is the first step in defining an effective test process. Several factors must be considered:

- **Project Lifecycle:**
  - **Greenfield Implementation**: Involves setting up SAP S/4HANA from scratch, requiring extensive testing of new configurations and integrations.
  - **Brownfield Migration**: Focuses on upgrading an existing SAP ECC system, with significant emphasis on regression testing and data migration validation.
  - **Hybrid Projects**: Combine elements of greenfield and brownfield, necessitating a mix of new functionality testing and legacy system validation.
- **Test Levels and Types:** Testing levels include unit, integration, system, and user acceptance testing (UAT). Additionally, test types such as performance, security, and compliance testing must align with project goals.

- **Business Landscape:** Integration with external applications such as Mobile apps, CRM and other systems.
- **Operational Constraints:**
    - o **Resource Constraints**: Availability of skilled testers or automation experts.
    - o **Cost Constraints**: Budget limitations influence the extent of automation and test coverage.
    - o **Operational Constraints**: Business operations that might limit system downtime or testing windows.
- **Organizational policies and governance standards:**
    - o Each organization has policies that influence the test process, such as compliance with industry standards, security mandates, or data privacy regulations.
    - o For example, adhering to GDPR requires extensive validation of data handling in SAP systems.

Understanding Test Coverage

Test coverage is a vital aspect of software testing that evaluates how thoroughly the software has been tested against its requirements, user stories, and technical designs. It provides a clear measure of how much of the test basis - the foundational artifacts such as requirements, user stories, design documents, and code—has been addressed through testing. This helps identify gaps in testing and ensures that all critical areas of the system are verified.

The test basis serves as the blueprint for creating test cases, encompassing everything from functional requirements to regulatory standards. "Coverage items" are the specific elements within this test basis, such as user stories, code modules, or communication paths, that need to be validated. For instance, in system-level testing, testers might ensure all user stories are exercised, while component testing might focus on code modules and branches. Coverage is quantified as a percentage, making it easy to track testing progress and highlight untested areas.

Beyond technical specifications, test coverage also extends to environmental and user-related aspects. For example, Fiori applications might need testing across different devices and browsers to ensure compatibility, while user-centric testing ensures diverse personas and success criteria are considered. Measuring these additional dimensions of coverage builds stakeholder confidence, demonstrating that the software is robust and operational risks are minimized.

Test coverage is more than a measure of completeness; it is a strategic tool for achieving testing objectives. It aligns testing efforts with business priorities, identifies untested areas, and ensures that the software meets both technical and user expectations. By continuously measuring and improving test coverage, teams can deliver high-quality, reliable software.

Test Activities and Tasks

A test process involves several interconnected activities, each playing a crucial role in ensuring software quality.

- **Test Planning** sets the foundation by defining the scope, objectives, and approach for testing. This activity establishes a clear direction for the testing effort, ensuring alignment with project goals and constraints.
- **Test Monitoring and Control** ensure that testing activities are on track. By regularly assessing progress, deviations from the plan can be identified early, allowing timely adjustments to stay aligned with project timelines.
- **Test Analysis** identifies the conditions to be tested and prioritizes them based on risk and importance. In SAP S/4HANA projects, this could involve analyzing key business processes like procure-to-pay or order-to-cash to identify critical testing areas.
- **Test Design** translates analysis into actionable test cases and scripts. These are the detailed steps that testers will follow to validate functionality.
- **Test Data Planning** focuses on preparing accurate and relevant data for testing.
- **Test Execution** involves running the test cases, capturing the results, and reporting any defects. For SAP hybrid projects, parallel testing can validate the consistency and performance of the new system alongside the existing one.
- **Test Completion** wraps up the process by summarizing outcomes, archiving artifacts, and documenting lessons learned. This ensures a clear understanding of what was achieved and areas for improvement in future projects.

Test Work Products are Essential

'*Work products*' is the generic name given to any form of documentation, informal communication or artefact that is used in testing. When testing is more formal, the majority of work products may be written documentation; when testing is very informal, the corresponding work product may just be a note in someone's mobile phone.

Test work products can be captured, stored, and managed in configuration management tools, or possibly in test management tools or defect management tools. The following is a list of standard work products across test activities and tasks.

- **Test planning** work products include test plans. A test plan is a planning document that contains information about what is intended to happen in the future and is similar to a project plan. It does not contain details of the test conditions, test cases, or other aspects of testing. A typical test plan includes information about the test basis, entry and exit criteria.

- **Test monitoring and control** work products include different types of test reports. For example, test progress reports, and summary reports are created on a regular basis to keep stakeholders informed about the progress. The work products in this activity must address project management concerns such as budget and schedule, task completion, resource allocation, usage, and effort.
- **Test analysis** work products include mainly test conditions, as these are the output of a test analysis activity. Each test condition is ideally traceable to the test basis.
- **Test design** work products include test cases, test environment readiness, and identification of tools.
- **Test data planning** work products include test data management. It includes defining test data strategy, and test data creation.
- **Test execution** work products include test procedures, test suites, test execution schedule, test execution reports, and defect reports. At this point, we want to know what happened when the tests were run. We want to know about any problems encountered that may have blocked some tests running.
- **Test completion** work products include test summary reports, action items for improvement, change requests, and product backlog items. Test completion work products give closure to the whole of the test process and should provide ongoing ideas for increasing the effectiveness and efficiency of testing within the organization for future.

Effective Traceability Between Test Work Products

Effective traceability ensures that work products are interconnected and aligned with project objectives. Bi-directional traceability allows for tracking a requirement through test conditions and test cases to test execution results, and vice versa. This cross-linking of work products enhances the test process in multiple ways. It aids in measuring and reporting test coverage, allowing stakeholders to see how well requirements are validated and how defects are linked to them.

Good traceability supports the following critical aspects of testing:

- It enables impact analysis by identifying the requirements and systems affected by changes.
- It ensures that testing is auditable and allows the measurement of coverage against governance standards.

- Coherent test progress and summary reports can be generated, presenting stakeholders with clear, actionable insights.
- By relating technical testing aspects to business terms, traceability fosters better stakeholder understanding.
- Additionally, it provides key data to evaluate product quality, process efficiency, and progress against business goals.

Pro Tip: *In high-regulation* SAP S/4HANA *projects, the traceability matrix created by testers proved invaluable during compliance audit reviews.*

To maintain effective traceability, test management or Application Lifecycle Management (ALM) tools can be leveraged. Many tools support traceability features, which automate the linking of work products and simplify impact analysis. Automated traceability is essential for managing complex projects, as manual methods are unsustainable at scale. Ensuring that traceability is automated not only streamlines the testing process but also enhances consistency and reliability in reporting and decision-making.

Risks and Testing

A risk in a project is defined as the possibility of a negative or undesirable outcome that could impact the quality, timeline, cost, or overall success of the software development process. These risks, arising from technical, operational, or business contexts, necessitate robust management strategies to ensure project success. In SAP S/4HANA projects, risks are typically classified into two broad categories: **product risks** and **project risks**.

Product Risks

Product risks relate to the system or software under development and the possibility of failing to meet customer, user, or stakeholder expectations. These risks can manifest in various forms:

- **Functional Failures:**
    - Missing or incorrect functionalities, such as unfulfilled business requirements or errors in critical modules like finance or logistics.
    - **Example**: An accounts payable module might fail to process transactions correctly due to errors in calculation logic.
- **Data Integrity and Quality Issues:**
    - Problems such as data migration errors, data conversion issues, and violations of data standards.

  - **Example**: A retail company's data migration from SAP ECC to S/4HANA revealed duplicate entries in product master data, leading to supply chain inefficiencies.
- **Quality Attribute Failures:**
  - Non-functional aspects, including performance, security, usability, and reliability.
  - **Example**: Response times in a high-performance transaction processing system may degrade under load, leading to customer dissatisfaction.
- **User Experience (UX) Gaps:**
  - The system may fail to meet user expectations for simplicity and ease of use.
  - **Example**: Users may struggle with Fiori-based interfaces if they are not intuitive or aligned with business workflows.

Project Risks

Project risks pertain to the management and execution of the testing process itself. These risks can hinder the testing effort or the overall project timeline, budget, and outcomes. Common project risks include:

- **Project Issues:**
  - **Delays in Deliverables**: Test items or environments may not be delivered on time.

    Example: Logistics or product quality issues may block critical tests.
  - **Budget Constraints**: Reallocation of funds or cost-cutting measures may result in insufficient resources for testing.
  - **Late Changes**: Significant product changes can invalidate test cases and require rework.
- **Operating Model Challenges:**
  - **Staffing Issues**: Insufficient skills or personnel can impede effective testing. For example, lack of training in automation tools can lead to inefficiencies.
  - **Conflict Among Teams**: Misalignment between vendors or internal teams may affect productivity.
- **Political and Communication Issues:**
  - **Inadequate Communication**: Poor articulation of testing needs or results to stakeholders.
  - **Neglected Follow-ups**: Failure to act on defects identified during testing.

- **Technical Challenges:**
  - **Ambiguous Requirements**: Vague or conflicting requirements may lead to ineffective test coverage.
  - **Environment Readiness**: Test environments may be unavailable or misconfigured. Setting up virtualized environments can impact the timelines unless this is clearly mentioned in the Test Plan.
  - **Defect Accumulation**: Poor defect management can result in significant technical debt.
- **Supplier Dependencies:**
  - **Third-Party Failures**: Delays or quality issues with vendor deliverables can disrupt the project.

Risks are an inherent aspect of any SAP S/4HANA implementation. However, with a structured approach to testing, these risks can be identified, prioritized, and mitigated effectively. Product risks challenge the system's ability to meet user and business expectations, while project risks threaten the successful execution of the testing effort.

Conclusion

As we conclude this chapter, it is necessary to recognize that testing is not a standalone activity but an integral part of the broader software development process. Its effectiveness depends on how well it aligns with project goals, risk management strategies, and stakeholder expectations.

In the next chapter, we will delve deeper into the software development life cycle models and their impact on testing. We will explore various software development life cycle models, test types, and the defect life cycle.

References

- ISTQB Foundation Guide: https://www.istqb.org/
- Foundations of Software Testing by Dorothy Graham, Rex Black, and Erik van Veenendaal
- Inside SAP S/4HANA podcast: https://podcast.opensap.info/inside-sap/
- Cost of finding bugs: https://www.functionize.com/blog/the-cost-of-finding-bugs-later-in-the-sdlc
- Economic Impacts of inadequate infrastructure for Software testing: https://www.nist.gov/system/files/documents/director/planning/report02-3.pdf

CHAPTER 6

Testing in the Software Development Life Cycle

Introduction

Testing is an integral part of the Software Development Life Cycle (SDLC). The chosen SDLC model significantly influences how testing is structured and executed. Given the diverse forms of testing - each serving different objectives within the development process, it is essential to clearly define and understand the various test levels and types to ensure effective Quality Engineering (QE) or Quality Assurance (QA).

From traditional waterfall methodologies to Agile and DevOps, testing integrates with every phase of the SDLC, adapting to diverse models and technological advancements.

Structure

This chapter provides a comprehensive exploration of the SDLC, and examines how Quality Assurance integrates holistically throughout each phase.

- Software Development Life Cycle
- Test Levels
- Test Types
- Test Management
    - Test Operating Model
    - Test Planning

- Risk Management
- Test Monitoring and Control
- Defect Life Cycle

Software Development Life Cycle

The SDLC represents the journey of software from concept to delivery and maintenance. Each SDLC model defines specific stages and their sequence, impacting how testing is planned and executed.

Let us explore three categories of software development life cycle models: Sequential, Incremental, and Iterative.

Sequential Development Models

Sequential development models follow a linear progression through discrete, successive phases, with no overlap between them. The next phase begins only after the previous one is complete. These models are best suited for projects with well-defined requirements and minimal expected changes.

Waterfall Model

The waterfall model is one of the earliest and most straightforward SDLC approaches. The Waterfall model is one of the earliest and most structured approaches to the software development life cycle (SDLC). It follows a linear, sequential progression, where each phase flows naturally into the next–much like a cascading waterfall.

The process begins with a feasibility study at the top, and systematically moves through key stages, including design, development, build, and testing, before culminating in deployment to the live environment. Testing in this model often occurs towards the end of the cycle, which may delay defect detection until close to the live implementation date. Feedback and iterations are challenging to incorporate, making it less flexible for dynamic requirements. The following are the typical phases followed in the model:

1. **Requirements Analysis:** In this initial phase, all possible requirements of the system to be developed are gathered and documented. This phase is crucial as it sets the foundation for the entire project.

2. **Design:** Based on the requirements gathered, the system's architecture and design are created. This includes both High-Level Design (HLD) and Low-Level Design (LLD).

3. **Implementation:** During this phase, the actual source code is written based on the design documents. Developers create the software components and integrate them.
4. **Testing:** After implementation, the software is tested to identify any defects or issues. This phase ensures that the software meets the specified requirements and functions correctly.
5. **Deployment:** Once testing is complete and the software is deemed ready, it is deployed to the production environment for end-users.

The waterfall model may be used for smaller projects within the SAP ECC to SAP S/4HANA migration initiatives, where requirements are well-defined, and minimal changes are expected.

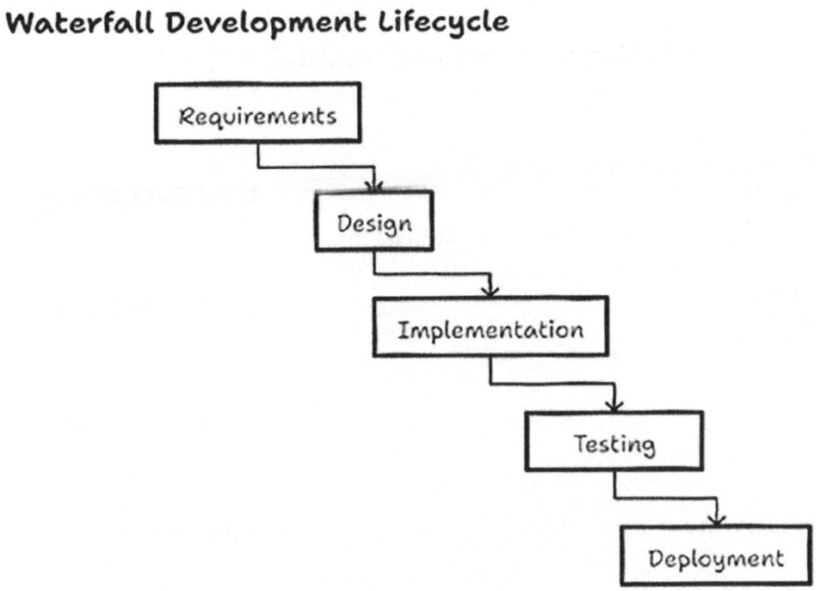

Figure 6.1: *Waterfall Model*

V-Model

The V-model was developed to address some of the limitations experienced with the traditional waterfall approach, particularly the delayed detection and lead times caused by testing being deferred to the end of the project. The V-model provides guidance on how testing can begin as early as possible in the life cycle. It also demonstrates that testing is not solely an execution-based activity. Instead, several preparatory activities, such as test design and planning, occur in parallel with development. Testers collaborate closely with developers and business analysts to create a set of test deliverables, ensuring thorough validation.

The work products produced during each development phase form the basis for testing at corresponding levels. For instance, requirements specifications are validated through acceptance testing, while system design outputs inform system testing. By initiating test design early, defects can often be identified in foundational documents, such as requirements or design artifacts. An effective practice is involving testers during the review of these documents to identify and address issues proactively. The V-model effectively integrates verification and validation throughout the life cycle. Early validation occurs during stages such as requirements reviews, while later stages involve activities such as user acceptance testing. This systematic approach helps ensure quality at every step, mitigating risks and reducing late-stage surprises.

The V-model is particularly useful for ERP implementations or upgrades in SAP, where every stage, from requirements gathering to deployment, demands thorough validation.

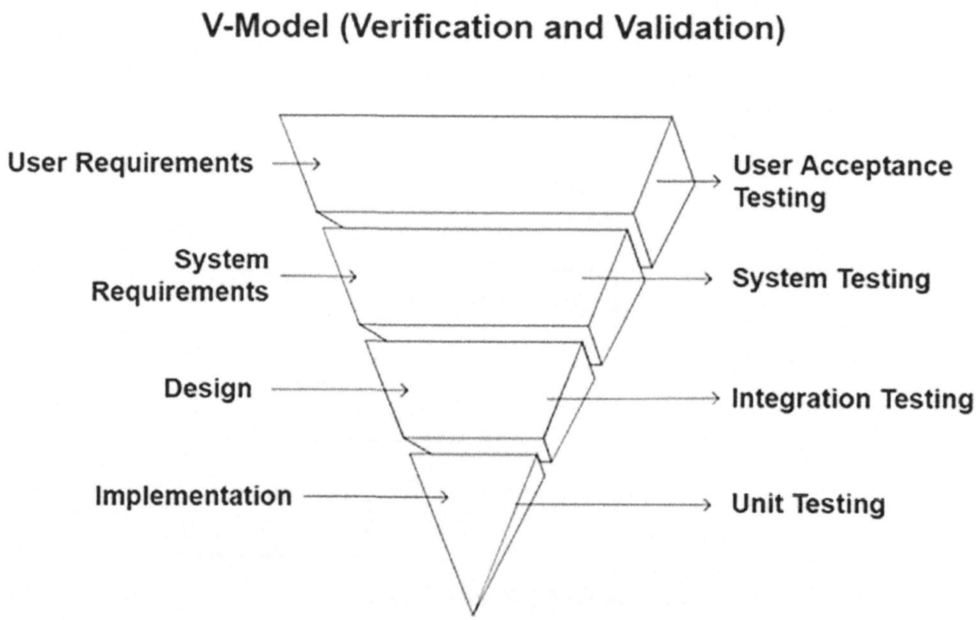

Figure 6.2: *V-Model*

Incremental Development Models

Incremental models focus on delivering software in smaller, manageable portions called increments. Each increment represents a subset of the system's functionality, with development and testing activities performed for each increment. This approach ensures early delivery of partially functional software, allowing for feedback and adjustments during subsequent increments.

Rapid Application Development (RAD)

RAD emphasizes the quick delivery of functional prototypes and incremental releases, with a strong focus on user feedback. Testing is integrated into the prototyping and incremental delivery process to ensure high-quality outputs. Phases of the RAD model are as follows:

- **Business Modeling**: Identifies business functions and information flow to determine data requirements and processes.
- **Data Modeling:** Analyzes the information obtained during business modeling and defines data objects and their relationships.
- **Process Modeling**: Converts data objects into processes to achieve business objectives and optimize workflows.
- **Application Generation:** Develops the system using reusable components, tools, and automated development features.
- **Testing and Turnover:** Conducts iterative testing of prototypes and ensures the final product meets business needs through continuous user feedback.

The incremental model may be used in implementing SAP Greenfield initiatives where functional modules are developed in phases, such as deploying SAP Finance first, followed by SAP Sales and Distribution. This phased approach allows organizations to adapt to the new system incrementally.

Iterative Development Models

Iterative models emphasize repetition and continuous improvement, allowing teams to adapt to changing requirements and incorporate feedback more effectively. These models are ideal for projects with evolving needs and where flexibility is key. In terms of developing software, a purely iterative model does not produce a working system until the final iteration.

The following figure presents the Iterative Software Development Life Cycle (SDLC) and highlights how testing expands with each iteration.

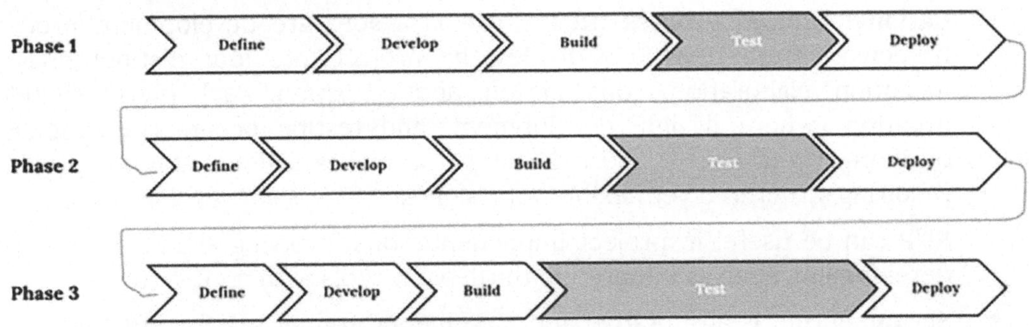

Figure 6.3: *Iterative Model*

With iterative and incremental life cycle models, early planning helps extend the scope of the test process further ahead, ensuring a strategic testing approach. However, these models come with some common challenges:

- **Increased Regression Testing**: Each iteration or increment necessitates the testing type (Regression Testing) to ensure new changes do not adversely affect previously developed components.
- **Defects Coverage**: Defects identified in areas outside the immediate iteration or increment require careful tracking to prevent neglect.
- **Less Thorough Testing**: As scope increases, testing resources may stretch thin, leading to less thorough coverage.

Since iterative development delivers portions of the system incrementally, parts of the application will reach a level of completion sooner and may be released for feedback from customers or users. This feedback loop helps refine future iterations. Regression testing becomes a vital component of the process, as previously developed parts need verification to ensure their functionality remains intact. The more iterations involved, the higher the regression testing demand, making test automation a valuable practice for maintaining efficiency and consistency.

Defects identified in the currently developed or tested portions are handled promptly. However, issues found during regression testing of previously developed parts, or those discovered incidentally, can sometimes fall outside the immediate scope. Without a robust defect management process, such issues risk being overlooked. Ensuring thorough documentation and tracking of all defects, regardless of their origin, is critical for sustained quality assurance.

Additionally, iterative models can lead to less formal testing, as smaller parts of the system may seem less critical. This perception can undermine testing rigor, particularly for regression tests. Addressing these challenges requires establishing structured testing practices and leveraging automation to ensure consistency and thoroughness throughout the project lifecycle.

The following are some of the example models that follow iterative development:

- **Rational Unified Process (RUP):** RUP is a software development process framework from IBM. RUP divides the project into four distinct phases: inception, elaboration, construction, and transition. Each phase includes iterations where design, development, and testing occur. The emphasis on iterative refinement and risk mitigation makes RUP suitable for projects requiring structured yet flexible approaches.

  RUP can be useful in project implementations involving significant custom development, such as integrating third-party tools with core systems.
- **Scrum:** Scrum is an iterative and incremental framework for effective team collaboration, which is typically used in Agile development, the most well-

known iterative method. Scrum (and Agile) is based on recognizing that change is inevitable and taking a practical empirical approach to changing priorities.

Scrum is an Agile framework that organizes work into small units called sprints, typically 2-4 weeks long. Teams collaborate in daily stand-ups, and testing occurs within each sprint to ensure the delivery of potentially shippable increments. The development teams typically are small, 3–9 people, and cross-functional, that is, they include people who perform various roles, and often individuals take on different tasks such as testing within the team.

Scrum is highly relevant for SAP cloud projects, such as SAP Analytics Cloud dashboards, where incremental delivery aligns with dynamic reporting needs.

- **Spiral Model:** The spiral model combines iterative development with systematic risk analysis. Each cycle includes planning, risk assessment, development, and testing, ensuring risk-driven decision-making. Prototypes may be developed as a way of addressing risks; these prototypes may be kept and incorporated into later cycles, or they may be discarded, or they may be reworked as part of the next cycle.

  The visual of the Spiral model shows development starting small from the center and moving in a circular way clockwise through the four stages. Each succeeding cycle builds outwards in a spiral through the phases, developing more functionality each time. The key driver for the Spiral model is that it is risk-driven.

  Spiral models are rarely used in SAP projects due to their complexity, but they might be considered for large-scale, multi-phased SAP rollouts where risk management is critical.

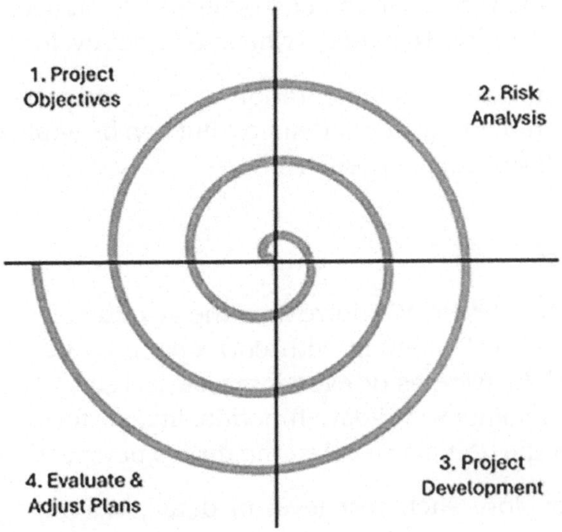

Figure 6.4: *Spiral Model*

- **Kanban:** Kanban came from an approach to work in manufacturing at Toyota. Kanban focuses on visualizing work in progress, limiting work items, and optimizing flow. A Kanban board has columns for different stages of work, from the initial idea through the development and testing stages to final delivery to users. The tasks are put on sticky notes which are moved from left to right through the columns, such as an assembly line for cars.

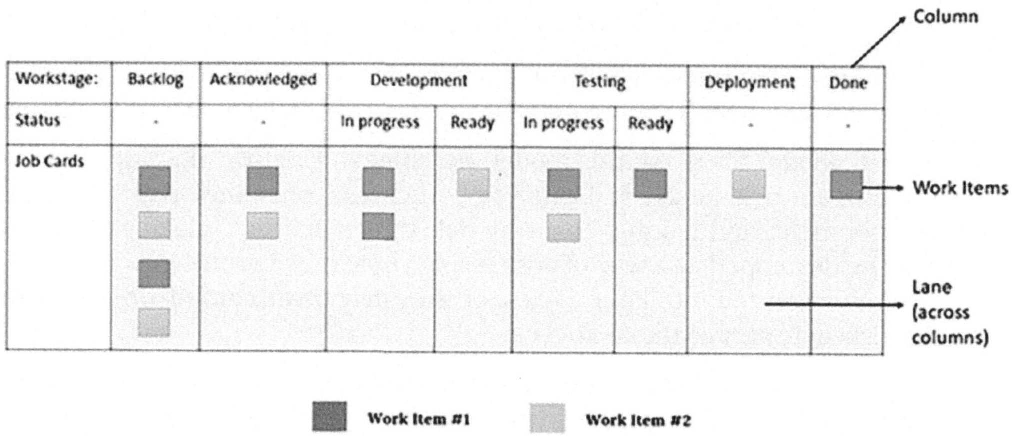

Figure 6.5: *Kanban Model*

A key principle of Kanban is to have a limit for work-in-progress activities. If we concentrate on one task, we are much more efficient at doing it, so this approach is less wasteful than trying to do little bits of lots of different tasks. This focus on eliminating waste makes this a lean approach.

There is also a strong focus on user and customer needs. Hence, Testing is integrated as a continuous activity rather than occurring in distinct cycles.

Kanban is less common in SAP implementation-specific projects due to requirements complexity and cross-functional dependencies. But can be applied to manage support tickets or ongoing SAP system maintenance.

Test Levels

When we talk about test levels, we delve into the structured activities performed at distinct stages of the SDLC, aligning with corresponding development levels–from components to complete systems or even interconnected systems of systems. These test levels act as checkpoints to validate functionality, performance, and compliance, ensuring quality from the granular level to the macro perspective.

In this section, we explore each test level in detail, examining its objectives, test basis, typical defects or failures it aims to uncover, and its relevance in SAP and SAP S/4HANA projects. By clearly defining these levels, organizations can identify gaps, prevent overlaps, and ensure efficient, comprehensive validation.

Component Testing

Component testing, often referred to as unit testing, focuses on verifying individual units or components of a software system. These units, typically the smallest testable parts of the application, are isolated to ensure that their behavior aligns with the design and requirements.

The objectives of component testing include:

- Mitigate risk and build confidence in the quality of a component.
- Verify the functionality of individual software components.
- Validate adherence to technical specifications.
- Detect and resolve the component.
- Prevent defects from escaping to later stages of testing.

Component testing focuses on verifying individual parts of the software on their own, without involving the entire system. Depending on the development stage and system design, this testing is performed in isolation. To achieve this, testers often use mock objects, stubs, or drivers to stand in for the parts of the software that are not yet available, allowing them to simulate interactions between components in a straightforward way. Test cases at this test level are derived from test basis such as software design, data structures, classes, and code specifications.

Typical defects and failures include:

- Incorrect functionality
- Syntax errors in code
- Incorrect data handling
- Interface mismatches

A typical example is unit-testing an ABAP function module that performs VAT calculations -mock inputs for diverse tax categories to catch logic errors before integration.

In SAP S/4HANA, component testing might involve testing a single ABAP program, ensuring that it processes financial data correctly, or validating custom Business Application Programming Interfaces (BAPIs) for specific business logic.

Tools typically used:

- ABAP Unit for testing ABAP programs.

- JUnit or TestNG for Java-based components in SAP.
- SAP ATC (ABAP Test Cockpit) for static code analysis and unit testing.

Integration Testing

Integration testing verifies the interactions between integrated components, ensuring that they work together as intended. This test level emphasizes data flow, communication, and interfaces.

In one SAP S/4HANA rollout, the team caught a critical defect when testing the handoff between SAP SD and a third-party logistics provider. The custom interface was dropping special characters and it led to failed shipments.

Integration tests are typically based on the software and system design, the system architecture (essentially relationships between components or objects) and the workflows or use cases by which the stakeholders will employ the system. There will be more than one level of integration testing, and it may be carried out on test objects of varying sizes. For example:

- **Component integration testing** verifies the interactions between software components and is done after component testing. It is a good candidate for automation. In an iterative and incremental development, both component tests and integration tests are usually part of continuous integration, which may involve automated build, test and release to end users.

  Example: Testing the integration between the Sales Order Processing component (VA01) and Availability Check (ATP) functionality within the SD module.

- **System integration testing** verifies the interactions between different systems, packages and microservices, and may be done after system testing. System integration testing may also verify interfaces to and provided by external applications.

  Example: Testing the end-to-end interface between SAP S/4HANA and a third-party warehouse management system (WMS).

The objectives of integration testing include:

- Mitigate risk, for example, by testing high-risk integrations first.
- Building confidence in the quality of the interfaces.
- Finding defects in the interfaces themselves or in the systems being tested together.
- Prevent defects from escaping to later stages of testing.

Test cases at this test level are derived from test basis such as system design specifications, sequence diagrams, interface protocol specifications, use cases, system architecture, and external interface definitions.

Integration testing in the SAP world spans a range of scenarios, from simple connections to complex, multi-system integrations. The scope of integration significantly impacts testing complexity. At one extreme, big-bang integration involves testing all components or systems simultaneously after integration, but this approach often carries significant risk due to the difficulty in isolating failures to specific interfaces. At the other end, incremental integration testing integrates and tests components or systems step by step. This approach is generally preferred, as it allows for early defect detection and reduces the risk of late discovery of major issues.

The best strategy depends primarily on the architecture, with high-risk interfaces prioritized for early testing. Incremental integration testing, particularly in iterative development, often forms part of continuous integration, where existing tests are reused as part of regression testing. While developers typically handle component integration testing, system integration testing is the responsibility of testers who validate end-to-end workflows and external interfaces

Tools typically used in SAP testing at this level are:

- SAP Solution Manager or SAP Cloud ALM for streamlining test management processes.
- Postman for API testing.
- SAP Integration Suite for validating integration flows.
- Various open-source frameworks or commercial test automation tools such as Microfocus, Tricentis, UiPath, Worksoft, INT4, and so on.

System Testing

System testing evaluates the complete, integrated system to verify that it meets the specified requirements. It ensures that the application behaves as expected in an environment that closely mirrors production. The focus here is on end-to-end tasks that the system should perform, including non-functional aspects, such as performance, security, and reliability. An end-to-end test may include all of the steps in a typical transaction, from logging on, accessing data, placing an order, and so on to logging off and checking order status in a database.

Typically, system-level tests are automated to provide a regression suite to ensure that changes have not adversely affected existing system functionality. The test environment is important for system testing; it should correspond to the final production environment as much as possible.

The objectives of system testing include:

- Mitigate risk, for example by verifying whether functional and non-functional behaviors of the system are as they should be.
- Validate end-to-end system behavior.
- Building confidence in the quality of the system as a whole.
- Preventing defects from escaping to production.

Test cases at this test level are derived from test basis such as software or system requirements specifications, risk analysis reports, use cases, epics/user stories, state diagrams, and user manuals.

Some of the system testing use cases in SAP S/4HANA projects are:

- Verifying business processes such as Order-to-Cash for workflow execution, data consistency, and compliance with business logic
- Verifying customer order management journey involving the SAP and Salesforce systems.
- Verifying procurement process between SAP S/4HANA and Ariba for supplier approvals, and financial reconciliations.

Examples of defects and failures that can typically be revealed by system testing include:

- Incorrect functional or non-functional behavior in the system.
- Incorrect control and/or data flows within the system.
- Failure to carry out end-to-end functional tasks.
- Failure of the system to work properly in the production environments.
- Failure of the system to work as described in system and user manuals.

System testing requires a well-controlled test environment, ensuring proper management of software versions, tools, and test data. To effectively identify potential issues, the test environment should closely mirror the final production environment. This alignment minimizes the risk of environment-specific defects going undetected during testing.

Tools typically used in SAP testing at this level are:

- Tricentis, Microfocus (Open Text), Worksoft, and UiPath
- SAP Cloud ALM, SAP Solution Manager for test management

User Acceptance Testing

User Acceptance testing validates that the system meets business requirements and is ready for deployment. It is often the final testing phase before the system goes live.

When system testing (and possibly system integration testing) is completed and most defects have been corrected, the system is delivered for acceptance testing. Acceptance tests aim to determine whether the system is ready for release and deployment to end-users or customers. Although defects may still be identified at this stage, finding numerous defects signals major problems and significant project risks.

The primary focus of acceptance testing is validation - ensuring the system is suitable for real-world use by its intended users. This involves assessing how well the system meets business needs, regulatory and legal requirements, and compliance with established standards. Ideally, these aspects are addressed earlier during other levels of testing, with acceptance testing serving as confirmation.

The objectives of acceptance testing include:

- Establishing confidence in the quality of the system as a whole.
- Validating that the system is complete and will work as expected.
- Verifying that functional and non-functional behaviors of the system are as specified.

The following are the work products used as a test basis for the various forms of acceptance test design and development including user or business requirements, business processes, use cases, system or user documentation, and risk analysis reports.

Examples of risks that can typically be revealed by acceptance testing include:

- Misaligned system workflows with business or user requirements
- Usability issues
- Business rules are not implemented correctly
- Missing critical features
- System does not satisfy contractual or regulatory requirements
- Non-functional failures, including security vulnerabilities, inadequate performance efficiency under high load, or improper operation on a supported platform.

In SAP projects, User Acceptance Testing is primarily the responsibility of business users or key stakeholders, though other parties may also be involved. This phase ensures that the system meets business requirements and is ready for deployment. Key questions addressed during acceptance testing include: "Is *the system ready for go-live*?" and "*Are there any critical business risks remaining*?" The focus is primarily on validation - confirming that the solution is fit for purpose–rather than defect detection, which is the primary goal of earlier testing phases.

Acceptance testing in SAP projects can take place at multiple stages, depending on the context and objectives. For example:

- An SAP S/4HANA quarterly release may undergo acceptance testing after installation or integration to ensure compatibility and business readiness.
- Usability acceptance testing of a specific component may be conducted during component testing to validate user experience and interaction.
- Acceptance testing of a new functional enhancement may be performed before system testing to confirm alignment with business requirements before broader validation.

Examples of Acceptance Testing use cases in SAP S/4HANA projects include:

- **SAP Fiori Application Testing**: Validating that a custom SAP Fiori application meets end-user expectations, including usability, responsiveness, and alignment with business workflows.
- **Central Finance Validation**: Ensuring that a newly implemented Central Finance system in SAP S/4HANA adheres to business requirements for financial consolidation and reporting.
- **Payroll Integration**: Verifying that SAP S/4HANA integrates seamlessly with a payroll system (e.g., Workday), ensuring accurate salary calculations and compliance with local tax regulations.
- **Regulatory Compliance:** Testing SAP processes to ensure adherence to industry-specific regulations, such as GDPR or SOX compliance, for data security and auditing.
- **End-to-End Process Validation**: Conducting acceptance tests for an entire Order-to-Cash (O2C) workflow, ensuring all steps, from order creation to invoicing, meet stakeholder expectations.

Tools typically used in SAP testing at this level include:

- Enterprise Test Automation tools such as Microfocus, Tricentis, Worksoft, and UiPath
- Jira, MS Office tools, SAP Cloud ALM, SAP Solution Manager for managing manual tests.

Pro Tip: *Invite super users to prepare real-life scenarios. In a finance-driven transformation project, Test Manager used the last quarterly close as their UAT playbook and it helps uncover reports with filtering issues before go-live.*

Here is a high-level summary highlighting key contrasts to distinguish the four test levels:

Aspect	Component Testing	Integration Testing	System Testing	Acceptance Testing
Key Objectives	Verify functionality of individual components.	Validate interactions between integrated modules.	Validate end-to-end system behavior.	Confirm readiness for deployment and business use.
Test Basis	Component designs, data models, technical specs.	Interface designs, workflow specifications.	Functional and non-functional requirements.	Business requirements, user stories, and contracts.
Test Objects	Individual software units (e.g., ABAP programs).	Interfaces between modules or systems.	Entire integrated system.	Full system as per user and business needs.
Typical Risks Revealed	Syntax errors, logical errors, data issues.	Data mapping errors, interface mismatches.	Missing functionalities, performance issues.	Misaligned business requirements, usability gaps.
Tools Used	ABAP Unit, SAP ATC, JUnit, TestNG.	SAP Solution Manager, Postman, SAP Integration Suite, INT4, UiPath, Tricentis, Worksoft	SAP Test Automation Framework, SAP Cloud ALM or Solution Manager, Tricentis, UiPath, Microfocus, Worksoft, Selenium, JMeter.	SAP Cloud ALM, SAP Solution Manager, Jira, MS Office, UiPath Test Suite, Tricentis, Worksoft, Microfocus

Figure 6.6: *Summary of Test Levels*

Test Types

In this section, we will explore the diverse landscape of Test Types that evaluate what a system does (functional testing), how well it does it (non-functional testing), and how it responds to changes (confirmation and regression testing). With SAP's complexity and frequent integrations with third-party systems, understanding and optimizing these test types across test levels is crucial to ensuring seamless operations.

A test type is defined by its specific objective, whether it's evaluating a system's functionality, assessing non-functional qualities including reliability or usability, analyzing its structure and architecture, or verifying changes. Change-related tests can focus on confirming bug fixes (confirmation testing) or detecting unintended side effects (regression testing). The way testing is structured depends on the objective. For example, testing a component for performance follows a different approach than testing it for decision coverage. Each test type serves a distinct purpose, ensuring a well-rounded validation of the system. In SAP, this distinction is vital when testing diverse functionalities, such as validating high-performance queries in SAP HANA versus verifying logical decision paths in ABAP workflows.

Functional Testing

Functional testing ensures that the system operates as intended by validating its features and business processes. This is typically described in work products such as business requirements specifications, functional specifications, use cases, epics or user stories. Functional tests are based on the functions described in these documents and may be performed at all test levels.

Functional testing could be approached from different perspectives, the two main ones being requirements-based and business-process-based.

- **Requirements-based testing** uses a specification of the functional requirements as the foundation for test design. A good starting point is to use the table of contents from the requirements specification to create an initial inventory of items to test (or not to test). Requirements can also be prioritized based on risk criteria, ensuring that the most critical and impactful tests are included in the effort. For instance, in a SAP implementation, prioritizing tests for financial closing processes in the Finance (FI) module ensures readiness for key business operations.
- **Business-process-based testing** leverages knowledge of the system's business processes, which describe the scenarios involved in daily operations. For example, in an SAP personnel and payroll system, the business process might include hiring an employee, processing their payroll regularly, and managing their exit. These scenarios guide the creation of test cases and models, such as process models or state transition diagrams. User scenarios, originating from object-oriented development, often align with these business tasks. Testing the procure-to-pay process in SAP S/4HANA, for example, ensures that the system supports end-to-end procurement workflows seamlessly.

In some instances, functional testing may require specific skills and domain knowledge, particularly for complex application landscapes such as SAP with industry-specific business processes. For example, in an SAP implementation for the oil and gas sector, testing workflows for geological modeling and equipment maintenance requires a deep understanding of domain-specific processes. Similarly, in the automotive sector, testing SAP systems to support just-in-time inventory management or automated production scheduling demands expertise in lean manufacturing principles. These examples highlight the importance of the domain expertise to achieve functional accuracy and reliability in SAP landscapes. This is why this book dedicates several chapters at the beginning to explore SAP landscapes in depth, setting the foundation for effective testing strategies.

Non-Functional Testing

Non-functional testing verifies the quality attributes of a system, focusing on how well or how efficiently something is done. Unlike functional testing, which evaluates what the system does, non-functional testing measures attributes such as performance, usability, and reliability on a quantifiable scale. For example, testing response time or transaction throughput provides measurable insights into system efficiency.

Non-functional testing, much like functional testing, is performed across all test levels. It encompasses a wide range of test types, including but not limited to performance testing, load testing, stress testing, usability testing, maintainability testing, reliability testing, portability testing, and security testing. Essentially, it evaluates how well the system operates under various conditions.

In the context of SAP landscapes, non-functional testing is indispensable. For instance:

- **Performance Testing:** This evaluates how well SAP systems handle peak workloads. A common scenario is assessing system behavior during Black Friday sales, where transaction volumes spike significantly.
- **Security Testing:** Ensures compliance with stringent data protection standards, such as testing role-based access for sensitive financial data in SAP S/4HANA.
- **Usability Testing:** Focuses on user experience in SAP Fiori apps, ensuring that navigation and accessibility meet user expectations.
- **Reliability Testing:** Verifies system stability under continuous operation, such as overnight batch jobs in SAP systems.

The thoroughness of non-functional testing can often be gauged by its coverage of non-functional requirements. Establishing traceability between test cases and these requirements can help identify coverage gaps. For example, ensuring that all performance metrics outlined in the requirements are adequately tested and validated reinforces system reliability and robustness. By quantifiably measuring system attributes, non-functional testing sets the foundation for high-performing SAP landscapes. Non-functional tests validate the system's performance, usability, security, and reliability.

Common tools used: Apache JMeter, Open Text, Tricentis, Applitools, UiPath, and Worksoft.

White-Box Testing

White-box testing examines the internal structure or implementation of a system or its components. This includes analyzing code, control flows, data flows, and business processes. Often referred to as structural or glass-box testing, it focuses on understanding the inner workings of the system.

This type of testing is frequently used to measure the thoroughness of testing by assessing the coverage of specific structural elements or coverage items. White-box testing can occur at any test level but is most commonly applied at component testing and component integration testing. At higher levels, such as system or acceptance testing, it is less common but may still be relevant, especially for validating complex business process logic.

For SAP landscapes, white-box testing can involve:

- **Component-Level Testing:** Measuring code coverage of ABAP customizations or SAP BAPI implementations. Tools can identify untested code segments, such as unused statements or missed decision points, enabling additional tests to achieve comprehensive coverage.
- **Component Integration Testing:** Focusing on system architecture elements, such as call hierarchies and interfaces between components. For example, validating that SAP's integration with external payment systems functions as intended, with all interfaces thoroughly tested.
- **Business Process Testing:** Using business models, such as process flows or decision trees, as the test basis. For instance, testing the complex approval workflows in SAP Workflow to ensure all conditional paths are executed.

A variety of tools can support white box testing in SAP environments by enabling thorough analysis and test execution. These include:

- **SAP ABAP Test Cockpit (ATC):** Helps analyze and ensure code quality by identifying performance bottlenecks, security vulnerabilities, and syntax errors in ABAP code.
- **SAP Code Inspector:** Offers customizable checks for ABAP code, enabling developers to validate coding standards and identify potential issues.
- **JUnit or NUnit:** Useful for unit testing of custom Java-based or .NET components in SAP integrations.
- **SonarQube:** Integrates with SAP to measure code quality, maintainability, and security metrics for custom ABAP developments.
- **Eclipse with ABAP Development Tools (ADT):** Supports dynamic analysis and debugging for custom ABAP applications, enhancing white-box testing efforts.

Change-Management Testing

Change-management testing is slightly different than others because if you have made a change to the software, you will have changed the way it functions, how well it functions (or both), and its structure. This category of testing ensures that modifications to the system work as intended and do not introduce new issues. It is important in dynamic SAP landscapes, where updates, enhancements, and integrations frequently occur.

For example, when SAP S/4HANA receives a major upgrade every quarter, change management testing ensures that all new features function correctly, and that existing workflows, such as financial closing processes or order-to-cash cycles, remain unaffected. We are looking here at the specific types of tests relating to these changes, even though they may include all other test types. There are two things to be particularly aware of when changes are made: the change itself and any other effects of the change.

- **Confirmation Testing:** Confirmation testing verifies that specific changes, such as patches, configuration updates, or enhancements, have been implemented successfully. This involves re-executing the test that initially detected the defect to ensure the issue has been resolved. For instance, if a defect in SAP's Sales and Distribution (SD) module caused incorrect pricing logic in generated invoices, confirmation testing would ensure that the updated pricing logic is now correctly applied.

  It is important to note that successful confirmation testing proves that the specific defect has been fixed in the tested area, but it does not guarantee the overall correctness of the system. Other parts of the system could be inadvertently affected by the fix, which is where regression testing comes into play to identify and mitigate such risks.

- **Regression Testing:** Regression testing ensures that changes to the system do not negatively impact existing functionality. In SAP landscapes, this is crucial during quarterly updates, where enhancements to modules such as Finance (FI) or Material Management (MM) could inadvertently affect other integrated workflows.

  Organizations typically maintain a regression test suite, a collection of test cases, specifically designed for regression testing. These test cases focus on broadly validating system functionality rather than delving into granular details. Regression test suites are relevant across all testing levels, from component to integration, system, and acceptance testing. For example, during an SAP S/4HANA quarterly update, regression testing might verify that updates in the Finance (FI) module do not disrupt critical processes in Sales and Distribution (SD) or payroll workflows in SAP SuccessFactors. A well-maintained regression test suite ensures that these workflows operate seamlessly after updates.

  The key elements to consider in regression testing are:

  - **Automation-Friendly:** Since regression testing often involves repeating tests with every system change, it is ideal for automation. Automated tools such as Tricentis Tosca or UiPath Test Cloud can execute these tests efficiently and reliably.
  - **Selective Execution:** For large regression test suites, it is often impractical to run all tests manually. Instead, subsets of tests are executed based on the scope of changes, prioritizing areas most impacted by recent updates.

 - **Agile Alignment:** In Agile projects, regression testing aligns with iterative development cycles. Select tests are executed during each sprint to validate both new features and existing functionality.

Pro Tip: *In a global SAP rollout, decentralized teams can create duplicate test scripts for the same processes. Consolidating efforts using a centralized repository can reduce redundant work and improve test coverage consistency.*

Maintenance Testing

Maintenance testing ensures that SAP systems remain functional, efficient, and adaptable over time. This type of testing focuses on validating changes made to operational systems, whether they result from planned enhancements, emergency fixes, migrations, or software retirements.

Effective maintenance testing requires careful planning. This includes not only scheduled releases but also urgent hotfixes. For example, SAP S/4HANA may require urgent updates to address regulatory compliance changes or planned enhancements, such as a new feature in the Finance (FI) module. Maintenance testing validates these updates without disrupting core business processes.

A major component of maintenance testing is **impact analysis**, which determines how changes affect the existing system and helps focus testing efforts where they are most needed. For instance:

- When updating the SAP SD module, impact analysis identifies areas such as pricing logic or order workflows that may be unintentionally affected.
- During a global rollout of SAP enhancements, tools such as SAP Business Process Change Analyzer (BPCA) help pinpoint impacted business processes.

The scope of maintenance testing depends on several factors, which influence the test types and test levels. The factors are:

- **Degree of Risk:** Self-contained changes carry lower risk compared to updates affecting highly integrated components.
- **System Size:** Larger systems typically require more extensive regression testing than smaller ones.
- **Change Size:** The magnitude of changes determines the amount of direct testing required, while regression testing depends more on the system size.

There are a number of factors that make impact analysis more difficult:

- Outdated or missing documentation, such as business requirements or architecture diagrams.

- Lack of up-to-date test cases or bi-directional traceability between tests and requirements.
- Limited tool support or insufficient domain knowledge among team members.
- Poor software maintainability, making changes harder to test.

Pro Tip: *Embed risk-based testing as a non-negotiable practice. Industry research shows that risk-focused approaches help organizations overcome resource limitations and focus on what matters most, particularly in large or regulated SAP environments.*

Some of the common tools used for impact analysis in the SAP S/4HANA landscape are: SAP Business Process Change Analyzer (BPCA), Tricentis Live Compare, UiPath Change Impact Analysis, Worksoft Impact, KTern, and Panaya Change Analysis for SAP.

Test Management

Managing the Quality Assurance programs in SAP landscapes is a complex but crucial task. Ensuring quality in SAP projects isn't just about running tests – **it's about orchestrating hundreds of moving parts with precision**. As an SAP program manager or Test Manager, your ability to plan, govern, and steer testing can make or break the project's success. In this section, we explore the core pillars of SAP test management with practical examples to guide you through this essential responsibility.

Test Operating Model

The test operating model defines the processes, tools, and resources required to execute an effective and scalable testing strategy. It ensures alignment with SAP's business objectives, and supports the delivery of high-quality SAP implementations, upgrades, or maintenance activities. It includes the establishment of test teams, allocation of responsibilities, and the selection of tools and methodologies to align with SAP's specific needs.

The key components of a test operating model include team structure, people, tools, and test environment.

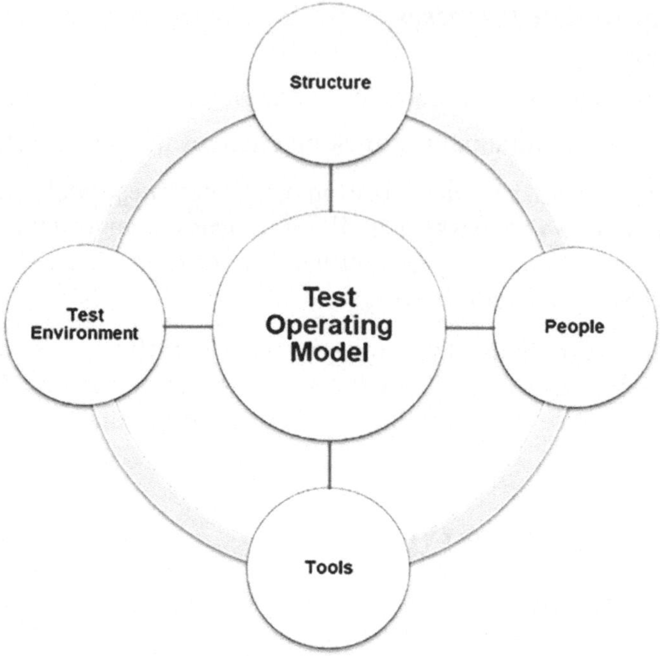

Figure 6.7: *Test Operating Model*

Test Team Structure (Centralized versus Decentralized Testing)

A well-defined structure for your testing team ensures that everyone contributes effectively to the testing effort. In a global SAP rollout, a centralized operating model is often ideal for ensuring consistency across regions. For instance, a multinational company implementing SAP S/4HANA might establish a centralized test team to define and manage test scripts for core processes such as procure-to-pay and order-to-cash. These scripts can then be adapted by local teams to accommodate regional requirements, creating a balance between global consistency and local relevance.

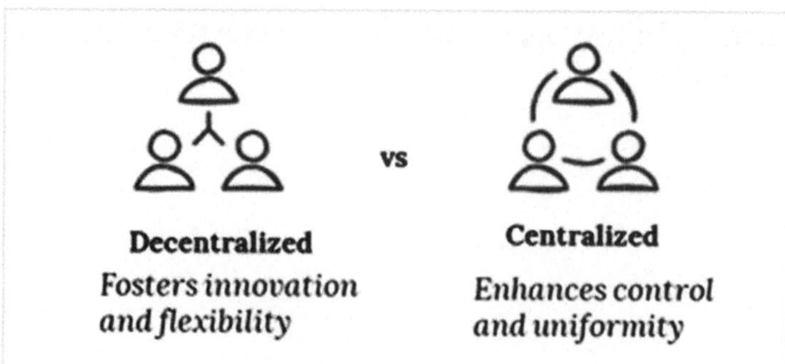

Figure 6.8: *Team Structures*

People

The success of a test operating model heavily depends on the roles, responsibilities, and capabilities of the team involved. Key considerations include:

Clear Roles and Responsibilities:

- **Test Manager:** Oversees the entire testing lifecycle, ensuring all testing phases align with project objectives. For example, in an SAP S/4HANA migration, the Test Manager ensures proper execution of functional, performance, regression testing and UAT.
- **Test Leads:** Coordinate specific areas of testing, such as managing integrations between SAP modules such as Finance (FI) and Materials Management (MM).
- **Functional Testers:** Focus on validating SAP modules such as SAP SuccessFactors for HR processes or SAP SD for order management.
- **Automation Engineers:** Develop and execute automated test scripts for repetitive tasks, such as weekly regression testing, and impact analysis.
- **Business Analysts:** Provide domain knowledge and validate test scenarios against business requirements, such as compliance-driven processes in SAP FI.

Effective Capability: Building a capable testing team involves:

- Training team members on SAP-specific tools such as Solution Manager, BPCA, or automation tools.
- Ensuring cross-functional expertise, enabling testers to understand integrations between modules (e.g., SAP SD and SAP MM).
- Establishing clear onboarding practices to familiarize new team members with SAP landscapes and the test operating model.
- Encouraging collaboration across global teams to share knowledge and standardize best practices in SAP projects.

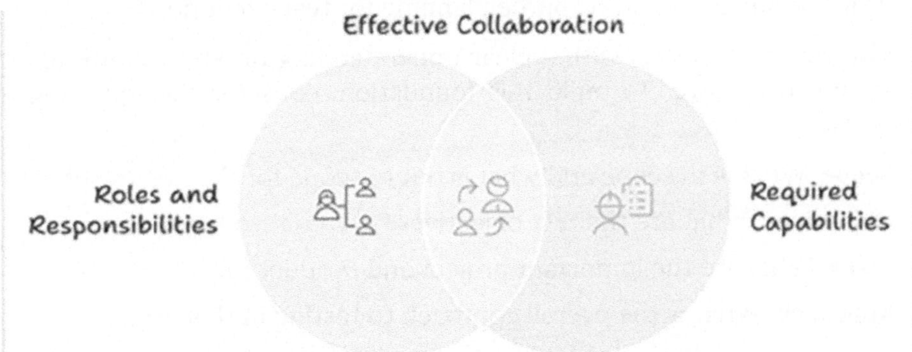

Figure 6.9: *Team Capability Framework*

Tools (Testing Tools or Frameworks)

An effective operating model must also incorporate a robust test automation strategy. For example, leveraging automation tools ensure streamlined and efficient integration testing, system testing, and regression testing for quarterly SAP upgrades, reducing manual effort and ensuring faster release cycles.

Test Environment Management

Managing test environments is a crucial aspect of the operating model. For SAP landscapes, maintaining well-synchronized environments such as Development (DEV), Quality Assurance (QA), and Production (PROD) ensures accurate validation of configurations, system integrations, and data migrations. For example, a QA environment mirroring the production setup is vital for testing high-risk customizations in SAP S/4HANA.

Test Planning

A test plan serves as the project plan for all testing activities in an SAP S/4HANA implementation or upgrade. It is not a test design specification, a collection of test cases, or a set of test procedures. Instead, it provides a structured roadmap that defines the testing scope, objectives, approach, timelines, roles, responsibilities, and dependencies.

Test plans ensure alignment across stakeholders - testers, test managers, SAP program managers, and business users - by establishing:

- A shared understanding of what needs to be tested and why.
- Clear responsibilities and expectations for different testing phases.
- A structured approach to managing test execution, risks, and reporting.
- Defined entry and exit criteria to control the flow of testing activities.
- Realistic timelines and resource planning for test execution.

An effective test plan begins with a clear understanding of why you are testing and what you aim to achieve. To build this foundation, consider the following guiding questions:

- **Scope:** What is in scope and what is out of scope for this testing effort?
- **Objectives:** What are the test objectives?
- **Risks:** What are the important project and product risks?
- **Approach:** What is the overall approach to testing in this project?

- **Prioritization and Resources:** How do we decide what to test, what people and other resources are needed to perform test activities, and how all test activities will be carried out?
- **Criticality:** What is most critical for this product and project?
- **Metrics:** What metrics will be used for test monitoring and control? (more on test monitoring in the next section)
- **Budget:** What is the budget for all test activities?
- **Documentation:** What should be the level of detail and structure for test documentation?

Answering these questions upfront ensures that the test plan is purposeful, aligned with project goals, and able to guide the team confidently through the testing process.

Sometimes test teams tend to use test planning, test strategy, and test approach interchangeably, but they have distinct roles in SAP S/4HANA projects:

Aspect	Test Strategy	Test Approach	Test Plan
Key Objectives	Establishes a high-level framework for testing across projects, ensuring consistency, governance, and best practices.	Defines the specific methodologies, tools, and processes for executing testing in a particular project.	Provides a detailed roadmap for test execution, covering scope, schedule, resources, and success criteria.
Scope	Organization-wide or program-wide	Project-specific	Project-specific, covering all testing phases
Ownership	Typically created by senior test managers or the Testing Center of Excellence (TCoE).	Defined by test managers or leads based on the project needs.	Created by the test manager for the project and approved by stakeholders.
Key Components	Testing methodologies, automation guidelines, risk management, compliance, and governance.	Test execution methods (manual vs. automation), test data handling, environment setup, and defect management approach.	Test scope, objectives, schedule, resources, risks, dependencies, and success criteria.
Examples	Defines that all SAP projects follow a risk-based testing approach and leverage automation for regression testing.	Specifies that the project will use risk-based testing with a focus on automating regression and UAT test cases.	Outlines that SIT will begin in Week 4, UAT in Week 6, and defines entry/exit criteria, resource allocation, and execution timelines.

Figure 6.10: *Test Strategy versus Test Approach versus Test Plan*

A couple of test plans are made available for your reference at our resources library here: **https://github.com/ava-orange-education/Mastering-SAP-S-4HANA-Quality-Assurance**

Risk Management

In simple terms, risk is the possibility of a negative or undesirable outcome. In the future, a risk has some likelihood between 0% and 100%; it is a possibility, not a certainty. In the past, however, whether the risk has materialized or not; the likelihood of a risk in the past is either 0% or 100%.

Imagine an SAP S/4HANA project preparing for go-live. A minor configuration issue in the Purchase Order workflow might seem like a low-risk problem - just like catching a common cold. Most SAP implementations encounter small configuration hiccups, and for a well-prepared business, these are quickly resolved with minimal disruption.

But now, consider the same issue in a highly regulated industry such as pharmaceuticals or banking, where a single incorrect purchase approval could violate compliance laws or delay mission-critical deliveries. Suddenly, what seemed like a minor inconvenience became a high-risk scenario, potentially leading to financial penalties, supply chain disruptions, or audit failures.

This is why risk assessment in SAP projects is not just about identifying issues – it is about understanding the impact in the real-world business context. A bug in a non-critical report may be low risk, but the same issue in financial postings before a quarterly audit could be catastrophic. Risk is not just about the probability of failure-it is about the consequences of failure.

Testing plays a pivotal role in risk management by ensuring that SAP S/4HANA solutions meet business requirements, function seamlessly across integrated systems, and maintain data integrity while complying with security and regulatory standards. SAP S/4HANA testing must account for various risks that can impact project success. The following are the key risk categories:

- **Functional Risks**
    - Misalignment between system behavior and business requirements.
    - Insufficient test coverage for end-to-end business processes.
- **Integration Risks**
    - Failures in interfaces between SAP and non-SAP systems (for example, SAP Ariba, SuccessFactors, third-party banking solutions).
    - API or middleware inconsistencies lead to data synchronization issues.
    - Cross system testing gaps in hybrid landscapes.
- **Data Migration Risks**
    - Incorrect or incomplete migration of master and transactional data.
    - Data integrity issues cause reporting and reconciliation failures.
    - Performance bottlenecks in data transfer between legacy and S/4HANA systems.

- **Performance and Scalability Risks**
  - o System response time degradation under peak loads.
  - o Poor performance of custom reports and transactions.
- **Security and Compliance Risks**
  - o Unauthorized access to sensitive business data.
  - o Inadequate Role-Based Access Control (RBAC) configurations.
  - o Non-compliance with industry regulations (for example, GDPR, SOX).
- **Regression Risks**
  - o New enhancements impacting the existing functionality.
  - o Custom code incompatibility with SAP updates.
  - o Business processes are failing due to configuration changes.
- **Test Execution and Resource Risks**
  - o Limited availability of business SMEs for UAT.
  - o Dependency on unstable test environments.
  - o Delays due to inadequate test data provisioning.

Thus, to mitigate risks, it is rarely practical to test every possible scenario in an SAP S/4HANA system. That's why Risk-Based Testing (RBT) is so valuable. RBT helps you focus your testing on the most critical and high-risk areas, ensuring that what matters most to the business is tested thoroughly. Instead of spreading efforts evenly across all features, you prioritize areas with the greatest potential impact. To effectively identify, assess, and manage these risks, refer to the simple table provided here:

Risk Category	Risk Description	Business Impact	Risk Level	Mitigation Plan	Owner	Status
Functional	Inconsistent tax calculation in SAP Finance module	High	Critical	Conduct end to end pricing calculation test cases	Finance SME	Open
Integration	Failure in API connection between SAP S/4HANA and 3rd party CRM	High	High	Conduct integration testing, and implement service virtualization mechanism	Integration Lead	Open
Data Migration	Data inconsistency in customer master records post migration	High	Critical	Perform data validation and reconciliation before cutover	Data migration Team	Open
Performance	High response time for financial reconciliation reports	Medium	Medium	Conduct performance testing and load testing	Performance test lead	Open

Figure 6.11: *Risk-Based Testing Template*

Defect Life Cycle

A defect is any instance where the system does not behave as expected. For example, according to business requirements, creating a sales order in SAP should automatically trigger an availability check and confirm the order without any errors.

During testing, however, you observe that while the order is created successfully, the availability check fails, leaving the order unconfirmed. This is a clear deviation from the expected functional behavior. Such defects can impact downstream processes involving delivery scheduling and billing, and must be promptly addressed by involving functional consultants, developers, and business stakeholders to ensure smooth business operations. Within the QA life cycle, defects follow their own distinct life cycle. In a typical SAP project, this defect life cycle includes the following stages:

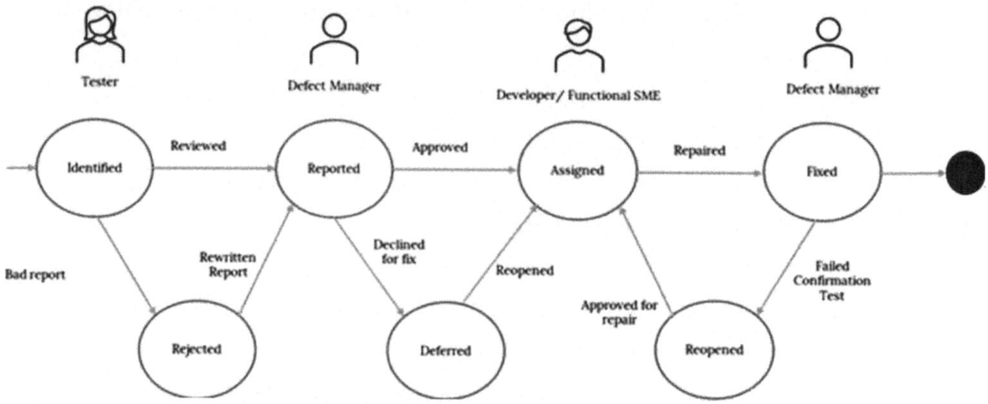

Figure 6.12: *Defect Life Cycle*

The following figure covers the owner-personas in SAP projects who guide the direction of a defect at various stages:

Defect Life Cycle Stage	Owner-Persona
Defect Identification	Functional Tester / Performance Tester
Defect Logging	Tester / Test Lead
Defect Triage	Defect Manager, Business Analyst, Developer
Assignment	Defect Manager
Defect Analysis	Developer / Configuration Specialist
Defect Fixing	Developer / Configuration Specialist
Defect Validation	Tester
Defect Closure	Defect Manager/ Test Lead

Figure 6.13: *Owners at Various Stages of a Defect*

Test Monitoring and Control

Effective test monitoring and control processes ensure that the testing activities align with project objectives, providing insights into testing progress and enabling informed decision-making to mitigate risks as well as optimize system quality.

Test monitoring involves systematic observation, recording, and reporting of testing activities to assess progress, performance, and compliance with predefined goals. It is a dynamic process that requires continuous evaluation to ensure alignment with the project objectives.

The core activities involved in test monitoring and control for SAP S/4HANA projects are:

- **Test Execution Tracking:** Capturing the status of test cases, including pass, fail, and gaps.
- **Defect Monitoring:** Recording and analyzing defect data to prioritize and resolve issues.
- **Coverage Analysis:** Ensuring that all critical business processes and system requirements are adequately tested.
- **Risk Management:** Identifying high-risk areas and assessing the impact of unresolved defects.

Metrics are the way you continue to monitor and control quality outcomes. They provide objective measurements that facilitate the evaluation of testing progress and effectiveness. In the context of SAP S/4HANA projects, test metrics enable stakeholders to gauge the quality of testing efforts and system readiness. For comprehensive insights, these metrics are organized into five categories:

- **Test Execution Metrics:** These metrics monitor the progress of test execution and help assess whether testing activities are proceeding as planned.
    - **Test Execution Coverage:** Measures the percentage of test cases executed out of the total planned. A high coverage percentage indicates thorough execution, while low coverage may signal potential delays.
    - **Pass/Fail Rate:** Indicates the proportion of test cases that pass versus those that fail.
- **Defect Metrics:** Defect-related metrics provide visibility into system quality and the effectiveness of testing efforts.
    - **Defect Detection Percentage (DDP):** Relative comparison of production defects to test defects. This helps to monitor the effectiveness of the test process.

      DDP = defects detected by testers/(defects detected by testers + UAT +Prod)

  - **Defect Density:** The number of defects per functional area. A high density may indicate areas requiring additional scrutiny.
  - **Defect Severity Distribution:** The proportion of defects categorized by severity levels (e.g., critical, major, minor).
  - **Defect Resolution Time:** The average time taken to resolve reported defects.
- **Requirements Metrics:** These metrics monitor the completeness of testing efforts and ensure that critical areas are adequately validated.
  - **Requirements Coverage:** Percentage of system requirements successfully validated by testing. *Example*: Achieving 95% requirements coverage ensured that all mandatory functionalities were operational.
  - **Business Process Coverage:** Measures the proportion of key business processes tested. *Example:* Full coverage of the "`Order to Cash`" process mitigates risks in any SAP S/4HANA deployment.
- **Efficiency Metrics:** Efficiency metrics monitor the productivity of the testing process and the utilization of resources.
  - **Test Case Execution Rate:** Number of test cases executed per day or per testing cycle. **Example**: Increasing the execution rate by 20% through automated testing streamlined the system validation phase.
  - **Resource Utilization:** The percentage of allocated testing resources actively engaged. **Example**: Monitoring utilization rates highlighted underused resources, allowing better allocation.
- **Risk Metrics:** These metrics highlight potential risks and help you monitor the areas that need focused attention.
  - **Open Defects:** The number of unresolved high-severity defects.
  - **Example**: Monitoring open defects during the final test phase ensured timely escalation and a smoother go-live.
  - **Risk Impact Analysis:** Evaluates the potential impact of unresolved issues on business operations.

Customer Example: In a large-scale SAP testing project for a multinational manufacturing enterprise, test monitoring played a pivotal role in identifying and resolving a critical bottleneck. Daily tracking of test execution rates revealed a persistent backlog in integration testing caused by incomplete data preparation. By leveraging these insights, the project team swiftly prioritized data preparation tasks and escalated dependencies for faster resolution. This proactive approach not only accelerated test completion but also ensured the project stayed on track for timely delivery, safeguarding key business milestones.

The following figure offers an analytical view of test metrics with context and interpretation:

Metric	Definition	Value	Interpretation and Implications
Test Execution Coverage	% of test cases executed	85%	Indicates strong progress but signals room for completion
Defect Density	Defects per 100 test cases	1.2	Suggests moderate complexity; further investigation needed
Defect Severity Distribution	High, Medium, Low counts	10/20/5	Highlights areas needing immediate priority
Requirements Coverage	% of requirements validated	92%	High coverage; supports business process continuity
Defect Resolution Time	Avg. days to resolve a defect	3 days	Efficient defect management contributing to project agility
Risk Impact Analysis	Risk potential of unresolved defects	Moderate	Suggests careful monitoring of pending high-severity issues

Figure 6.14: *Test Metrics with the Analytical View of Context and Interpretation*

In the olden days, test program managers spent several days collecting data from various teams and data sources across the SAP projects and preparing these metrics. However, times have changed. Especially with the accessibility of Gen-AI, you can now have these details available to you almost instantly - provided your teams follow some best practices. The future looks very promising for test management, with AI and GenAI-based solutions poised to revolutionize how quality outcomes are monitored and controlled. We will explore these advancements further in *Chapter 8, Tools and Technologies for SAP Testing*.

Conclusion

In this chapter, we explored the foundational aspects of testing in SAP S/4HANA projects, emphasizing that testing is not merely about test cases. We examined how testing integrates into different SDLC models, from Waterfall to Agile and DevOps, and how it adapts to suit various SAP project approaches.

We covered the key topics such as test levels, test types, and test management, delving into critical areas including operating models, planning, risk management, test monitoring, and defect lifecycle management. To support your understanding, we included several SAP examples.

In the next chapter, we will explore test design and core design techniques used for SAP testing projects.

References

- https://www.istqb.org/certifications/certified-tester-foundation-level-agile-tester-ctfl-at/
- (Book) Introduction to SAP S/4HANA
- https://elearning.sap.com
- https://www.iso.org/
- https://www.jait.us/uploadfile/2021/0331/20210331111256770.pdf
- https://www.panaya.com/blog/sap/optimizing-sap-s-4hana-testing-tips-tools/
- https://www.codasol.com/sap-s-4hana-migrations/
- https://ktern.com/article/sap-s4hana-testing/

Chapter 7
Test Design

Introduction

Testing every possible function in SAP applications or business processes is impractical. However, this does not mean that quality teams should settle for a set of test cases without knowing their effectiveness in SAP applications. Poorly designed tests can lead to gaps in coverage, inefficiencies, and increased costs due to defect resolution at later stages of the project life cycle.

Hence, test design forms the backbone of software testing, ensuring that test cases comprehensively validate business requirements, while optimizing testing efforts. In the SAP application landscape, well-structured test design helps prevent defects earlier in the cycle, improves test efficiency, and enhances the overall user experience.

Structure

This chapter explores the philosophy of test design, and various test design techniques that can be used to build comprehensive tests for SAP S/4HANA projects, illustrated with relevant examples:

- Common Traps
- Test Design Best Practices
- Test Design Techniques
- User Acceptance Test Design (UAT)
- AI-Powered Test Design
- Standard KPIs in Test Design
- Test Design Cheat Sheet

Common Traps

Before diving into the test design techniques, it is important to recognize common traps that can undermine the effectiveness of SAP test design. According to a recent Capgemini report, up to 30% of SAP project failures are attributable to insufficient or misaligned testing, leading to substantial cost overruns and business disruptions.

A notable SAP S/4HANA migration failure occurred at a major European retailer, which faced severe disruptions post-go-live due to poor test design. Testing focused only on basic functional validations, neglecting comprehensive end-to-end process coverage. For example, during the first week after go-live, customers ordering promotional items online were charged full price because **key SAP SD pricing rules were not validated**, resulting in incorrect discounts being applied. Additionally:

- **Warehouse operations stalled** when SAP EWM integration tests were skipped, leading to stock mismatches and undelivered orders.
- **User Acceptance Testing (UAT)** was treated merely as a final checkpoint, rather than an iterative process, delaying defect discovery until production.
- **Automated regression testing was insufficient**, missing critical data inconsistencies in migration scripts that disrupted order-to-cash processes.

This failure highlights the importance of robust test design strategies, including risk-based prioritization and comprehensive business process validation.

Teams often defend their existing SAP test design approaches, falling into familiar traps that experienced practitioners recognise all too well. Some of the most common include:

- **"My testing is done by SAP developers":** Remember, developers typically focus on unit testing, which often misses integration, and business process issues. While unit tests ensure that individual functions work as expected, they do not validate how different SAP modules interact. For example, a developer might confirm that an invoice can be generated in SAP S/4HANA but overlook whether it aligns with order-to-cash workflows, potentially leading to discrepancies in financial reconciliation.
- **"My testing is handled by a partner":** Maintenance teams focus on ensuring system stability, but they are not typically involved in validating new business processes or major configuration changes. This can result in outdated test cases that do not align with the evolving SAP landscape. For instance, a maintenance team may verify that a purchase order can still be created post-upgrade but fail to test the impact of new approval workflows, causing operational delays.
- **"Our UAT will catch everything":** Relying solely on User Acceptance Testing (UAT) as the primary quality checkpoint increases the risk of late defect discovery. UAT is designed to validate business workflows, not detect fundamental system flaws. At a global pharmaceuticals firm, incorrect tax

calculations were only caught in UAT, requiring last-minute code fixes, and delaying go-live by three extra weeks.

- **"We have enough automated tests":** Automated tests are essential for regression and efficiency, but they do not replace structured manual testing. Many critical business scenarios, such as compliance validation and exception handling, require exploratory testing. For example, an automated script might verify that a material can be issued in SAP MM but miss an edge case where a specific batch allocation rule prevents issue processing.
- **"We test only based on business user inputs":** While business user insights are valuable, they are often limited to known use cases, leaving blind spots in validation. Structured test design techniques, such as risk-based and equivalence partitioning, help ensure broader coverage. For example, an HR business user might validate basic payroll runs in SAP SuccessFactors but overlook performance testing under peak processing loads, leading to unexpected system slowdowns during payroll cycles.

Addressing these common traps is critical to establishing a structured and resilient SAP test design strategy.

Pro Tip: *Always map automated test coverage to business-critical risk areas. Even robust automation often misses high-impact scenarios. Use exploratory sessions to probe undocumented process flows.*

Test Design Best Practices

A well-structured test design framework ensures that testing efforts are directed toward the most critical areas, balancing risk, cost, and time. An effective test design approach is defined by the following key elements:

- **Clear Objectives and Scope:** Test design should align with business and technical requirements, ensuring that key functionalities and critical workflows are validated.
- **Risk-Based Prioritization:** Focusing on high-risk areas first ensures that defects with the most significant impact are identified early in the testing process.
- **Coverage and Traceability:** Mapping test cases to business requirements helps ensure completeness and aids in impact analysis when changes occur.
- **Test Data Management:** Well-managed test data ensures that test scenarios mimic real-world conditions, and remain reusable for regression testing.
- **Reusability and Maintainability:** Designing modular test cases allows reuse across different test cycles, reducing effort and improving efficiency.

- **Balance between Manual and Automated Testing:** Identifying which test cases should be automated versus manually executed enhances overall test efficiency and accuracy.

Thus, by embedding these foundational principles, teams can establish a robust test strategy that drives efficient, effective, and reliable test execution.

Test Design Techniques

This section explores nine key test design techniques with real-world SAP S/4HANA test case examples.

Equivalence Partitioning

Equivalence partitioning is a black-box testing technique that divides input data into partitions where the system behaves similarly. The idea is to optimize the number of test cases by selecting one representative from each partition.

Best for: Validating SAP Fiori/UI5 forms, SAP S/4HANA transactions, and input fields.

The following is an example of using equivalence partitioning for testing a Sales Order Quantity field, and discounting procedures in SAP S/4HANA: when the quantity is 100 or more, the system should automatically add a special pricing condition (for example, a special discount).

- **Business Rule:**

  a. **Invalid Inputs**: Quantities less than 1 (for example, 0, negative numbers) are not allowed.

  b. **Valid Inputs (No Special Discount)**: Quantities between 1 and 99 should be accepted normally without any additional pricing adjustments.

  c. **Valid Inputs (Special Discount Applied)**: Quantities of 100 or more should trigger an automatic special pricing condition.

- **Test Case #1 – Regular Quantity without Special Discount:**

  Step 1: Launch Sales Order T-code in SAP S/4HANA.

  Step 2: Enter a quantity value within the range 1–99 (example, 50).

  Step 3: Save the order.

  Expected Outcome:

  - The order is accepted and processed normally.
  - No special discount or pricing condition is applied.

- **Test Case #2: High Quantity Triggering Special Discount**

  Step 1: Launch Sales Order T-code in SAP S/4HANA.

  Step 2: Enter a quantity value of 120 (which is 100 or more).

  Step 3: Save the order.

  Expected Outcome:

  - The order is accepted and processed.
  - A special pricing condition (example, a discount rate automatically applied) is added to the order due to the high quantity.

- **Test Case #3: Invalid Quantity**

  Step 1: Open the Sales Order module in SAP S/4HANA.

  Step 2: Enter a quantity of 0 or a negative number (example, 5).

  Step 3: Attempt to save the order.

  Expected Outcome: The system rejects the input, displaying an error message indicating that the quantity must be at least 1.

Using equivalence partitioning in this example allows you to cover a broad range of inputs, while ensuring that:

- Invalid inputs are properly rejected.
- Regular inputs are processed without unexpected pricing conditions.
- High-volume orders trigger the desired business logic of applying a special discount automatically.

This clear segregation into equivalence classes reduces the number of test cases, while ensuring comprehensive coverage of both normal and special pricing scenarios in SAP S/4HANA.

Boundary Value Analysis

Boundary Value Analysis (BVA) focuses on testing at the edges of input ranges. Since defects often occur at boundaries, testing just inside, on, and just outside these boundaries is essential.

Best for: Validating SAP Fiori/UI5 forms, SAP S/4HANA transactions, and input fields.

The following is an example of using a production order in the manufacturing module where the order quantity must lie between 50 and 500 units.

- **Business Rule:**

  a. Validate the boundary conditions for Production Order Quantity.

b. Determine Boundary Values:
   - **Lower Boundary**: 50 (minimum valid)
   - **Upper Boundary**: 500 (maximum valid)
   - **Just Below Lower**: 49
   - **Just Above Upper**: 501

- **Test Case #1: At Lower Boundary**

  Step 1: Launch Production Order T-code in SAP S/4HANA.

  Step 2: Enter a quantity 50 Units.

  Step 3: Save the order.

  Expected Outcome: The order is accepted and processed.

- **Test Case #2: Below Lower Boundary**

  Step 1: Launch Production Order T-code in SAP S/4HANA.

  Step 2: Enter a quantity 49 Units.

  Step 3: Attempt to save the order.

  Expected Outcome: The order is not accepted, and the system shows an error.

- **Test Case #3: At Upper Boundary**

  Step 1: Launch Production Order T-code in SAP S/4HANA.

  Step 2: Enter a quantity 500 Units.

  Step 3: Attempt to save the order.

  Expected Outcome: The order is accepted and processed.

- **Test Case #4: Above Upper Boundary**

  Step 1: Launch Production Order T-code in SAP S/4HANA.

  Step 2: Enter a quantity 501 Units.

  Step 3: Attempt to Save the order.

  Expected Outcome: The order is not accepted, and the system shows an error.

Pro Tip: *In SAP master data screens, boundaries often shift after upgrades. Regularly review business rules, as hardcoded min/max values can subtly change with new releases.*

Decision Table Testing

Decision table testing is a black-box testing technique, meaning it tests the system's behavior without looking at its internal code. It uses a table representation to effectively validate how the system responds to different input combinations, making it useful for complex systems with multiple conditions.

How it works

- **Conditions**: The input variables that affect the system's behavior.
- **Actions**: The system's responses based on the conditions.
- **Rules**: The combinations of conditions and their corresponding actions.

Best for: Complex business rules in pricing, tax calculations, and payroll in SAP as well as its integrated applications.

Let us look at a use case where a customer gets a discount based on customer type, order value, and promotion eligibility.

Customer Type	Order Value	Promo Applied?	Discount (%)
Regular	< 1000	No	0%
Regular	>= 1000	Yes	5%
VIP	<1000	Yes	7%
VIP	>=1000	No	5%

Table 7.1: *Decision Table Testing – Conditions/Actions/Rules*

Here are the test cases that you may design based on this test design technique.

Test ID	Test Case Description	Business Rule
1	Verify that no discount is applied for a regular customer with an order value below $1000 without a promo.	Regular Customer, Order Value < 1000, No Promo.
2	Verify that a 5% discount is applied when a regular customer places an order above $1000 with a promotion.	Regular Customer, Order Value ≥ 1000, Promo Applied.
3	Verify that a 7% discount is applied when a VIP customer places an order below $1000, but a promo is active.	VIP Customer, Order Value < 1000, Promo Applied.
4	Verify that a 5% discount is applied when a VIP customer places an order above $1000 without any promotion.	VIP Customer, Order Value ≥ 1000, No Promo.
5	Attempt to create an order for an unregistered customer type.	Invalid Customer Type (Negative Testcase).

6	Apply an expired promo code to an order.	Promo Code Expired (Negative Testcase).
7	Verify the discount reversed, and the promotion quota restored for a cancelled order.	Order Cancellation After Discount Applied (Negative Testcase).

Table 7.2: *Decision Table Testing – Test Cases*

State Transition Testing

State transition testing is a black-box testing technique that checks how a system changes state in response to inputs or events. It can be used with business requirements where outputs depend on both current and previous inputs.

How it works

- In state transition testing, you observe how a system behaves when given different input conditions in a sequence.
- You provide both positive and negative input values.
- You focus on the input given to the system, the state it goes to, and the output it produces.

Best for: SAP workflow-based modules (for example, Purchase Requisition Approvals, Employee Onboarding integrated with SAP SuccessFactors or Workday).

Employee onboarding is a workflow-driven process where an employee's status transitions through various states based on approvals, document verification, compliance checks, and IT provisioning. Let us look at this HR use case for test design using State Transition Testing.

State Transition Flow

1. New Hire Initiated → HR enters employee details in Workday, and the record syncs to SAP SuccessFactors.
2. HR Review → HR verifies employee details (job title, salary, department, benefits, and so on).
3. Compliance Check → Background checks, tax forms, and legal verifications are completed.
4. IT Setup → Employee accounts are provisioned in SAP and integrated systems.
5. Onboarding Complete → Employee receives credentials for necessary applications.

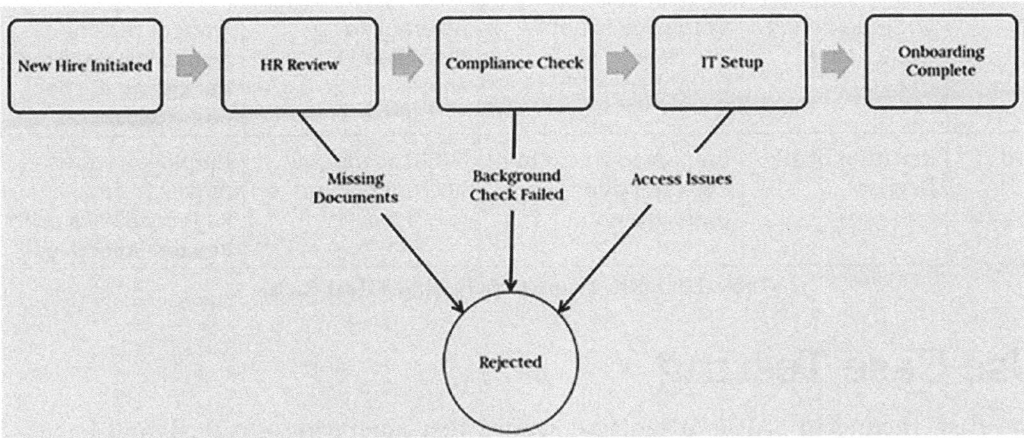

Figure 7.1: *State Transition Flow – Employee Onboarding*

Here are the test cases that you may design based on this test design technique.

Test ID	Test Case Description	Precondition	Action	Expected Outcome
1	New Hire Initiation	Employee record is entered.	Sync data between SAP and Success Factors.	Employee Status updates to **`New Hire Initiated`**.
2	HR Review Approval	Employee in New Hire Initiated Status.	HR Reviews and approves.	Employee moves to **`HR Review Approved`** state.
3	Background check cleared	Employee in HR Review approved state.	Compliance team approves background checks.	Employee moves to **`Compliance Check Passed`**.
4	IT Setup completed	Employee in Compliance Check passed state.	IT provisions systems access.	Employee moves to **`Onboarding Complete`**.
5	HR Review Rejection	Employee in New Hire Initiated Status	HR finds missing documents and rejects	Employee status moves to **`Rejected`**
6	Background check failure	Employee in HR Review Approved state	Background check fails	Employee status moves to **`Rejected`**
7	IT Setup Failure	Employee in Compliance Check Passed state	IT Provision fails	Employee status moves to **`Rejected`**
8	HR Approval before New Hire Initiation	Employee does not exist in system	Attempt to approve HR Review	System throws an error: "**`No record found`**"

9	IT Setup Before Compliance Check	Employee is not yet cleared in Compliance Check	Attempt to provision IT access	System rejects request: "**Employee background check not completed**"
10	Re-attempt HR Review	Employee status in Rejected due to lack of documents	HR fixes missing documents and re-approves	Employee status moves from **Rejected** back to **HR Review Approved**

Table 7.3: *State Transition Testing – Test Cases*

Use Case Testing

Use case testing in SAP is a method where test scenarios are designed based on typical user interactions and business processes. It simulates real-world workflows to ensure that the system functions as expected across end-to-end processes.

Key Aspects of Use Case Testing

- **Real-World Scenarios:** Test cases mirror actual user operations, covering standard workflows, edge cases, and exceptions to validate system behaviour in practical conditions.
- **Process-Centric Validation:** Instead of isolated functional tests, use case testing evaluates how different SAP modules interact, ensuring seamless process execution.
- **Comprehensive Documentation:** Test scenarios are documented as "**use cases**," detailing user actions, system responses, and expected outcomes for each step, aiding in repeatability and traceability.

Best for: Validating real-world user journeys.

Let us look at test case design for a procurement officer journey, while managing purchase orders.

Test ID	Test Case	Expected Result
1	Attempt to create a PO.	PO should be created successfully.
2	Attempt to create a Purchase Order without a Purchase Requisition.	System should block PO creation, and show errors, if any.
3	Assign PO to an inactive vendor.	System should block vendor selection.
4	Release PO above threshold limit without approval.	System should block PO release until proper authorization.

Table 7.4: *Use Case Testing – Test Cases*

Interface (API and Integration) Testing

In a SAP landscape, interface testing ensures seamless communication between SAP and non-SAP systems, verifying that the data is correctly exchanged across various integrations. Since SAP environments often interact with third-party applications, legacy systems, and cloud platforms, robust interface testing is critical for process integrity, data accuracy, and system reliability. These tests validate that data flows correctly, system interactions function as expected, and security and performance requirements are met.

Best for: Testing SAP Cloud Platform (BTP), SAP CPI integrations, and non-SAP connectors.

Key Interface Types in SAP

- **Intermediate Documents (IDocs)**: Used for asynchronous data exchange between SAP systems or with external applications.
- **Business Application Programming Interfaces (BAPIs)**: Allow external applications to access SAP business processes.
- **Remote Function Calls (RFCs)**: Enable real-time communication between SAP and non-SAP systems.
- **OData and REST APIs**: Facilitate web-based integrations, especially in SAP Fiori and S/4HANA environments.
- **Process Integration/Process Orchestration (SAP PI/PO)**: Middleware that connects SAP with third-party systems.
- **Cloud Connectors and SAP Integration Suite**: Support hybrid integration scenarios between on-premises and cloud solutions.

Here is a list of example test cases for validating the Sales Order Interface functionality between SAP and a non-SAP based logistics system.

Test ID	Test Case	Description	Expected Result
1	Valid Data Exchange	Send an order from SAP to a third-party logistics system via IDoc	Order is successfully received and acknowledged
2	Invalid Order Format	Send an order with missing fields	System logs an appropriate error and rejects the IDoc
3	Performance Test	Process 1000 orders in bulk	Orders are processed within SLA time
4	Security Test	Attempt unauthorized access to API	Access is denied with appropriate error message

Table 7.5: *Interface Testing – Test Cases*

Best Practices for SAP Interface Testing

- **Use realistic test data**: Avoid hardcoded values; leverage actual business scenarios.
- Automate interface validation.
- **Perform negative testing**: Simulate failures to check how the system reacts.
- **Coordinate with business and technical teams**: Ensure test cases cover both functional and integration aspects.

Business Process Testing (BPT)

Business Process Test Design (BPT) is an end-to-end validation approach that ensures real-world business scenarios work as expected across SAP and non-SAP systems. Unlike Use Case Testing that validates individual user journeys, BPT verifies workflows across multiple users - ensuring seamless integration, compliance, and business continuity.

Here is a quick comparison chart on BPT vs Use Case Testing for clearer understanding.

Aspect	Use Case Testing	Business Process Testing
Focus	Single user action	End-to-end process
Scope	One Interaction at a time	Multi-step, cross functional workflow
Validation	Functional correctness	Process consistency and integration

Table 7.6: *BPT vs. Use Case Testing*

BPT is one of the most common test design techniques used in SAP landscapes, and is best suited for the following examples:

Business Process	SAP Modules Involved	Systems Involved
Procure-to-Pay (P2P)	MM (Materials Management), FI (Finance), and AP (Accounts Payable).	SAP S/4HANA, Ariba, Vendor portals, and Banks.
Order-to-Cash (O2C)	SD (Sales and Distribution), FI, and CRM (Customer Relationship Management).	SAP S/4HANA, Salesforce, and Payment Gateways.
Hire-to-Retire (H2R)	Success Factors, HR, and Payroll.	SAP, Success Factors, and Benefit Providers.
Supply Chain Management (SCM)	PP (Production Planning) and EWM (Extended Warehouse Management).	SAP S/4HANA, MES, IoT devices, and 3PL systems.

Table 7.7: *Business Processes*

Here is a list of the commonly designed test cases for Procure-to-Pay using BPT:

Test ID	Objective	Test Steps	Expected Result
1	Purchase Requisition (PR) creation and approval	• Create PR in SAP Fiori App. • Assign Cost Center and GL Accounts. • Submit Approval Workflow.	• PR is routed to the correct approver. • Approved PR is converted to Purchase Order (PO).
2	PO creation and Vendor Selection	• Convert PR to PO in SAP S/4HANA. • Select preferred vendor in SAP MDG. • Send PO to SAP Ariba. • Vendor accepts the PO.	• PO is successfully created and sent to the correct vendor. • Vendor acknowledges PO in SAP Ariba.
3	Posting Goods Receipt (GR)	• Warehouse team receives goods in SAP EWM. • Post GR against the PO. • Verify stock updates in SAP MM inventory. • Check if GR triggers invoice verification.	• Goods are received and updated SAP MM. • Stock levels are updated in the warehouse. • SAP matches the PO and GR for invoice processing.
4	Three-way matching for invoice processing	• Vendor submits the invoice in SAP Ariba. • Validate the invoice with PO and GR. • Send the invoice for manual review in case of discrepancy.	• System rejects the invoices that do not match PO and GR. • Matched invoices are approved for payment.
5	Vendor Payment processing	• Generate vendor payment batch in SAP S/4HANA FI-AP. • Send payment instruction to bank via API. • Verify bank payment confirmation. • Verify vendor account updated.	• Verify the payment status. • Verify invoice status changed to Paid. • Verify bank confirmation.

Table 7.8: *Business Process Testing – Test Cases*

Pro Tip: *In a recent SAP S/4HANA rollout, cross-functional 'war room' testing sessions brought together users from finance, supply chain, and compliance. This broke down silos, surfacing process-blocking defects earlier, and increasing user buy-in.*

Exploratory Testing

Exploratory test design technique is an unscripted, experience-based testing technique that focuses on identifying defects through real-world user interactions, rather than predefined test cases. In a SAP S/4HANA landscape, where complex ERP processes, custom enhancements, and integrations exist, exploratory testing plays a crucial role in uncovering hidden issues that structured testing might miss.

Why are issues missed with structured testing?

Structured testing relies on predefined test cases created from known requirements, and expected system behaviours. While this ensures coverage of documented scenarios, it has certain limitations such as:

- **It tests only what is known.** Structured test cases are based on documented requirements, leaving gaps for scenarios that were not anticipated during design.
- **Real-world variations are often overlooked.** Users interact with the system in diverse and unpredictable ways that scripted tests do not capture.
- **Dynamic integration issues can go undetected.** Especially in SAP S/4HANA, where multiple modules and external systems interact, unexpected data flows or timing issues may not be covered in structured test cases.
- **Assumptions remain unchallenged.** Structured tests validate expected behaviour, but exploratory testing challenges assumptions, revealing defects in edge cases and unusual workflows.

Exploratory testing can be used in the following areas:

- Custom SAP enhancements (Z-Programs, Reports, and Workflows)
- SAP Fiori Apps
- SAP Business Process Workflows (PR, PO, and Invoice Workflows)
- SAP Upgrades and Patches
- SAP Security and Authorization

Here is a list of the sample exploratory test cases focusing on unpredictable behavior, integrations, and edge cases:

Test ID	Objective	Test Approach	Expected Result
1	Month-end finance report (Z-report) should return 100,000+ records within 5 seconds.	• Execute z-report with custom filters. • Test the impact of large datasets.	• The report should return results in 5 seconds. • No memory dumps or time outs should occur.

2	Verify that the master data is transferred without duplicates during SAP ECC and SAP S/4HANA migration.	• Manually compare migrated records between ECC and S/4HANA. • Modify a migrated vendor record in SAP S/4HANA, and check for inconsistencies. • Create new transactions (example, Purchase Orders) using the migrated master data. • Enter invalid or incomplete data, and observe system behavior.	• No duplicate vendors or materials should exist post-migration. • No master data should be corrupted or missing key attributes (example, payment terms). • System should prevent incorrect vendor selection due to incomplete data.
3	Only Finance Managers should be able to approve vendor payments.	• Attempt to approve a payment as a non-Finance user. • Test for Segregation of Duties (SoD) violations. • Simulate an inactive user trying to log in, and approve payments.	• Unauthorized users should be blocked from approving payments. • SAP GRC logs should capture all access violations. • The system should prevent SoD conflicts (for example, the same user cannot create and approve a payment).

***Table 7.9**: Exploratory Testing – Test Cases*

User Acceptance Test Design (UAT)

User Acceptance Testing (UAT) is the final validation phase in an SAP project, where business users (end users) verify that the system meets their requirements before go-live. UAT ensures that:

- The SAP system aligns with real-world business workflows.
- End users can perform their daily tasks without issues.
- The solution is ready for deployment.

Why is UAT critical in SAP applications?

- **Multiple teams are involved:** SAP projects often include different system integrators, consultants, and vendors working on various modules. UAT ensures that everything works together as expected.
- **Earlier testing does not cover everything**: Technical and functional tests check if the system works as designed, but UAT confirms it works for real business tasks.

- **Fixing issues early saves cost:** Finding defects in UAT is much cheaper than discovering them after go-live.
- **End-user confidence**: UAT gives business users a chance to use the system before launch, provide feedback, and build confidence.
- **Compliance checks:** UAT ensures that the system meets legal and regulatory requirements before it goes live.

Best Practices for UAT Design

- **Base test cases on real business scenarios:** Ensure that test cases reflect actual day-to-day tasks and workflows, not just blueprint requirements.
- **Cover end-to-end process flows:** Design test cases that span across modules to validate complete business processes.
- **Use realistic, production-like data:** Testing with real-world data uncovers data issues, and builds user confidence.
- **Prioritise high-risk and critical processes:** Focus efforts on processes that, if failed, would have the greatest business impact.
- **Write clear, user-friendly test cases:** Use simple business language so that end users can execute tests independently and confidently.

Here is a case study of a SAP customer where a well-structured test strategy prioritized UAT, ensuring business continuity and a smooth SAP S/4HANA upgrade.

- **Customer**: Fortune 500 manufacturer of industrial explosive machinery components.
- **Project**: SAP S/4HANA upgrade from 1709 to 2210.
- **Business Risk**: A one-day delay could lead to:
  - Loss of market share to competitors.
  - Revenue loss from incorrect pricing and deal registration.
  - Supply chain disruptions, affecting production schedules.
- **Project Life Cycle Model**: Iterative Development and Testing.
- **SAP Landscape**: 5-tier (Dev, QA, Integration, UAT, and Prod).
- **Test Volume**: 10000 + Test Cases.
- **Test Coverage**: O2C, P2P, Supply Chain, Finance, Supplier and Distributer Workflows, SAP Fiori and Custom Developments.
- **UAT Volume**: 3,000 + UAT test cases executed by business users per test cycle.

The following are some of the UAT test samples used by the customer, mentioned above.

Test ID	Process	Test Case
1	O2C	Create sales order, and validate correct pricing, taxation, and ATP checks.
2	O2C	Generate customer invoice, and validate correct financial postings in FI-AR.
3	Manufacturing and Supply Chain	Run MRP live, and validate production planning changes.
4	Manufacturing and Supply Chain	Validate new Predictive Material and Resource Planning (pMRP) introduced in 2210.
5	FI and CO	Execute Foreign Currency Revaluation (`FAGL_FC_VAL`) with 2210 exchange rate updates.
6	Custom Developments	Run batch jobs, and validate performance with SAP BTP-based enhancements.

Table 7.10: *Customer Example* - UAT Test Cases

AI-Powered Test Design

With the advent of Artificial Intelligence (AI), test design has evolved to become more efficient, accurate, and less time-consuming. While traditional methods are reliable, they struggle to keep pace with the demands of tight timelines, comprehensive risk coverage, and cost constraints. Industry analysts report that AI-driven test design accelerates test coverage for regression cycles, and reduces missed defects by over 20%.

This section explores how AI can be effectively leveraged to design test cases for SAP S/4HANA, including practical example prompts and prompt chains to guide you through the process.

Step-by-Step Instructions to Generate Test Cases Using AI Tools

Step 1: Define scope and objectives - Clearly define the scope and objectives of your testing effort. This includes identifying the modules, processes, and integrations that need to be tested.

Step 2: Create context for test design - Provide documentation and business process details. This ensures comprehensive coverage of all scenarios.

Prompt example: *Focus on the financial accounting and sales distribution modules. Include key objectives such as custom report validation, and integration testing.*

Step 3: Prioritize test cases – Clearly state the type of test cases to be designed. For example, approval workflow validations, business process test cases, and so on.

Step 4: Change management – In case you are trying to consolidate your existing test cases using the new changes released by SAP, then provide the context for change requests and the existing test cases.

Step 5: Refine test cases – Always review and validate the test cases generated by AI to ensure that they align with your requirements. Use AI outputs as a starting point, and then refine and enhance them with your expertise.

Example Prompt Chains

- **Prompt Chain #1: End-to-End Test Case Generation**

  Define Scope: "*Define the scope of testing for an SAP S/4HANA migration project, focusing on the financial accounting and sales distribution modules.*"

  Create Context: "*Generate a set of test cases for the financial accounting processes based on attached documentation – Business Requirements Document and Business Process Diagram*"

  Generate Test Case: "*Include scenarios for data migration, custom report validation, and integration with other modules.*"

  Prioritize Test Cases: "*Identify high-risk areas for testing in the financial accounting module, and prioritize the generated test cases accordingly.*"

  Validate and Refine: "*Review and refine the test cases for the financial accounting module to ensure that they cover all critical scenarios.*"

- **Prompt Chain #2: Risk-Based Test Case Generation**

  Identify High-Risk Areas: "*Identify high-risk areas for testing in an SAP S/4HANA upgrade project, focusing on integrations, and custom code specifications provided.*"

  Generate Test Cases: "*Generate test cases for the identified high-risk areas, including edge cases and failure scenarios.*"

  Prioritize Test Cases: "*Prioritize the generated test cases based on the level of risk and potential business impact provided in the business-risk-matrix.*"

Validate and Refine: "*Review and refine the test cases for the high-risk areas to ensure that they are comprehensive and accurate.*"

- **Prompt Chain #3: State Transition Test Design for O2C Process**

  Define Scope: "*Define the scope of state transition testing for the order-to-cash process in SAP S/4HANA, focusing on order creation, approval, shipment, and invoicing.*"

  Generate Test Cases: "*Generate state transition test cases for the order-to-cash process, including all possible transitions and edge cases.*"

  Prioritize Test Cases: "*Identify high-risk transitions in the order-to-cash process, and prioritize the generated test cases accordingly.*"

  Validate and Refine: "*Review and refine the state transition test cases to ensure that they cover all critical scenarios and transitions.*"

- **Prompt Chain #4: Boundary Value Analysis for Finance Process**

  Define Scope: "*Define the scope of boundary value analysis for the financial accounting process in SAP S/4HANA, focusing on fields - account balances, tax rates, and currency conversions.*"

  Create Context: "*Generate test cases based on the specific business logic provided in the user story document and functional specification.*"

  Generate Test Cases: "*Generate test cases using boundary value analysis for the financial accounting module, including minimum, maximum, and edge values.*"

  Prioritize Test Cases: "*Identify high-risk fields in the financial accounting module, and prioritize the generated test cases accordingly.*"

  Validate and Refine: "*Review and refine the boundary value test cases to ensure that they cover all critical scenarios and edge* values."

These prompt chain examples have been tested across various Large Language Model (LLM) applications, including OpenAI, Anthropic, and DeepSeek. The results were consistently effective, with well-structured and formatted outputs that met the requirements for SAP S/4HANA test design.

However, while AI-powered test design offers significant advantages, it is essential to address customer concerns related to data security, governance, and compliance. The following best practices will help you implement AI capabilities responsibly within your SAP projects, ensuring both innovation and adherence to organisational standards.

- **Data Security and Privacy:** Ensure that all data used by AI tools is encrypted, both at rest and in transit, to protect sensitive information. Ensure that your

AI tools comply with data protection regulations such as GDPR, CCPA, and industry-specific standards.

- **Start Small:** Begin by using AI for specific modules or processes, and then gradually expand its use across the entire project.
- **Collaborate with AI:** Treat AI as a collaborative partner. Use its outputs as a starting point, and then refine and enhance them with your expertise.
- **Validate AI Outputs:** Always review and validate the test cases generated by AI to ensure that they align with your requirements.
- **Invest in Training:** Learn how to use AI tools effectively, and stay updated on the latest advancements in AI-powered testing.
- **Measure Success:** Track key metrics such as test coverage, defect detection rates, and time savings to demonstrate the value of AI-powered test design.

Pro Tip: *While AI-generated test cases boost coverage, you may want to always review the results for gaps or redundant cases. AI may skew toward previously over-tested areas, if not balanced with the current business risk mapping.*

Standard KPIs for Test Design

In medium to large-scale SAP S/4HANA testing projects, continuously measuring the quality of test design is essential to reduce business risk, and ensure project success. Test managers rely on Key Performance Indicators (KPIs) to gain quantifiable insights into the quality, coverage, and efficiency of testing. These KPIs help identify gaps, optimise resources, and support data-driven decisions to improve testing outcomes.

As per the recent World Quality Report, best-in-class QA organizations aims for at least 85% requirement coverage, >60% automation in regression packs, and early defect detection rates of 75% or above.

Test Coverage

- **What is it**? The percentage of business requirements, processes, and functionalities covered by test cases.
- **Formula**: (Number of Requirements Covered by Test Cases/Total Number of Requirements) * 100
- **Why It Matters:**
    - Ensures that all critical business processes and functionalities are tested.
    - Identifies gaps in test design that could lead to untested scenarios.

Requirement Traceability

- **What is it**? The percentage of test cases mapped to specific business requirements.
- **Formula**: (Number of Test Cases Mapped to Requirements/Total Number of Test Cases) * 100
- **Why It Matters**:
  - Ensures that test design aligns with business objectives.
  - Facilitates impact analysis during changes or enhancements.

Test Case Reusability

- **What is it**? The percentage of test cases that can be reused across different phases or projects.
- **Formula**: (Number of Reusable Test Cases/Total Number of Test Cases) * 100
- **Why It Matters**:
  - Measures the efficiency of test design in creating reusable assets.
  - Reduces efforts and cost in future projects.

Pro Tip: *If reusability falls below 30%, conduct workshops to modularize test assets, and reduce duplication.*

Test Design Productivity

- **What is it?** The number of test cases designed per unit of time (for example, per day or per week).
- **Formula**: Total Number of Test Cases Designed/Total Time Spent on Test Design
- **Why It Matters**:
  - Evaluates the efficiency of the test design process.
  - Helps identify bottlenecks or resource constraints.

Test Automation Coverage

- **What is it?** The percentage of test cases automated compared to the total number of test cases.
- **Formula**: (Number of Automated Test Cases/Total Number of Test Cases) * 100
- **Why It Matters**:
  - Measures the efficiency of test design in supporting automation.
  - Higher automation coverage reduces manual effort, and accelerates testing.

Defect Detection Percentage (DDP)

- **What is it?** The percentage of defects detected during testing compared to the total defects found (including post-production).
- **Formula:** (Defects Detected During Testing /Total Defects Detected) * 100
- **Why It Matters:**
  - Measures the effectiveness of test design in identifying defects early.
  - A high DDP indicates robust test design, reducing the risk of defects in production.

Pro Tip: *Use the following checklist to evaluate your test-design: Are all high-risk areas covered by at least one test case? Is each test case mapped to a specific business requirement?*

Several templates and test design documents are made available for your reference at our resources library here: **https://github.com/ava-orange-education/Mastering-SAP-S-4HANA-Quality-Assurance**

Conclusion

This chapter explored the fundamental principles, methodologies, and best practices to enhance test effectiveness, and mitigate risks early in the development cycle. By addressing common pitfalls, integrating AI-driven test design approaches, and strengthening User Acceptance Testing (UAT) strategies, it provides a practical framework for designing robust test cases.

Additionally, the inclusion of standardized KPIs equips quality teams with the tools needed to align test coverage with business and compliance requirements, ensuring a smooth and successful SAP system deployment.

In the next chapter, we will explore the tools and technologies that QA teams commonly use in SAP S/4HANA projects to drive efficiency, coverage, and quality outcomes.

References

- Foundations of Software Testing – ISTQB Guide
- SAP S/4HANA Conversion Guide
- Learning.SAP.COM
- https://training.sap.com/course/calm20-sap-cloud-alm-for-implementation-classroom-001-g-en/
- Inside SAP S/4HANA Cloud for referring to various customer case studies and User Presentations - https://open.spotify.com/show/2lW4pQEhgLuoadLVSBpi4w

CHAPTER 8
Tools and Technologies for SAP Testing

Introduction

To navigate the large SAP testing projects, tools and technologies play a vital role in ensuring a smooth and efficient testing process. This chapter explores the tools that testing teams commonly use, or may typically consider to build seamless test feedback cycles. These tools are essential for ensuring efficiency, accuracy, and collaboration throughout the testing process.

Successful QE/QA teams are often seen leveraging a variety of tools to optimize the test life cycle across SAP S/4HANA projects. While the specific tools may vary between implementations, a strong understanding of their core functionalities and benefits enables these teams to address SAP testing challenges effectively. The following overview highlights the key tools commonly used to support a smooth and efficient testing process.

This chapter does not advocate for any specific tool or technology. Instead, it explores common patterns across various solutions from an objective standpoint, empowering project teams to assess and select the best fit for their unique needs.

Structure

This chapter explores the key tools commonly used to support a smooth and efficient testing process. They include:

- Common Traps with Tools
- Test Management Tools
- Test Automation Tools
    - Functional
    - Non-Functional
    - Interfaces

- Change Management Tools
- AI Testing Tools
- Architecture Patterns of SAP Testing Tools
- Three-dimensional Tool Evaluation Criteria
- Evolution of Test Automation in SAP Projects

Common Traps

Despite the clear benefits, many SAP teams hesitate to invest in appropriate testing tools. Here are the five most common reasons:

- **Cost Concerns**
    - **Justification**: "*We do not have the budget for expensive testing tools.*"
    - **Reality**: While the upfront cost may seem high, not investing in automation and test management tools often leads to higher long-term costs due to rework, production defects, and delayed releases. Many modern tools offer scalable pricing models to fit different budgets.
- **Comfort Zone and Resistance to Change**
    - **Justification**: "*Our current testing methods work fine; why change?*"
    - **Reality**: Many SAP teams are comfortable with manual testing or legacy tools, and resist adopting new solutions. However, as SAP S/4HANA evolves, manual methods become insufficient, leading to gaps in coverage and inefficiencies.
- **Lack of In-House Skills**
    - **Justification**: "*Our team lacks the expertise to use these advanced tools.*"
    - **Reality**: While there may be a learning curve, most modern test automation tools offer low-code/no-code solutions that require minimal technical expertise. Investing in upskilling ensures long-term efficiency gains.
- **Dependency on External Testing Teams**
    - **Justification**: "*We rely on external vendors for testing.*"
    - **Reality**: Relying solely on external teams can lead to a lack of internal control over the quality process. Having in-house tools empowers SAP teams to execute tests faster, and reduces dependency risks.
- **Overconfidence in the Existing Processes**
    - **Justification**: "*We have a robust testing methodology, and our teams already do extensive testing.*"

- o **Reality**: Even with strong manual processes, human errors and inefficiencies creep in. Automation and structured testing tools provide scalability, consistency, and enhanced test coverage beyond manual capabilities.

Test Management Tools

Test management plays a crucial role in connecting test life cycles with the key SAP stakeholders - business, functional, development, and QA teams. Without a structured test management tool or framework, organizations risk creating testing silos, leading to inconsistent quality across SAP processes. An effective test management tool bridges these gaps, ensuring alignment, traceability, and streamlined defect resolution.

The following figure illustrates how test management is streamlined for SAP projects by mapping the test life cycle to the key personas involved.

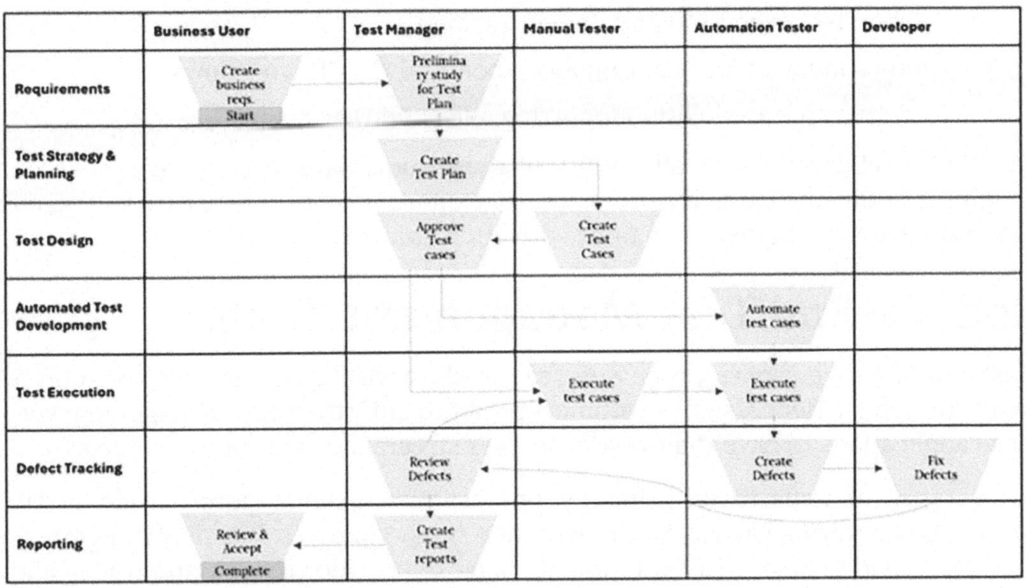

Figure 8.1: *Test Management Process Flow*

This section explores the key test management tools within the SAP ecosystem, categorized into three types:

- **SAP-provided tools** that include test management as part of broader application lifecycle management (ALM). For example, SAP Solution Manager, and SAP CloudALM.
- **End-to-End test management tools** that integrate testing processes with SAP lifecycle management solutions. For example, Atlassian Jira, Tricentis qTest, OpenText ALM, UiPath Test Manager, Panaya, and so on.

- **Independent test management tools** used primarily by testing teams with little or no integration with SAP environments. For example, open-source test management tools, defect management tools, and so on.

SAP-Provided ALM Tools

SAP offers a couple of built-in tools that manage test processes alongside broader application lifecycle management (ALM) capabilities. These tools are provided to SAP customers as part of their SAP landscape, either through cloud-based subscriptions or as part of their on-premise SAP infrastructure.

The following SAP tools are quite commonly used in testing – SAP Cloud ALM and SAP Solution Manager (SolMan). Both of them offer capabilities that almost cover all the phases of testing though it is just manual testing. The key capabilities include:

- Test planning aligned with business processes.
- Built-in test execution and defect tracking.
- Integration with SAP's automation tools and CI/CD workflows.
- End-to-end traceability, supporting agile and DevOps testing.

The high-level architecture and utility of these tools have already been covered in Chapter 2. In the upcoming chapters, we will explore how these tools are leveraged by successful Quality Engineering teams with appropriate case studies.

End-To-End Test Management Tools

Most often, SAP business processes seamlessly navigate across SAP and non-SAP application stack. Hence, some customers prefer to unify their test management across these applications to have their test processes streamlined across the enterprise.

These types of tools focus primarily on test management across wide array of applications covering various implementation methodologies. But they integrate well with SAP Cloud ALM and SAP Solution Manager to provide visibility and traceability.

Some of the most common test management tools are: Atlassian Jira, Microfocus ALM, Tricentis qTest, UiPath Test Manager, and Panaya.

All of these tools offer capabilities for seamlessly integrating with SAP focused test projects, along with business process testing, as well as regression test projects.

- Test case repository and execution tracking.
- Defect management linked to SAP transports.
- Risk-based testing.
- Dashboards for visibility across teams.

- Integration with SAP and several non-SAP applications.

Independent Test Management Tools

In some small to medium sized testing projects, organizations tend to choose independent test management tools such as open-source test management tools, or in some cases as simple as Excel could be leveraged too. This type of test management solution covers just a basic need like:

- Manual test case tracking
- Defect management
- Test data sources

Let us understand the benefits of an effective test management through a real customer story. A global pharmaceutical company undergoing an SAP S/4HANA migration needed to streamline their test management to replace their fragmented, manual testing processes.

- **Challenges with the current state:**
  - o Inconsistent test tracking across multiple business units.
  - o Poor defect resolution workflows, delaying releases.
  - o Limited test automation integration, leading to excessive manual work.
- **Solution Implemented:**
  - o Implemented SAP Cloud ALM for end-to-end test management.
  - o Connected SAP BPCA to assess the impact of changes, and prioritize testing.
  - o Integrated enterprise test automation tools to optimize test execution.
- **Results Achieved:**
  - o 60% reduction in testing efforts through automation and centralized test management.
  - o Faster defect resolution with real-time collaboration between testing and development teams.
  - o Consistent test tracking and compliance across SAP business units.
  - o Accelerated go-live by two months, improving business continuity.

For more customer case studies, please refer: https://support.sap.com/en/alm/sap-cloud-alm/sap-cloud-alm-references.html

How Do You Choose Your Test Management Tool:

While there is no one right way of managing SAP test projects, the following list of essential evaluation factors can guide you in evaluating the right test management tool for your SAP project:

Aspect	Description
Cost and Licensing	Subscription vs. one-time licensing fees, scalability costs, and hidden expenses (maintenance, upgrades).
Technology and Architecture	Cloud vs. on-premises, compatibility with SAP landscape (S/4HANA, ECC), and API availability.
Ease of Use and Learning Curve	Intuitive UI, training availability, and adoption speed.
Integration Capabilities	SAP Cloud ALM/Solution Manager integration, CI/CD compatibility, and automation framework support.
Test Automation and Execution	Manual and automated test support, scheduling, and execution tracking.
Defect Management and Traceability	Real-time defect tracking, integration with Jira and SAP transport management.
Compliance and Security	Regulatory adherence (GDPR, ISO 27001), role-based access, and audit logging.
Scalability and Performance	Performance under heavy test loads, multi-project support.
Customization and Flexibility	Custom fields, workflows, and reporting dashboards.
Vendor Support and Community	Customer support, user communities, and product roadmap.
AI Innovations	AI capabilities for reporting, test design, data security, and anonymization.

Table 8.1: *Test Management Tool – Evaluation Checklist*

Pro Tip: *Always pilot new tools with a cross-functional team to reveal hidden integration gaps early.*

Test Automation Tools

Manual testing often falls short at many test levels. It is not a reliable or scalable approach to deliver the test coverage required for SAP projects within tight project timelines. According to Gartner's 2024 Market Guide for Application Testing Services, enterprises automating SAP business process tests report 40–60% cycle time reduction compared to manual efforts.

This section explores key test automation tools leveraged within the SAP ecosystem, categorized into three types:

- **Functional Test Automation Tools** are designed to automate end-to-end test cases covering functional aspects of business requirements. Some of the common test platforms used in SAP are Tricentis, Worksoft, UiPath, OpenText (aka Microfocus), Panaya, KTern, and Selenium-based Opensource tools.

- **Non-Functional Test Automation Tools** are designed to validate aspects such as performance, scalability and reliability under various conditions. For example, tools like Apache JMeter, Microfocus LoadRunner, Tricentis Neo Load, UiPath, and Worksoft.
- **Interfaces Test Automation Tools** used primarily to validate data exchange and integration between SAP S/4HANA and external systems, ensuring seamless communication via APIs, IDocs, or other interfaces. Common tools include SmartBear SoapUI, Postman, SAP PI/PO, and INT4 IFTT, and so on.

The following figure illustrates how test automation is typically operationalized within the SAP projects connecting the test life cycle and the personas involved.

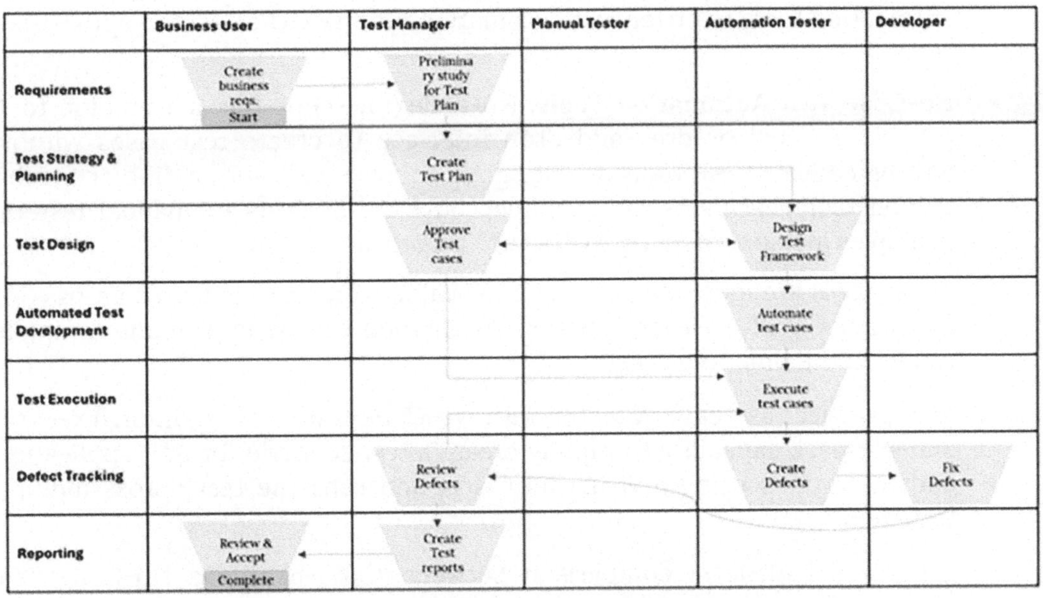

Figure 8.2: *Test Process Flow with Test Automation Tools*

Functional Test Automation Tools

Functional test automation tools are typically used in SAP projects to make test processes efficient and mitigate many of the common risks that arise with manual testing:

- Reducing test execution time, and improving efficiency.
- Ensuring consistent and repeatable test validations.
- Enhancing test coverage across various SAP modules.

- Accelerating release cycles, and minimizing risks.
- Freeing up business users for more value-added tasks.

SAP functional test automation tools fall into two primary categories:

- **Code-Based Test Automation Tools:** Code-based test automation tools require testers or developers to write scripts or codes to automate test cases. These tools provide frameworks and libraries to interact with the Application Under Test (AUT) programmatically. Examples include Selenium, Cypress, Playwright, and Appium.

  These tools are ideal for coder or programmer personas. If your test capability is built with these personas, you may consider the code-based test automation tools. However, these code-based functional test automation tools have technology limitations, and they typically only work for SAP Web-based applications due to which, you may want to leverage other test automation tools to cover test automation for SAP GUI, Desktop apps-based testing.

- **No-Code Test Automation Tools:** No-code/low-code test automation tools provide a visual or drag-and-drop interface to create test cases without writing codes. These tools are designed to make test automation accessible to non-technical users (for example, business analysts or manual testers). Examples include Tricentis, Worksoft, UiPath, and so on.

  These tools are ideal for building and scaling your testing teams across SAP landscapes. With ease-of-use, test automation can be implemented rapidly, reducing the time to market.

  As a practical use case, a tester with No-Code tool uses traditional record-and-playback capability to rapidly create a test scenario for SAP application, adds assertions using a visual interface, and runs the test across multiple browsers.

  Here is a high-level comparison between Code-based vs No-Code Test Automation tools:

Aspect	**Code-based Tools**	**No-Code/ Low-code Tools**
Ease Of Use	Requires programming expertise	No coding skills required; User friendly interface
Flexibility	Highly flexible for complex processes – mobile & CI/CD	Limited flexibility for advanced use cases
Speed for Testing	Slower (requires skilled resources)	Faster (drag-and-drop and Record-and-Playback)

Maintenance	High – requires manual updates	Often includes self-healing capabilities
Target users	Developers, SDETs, Technical testers	Manual testers, Business users
Cost	Low-cost. Often open-source	Can be expensive

Table 8.2: *Code-based vs No-Code based Test Automation Tools*

Choosing the right test automation tool can make or break your SAP project's quality outcomes. The following list highlights the essential aspects that successful teams prioritize when evaluating tools to ensure scalability, efficiency, and long-term value:

Aspect	**Description**
SAP Compatibility	Native support for SAP GUI, SAP Fiori, SAP S/4HANA, and other interfaces
Ease of Use	Can be adopted by current testing and business teams
Integrations	Support for continuous testing in Agile environments
Technology Support	Support for automating various technologies including SAP
AI and Smart testing	AI-driven automation for self-healing and intelligent test execution
Reusability	Ability to reuse test assets across SAP upgrades, and releases
Maintenance	Ability to reduce script maintenance times due to technical and functional updates to SAP systems
Scalability	Capability to handle large-scale SAP test scenarios
Licensing Model	Total cost of ownership, including licensing and maintenance

Table 8.3: *Functional Test Automation Tools – Evaluation Checklist*

To truly grasp the value of a well-executed test automation strategy, let us explore a customer case study that highlights how modern QA teams are accelerating quality, reducing risk, and transforming their SAP project outcomes: A leading energy company undergoing an SAP S/4HANA transformation faced significant testing challenges, including manual effort, long testing cycles, and inadequate test coverage. They chose No-Code test platform to automate their functional testing.

The benefits reported include:

- 60% reduction in test execution time.
- 40% improvement in test coverage across SAP modules.
- Seamless integration with CI/CD pipelines, enabling faster releases.
- Reduction in test maintenance efforts with AI-driven automation.

Operating Model

The company implemented a centralized test automation framework integrated into their SAP project lifecycle. The architecture included:

- **Test Design and Management:**
    - Test automation platform integrated with SAP Solution Manager.
    - Business process models used for designing manual and automated test cases.
- **Test Execution:**
    - Tests are scheduled on a periodic basis in SAP landscapes (Dev, QA, and Pre-Prod).
    - AI-powered self-healing for resilient test execution, and to reduce maintenance efforts.
- **Defect Management and Reporting:**
    - Test Automation framework integrates with Jira for defect tracking.
    - Real-time test dashboards for visibility into test results.
- **Continuous Integration and Deployment:**
    - Automated test execution triggered via GitHub Actions and Jenkins.
    - Support for SAP transport validation, and release readiness.

Thus, by integrating automation into their SAP testing strategy, the company achieved higher efficiency, improved test reliability, and accelerated their SAP rollout.

Non-Functional Test Automation Tools

While functional testing ensures that business processes work as intended, it is non-functional testing that safeguards the system's stability, performance under pressure, security, and regulatory compliance. In today's high-stakes SAP S/4HANA landscapes, automating non-functional tests is not optional– it is critical for meeting strict SLAs, minimizing risk, and controlling costs. The following are key non-functional testing methodologies that every SAP program should consider integrating into its quality strategy.

- **Performance and Scalability Testing:** SAP systems often serve thousands of users, requiring rigorous performance testing to ensure smooth operations during peak loads.
- **Security and Compliance Testing:** With increasing cybersecurity threats and regulatory requirements (example, GDPR, SOX), automated security testing helps in identifying the vulnerabilities early.

- **High Availability and Disaster Recovery Testing:** Automating tests for failover, redundancy, and backup validation ensures system resilience.
- **Regression and Upgrade Validation:** Frequent SAP updates necessitate regression testing to validate performance, security, and stability without manual overhead.
- **Continuous Testing and DevOps Integration:** Modern SAP deployments leverage DevOps, making test automation critical for integrating non-functional testing into CI/CD pipelines.

  The following are commonly used non-functional test automation tools found in SAP projects, categorized by their core capabilities to help teams address performance, security, compliance, and system resilience more effectively.

Aspects	Common Tools
Performance Testing Tools	**LoadRunner (Micro Focus)**: Simulates virtual users to assess SAP system scalability. **JMeter (Apache)**: Open-source tool for load and performance testing. **Neoload (Tricentis)**: Offers cloud-based performance testing for SAP. UiPath: Provides comprehensive cloud infrastructure to build and execute load.
Security Testing Tools	**SAP Code Vulnerability Analyzer**: Identifies security flaws in SAP ABAP code. **Fortify (Micro Focus)**: Provides static and dynamic security testing. **Qualys**: Scans for vulnerabilities and compliance issues.
Resilience Testing Tools	**Chaos Monkey (Netflix OSS)**: Tests SAP system resilience by injecting failures. **Gremlin**: Simulates real-world outages and disruptions.
Miscellaneous Tools	**SAP Data Services**: Manages test data for non-functional testing. **Delphix**: Provides test data virtualization and masking.

Table 8.4: *Non-functional Test Automation Tools*

When it comes to selecting the right non-functional test automation tools, successful teams are often seen focusing on what truly drives outcomes. The following criteria represent the critical factors that guide informed decision-making–ensuring scalability, operational efficiency, risk reduction, and long-term value across SAP landscapes.

Aspects	Description
SAP Compatibility	The tool should natively support SAP UI technologies (Fiori, SAP GUI, and WebDynpro).
Scalability	Ability to simulate high loads, and scale for enterprise use.
Integration with DevOps Pipelines	Compatibility with CI/CD tools like Jenkins, Azure DevOps.
Cost and Licensing	Open-source vs. commercial licensing models.
Ease of Use and Skill Requirements	Can be adopted by current testing and business teams
Support for Cloud and Hybrid Environments	Able to support all deployment models and architectural landscapes
Security & Compliance Features	Ensuring adherence to industry regulations

Table 8.5: *Non-functional Test Automation Tools – Evaluation Checklist*

Let us understand how an effective test automation strategy helps companies through a real customer case study:

A global manufacturing company running SAP S/4HANA faced challenges with performance bottlenecks and security vulnerabilities during a major system upgrade. Their challenges include:

- Performance issues under peak load during order processing.
- Security compliance gaps in SAP custom code.
- High manual effort in non-functional testing cycles.

To address these challenges, their centralized QA team adopted a hybrid test automation approach integrating:

- Automate performance testing (simulating 10,000 users).
- Automate static code analysis and security compliance.
- Integrating functional automated tests into their DevOps pipeline.

To achieve optimum results with this SAP project, QA program management function chooses:

- **Test Automation Framework:** A centralized automation framework integrating Performance, Code Analysis, and functional test automation tools.
- **CI/CD Integration:** Automated non-functional tests triggered on every SAP transport request.
- **Performance and Security Dashboards:** Real-time reporting via SAP Analytics Cloud.

- **Parallel Execution on Cloud:** Leveraged AWS test environments for scalability.

The customer reported the following results:

- 40% reduction in performance testing cycle time.
- 50% decrease in security vulnerabilities in SAP custom code.
- 30% cost savings in test execution and infrastructure.

The case study illustrates how a structured approach to test automation can enhance SAP project success. Investing in the right test automation strategy can future-proof SAP landscapes against performance and security challenges.

Interface Test Automation Tools for SAP Projects

Interface testing is used primarily to validate data exchange and integration between SAP S/4HANA and external systems, ensuring seamless communication via APIs, IDocs, or other interfaces. Given the complexity of SAP environments, manual testing is not feasible for maintaining accuracy, speed, and scalability.

Some of the key benefits of test automation include:

- **Ensuring Data Integrity**: Automated tests validate data consistency across integrated systems.
- **Accelerating Testing Cycles**: Reduces regression testing time, and improves project timelines.
- **Reducing Defects in Production**: Identifies integration issues early.
- **Improving Compliance and Auditability**: Provides traceability for regulatory standards.

Different types of test automation tools are available for SAP interface testing, catering to the following varied integration needs:

Aspects	Common Tools
API and Web Service Testing Tools	ReadyAPI, Postman, SAP PI/PO, INT3 IFTT, UiPath, Tricentis and so on. These are best for validating REST, SOAP-based APIs, and SAP Gateway OData services.
RPA tools	UiPath, Automation Anywhere, SAP Build, and Blue Prism These are best for automating interactions with SAP GUI when APIs are not available.
Service Virtualization and Mocking Tools	Parasoft, Micro Focus, Tricentis. INT4, and Postman. These are best for external services when live systems are not available.

Table 8.6: *Interface Test Automation Tools*

Let us understand how an effective test automation strategy helped a large energy company through a customer case study:

A global energy company running SAP S/4HANA faced challenges in testing integrations with external vendors, financial institutions, and supply chain partners. Manual testing resulted in slow deployments and high defect rates in production.

Their QA team implemented an Automated Interface Testing Framework to solve this problem. The company deployed API test automation tools, and RPA tools to automate SAP interface testing, focusing on API validation, performance testing, and data integrity checks.

To address these challenges, their centralized QA team adopted a hybrid test automation approach integrating:

- **Test Automation Center of Excellence (CoE)**: Established governance and reusable test assets.
- Hybrid Test Automation Approach:
  a. API testing for SAP OData, IDocs, and BAPI calls.
  b. End-to-end integration testing covering multiple touchpoints.
  c. Service virtualization for unavailable external systems.
- Integration with CI/CD Pipelines:
  a. Automated tests triggered in Jenkins.
  b. Real-time dashboards for tracking test results and system health.
- Shift-Left Testing: Early testing in development cycles to reduce, rework and defect costs.

The company reported the following business impact:

- 30% Faster Deployment Cycles
- 50% Reduction in Testing Costs
- 90% Test Coverage of Critical Interfaces
- Zero Major Defects in Production for 6 Months

Interface test automation is critical for ensuring reliable, high-performance SAP S/4HANA integrations with external systems. By implementing a structured automation framework, businesses can significantly improve test efficiency, system stability, and compliance in their SAP projects.

Automating Change Management and Transport Management

Managing changes in a SAP S/4HANA environment is no small feat – it demands rigorous testing to protect business continuity. At the heart of it lie Change Management and Transport Management which govern how updates, configurations, and new functionalities move across complex SAP system landscapes. To stay ahead of risk, successful QA leaders are embracing test automation as a core part of their change strategy – validating every change before it reaches production.

Integrating Test Automation with Change Management processes is critical for achieving:

- **Reduced Business Disruptions:** Automated testing safeguards critical processes from unintended impacts.
- **Faster Release Cycles:** Continuous testing accelerates delivery, and reduces go-live delays.
- **Stronger Compliance:** Automated test documentation supports audits and regulatory requirements.
- **Lower Costs:** Automation cuts down manual testing efforts, freeing up resources, and reducing testing spend.
- **Improved Test Coverage:** End-to-end Automated regression tests validate end-to-end processes efficiently.

Change Management automation tools in SAP projects are categorized into distinct groups based on their core capabilities, each tailored to address specific needs within the system landscape, and drive streamlined, risk-free change processes.

Aspects	Common Tools
SAP Tools	**SAP TMS (Transport Management System)**: To manage transport across SAP landscapes. **SAP CTS+ (Change and Transport System Plus)**: To manage changes across heterogenous landscapes, including Java, ABAP, and non-SAP systems. **SAP ChaRM (Change Request Management)**: Centralized change management with workflow approval. **SAP Retrofit**: To synchronize changes between SAP systems. **SAP CTM (Cloud Transport Management)**: To manage changes across SAP cloud applications, including SAP BTP, SAP S/4HANA Cloud, and so on. **SAP Focused Build**: To achieve agile change management with DevOps support. **SAP Focused Run**: To proactively monitor systems and transport. **SAP gCTS (Git enabled Change and Transport System)**: Uses Git for ABAP transport management. These various tools can be commonly seen in SAP landscapes for agile delivery.

Third Party Tools used in Transport Management Process	**Jenkins (with SAP Plug-in)**: To automate SAP transport in CI/CD pipelines. **Azure DevOps for SAP**: To manage SAP transport using Microsoft DevOps tools. **ServiceNow Change Management for SAP**: To track and automate SAP changes. Best for ITSM-driven change governance. **Rev-Trac**: To enforce transport sequencing, conflict detection, and automated workflow-based approvals. **Basis Technologies ActiveControl**: To automate transport and rollback mechanisms. **Panaya Change Intelligence**: Provides impact analysis, risk assessment, and test recommendations. **Tricentis Live Compare**: To analyze the impact of the transport, and to help QA teams to optimize test cycles. **UiPath Change Impact Analysis**: To analyze the impact of the transport, and to help QA teams to optimize test cycles. **Worksoft Impact**: To analyze the impact of the transport, and to help QA teams to optimize test cycles.
Governance, Risk, and Compliance (GRC) tools	**SAP Access Control (GRC)**: To ensure change compliance by restricting unauthorized transport, and to enforce SoD (Segregation of Duties) policies. **Xiting Authorizations Management Suite**: To manage SAP roles doing the changes.

Table 8.7: *SAP Change or Transport Management Tools*

An in-depth understanding of both SAP-native and third-party transport management tools is critical for QA teams to drive efficiency and quality across the entire SAP lifecycle, such as:

- **Optimize QA Processes:** By understanding how SAP changes are managed, QA teams can align their testing strategies with the transport lifecycle, enabling proactive test planning and automation that minimizes surprises during deployment.
- **Seamless Tool Integration:** Modern SAP change management integrates with CI/CD, test automation, and impact analysis tools. QA teams that leverage these integrations can automate regression testing, accelerate defect resolution, and improve release confidence.
- **Break Down Siloed QA Operations:** Traditionally, QA teams operated in isolation, testing after development and transport completion. Now, by embedding testing within SAP change management processes (for example, via ChaRM, Rev-Trac, or ActiveControl), teams can shift left, collaborate closely

with SAP functional and basis teams, and validate transport before they even reach production.

- **Strengthen Governance and Compliance**: With tools like SAP GRC, ServiceNow, and SAP ChaRM enforcing stringent change approvals, QA teams can ensure that testing serves as a critical quality gate, reducing risk, and ensuring compliance before changes go live.

  To demonstrate the power of a well-structured test automation framework, let us explore a real transformation project led by a major Energy and Utilities company–a journey that redefined how SAP testing is executed, particularly around transport and change management. A large Energy and Utilities company faced significant bottlenecks in its SAP release process. Their SAP landscape include SAP S/4HANA, SAP Ariba, and SAP Success Factors. Manual testing slowed down validation, while defects often surfaced late in production, causing business disruptions.

  To address these challenges, the company implemented a test automation framework built on No-Code test automation tools, tightly integrated with SAP ChaRM (Change Request Management) to automate regression testing at every stage of transport movement.

The key components of the solution included:

- No-Code testing tools embedded within SAP Solution Manager to trigger automated regression tests after each transport.
- API-based testing for backend validation.
- Automated UI testing for SAP Fiori applications to ensure front-end consistency.
- Automated test execution integrated with Azure DevOps and Jenkins, triggered immediately upon transport approval.
- Continuous feedback loop ensuring defects were identified early in the development lifecycle.

The adoption of the test framework and its integration with SAP change management processes significantly improved testing efficiency and quality. The business impact reported were:

- **30% Faster Release Cycles**: Automated tests validated transports within hours, instead of days.
- **40% Reduction in Defects**: Early defect detection prevented issues in production.
- **Significant Cost Savings**: Reduced reliance on manual testing.

AI Testing Tools

The evolution of software testing has brought forth a new class of intelligent and autonomous testing solutions known as Agentic Testing Tools. Capgemini's recent SAP Quality Maturity Benchmark finds organizations integrating AI-centric test automation tools consistently rank higher in business process coverage, and release velocity.

Unlike conventional tools that rely on static test scripts and manual intervention, these tools dynamically learn, self-heal, and execute tests based on real-time system behavior, making them ideal for SAP S/4HANA transformations.

Traditional Testing Tools vs AI Testing Tools

Traditional test automation is rule-based, and requires testers to create and maintain scripts that may break with UI or API changes. These tools:

- Have high maintenance costs due to frequent test script updates.
- Struggle with dynamic UI changes in SAP Fiori or custom applications.
- Depend on predefined test cases with limited adaptability.
- Lack real-time defect prediction and auto-correction mechanisms.

AI testing tools, on the other hand, provides QA teams a whole new set of tools to solve some of the complex testing use cases that include:

- **Self-healing automation:** Adapts to UI/API changes autonomously.
- **AI-powered test generation:** Dynamically creates new test cases based on system behavior.
- **Context-aware execution:** Tests are intelligently executed based on real-time data.
- **Intelligent defect triaging:** AI identifies the root cause of failures, and suggests corrective actions.
- **Scalability:** Enables large-scale test automation with minimal human effort.
- **Test Orchestration**: Intelligently prioritizes tests based on business risks, and schedules execution accordingly.

The following table covers various agentic tools and the capabilities that QA teams start to leverage across SAP test lifecycle.

Test Life cycle	Agentic Testing Tools/Capabilities
Requirements Management	**SAP Signavio**: Process modelling and test scenario discovery **Polarion**: Requirements traceability **TestModeller.ai**: AI-driven model based test generation **UiPath Test Cloud**: Agentic capabilities for requirements quality analysis and test generation
Test Development (Automation)	**UiPath Test Cloud**: Automatic functional and regression test development for UI, API, and backend **Tricentis Tosca**: Model-based SAP test development with self-healing capabilities **ACCELQ**: Autonomous test generation
Test Execution	**UiPath Test Cloud**: Self-Healing, Elastic Execution **Tricentis**: AI-driven test execution **Worksoft**: Self-Healing and Test Data Management
Impact Analysis	**UiPath Change Impact Analysis**: AI-based impact analysis and test execution **Tricentis Live Compare**: AI-powered transport risk analysis **Panaya**: AI powered impact analysis for SAP changes
Performance Testing	**LoadRunner**: Predictive analytics-driven performance testing **NeoLoad**: AI-driven SAP load testing **UiPath**: Agentic Performance Testing
Security Testing	**Synopsys Seeker**: AI-powered run time security testing **Checkmarx**: Static code security testing with AI analytics **Qualys**: AI driven vulnerability management for SAP landscapes
Reporting	**UiPath Test Cloud**: AI-driven predictive analytics and notifications **Tricentis qTest**: AI-driven SAP test management and reporting tool

Table 8.8: *Agentic Testing Tools for SAP S/4HANA Projects*

As agentic test automation tools for SAP S/4HANA continue to emerge, it is essential to carefully evaluate the following key factors to ensure that you choose a solution that aligns with your project's goals, complexity, and long-term roadmap.

Aspect	Description
AI Capabilities	Does it offer self-healing and autonomous test case generation? Can it dynamically adapt to SAP Fiori/UI5, SAP GUI, and APIs? Is it capable of integrating with custom AI models?
Integration with SAP landscape	Does it integrate with SAP Solution Manager, CI/CD pipelines, and test management tools? Can it sync with SAP Test Automation Frameworks (TTA)?
Scalability and Performance	Can it efficiently handle SAP enterprise applications? Does it support cloud-based execution?
SAP-specific support	Can AI automate SAP GUI, WebDynpro, Fiori, and ABAP-based applications? Does it support SAP BTP and S/4HANA-specific test scenarios?
Cost and Licensing	Is the pricing model scalable for enterprise-wide SAP adoption? Does it align with project budgets and ROI expectations?
Security and Compliance	Does it comply with enterprise security and regulatory policies? Is it suitable for highly regulated SAP environments?
Reporting and Analytics	Does it provide AI-driven insights and automated dashboards? Can it generate intelligent defect reports?

Table 8.9: *Agentic Testing Tools – Evaluation Checklist*

Agentic testing tools redefine how SAP testing is approached, moving from static automation to AI-driven, self-adaptive strategies. Thus, whether it is SAP S/4HANA migrations, or business process transformations, these tools enhance efficiency, resilience, and scalability.

Evolution of Testing in SAP Projects

Imagine SAP testing teams as time travellers, journeying through distinct eras of testing practices. Each era represents a leap in efficiency, capabilities, and outcomes. Let us explore this journey together, understanding how we arrived at today's AI-powered testing landscape, and what it means for your SAP projects.

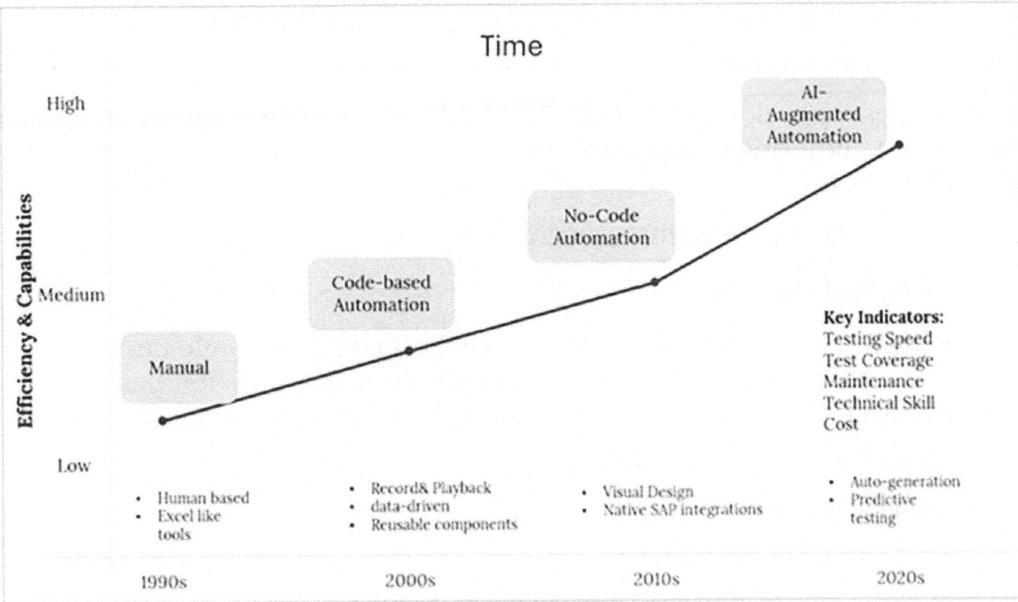

Figure 8.3: *Evolution of SAP Testing*

Era 1: Manual Testing (1990s–2000s)

"Click, observe, document—repeat."

Testing started with teams manually clicking through SAP screens, following test scripts, and noting results by hand.

- Business users were pulled away from their jobs for weeks.
- Test cases lived in binders and spreadsheets.
- Regression testing could take months.
- Performance testing was rare.

Impact: Testing became time-consuming and error-prone as SAP systems evolve architecturally and functionally. Success depended on human diligence.

Era 2: Code-based Automation (2000s–2010s)

"Testing meets engineering"

As SAP systems got more complex, automation tools like HP QTP, HP LoadRunner eCATT, SoapUI, and Selenium emerged. Testing matured with structured frameworks and reusable components.

- Common tasks could be recorded and replayed.
- Reusable Components.
- Keyword and Data-driven designs.

- End-to-end business process testing, not just isolated transactions.
- Interface and performance testing became possible.

Impact: Regression cycles shrank by 60–70%, and test consistency improved. Specialist roles like test automation engineers emerged. But scripts were fragile and required high maintenance.

Era 3: No-Code Automation (2010s–2020)

"Empowering business users."

No-code platforms democratized testing. Now business users could design and run automated tests, even for interfaces. Testing platforms that powered this innovation were - Worksoft, Tricentis, Microfocus, Panaya, Postman, Ready API, and Jmeter.

- Visual test design and pre-built content
- Minimal test skills required
- Built-in SAP integrations
- Performance testing visualization via dashboards
- Integration with CI tools
- Service virtualization for interface testing

Impact: Test automation exploded. Business users actively participated, though complex and custom scenarios still required support.

Era 4: AI-Augmented Testing (2020–Now)

"Machines learn what to test."

AI is now transforming the entire testing lifecycle. From generating test cases to predicting failures, smart tools are reshaping how and *what* we test. This era is powered by innovative automation platforms such as UiPath, Tricentis, Worksoft, INT4, Functionize, Lambda Test, Parasoft, Postman, Dynatrace, and BlazeMeter.

- Self-healing scripts and test generation from usage data.
- Predictive and risk-based testing.
- Real-time performance monitoring and anomaly detection.
- Autonomous interface mapping and testing.

Architecture Patterns of SAP Testing Tools

One of the most underestimated factors when choosing a SAP testing tool is its architecture. While features and automation capabilities often dominate the conversation, it is the tool's architectural foundation that truly determines its long-term value. A well-aligned architecture can seamlessly integrate with your existing processes, infrastructure, and team workflows—amplifying testing efficiency and delivering meaningful outcomes. Conversely, a tool with a mismatched architecture can quickly become a siloed, underutilized component that adds complexity rather than reducing it. To make an informed decision, let's examine the three core architecture patterns commonly found in SAP testing tools—and how each one can influence your project's success.

On-Premises Client-Server Architecture

Traditionally, SAP testing tools followed a client-server model, where a central server managed test cases, execution, and reporting, while users accessed the system through desktop clients. This architecture works well for organizations that require complete control over their test environments and data—especially those running SAP ECC with strict regulatory requirements.

- **Best suited for:** Enterprises with legacy SAP systems, security-driven industries like banking and pharmaceuticals.
- Can flow well with siloed or centralized testing teams.

Cloud-Native or SaaS-Based Architecture

With the rise of SAP S/4HANA Cloud, testing tools have evolved into cloud-native platforms that offer AI-driven automation, scalability, and seamless integration with DevOps pipelines. These tools eliminate infrastructure maintenance, and enable teams to collaborate globally, while automating test execution across SAP and non-SAP applications.

- **Best suited for:** Organizations adopting SAP S/4HANA Cloud, Agile, and DevOps methodologies.
- Can flow well with centralized or federated testing teams

Hybrid Architecture

Many enterprises are in a transition phase, moving from on-premises SAP landscapes to cloud-based solutions. A hybrid architecture allows businesses to retain test execution agents on-premises, while leveraging cloud-based test management, AI-driven analytics, and reporting. This balances security concerns with the flexibility of cloud testing.

- **Best suited for:** Enterprises shifting from SAP ECC to S/4HANA Cloud, requiring a mix of on-premises control and cloud-based scalability.

- Can flow well with all types of testing teams but requires a strong governance policy to ensure standardization of practices.

Here is a comprehensive diagram that visually represents the architecture patterns of SAP Testing tools described in this section.

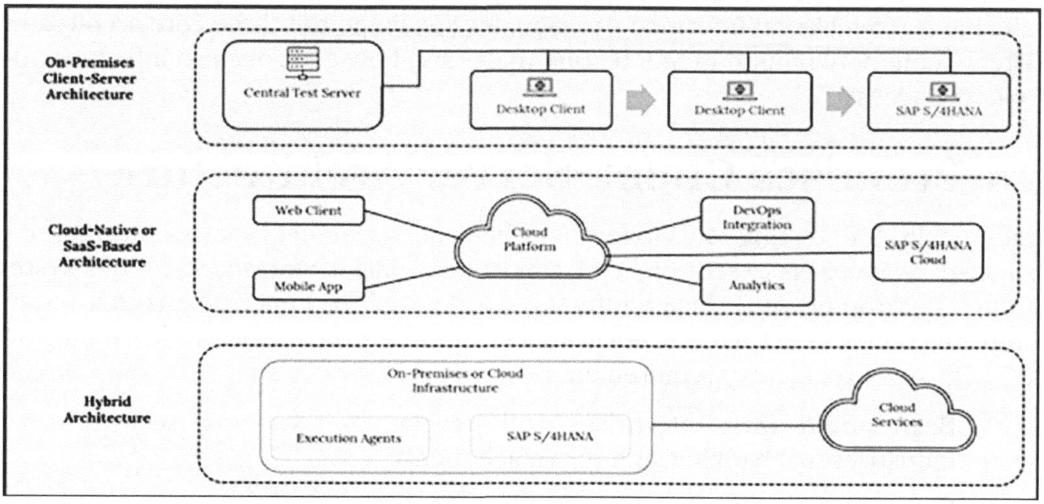

Figure 8.4: *SAP Testing Tool Architecture Patterns*

The architecture of a testing tool is not merely a technical choice—it plays a pivotal role in how effectively teams can conduct testing, integrate systems, and scale automation initiatives. Whether the environment is on-premises, cloud-native, or hybrid, selecting the right architectural fit is essential for seamless adoption, cost optimization, and enhanced quality engineering outcomes in SAP projects. The following section explores objective criteria for selecting the right tools through a three-dimensional lens: People, Processes, and Capabilities.

Evaluation of Tools

A key principle observed across high-performing SAP testing teams is this: no single tool delivers 100% of what is needed. The strength of a team's expertise lies in the trade-offs it makes. Each tool brings distinct advantages and inherent limitations, and the success of any selection depends on a clear understanding of the value it delivers versus the compromises it requires.

In the context of SAP S/4HANA transformations, cloud migrations, and continuous delivery models, tool evaluation must go beyond checklists of features or cost considerations. The right testing tool must integrate effortlessly within the SAP ecosystem, supporting complex end-to-end business process validations, SAP UI automation, API testing, and regulatory compliance.

This is why a three-dimensional evaluation framework–centered on People, Processes, and Tools–has proven vital. It enables organizations to make informed, strategic choices that reflect not only technical alignment but also the long-term implications for teams, operational workflows, and overall business outcomes.

People Dimension:

Aspect	Description
Skills and Competency	Do we have in-house expertise for the tool, or will we need external training? Is the tool easy to learn for manual testers and functional consultants? Does it require specialized scripting knowledge or low/no-code capabilities? What is the tool's learning curve for business users, testers, and developers? Does the vendor provide sufficient training resources and certification programs?
Collaboration and Adoption	Can SAP functional consultants, business users, and testers work together within the tool? Does it integrate into SAP Solution Manager (SolMan) Test Suite or SAP Cloud ALM for defect and test case management? Does it support business-driven testing to enable SAP super users to define and validate test cases? Is the tool's reporting and dashboarding tailored to SAP testing KPIs (for example, test execution, risk-based testing coverage, and defect trends in SAP modules)? How does the tool enable collaboration across SAP Basis, Security, and Integration teams?
Change Management and Support	How much effort is required to onboard SAP project teams onto this tool? Does the vendor provide SAP-specific testing best practices and community support? Is it optimized for SAP Agile and DevOps practices, supporting rapid SAP releases? Can it integrate seamlessly with the existing SAP ALM (Application Lifecycle Management) workflows? Is there an internal champion within the organization who can drive adoption?

Table 8.10: *Evaluation of Tools - People Dimension*

Process Dimension:

Aspect	**Description**
SAP Test Strategy Alignment	Does the tool align with SAP S/4HANA transformation testing, including ECC to S/4HANA migration? Can it support all testing types required in SAP projects (Unit, Integration, Regression, UAT, Performance, and Security)? How well does the tool integrate with SAP-specific requirements? Can it test SAP and non-SAP applications together, ensuring end-to-end business process validation? Does it support SAP Business Process Testing (BPT) across FI, MM, SD, PP, SCM, and HR modules?
Test Execution and Automation for SAP	Can it automate SAP UI interactions for SAP GUI, SAP Fiori, WebDynpro, and SAP NWBC? Does it support SAP API testing (OData, RFC, IDoc, BAPI, SOAP)? How well does it handle data-driven testing for SAP transactions (SE16, AL11, LSMW, BDC, Fiori Apps, and so on)? Does it provide AI-driven or self-healing automation for SAP screen changes? How effectively does it manage SAP test data without relying on production data?
SAP Test Management	Does it support SAP Solution Manager and SAP Cloud ALM integration for test execution and defect tracking? Can it link test cases to business processes in SAP Signavio or BPM tools? Does the tool support SAP audit, compliance, and risk-based testing approaches (for example, SOX, GxP, and GDPR)? Can it align with SAP's continuous integration and DevOps pipelines for faster testing?
Performance and Load Testing for SAP	Does the tool support SAP-specific performance testing? Can it simulate thousands of concurrent SAP users executing transactions? Does it work for SAP HANA database performance benchmarking?

***Table 8.11:** Evaluation of Tools – Process Dimension*

Tool and Technology Dimension:

Aspect	**Description**
Technical Capabilities	Does the tool support SAP ECC, SAP S/4HANA (Cloud, Private Cloud, On-Premises), and SAP BTP? Can it handle SAP UI automation across different deployment types (Fiori, GUI, and WebDynpro)? How well does it support SAP test data management (TDM) and synthetic data creation? Does it have pre-built automation libraries for SAP transactions and common processes? Can it handle SAP custom enhancements, extensions, and third-party integrations?
Integration and Extensibility	Can the tool integrate with SAP ALM and 3rd party ALM tools (SAP Solution Manager, SAP Cloud ALM, Jira, Service Now, and Microsoft ADO)? Does it support API-based test automation for SAP interfaces (OData, BAPI, RFC, and IDoc)? Can it work with CI/CD pipelines for SAP (Jenkins, Azure DevOps, and GitHub Actions)? Does it support ServiceNow, Jira, or other ITSM tools for SAP defect tracking?
Cost and Licensing	What is the Total Cost of Ownership (TCO) for SAP projects, including licensing, support, and maintenance? Does the tool offer a flexible licensing model (user-based, execution-based, pay-per-use)? What hidden costs exist (SAP connector fees, cloud costs, additional integration costs)? How does it compare with SAP native testing tools (for example, CBTA, eCATT, and TTA) in terms of ROI? Does the vendor offer a trial or Proof-of-Concept (POC) specific to SAP testing?
Scalability and Performance	Can it scale to global SAP implementations with multi-region support? How well does it handle high-volume SAP regression testing across multiple landscapes? Does it support cloud-based SAP S/4HANA and hybrid environments?

Security and Compliance	Does it comply with SAP security policies (authentication, authorization, encryption)? Can it manage SAP role-based access for test data and scripts? How does it handle test data masking for SAP compliance (GDPR, SOX, and HIPAA)?
AI and Agentic Capabilities	Can the tool generate test cases autonomously based on SAP transaction logs and business process models? Can the tool generate test data based on master data and transaction data models? Does it support predictive test execution schedules? Can AI assistant autonomously troubleshoot test failures, and notify the stakeholders?

Table 8.12: *Evaluation of Tools – Tool Dimension*

Test evaluation checklist is also made available for your reference at our resources library here: **https://github.com/ava-orange-education/Mastering-SAP-S-4HANA-Quality-Assurance**

Pro Tip: *Gartner predicts that by 2027, more than 70% of SAP testing processes will leverage AI-powered agentic workflows for adaptive test generation, particularly in cloud-native and hybrid SAP landscapes.*

Conclusion

In this chapter, we have explored the tools and technologies that play a crucial role in ensuring SAP S/4HANA quality assurance. From test automation platforms, change management tools, and AI-driven testing solutions, we have examined how organizations can build a robust and scalable testing ecosystem by using the 3-dimensional evaluation framework - balancing people, process, and technology trade-offs to drive efficiency, maintainability, and business alignment.

In the next chapter, we shall explore how to unlock the data-driven testing with efficient *Test Data Management*.

References

- SAP Cloud ALM customer case studies: https://support.sap.com/en/alm/sap-cloud-alm/sap-cloud-alm-references.html
- SAP Code Vulnerability Analyzer documentation - https://help.sap.com/docs/SAP_NETWEAVER_AS_ABAP_FOR_SOH_740/1a93b7a44ac146b5ad9b6fd95c1223cc/e6f9668fa26e4680955165acb2b0fb40.html
- LoadRunner Performance Testing whitepaper: https://community.opentext.com/cfs-file/__key/telligent-evolution-components-attachments/00-194-01-00-00-33-42-49/HP-LoadRunner-Best-Practices-.pdf
- Test Automation case studies across various tools
- SAP Transport Management Overview: https://www.sap.com/products/scm/transportation-logistics.html
- Enterprise Architecture with SAP by Anup Das, Peter Klee, and Johannes Reichel

Chapter 9
Test Data Management

Introduction

Gartner (2023) noted that *over 60% of SAP S/4HANA transformation projects report test delays due to poor data availability*. For years, SAP-driven enterprises have pursued the vision of becoming truly data-driven - consolidating systems, eliminating silos, and standardizing data structures. But with the shift to SAP S/4HANA, that ambition demands more than just collecting and storing data. It requires a deliberate, end-to-end strategy - from data creation to governance.

CIOs see data as a strategic asset that drives transformation. Yet in many SAP projects, one critical piece is often overlooked: A deep understanding of SAP's data models. When that is missing, test quality suffers, and it leads to fragmented test scenarios, which eventually result in unreliable outcomes.

On the flip side, QA teams that align their data strategy with test objectives consistently report smoother test cycles, reduced maintenance effort, and a tighter connection between testing and business priorities. In short, mastering data is not just good hygiene, it is a competitive advantage.

Structure

In this chapter, we will explore the Test Data Management with the following aspects:

- Common Misconceptions
- Data Organization in SAP
- Challenges with Test Data in SAP
- Characteristics of Good Test Data
- Create and Manage Test Data in SAP S/4HANA
- Test Data Management Best Practices
- Where To Look for SAP Data
- Customer Example with Key Data Structure (KDS)

Common Misconceptions

Test Data is often an overlooked aspect of SAP Testing, leading to failed test cases, inaccurate results, and project delays. Many testing teams fall into common misconceptions that disrupt the integrity of test execution and impact business outcomes. The following are five critical mistakes that lead to project inefficiencies, along with real-world examples illustrating their consequences.

My Business Team Provides the Test Data

Misconception: "*The business team owns the data, so they will provide accurate and sufficient test data for all scenarios.*"

Reality: While business teams understand data from an operational perspective, they may not anticipate all test coverage needs. Their data might lack edge cases, boundary conditions, and error scenarios, leading to incomplete testing.

Example: A finance team provides a set of customer invoices for testing a SAP FI-CO migration. However, they only include regular payment cases. The test team misses:

- Reversal scenarios
- Credit memos
- Cross-company transactions

Consequence: The system goes live, but reversals fail because no test cases validated the process.

Solution: Testing teams should define test data requirements proactively, and collaborate with business users to ensure data completeness.

Yahoo - My Test Data Works

Misconception: "*If the test data worked for one test cycle, it will work for all cycles.*"

Reality: Test data needs constant validation because SAP environments evolve with config changes, master data updates, and patches. A working data set in one cycle may fail in another.

Example: An SAP Order-to-Cash (O2C) scenario was successfully tested in the first cycle. However, during the next test cycle, a pricing condition changed in SD (T685 table), and the existing test data no longer matched the new pricing rules.

Consequence: Regression testing fails due to incorrect pricing, causing unnecessary debugging efforts.

Solution: Implement a test data refresh strategy, validating data before each test cycle.

No Worries - I Can Use Synthetic Test Data

Misconception: "*I do not need real production data; synthetic data is enough for testing.*"

Reality: Synthetic data can be useful but lacks the complexity of real-world SAP transactions. Many business processes rely on historical dependencies, master data relationships, and integrated flows that synthetic data often fails to replicate.

Example: A testing team creates synthetic financial postings (BKPF, BSEG tables) to simulate transactions. However, when real postings are processed in UAT, they fail because:

- The posting period is not open.
- Cost center mappings do not exist.
- **The system expects historical data references.**

Consequence: Testing gave a false sense of security, but real transactions failed in production.

Solution: Use masked or anonymized production data wherever possible, and supplement with carefully modelled synthetic data.

I Do Not Care - Test Data is Not My Problem

Misconception: "*Testers should focus on scripts; someone else will provide the test data.*"

Reality: Without ownership of test data, testing teams struggle with delays and inconsistent results. Waiting for functional teams or database admins to provide test data slows down testing cycles.

Example: A SAP S/4HANA migration project was delayed because testers relied on functional teams to provide customer master data for specific test cases. Functional team was overloaded with other priorities, and test execution was blocked for weeks due to missing test data.

Consequence: Project delays, lack of test coverage, and last-minute data scrambles leading to poor test quality.

Solution: Test teams should take proactive ownership of the test data:

- Self-service test data provisioning
- Test data subsets with proper governance
- Data automation tools for test setup

Yay - My Test Script Will Work Fine

Misconception: "*If my script works with one dataset, it will work with all datasets.*"

Reality: SAP test automation often fails due to hardcoded dependencies on specific data sets. A script tested with one type of material, customer, or GL account may break when new data is introduced.

Example: A tester automates a Purchase Order (PO) approval workflow, assuming that all vendors have the same payment terms (EKPO table). However, when tested with a different vendor, the PO fails due to:

- Different approval thresholds.
- Missing vendor-specific configurations.

Consequence: Test automation scripts fail unpredictably, increasing maintenance efforts. It leads to "*no-confidence*" on QA cycles.

Solution: Design data-driven test automation with:

- Parameterization of test data.
- Dynamic data retrieval from SAP tables.
- Variability testing across different data conditions.

In addition to these five critical misconceptions, here are a few more challenges that SAP testing teams should address:

- **Data Volume Problems:** Running full test cycles with excessive production data can slow down testing. Use data subsets by using the Equivalence Partitioning Technique explained in the Test Design chapter.
- **Compliance and Security Risks:** Using real customer/vendor data in non-prod systems can violate GDPR, CCPA, or internal security policies. Always mask the sensitive data.
- **Test Data Aging:** Old test data may not align with new SAP versions, configurations, or business processes. Refresh and validate the test data typically, once in every 12 months.
- **Lack of Negative Test Data:** Many teams focus only on happy path scenarios, missing validation for incorrect entries, missing values, or error-handling cases.

Avoiding these common test data pitfalls is crucial for successful SAP testing. **Testing teams must take ownership of data,** ensure test coverage across realistic scenarios, and adopt data-driven automation for reliability. By treating test data as a strategic asset, teams can significantly reduce test failures, improve test execution speed, and ensure robust SAP system validation.

Pro Tip: *Always create a data coverage checklist before requesting data from business users (covering edge conditions like reversals, blocked vendors, expired pricing, and so on).*

Data Organization in SAP

Effective Test Data Management (TDM) in SAP starts with a clear understanding of how data is structured. SAP data is broadly classified into Master Data, Transactional Data, and Configuration Data, each playing a crucial role in ensuring system integrity and accurate business operations.

The following table provides an architectural view of how data is classified, its function, and where it is stored in SAP:

Data Type	Purpose	Examples	SAP Tables	How to Access?
Master Data	Represents core business entities that remain stable over time	Customers, Vendors, Materials, and Business Partners.	MARA (Material Master), KNA1 (Customer Master), LFA1 (Vendor Master), and BP000 (Business Partner).	SE16N, SE11, and SAP Fiori Apps.
Transactional Data	Captures dynamic business operations that change frequently	Sales Orders, Purchase Orders, Deliveries, Invoices, and Financial Documents.	VBAK (Sales Order Header), VBAP (Sales Order Items), BKPF (Accounting Document Header), and BSEG (Accounting Document Items).	SE16N, SE11, SAP, and Fiori Analytical Apps.
Configuration Data	Controls how business processes function within SAP	Pricing conditions, Posting periods, Tax settings, and Workflows.	T685 (Pricing Conditions in SD), T001 (Company Codes), and T030 (Automatic Account Determination).	SPRO (Customization), SE16N, and SE11.

***Table 9.1:** Data Organization in SAP – Architectural View*

Master Data: This represents business entities that remain relatively unchanged. These are used across multiple modules to ensure consistency in business operations.

Technical Characteristics:

- Stored in core tables, usually persistent over time.
- Used across modules (SD, MM, FI, HR, and so on) to maintain uniformity.
- Typically requires governance to avoid duplication and inconsistencies.

Key Examples:

- **Material Master (MARA):** Contains material-specific data used in purchasing, inventory, and production.
- **Customer Master (KNA1):** Stores customer information for sales and billing.
- **Vendor Master (LFA1):** Used in procurement processes.

Where to Find Master Data?

- **SAP Tables**: MARA, KNA1, LFA1, and BP000.
- **SAP Fiori Apps**: "*Manage Business Partners*", and "*Display Material*".
- **T-Codes**: SE16N, MM03 (Display Material), and BP (Business Partner).

Pro Tip: *Encourage your teams creating controlled master datasets with multiple conditions (for example, blocked, credit-limit customers, and alternate units of measure for materials).*

Transactional Data: Transactional Data refers to business events recorded in the system, such as sales orders, invoices, payments, and stock movements.

Technical Characteristics:

- Short-lived compared to the master data.
- Drives real-time business processes (for example, Order-to-Cash, Procure-to-Pay, and so on).
- Often has high volume, and requires archiving strategies.

Key Examples:

- **Sales Orders (VBAK - Header, VBAP - Items)**: Generated during order processing.
- **Purchase Orders (EKKO - Header, EKPO - Items)**: Created in procurement.
- **Financial Documents (BKPF - Header, BSEG - Line Items)**: Stored in FI module.

Where to Find Transactional Data?

- **SAP Tables**: VBAK, VBAP, BKPF, BSEG, EKKO, and EKPO.
- **SAP Fiori Apps**: "*Manage Sales Orders*", and "*Display Purchase Orders*".
- **T-Codes**: VA03 (Display Sales Order), and ME23N (Display Purchase Order).

Pro Tip: *Consider multiple document types. For example, Testing Sales Orders should consider multiple order types (for example, OR = Standard Order, RE = Returns) instead of using just one order type.*

Configuration Data: This consists of customized settings that define how the SAP system operates according to a company's requirements. The data is maintained by SAP consultants or system administrators. These configurations do not change frequently.

- **Technical Characteristics:**
  - Maintained through SPRO (SAP Project Reference Object).
  - Stored in customization tables.
- Required for system-wide consistency but rarely changes in a stable environment with minimal unexpected changes and disruptions.
- **Key Examples:**
  - **Pricing Configuration (T685 - Pricing Conditions)**: Defines price determination in SD.
  - **Material Types (T134)**: Define material categories such as Raw materials and Finished goods.
  - **Company Codes (T001)**: Organizational units in FI.
  - **Account Determination (T030)**: Determines which GL account transactions post to.

Where to Find Configuration Data?

- **SAP Tables**: T685, T001, and T030.
- **SPRO Path**: "IMG → Sales & Distribution → Basic Functions → Pricing".
- **T-Codes**: SPRO, OBYC (Account Determination).

Challenges with Test Data in SAP

Test Data Management in SAP is not just about having some data; it is about having the right data at the right time to ensure accurate, efficient, and comprehensive testing. The following table summarizes the key considerations with real-world examples illustrating the impact of poor test data choices.

Aspect | Impact	Master Data	Transactional Data	Configuration Data
Test Data Volume	Moderate	High	Low
Data Generation	Pre-created	Real-time from transactions	System configuration
Dependency	Used by transactions	Depends on master/ configuration	No direct dependency but affects transactions
Test Data Refresh	Infrequent	Frequent	Rare
Archiving Strategy	Retained for long term	Archived periodically	Not archived

Table 9.2: *Data Organization in SAP – Test Data Considerations*

The combination of data refresh frequency, dependency management, and archiving directly drives both test reliability and maintenance overheads. Let us explore the tangible impact of test data using three anonymized customer case.

Customer Example 1: Master Data Inconsistencies

A large retail company was migrating from SAP ECC to SAP S/4HANA. The test team used a subset of customer master data (KNA1 table) for validation, assuming it was representative of real-world cases.

Issues Faced:

- The test dataset only included active customers, missing customers with credit blocks, blacklisted customers, and inactive accounts.
- When real customers were processed in production, the system rejected orders due to missing credit limit checks and partner determinations.
- Customer tax settings (KNVI table) were not aligned, leading to incorrect tax calculations in SAP FI.

Lessons Learned:

- Use a diverse dataset covering all business scenarios, not just active entities.
- Validate business rules dependent on master data such as credit checks and taxation.
- Leverage production-like anonymized master data.

Customer Example 2: Incorrect Transactional Data

A SAP MM (Materials Management) team was testing a Procure-to-Pay (P2P) process. The team used manually created synthetic Purchase Orders (POs) (EKKO and EKPO tables) for testing.

Issues Faced:

- The synthetic POs had no associated Goods Receipts (GRs) posted against them. As a result, no Goods Receipt Notes (GRNs) existed in the system, making invoice verification using MIRO infeasible—especially since the system was configured for goods-receipt-based invoice verification.
- The outdated vendor master (LFA1) led to payment blocks in SAP FI due to inactive or incorrect vendor statuses.
- The test data did not include multiple tax codes, causing tax mismatches between the POs and invoices.

Lessons Learned:

- Transactional data must be realistic and complete, including historical references.
- Use production-like purchase orders to validate end-to-end processes.
- Automate test data provisioning to avoid manual errors.

Pro Tip: *Transactional datasets must always include preceding and dependent steps. For example, P2P cannot be validated with isolated POs.*

Customer Example 3: Configuration Data Misalignment in SAP SD Pricing

A large company was implementing SAP S/4HANA Sales and Distribution (SD) with complex pricing rules (T685 table). During UAT, the testers created synthetic sales orders (VBAK and VBAP tables) assuming pricing would remain consistent.

Issues Faced:

- The pricing conditions used in test cases were outdated due to a recent business pricing policy change.
- New pricing conditions applied in production resulted in order pricing mismatches and unexpected discounts.
- The automation scripts failed because they relied on fixed price conditions instead of fetching dynamic pricing from SAP tables.

Lessons Learned:

- Keep configuration data aligned with real-time business changes.
- Refresh pricing configurations before major test cycles.
- Use dynamic test scripts to retrieve real-time pricing conditions from the system.

Pro Tip: *One global beverage company resolved this by linking automated test scripts directly with live pricing condition tables, dynamically fetching values, instead of hardcoding discounts.*

Characteristics of Good Test Data

Let us now explore this using a customer case study presented at SAP ASUG conference. A leading automotive manufacturer faced repeated test failures and production defects due to mismatched customer and pricing data. Their test cycles were long, unstable, and full of rework. By introducing an automated test data provisioning system aligned with business scenarios, they cut the test execution time by 50%, and saw a sharp decline in post-go-live issues.

This is not an exception – it is a repeatable pattern. Successful SAP projects consistently follow proven test data management practices. Here is what defines good test data in SAP S/4HANA environments:

- **Representative of Real Scenarios:** Data should mimic real-world business transactions, covering edge cases and exceptions.
- **Up-to-Date:** Ensuring fresh data before each test cycle prevents false positives/negatives.
- **Secure and Compliant:** Masking or anonymizing sensitive data protects against security breaches. According to Capgemini's WQR 2024, 53% of SAP customers rank GDPR and CCPA compliance as their biggest TDM challenge.
- **Scalable:** Capable of handling high transaction volumes without affecting system performance.
- **Readily Available:** Providing test teams with quick and reliable access to the relevant data.
- **Automation-Ready:** Dynamic and parameterized data supports stable automated testing.
- **Minimally Dependent on Production:** Reducing reliance on full production clones prevents unnecessary overhead.

Pro Tip: *Automate daily refresh of critical datasets (for example, open sales orders and vendor balances) so that testers do not waste time debugging stale records.*

Create and Manage Test Data in SAP S/4HANA

For a QA team, it is crucial to build great relationships with the SAP data team responsible for managing and structuring data within your SAP environment. No two SAP companies handle master data the same way, which means your SAP data team is your best ally to understand how master data, transactional data, and configuration data are maintained in your organization.

Once you have a clear understanding of how data is structured, you can leverage the following methods to create and manage the test data effectively:

Category	SAP Tools	Third-Party Tools
ETL and Data Extraction	SAP Data Services (BODS)	Informatica, Talend, Apache NiFi, and UiPath

Data Sub-setting	SAP TDMS	IBM InfoSphere and EPI-USE DSM
Data Masking	SAP Information Steward	Delphix and Informatica Masking
Data Refresh and Cloning	SAP TDMS, LSMW	EPI-USE DSM and Delphix
Synthetic Data	SAP Test Data Designer	GenRocket, Tonic.ai, and UiPath
UI and API Automation	SAP Solution Manager, SAP CloudALM	Tricentis, UiPath, Microfocus, and Worksoft
AI-Powered Test Data Management	SAP AI Core, SAP BTP	UiPath, Delphix DataOps, and Tricentis, KTern

Table 9.3: *Test Data Creation and Management Tools*

Let us examine a couple of practical customer scenarios where QA teams can effectively use proven methodologies to generate and manage high-quality test data.

Use Case 1: Creating Test Data for Material Availability in Sales Order Processing

To simulate real-world material availability scenarios in the Order-to-Cash (O2C) process, test data must include:

- **Material Master Data (MARA, MARC)**: Ensure stock availability.
- **Inventory Data (MB52, MARD)**: Maintain appropriate stock levels.
- **Customer Orders (VBAK, VBAP)**: Link material to open sales orders.

Methods to Create Data

- **ETL (Extract, Transform, Load) Tools**: Use SAP Data Services (BODS) to extract material master data from production, modify stock levels, and load it into the test environment.
- **API (BAPI) Methods**: Leverage `BAPI_MATERIAL_STOCK_REQ_LIST` to create stock requirements.
- **UI Automation**: Use SAP GUI scripts or RPA or Testing tools to simulate user actions for stock movements (MB1C, MIGO).

Pro Tip: *When simulating stock levels, also include "special stock" types (consignment, batch-managed). Many defects surface when stock rules are not covered.*

Use Case 2: Creating Test Data for Purchase Order Testing in an End-to-End Business Process

To simulate real-world purchasing process, a Procure-to-Pay (P2P) scenario requires test data that covers:

- Vendor Master Data (LFA1, LFB1)
- Purchase Requisitions (EBAN)
- Purchase Orders (EKKO, EKPO)
- Goods Receipts (MKPF, MSEG)
- Invoice Processing (BKPF, BSEG)

Methods to Create Data (These are mutually independent)

- **ETL Tools**: Extract live vendor and purchase data from production, and apply modifications before loading it into QA.
- **API (BAPI) Methods**:
  - Use `BAPI_PO_CREATE1` to generate purchase orders.
  - Use `BAPI_GOODSMVT_CREATE` to simulate stock receipts.
- **UI Automation**: Automate the creation of purchase orders and invoice verification using SAP Fiori Apps and robotic test automation frameworks.

Use Case 3: Synthetic Data for Validating Payroll Processing in SAP HCM

In an SAP HCM (Human Capital Management) payroll testing scenario, testers need employee payroll data but cannot use real employee salaries due to data privacy concerns (GDPR, CCPA, and so on).

To simulate real-world payroll data, a Hire-to-Retire (H2R) scenario requires test data that covers:

- **T-Code Used**: `PC00_M99_CALC_SIMU` (Payroll Simulation)
- **Key Tables**:
  - PA0008 (Basic Pay)
  - PA0014 (Recurring Payments/Deductions)
  - PA0015 (Additional Payments)
  - RT (Results Table for Payroll Calculation)

Methods to Create Synthetic Payroll Data

- **ETL Tools**: Tools like SAP Data Services (BODS) or Informatica can generate random but structured payroll records with salary bands, benefits, and tax deductions aligned with HR policies.
- **API (BAPI) Methods**:
  - **`BAPI_EMPLOYEE_ENQUEUE`**: Lock employee for processing.
  - **`BAPI_PERSDATA_CHANGE`**: Update personal data for test scenarios.

- **BAPI_PAYROLL_CALCULATE**: Simulate payroll calculations.

- **UI Automation**: SAP GUI Scripts or RPA tools or Test Automation tools can simulate a payroll administrator entering payroll changes manually.

Use Case 4: AI-Powered Test Data Agents in SAP S/4HANA Testing

With the rise of AI-driven automation, Test Data Agents are transforming how test data is generated, managed, and optimized in SAP S/4HANA testing. Test Data Agents leverage Machine Learning (ML) and Natural Language Processing (NLP) to dynamically create, analyze, and validate the test data, ensuring higher accuracy and reduced manual effort.

Let us explore further this use case with a customer example. We have referred to multiple customer presentations available at www.sap.com to provide you with a realistic methodology here.

A global consumer goods company was facing challenges with inconsistent test data when testing their Sales Order Management process. Manually setting up test data led to frequent failures due to missing customer credit limits, incorrect material stock levels, and pricing mismatches.

To solve this, their QA team has implemented an AI-powered Test Data Agent that:

- Analyzed historical transaction data from VBAK, VBAP, and KNA1 tables.
- Identified missing or inconsistent data for open sales orders.
- Automatically generated realistic customer profiles and orders using **BAPI_SALESORDER_CREATEFROMDAT2**.
- Validated stock availability using **BAPI_MATERIAL_STOCK_REQ_LIST**, and suggested replenishment.
- Updated pricing and discounts dynamically based on the existing SAP SD conditions (**T685**, **T683T**).

The architecture of the Test Data agent include:

- **SAP Business Technology Platform (BTP):** Served as the foundation for integrating AI capabilities into SAP S/4HANA, enabling the development and deployment of AI-driven applications.
- **Machine Learning (ML) Algorithms:** Employed to analyze historical transaction data, identify patterns, and detect anomalies within SAP modules.
- **SAP AI Core:** Utilized to manage and deploy AI models, facilitating the integration of machine learning capabilities into SAP applications.

- **SAP AI Launchpad:** Provided a centralized interface for monitoring and managing AI models, ensuring seamless operations and governance.
- **SAP Analytics Cloud (SAC):** Leveraged for advanced analytics and visualization, enabling real-time insights into test data and system performance.

Pro Tip: *Start by training your AI agent on one process (for example, Sales Orders) instead of enterprise-wide, then expand gradually. Otherwise, data drift and false positives overwhelm test cycles.*

By incorporating test data management strategy, QA teams can ensure full test coverage, security compliance, and efficient testing without relying on sensitive production data.

Test Data Management Best Practices

A well-defined test data strategy accelerates testing cycles and ensures compliance with data security regulations. Engaging with SAP Master Data Governance (MDG) teams is particularly critical in understanding the underlying data models, data structures, master data, transactional data, and configuration data - all of which influence test planning and execution. Without this engagement, test data may be incomplete, inconsistent, or misaligned with real-world business processes, leading to inaccurate test results and production issues.

Following are the best practices that successful SAP QA teams follow:

- **Engage with SAP Data Stakeholders**

  Collaborate early with SAP MDG, business process owners, functional consultants, and IT teams to gain a deep understanding of:

  - **Master Data:** Business-critical entities such as customers, vendors, materials, and financial accounts.
  - **Transactional Data:** Real-world business transactions such as orders, invoices, and payments.
  - **Configuration Data:** System settings that define business rules such as pricing conditions and tax codes.

  Engagement with MDG teams ensures alignment between test data and business realities, preventing costly defects downstream.

- **Define Test Data Requirements Early**

  - Work closely with business and functional teams to define how much and which type of data is required for testing, and ensure that it reflects real-world scenarios.

- Account for negative testing–not just the "`happy path`"–to validate error handling and security mechanisms.

- **Use Data Sub-setting Instead of Full Production Copies**
  - Extract only the relevant data for specific test cases, instead of cloning the entire production databases.
  - Apply filtering techniques to retrieve data by business unit, region, or functional module.

  This reduces data volume, minimizes compliance risks, and enhances test performance.

- **Implement Data Masking and Anonymization**
  - Protect the sensitive data such as financial transactions and personal details.
  - Utilize masking techniques such as encryption, tokenization, and data scrambling to ensure compliance with privacy regulations like GDPR and CCPA.

- **Automate Test Data Provisioning**
  - Reduce dependency on manual data preparation.
  - Enable self-service test data management for QA teams, enabling faster test execution.
  - Leverage RPA tools/ Data Automation tools to streamline the data provisioning.

- **Synchronize Data across Environments**
  - Ensure that there is a data consistency across DEV, QA, and UAT systems.
  - Enable test data reuse with minimal rework across multiple test environments, improving efficiency and test coverage.

By integrating these best practices and closely collaborating with SAP Data stakeholder teams, organizations can enhance the quality, accuracy, and reliability of the SAP test data.

Pro Tip: *A simple automation or an AI agent can be scheduled to refresh and mail "daily test data readiness" reports. It builds both transparency and tester trust.*

Where to look for SAP Data

You may realize by now that data is at the core of all SAP systems, influencing business processes, reporting, and automation. But what if you do not have direct access to SAP data experts to guide you? Can you still make progress in understanding SAP data models and structures?

Yes, while expert guidance is invaluable, you can take systematic steps to explore master data on your own. This section outlines a **testing cheat sheet** to help you investigate and choose the right SAP test data. However, keep in mind that this is not a substitute for a subject matter expert's advice on test data management.

Transaction Codes (T-Codes)

Transaction codes provide direct access to master data records within SAP GUI. The following are some commonly used T-codes:

- **PA20 - Display HR Master Data**: View detailed employee master data across various infotypes (read-only).
- **FI03 - Manage Banks**: Display bank master data after it is imported into SAP.
- **MM03 - Material Master**: Access material master records.
- **MD04 - Master Data Overview**: View real-time master data and stock levels.
- **VA03 - Sales Order Display**: Retrieve the sales order details.
- **FB05 - Financial Accounting**: View financial accounting documents.

SAP Fiori Apps

SAP Fiori provides modern web-based applications to manage and display the master data. Some useful apps include:

- **Manage Product Master Data (F1602)**: Search, view, edit, create, and copy product master data.
- **Manage G/L Account Master Data**: Access G/L account details via the SAP Fiori launchpad.
- **Manage Banks**: View and update the bank master data.

SAP Tables

The following SAP tables in SE16/SE11 can help with the master data:

- MARA (Material Master)
- KNA1 (Customer Master)
- LFA1 (Vendor Master)
- BKPF (Accounting Document Header)
- VBAK (Sales Order Header)
- AFKO (Production Order Header)

SAP Reports and Queries

- You may use SAP Query (SQVI/ SQ01) to generate reports on master data.
- You may also leverage standard SAP reports, for example, MB52, for material stock overview.

SAP Business Object Repository (BOR) and Custom ABAP Reports

If you have access to an ABAP team, you may want to use this approach to understand the data and its relationships. The BOR is a central access point for SAP business objects, and their BAPIs (Business Application Programming Interfaces). It defines and describes SAP business objects and interface types as well as their BAPIs.

- The BOR organizes SAP data into object types, allowing developers to understand the relationships between different data elements.
- Helps identify relationships between different master data objects.
- Typically used in Workflow and Automation Scenarios.
- In some cases, custom ABAP reports may be needed to extract specific master data views.

Use the following table as a handy reference to identify where specific data can be found within SAP T-Codes and Fiori Apps.

Master Data Object	Type	Description	T-Code / Fiori App
Material Master	Master	Details of materials used in procurement, production, and sales.	MM03 (GUI), and Manage Product Master Data (Fiori)
Vendor Master	Master	Details of suppliers and their business transactions.	XK03 (GUI), and Manage Supplier Master Data (Fiori)
Purchase Info Record	Master	Stores purchasing-related details of materials and vendors.	ME13 (GUI)
Customer Master	Master	Information about customers, including addresses and payment terms.	XD03, VD03 (GUI), and Manage Customer Master Data (Fiori)
Sales Pricing Conditions	Master	Defines pricing rules for sales transactions.	VK13 (GUI), and Manage Sales Prices (Fiori)

Sales Order	Transactional	Record of a sales transaction between a company and a customer.	VA03 (GUI), and Track Sales Orders (Fiori)
G/L Account Master	Master	General ledger account details used for financial reporting.	FS00 (GUI), and Manage G/L Account Master Data (Fiori)
Bank Master	Master	Details of banks used for financial transactions.	FI03 (GUI), and Manage Banks (Fiori)
Cost Center	Master	Defines areas where costs are tracked in an organization.	KS03 (GUI), and Manage Cost Centers (Fiori)
Storage Bin Master	Master	Defines storage locations within a warehouse.	LS03N (GUI), and Manage Storage Bins (Fiori)
Handling Unit	Transactional	Physical units in a warehouse used for logistics and shipping.	HU03 (GUI)

Table 9.4: SAP Data Lookup

Customer Example with Key Data Structure

In the SAP S/4HANA landscape, Key Data Structures (KDS) are foundational building blocks that define how business-critical data is organized, linked, and accessed across the system. These structures are not just tables or fields–they represent the core framework that supports end-to-end business processes, ensures data integrity, and enables seamless automation and analytics.

KDS can include master data (like customer, material, and vendor records), organizational data (such as company codes, plants, and sales areas), and transactional data structures (like sales orders, purchase orders, or billing documents). Understanding how these data structures interact is essential for building robust testing strategies, designing efficient processes, and avoiding downstream errors.

To illustrate this, let us take a fictional example of an ABC Fabrications Company, a mid-sized manufacturer transitioning to SAP S/4HANA. In this scenario, you will see real key data structures in action–such as how material master data links to plant-specific settings, how customer master data integrates with pricing conditions, and how transactional records flow through logistics and finance. This example will bring the abstract concept of key data structures to life, showing you exactly how they are modelled and leveraged in a real-world SAP S/4HANA project.

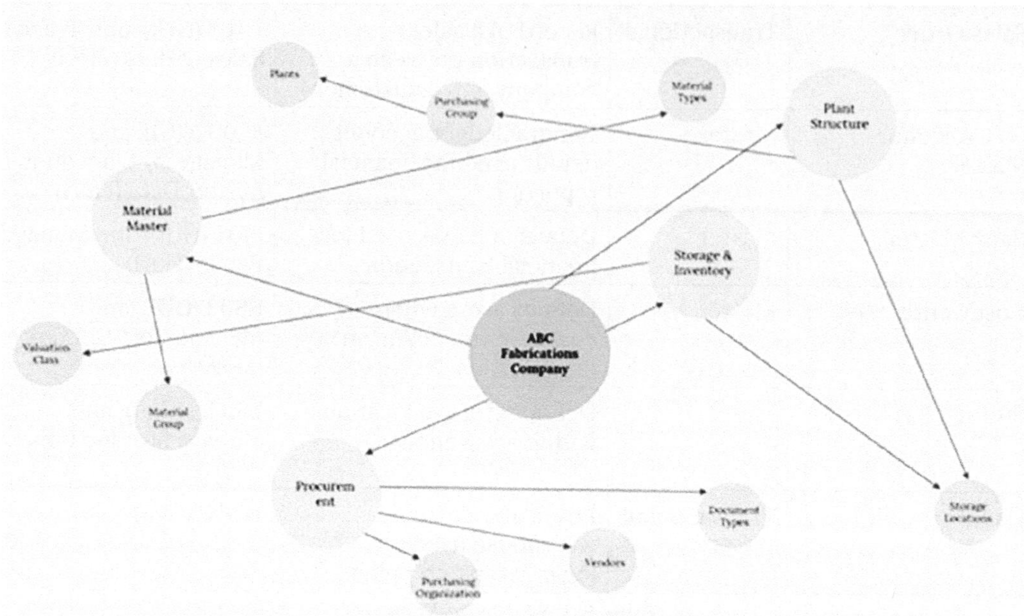

Figure 9.1: *Key Data Structure in a Fabrications Company That Uses SAP*

At ABC Fabrications, the QA team struggled to trace why purchase requisitions were not flowing into POs, until they mapped the KDS, and realized that the configuration of Plant and Purchasing Org linkages were missing. The following tables define data elements and their relationships:

Plant: This helps to verify that the plant-to-company code assignments are correct, as mismatches often break inventory, production, and financial postings during integration testing.

Company Code	Description	Plant	Storage Location	Purchasing Org	Country	Currency
Y020	ABC Fabrication LTD	Y023	Y023	Y020	Germany	EUR
Y020	ABC Fabrication LTD	Y024	Y024	Y020	Germany	EUR

Table 9.5: *ABC Fabrications – Plant*

Purchasing Org: This helps to ensure that purchasing org linkages are tested thoroughly, since incorrect mapping can prevent POs from flowing through approval and vendor management workflows.

Plant	Description	Purchasing. Org	Country
Y023	ABC Garage Division	Y020	Germany
Y024	ABC Heavy Equipment's	Y020	Germany

***Table 9.6:** ABC Fabrications – Purchasing Org*

Purchasing Group: This helps validate purchasing group assignments in test data to ensure cost approvals and sourcing rules route correctly across departments.

Company Code	Purchasing Group	Description
Y020	Y11	General
Y020	Y12	E and T
Y020	Y13	IT
Y020	Y14	Facilities
Y020	Y15	Finance
Y020	Y16	HR
Y020	Y17	Marketing
Y020	Y18	Quality

***Table 9.7:** ABC Fabrications – Purchasing Group*

Storage Location: Know your Storage Location setups early, as wrong assignments frequently cause goods movement and stock availability test failures.

Company Code	Plant	Description	Storage Location	Description
Y020	Y023	ABC Garage Division	Y023	General Store
Y020	Y024	ABC Heavy Equipment's	Y024	General Store

***Table 9.8:** ABC Fabrications – Storage Location*

Material Group: Include multiple material groups in test datasets, because incorrect grouping often impacts reporting, valuation, and procurement analytics.

Company Code	Material Group	Description
Y020	YYTE	Tyres
Y020	YPLM	Plumbing
Y020	YTUB	Tubes

***Table 9.9:** ABC Fabrications – Material Group*

Document Types: This helps in verifying document type ranges and configurations in test cycles to ensure requisitions, POs, and contracts are posted in the right sequences without authorization errors.

Doc. Type	Element	Description	From	To
Y2CR	Purchase Requisition	Capex PR for Y020	1000000	1005000
Y2SR	Purchase Requisition	Stock Item for Y020	1005001	1010000
Y2MR	Purchase Requisition	MRP PR for Y020	1010001	1015000
Y2CO	Purchase Order	Capex PO for Y020	100000	1005000
Y2SO	Purchase Order	Stock Item PO for Y020	1005001	1010000
Y2RQ	Request for Quotation	RFQ process for Y020	1000000	1005000
Y2QC	Contract	Quantity Contract for Y020	1010001	1015000
Y2VC	Contract	Value Contract for Y020	1015001	1020000
Y2LW	Schedule Agreement	SA with release for Y020	1010001	1015000
Y2LR	Schedule Agreement	SA without release for Y020	1015001	1020000

Table 9.10: *ABC Fabrications – Doc Types*

Material Types: Understand different material types, as misconfigured valuation classes or account references often trigger finance posting errors.

Material Type	Description	Valuation Class	Acc. Cat. Reference	Interval
YROH	Raw Material	YROH	YROH	Y1
YFRT	Finished Material	YFER	YFER	Y2
YHLB	Semi-finished material	YHAL	YHAL	Y3
YLEH	RTP material	YLEI	YLEI	Y4

Table 9.11: *ABC Fabrications – Material Types*

Business Partners: Know your vendor/customer/business partner role assignments, since missing or wrong BP roles cause process breakdowns in O2C and P2P testing.

BP Group	Account Group	Type	Number Range	From	To
Y2LV	Y2LV	Local Vendor	YA	1001001	1005000
Y2LS	Y2LS	Local Service	YB	1005001	1010000
Y2IV	Y2IV	Import Vendor	YC	1010001	1015000
Y2IS	Y2IS	Import Service	YD	1015001	1020000
Y2EV	Y2EV	Employee	YE	1020001	1025000
Y2VI	Y2VI	Intercompany Vendor	YF	1025001	1030000
Y2IC	Y2IC	Intercompany Customer	1030001	1035000	

Y2FV	Y2FV	Freight Vendor	YH	1035001	1040000
Y2SV	Y2SV	Service Vendor	YI	1040001	1045000

Table 9.12: *ABC Fabrications – Business Partners*

We hope these real-world KDS examples in this case provide a clearer perspective on how data operates holistically across an entire company - connecting departments, systems, and processes into a unified digital core.

To deepen your understanding of test data management in SAP landscapes, it is necessary to tap into the right knowledge sources. Hence, whether you are starting out or looking to refine your strategy, the following trusted resources offer expert guidance, practical insights, and real-world strategies to help you master test data management in SAP environments:

- **SAP Learning Hub:** Access a comprehensive repository of SAP training materials, including courses on test data management. https://learninghub.sap.com
- **openSAP:** Enrol in free Massive Open Online Courses (MOOCs) provided by SAP, covering various topics including test data management. https://learning.sap.com
- **SAP Community Blogs:** Read insights and strategies on formulating test data management enterprise strategies for SAP databases. https://community.sap.com

Conclusion

In recent studies by IDC and ASUG, companies with a clear Test Data Management (TDM) strategy reported 50% fewer UAT defects and 30% faster release cycles. For SAP S/4HANA programs, that can be the line between a smooth go-live and a painful one.

This chapter highlighted why TDM is more than a technical task, it is a business enabler. We explored how understanding SAP's data organization helps QA teams avoid common pitfalls such as incomplete, inconsistent, or non-compliant data. We discussed the core traits of good test data such as accuracy, scalability, security, and traceability - and how they directly impact quality and speed.

In the next chapter, we shift from **data readiness** to **test strategy design**, exploring how testing can start to become a true driver of agility and innovation.

Resources

- https://community.sap.com/t5/technology-blogs-by-members/master-data-lookups-in-sap-bw-routine/ba-p/13536150
- https://www.sap.com/india/products/data-cloud/master-data-governance/what-is-mdm.html
- https://en.wikipedia.org/wiki/SAP_NetWeaver_Master_Data_Management
- https://www.epiuselabs.com/client-story-sanofi-transforms-their-test-data-management-and-client-refreshes-on-sap-s/4hana
- https://sapinsider.org/type/case-studies/
- https://www.acquia.com/resources/customer-stories
- https://ktern.com/article/agentic-ai-and-ai-first-digital-transformation-2/
- https://www.sap.com/assetdetail/2024/10/0884897d-de7e-0010-bca6-c68f7e60039b.html
- https://www.tmap.net/wiki/sap-test-data-management
- https://sap.walkme.com/business-object-repository/#:~:text=What%20is%20a%20Business%20Object%20Repository%20in%20SAP?,Purchase%20Order

CHAPTER 10
SAP Test Strategy

Introduction

Capgemini's World Quality Report highlights that SAP transformations fail to achieve quality objectives when Testing is treated as an afterthought, instead of a strategic driver. A well-defined test strategy serves as the foundation for a structured and effective testing framework.

A robust SAP test strategy is integrated throughout the project lifecycle, enabling early detection of defects, minimizing performance bottlenecks, and ensuring regulatory compliance, all while keeping pace with the demanding project schedules. It anchors testing to business priorities, making quality a strategic driver, rather than a reactive checkpoint.

This chapter delves into the core pillars of an effective SAP test strategy, including testing governance, automation, risk-based testing, and cross-functional alignment. By formalizing this strategy, organizations can create a common vision for quality, foster ownership, and cultivate a test-driven culture that accelerates and de-risks the journey to SAP S/4HANA.

Structure

This chapter on Test Strategy is explored with the following aspects:

- Common Myths
- Critical Elements of a Test Strategy
- Test Project Estimation techniques
- Team and Capability

Common Myths

Skipping a test strategy might seem like a shortcut to save time and effort. But in reality, it often leads to delayed go-lives, higher defect resolution costs, and disruptive business impacts. Still, many organizations either overlook the importance of a structured test strategy or deprioritize it altogether. Why? A mix of misconceptions and practical challenges:

We do not have time or resources to create a test strategy

Test strategy development is often seen as an overhead, rather than a necessity. Project teams are always under pressure to meet aggressive timelines, prioritize execution over planning. Without a clear strategy, testing becomes reactive, leading to inefficiencies, duplicated efforts, and missed critical defects.

Customer Example: A retail company embarking on an SAP S/4HANA rollout found itself with just one tester for every nine other team members - well below the industry best practice of a 4:1 ratio. Lacking both the testing manpower and automation expertise, the team prioritized delivering features over structured planning. As a result, several critical integration bugs surfaced only after go-live, forcing emergency patches and overtime work, which ultimately cost more time and money than the initial "*savings*".

Pro Tip: *Even if timelines are short, a* ***one-page lean test strategy*** *can anchor the team. Capture just scope, risks, automation plan, and governance, this 4-block approach avoids analysis-paralysis later.*

Our SAP systems evolve too quickly, and so creating a test strategy is impossible.

Frequent system updates, agile development cycles, and evolving business processes make some teams believe a static test strategy is futile. However, a well-structured test strategy is not a one-time document but an evolving framework that adapts to changes, while ensuring consistency in quality assurance.

Customer Example: A global manufacturer using SAP Commerce Cloud adopted a "*just test what changed*" mindset because updates arrived monthly. Lacking a living test strategy, they routinely missed the regression impact of new releases. One missed update led to a critical order management failure in their live system, causing revenue losses until the issue was patched.

We use test automation, so everything is already documented.

Relying solely on automated test scripts as a substitute for a test strategy is a common misconception. Automation scripts capture test steps, but they do not define *why* certain tests are prioritized, *how* risks are mitigated, or *what* governance model ensures effective testing. A test strategy provides this overarching structure.

Customer Example: A tech firm invested heavily in Opensource framework-driven automation for SAP regression testing. However, with no overarching test strategy, nobody tracked which business-critical processes were (or were not) automated. During a regulatory audit, several mandatory controls lacked automated tests – and there was no clear rationale for gaps, exposing the organization to compliance risks.

Performance and security testing can be deferred

Organizations often push performance and security testing to later stages or treat them as optional (WHY)? Why? Scarcity of skilled testers, it requires complex process, and availability of time.

Customer Example: A financial services company delayed SAP S/4HANA performance testing until after go-live, believing other priorities came first. Only after their partner, and customers started experiencing system slowdowns did the team uncover batch processing bottlenecks. Emergency fixes required costly downtime and manual workarounds.

A well-planned test strategy always ensures alignment between testing efforts and business objectives, improving test efficiency, risk mitigation, and overall SAP S/4HANA project success.

Critical Elements of a Test Strategy

More than a document, Test Strategy is a shared reference point driving collaboration, consistency, and proactive quality management across the entire transformation journey. Now, we could walk through a theoretical breakdown of what goes into a test strategy document–but let us be honest, that would be dull and disconnected from reality. Instead, let us look at a real-world example.

A leading manufacturing enterprise recently undertook a brownfield migration from SAP ECC 6.0 to SAP S/4HANA. The company aimed to modernize its core business systems, while retaining critical customizations built over the years. This transformation was complex, with risks spanning data integrity, process continuity, system performance, and end-user adoption.

To manage these risks, and ensure a smooth transition, the company implemented a well-structured test strategy covering all key testing dimensions. In the following sections, we will use this example to illustrate the critical components of an effective test strategy–and how it played out across multiple workstreams.

Scope: Defining What is In and What is Out

The first and arguably most critical step in any test strategy is defining its **scope**. This means clearly establishing what will be tested, and what will not. Without a well-defined scope, testing efforts can easily become scattered, inefficient, and misaligned with business priorities, leading to missed risks and duplicate efforts.

In the case of our customer, the test scope was defined with precision to focus on the most business-critical and high-risk areas. Their test strategy included:

- **Validating Core Business Processes** such as Finance (FI), Procurement (MM), and Sales (SD).

- **Validating Data Migration** to ensure accuracy between SAP ECC and S/4HANA.
- **Integration Testing** for third-party applications.
- **Security and Compliance Testing** for regulatory adherence.

By defining this scope early in the project lifecycle, the team was able to direct efforts toward high-risk areas from the outset - ensuring better resource allocation, and helping to avoid costly surprises later in the project.

Test Approach: The Strategy behind Testing

The test approach outlines the methodology used to conduct testing processes efficiently. It outlines whether testing will be manual or automated, risk-based or exploratory, and how defects will be managed.

A well-defined Test Approach ensures:

- Early defect detection to avoid costly fixes later.
- Consistent and repeatable validation through automation.
- Alignment with business objectives to ensure a high-quality system upgrade.
- Seamless integration of test tools to automate execution, tracking, and reporting.

The test strategy is governed by key principles that ensure effective testing throughout the SAP S/4HANA migration lifecycle. Here are some of the standard test principles used in SAP projects.

- **Test Early:** Testing should start as soon as possible in the development lifecycle. The earlier defects are found, the cheaper and easier they are to fix.
- **Quality Control:** Minimizing testing gaps is key to a successful migration. Clear test objectives and adherence to entry and exit criteria ensure that all planned scenarios are executed.
- **Define Test Cases during Design and Build:** Test cases should be written alongside design and build activities to ensure that they align with business requirements.
- **Risk-Based Testing:** Not all tests are equal—some processes are more crucial than others. A risk-based approach prioritizes high-impact areas to ensure that defects in critical business processes are identified early.
- **Involve Business User Early:** Engaging business users early ensures that testing aligns with real-world scenarios, and users take ownership of the system.

- **Exercise End-To-End Business Process Testing Early and Often:** Testing should be structured around end-to-end process flows, rather than isolated modules, to identify integration issues early.
- **Use Approved AI Capabilities Only:** Testing should leverage the AI tools and capabilities that are approved by the organization.

The following graphical representation illustrates the integrated approach for our customer, ensuring that every phase of testing is connected, traceable, and efficient for the scope defined earlier.

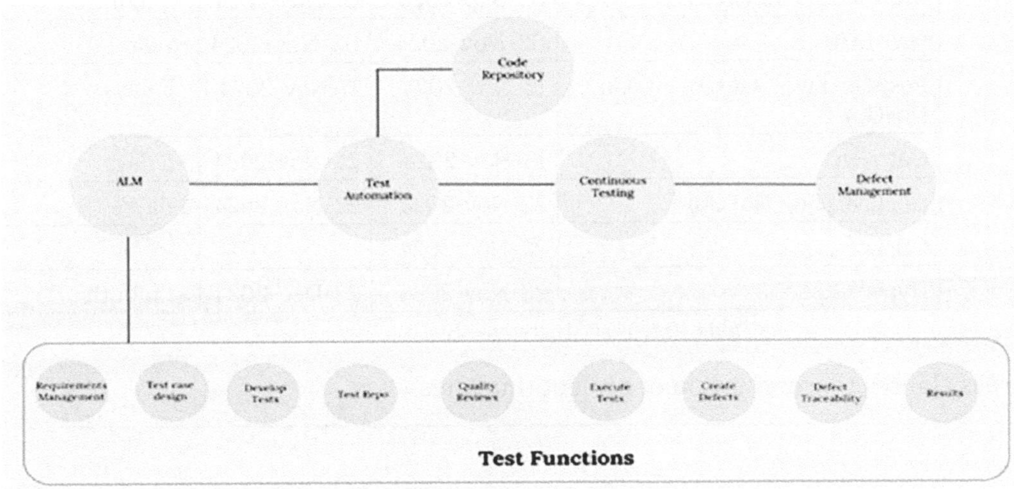

Figure 10.1: *Test Strategy – Test Approach*

Pro Tip: *Encourage teams to create a* **"Test Heatmap"** *(processes vs. risk/ complexity) to drive scope discussions with business stakeholders.*

Timelines: Aligning Testing with Project Phases

Testing is not a single event–it is a structured process that must align with project milestones. A well-defined testing timeline ensures that each phase gets the right focus at the right time.

This structured timeline allowed the customer to progressively mitigate risks, and address issues before go-live. The following table showcases the timelines for customer's testing project:

Testing Activities	Start Date	End Date	Duration
Test Discovery and Study	01-Feb-2024		
Complete Design and Build (Critical Tests)	01-Feb-2024	21-Jul-2024	~5.5 months

Test Automation Development	01-Mar-2024	15-Sep-2024	~6.5 months
Training for Business teams	03-Jul-2024	01-Sep-2024	~2 months
Testing (SIT)	11-Jul-2024	01-Sep-2024	~7 weeks
Exit SIT / Entry to UAT	01-Sep-2024	01-Sep-2024	~1 day
Testing (UAT)	04-Sep-2024	03-Nov-2024	~2 months
UAT Test Automation Execution	04-Sep-2024	03-Nov-2024	~ 2 months (parallel to UAT)
Knowledge Transfer	04-Sep-2024	01-Nov-2024	~2 months
UAT Exit	03-Nov-2024	03-Nov-2024	~1 day
Post Go-Live Assessment (Go/ No-Go)	13-Nov-2024	17-Nov-2024	~5 days
Cutover	18-Nov-2024	22-Nov-2024	~5 days
Go-Live (Go/ No-Go)	22-Nov-2024	22-Nov-2024	1 days
Go-Live	23-Nov-2024		
Hyper Care	23-Nov-2024	22-Dec-2024	~1 month

Table 10.1: *Test Strategy – Testing Timelines*

Here is Gantt's representation of project timelines.

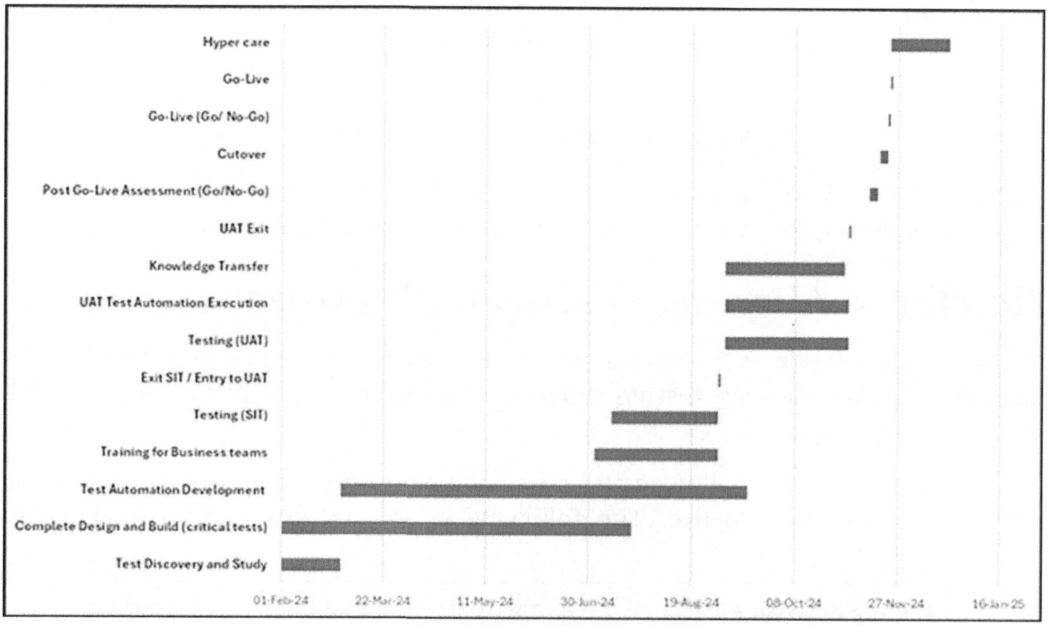

Figure 10.2: *Test Project Timelines – Gantt Chart Representation*

Pro Tip: *Always "ringfence" environments for UAT to avoid business fatigue. In one project, UAT overlapped with performance testing due to delays in SIT. This led to conflicting environment usage, frustrating business users.*

Test Phases: Breaking Testing into Manageable Stages

To avoid chaos, testing is divided into phases, each with its own objectives.

For customer convenience, these test phases are included in the test strategy:

- **System Integration Testing (SIT):** Verified end-to-end workflows across integrated systems.
- **User Acceptance Testing (UAT):** Business users tested real-world scenarios.
- **Performance Testing:** Assessed how the system handled peak loads.
- **Regression Testing:** Ensured stability after changes.

Breaking testing into phases helped the team catch defects early, avoiding costly rework closer to go-live.

The following table explains how and when these different test phases are planned to be carried out.

Testing Phase	Entry Criteria	Exit Criteria
System Integration Test (SIT)	• Environment has been setup (access/permissions) end to end, including connectivity with all interfacing parties. • Test resources are trained in the Solution operation required to complete testing. • All resources required to execute the Test cases and scripts have been identified, and are available. • All test data requirements have been identified and created within the Test environment as required. • All testing documentation written, reviewed and signed off by Business.	• All Test cases and data preparation are completed and reviewed. • Automation test results will be provided to the Functional Team. • All Defects are documented in SAP Cloud ALM. • There are no outstanding very high defects-showstopper and High-Critical defects opened. • Acceptance of test summary report for SIT.

Automation Testing	• Manual test cases should be baselined. • Feasibility test should be performed based on the application's technology stack. • Scenario Variants and Business Risks are defined and signed off by Business and IT SMEs. • Environment (Automation tool and Application supporting software's) should be ready. • Test Automation team is trained. • Test execution pass criteria are agreed. • Test data is available.	• All the Scenario Variants should be successfully automated. • Business and Functional Team provides signed off and approval on the automated test scenarios. • Automation test results are published in the relevant Test Phase Summary Report. • Automation Test Phase Summary Report is reviewed and approved by the Project Team. • Test Execution completion is 100%, and Pass Percentage is 100%.
User Acceptance Testing (UAT)	• UAT Environment has been setup (access/permissions). • Test teams monitor unattended executions and availability for defect resolution. • All resources required to execute the test cases and scripts have been identified, and are available. • All test data requirements have been identified and created within the test environment as required. • Test cases and scripts have been completed. • Configuration management processes are in place to accommodate any Software fixes, and application code version is updated as per the current production (if applicable), with the code required for the next production release. • There are no outstanding Severity 1 or 2 Defects from the SIT phase or previous phases, if a waiver was provided during previous phase. • Acceptance of an agreed number of outstanding Severity 3 or 4 Defects.	• All Test cases and Data preparation are completed and reviewed. • Automated Test cases documented in SAP Cloud ALM. • All Defects are documented in SAP Cloud ALM. • There are no outstanding defects of High or Critical or Showstoppers. • Acceptance of the outstanding Medium and Low Defects, and an associated action plan to resolve them. • Design documents updated to reflect any changes made as an outcome of testing. • Acceptance of Test Summary Report for UAT. • All Test cases have been executed, and results documented. • Unattended successful execution with 2 sets of positive and 2 sets of negative test data. • Test Reports (HTML) should be validated, and signed off by Business. • Test Execution Completion is at least 100%, and Pass Percentage is at 95%.

Table 10.2: *Test Strategy – Test Phases*

In one SAP program, the project manager said, "*We built the Ferrari but tested the tires separately from the engine.*" That is the danger of not doing end-to-end. Here are five (5) Golden Rules for SAP Testing:

- Shift-Left → Test early, design test cases during build.
- Risk-First → Focus where business exposure is the highest.
- End-to-End Always → Avoid silo testing.
- Business in the Loop → Involve users early.
- Governed AI → Only use approved AI in testing.

Roles and Responsibilities: Defining Who Does What

Testing is a team effort, and without clear roles, it can quickly become disorganized. This section outlines who is responsible for what, ensuring accountability.

For our customer/s, the key roles included:

- Test Manager - Owned the overall test strategy.
- Business Process Owners - Defined and validated UAT scenarios.
- Manual Testers (or Functional Consultants) - Executed business process validation.
- Integration Experts - Ensured third-party systems worked seamlessly.
- Test Automation Engineer – Managed automated test cases.
- Performance Engineers - Evaluated system scalability.

This structured approach ensured clear ownership, reducing bottlenecks during execution.

Test Automation: To Speed up Test Cycles

An effective test strategy is not just about planning–it is about executing testing efficiently, and accelerating cycles without compromising quality. This is where test automation approach plays a critical role in reducing the timelines of a project, and brings in efficiency and effectiveness to the quality.

For our customers, the key steps include:

- **Feasibility Study:** The following principles must be used to identify the good candidates for test automation:
    - **Repeatable**: Tests that need to be run against multiple environments, run against every release of the application such as Smoke Test and Regression Tests.

- **High-Business-Value**: Critical and high-volume functions that deliver increased value to the customers, and would cause considerable damage to the business, if they fail.
- **Frequently Used**: Functionality is commonly used that is high risk or high customer impact. For example, Create Emergency order.
- **Multiple Configurations**: Tests that need to be run against multiple SAP environments, Operating Systems and/or Browsers.
- **Large Volume**: Tests that require large amounts of data for the filling out of lengthy forms.

- **Test Design:** The Test Automation team conceptualizes the framework design, and commences test build with the identified automation testing tool installed in local machines. Tests will follow Modular and Data-Driven design to accelerate test development, and increase reusability.
- **Framework Elements:** Automated test design to consider reusing the Object Repository, Reusable Libraries, Execution Templates, Design Templates, and Test Data Templates.
- **Build:** Automated tests to be created with appropriate names for test cases, objects, and library components.
- **Test Execution:** Prior to test execution, always ensure that the test data is created and available.

Test Data Management: The Backbone of Reliable Testing

Reliable testing is only possible with realistic, well-managed test data. **Test data management** forms the backbone of quality assurance, ensuring scenarios are valid and results can be trusted–without compromising data security or compliance.

For our customer's SAP S/4HANA migration, the team implemented a comprehensive test data management strategy that included:

- **Selecting Representative Data Subsets**. Carefully chosen data sets were extracted to accurately reflect real-world usage, business processes, and edge cases from the production system. This approach allowed for robust testing without the risk of exposing sensitive customer or financial data.
- **Incremental Data Migration testing for validation**. Instead of a one-time data load, migration was performed incrementally in controlled waves. At each stage, automated validation steps ensured that the migrated data matched source values, helping to catch inconsistencies and errors early.
- **Automated Data Reconciliation Scripts to check consistency**. Specialized scripts compared source and target datasets to verify completeness and

consistency. These reconciliations formed a critical safety net, flagging any mismatched records before the testing began.

The following diagram illustrates how test data availability can be planned during test strategy phase.

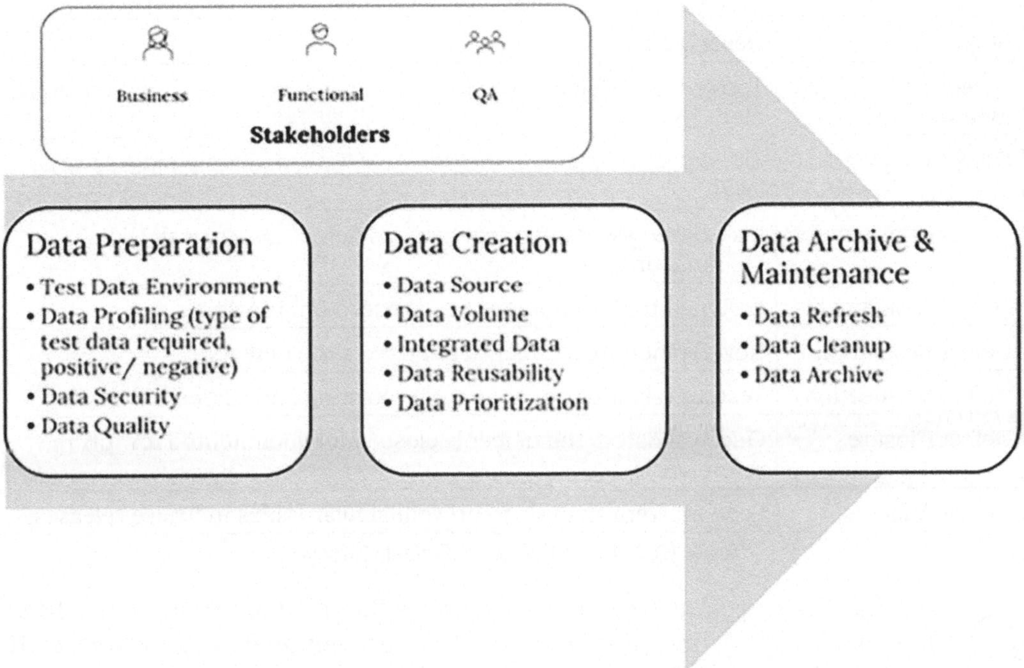

***Figure* 10.3:** *Test Strategy – Data Strategy*

Test Environment: Where Testing is Executed

Environment planning is essential for supporting testing across all test phases as SAP updates progress through different stages. The following table can provide realistic information that customers can include in their test strategy document to ensure structured and efficient test execution.

Test Phase	Environment
System Testing	EDQ
System Integration Testing 1	EDI1
System Integration Testing 2	EDI2
User Acceptance Test	EDU

***Table* 10.3:** *Test Strategy – Test Environment*

Defect Management: Track and Resolve Anomalies

A structured defect management process is critical to ensure that defects are logged, prioritized, and resolved efficiently. The Defect Lifecycle can clearly be highlighted for a customer:

Stage	Description
Defect Identification	Tester logs a defect with detailed steps, screenshots, and impacted modules.
Defect Logging	The defect is logged in the SAP ALM Tool, and assigned a severity level.
Defect Prioritization	Risk-based assessment categorizes defects as Critical, High, Medium, or Low.
Defect Assignment	Assigned to development teams based on priority.
Defect Resolution	Development team analyzes and fixes the defects.
Defect Verification	Testers validate the fix through retesting and regression testing.
Defect Closure	Once validated, the defect is closed and documented for future reference.
Defect Analysis	Post-mortem analysis to prevent similar issues in future releases.

Table 10.4: *Test Strategy – Defect Lifecycle*

Pro Tip: *The best practice is a "Defect Triage Board", daily 15-minute calls with functional + test + business users to drive accountability. According to IDC, unresolved critical defects account for 60–70% of SAP go-live delays.*

Defects are usually categorized based on business impact, and are highlighted as follows.

- **Critical Defects:** Block go-live, must be fixed immediately.
- **High-Severity Defects:** Impact business functions but have workarounds.
- **Medium-Severity Defects:** Minor impact, fixed in subsequent releases.
- **Low-Severity Defects:** UI-related or minor issues that do not affect core business functions.

User Acceptance Testing: Final Validation Phase

User Acceptance Testing (UAT) serves as the final checkpoint before the SAP S/4HANA goes live. Its primary goal is to validate that the configured solution, migrated data, and end-to-end business workflows function correctly in real-world scenarios–*from the perspective of the business users.*

For our customers, the UAT scope was carefully designed to reflect practical, high-impact use cases, and included the following focus areas:

- End-to-End Business Process Validation (for example, Order-to-Cash, Procure-to-Pay, and Record-to-Report).
- Validation of Role-Based Access Control to ensure correct user permissions.
- Realistic Data Testing using migrated production-like datasets.
- Integration Testing with Third-Party Systems (example, tax, finance, and supplier platforms).
- Performance Checks to assess system usability under normal operational loads.
- Regulatory and Compliance Validation ensuring adherence to industry standards.

A structured UAT not only validates system readiness - It also builds business confidence, drives adoption, and serves as a critical go/no-go decision point before production deployment.

Risk Management: Acknowledge and Mitigate Risks

Risk management ensures that high-impact failures are prevented before go-live. The Program Management function of SAP follows a structured approach to identify, assess, and remediate risks as early as possible.

For customers, the key risks are mitigated with the following highlighted approach.

Risk	Potential Impact	Mitigation Approach
Data Migration Risk	Incomplete or incorrect data, impact testing.	Perform multiple mock migrations and reconcile with the legacy data.
Integration Failures	Disruptions in external system connections.	Conduct early integration testing, and validate APIs.
Test Environment Instability	Frequent system crashes delaying testing.	Maintain dedicated, stable test environments.
High Defect Volume	Delays in go-live due to unresolved critical defects.	Daily defect triage meetings to track and resolve issues.
Performance Bottlenecks	System lags during high transaction loads.	Conduct performance testing before UAT completion.
Security and Compliance	Data privacy breaches or non-compliance issues.	Security testing and compliance validation before deployment.

Table 10.5: *Test Strategy – Risk Management*

A large mining company underestimated "*test environment instability*" as a risk. Midway, frequent refreshes caused test data mismatches, delaying UAT by 3 weeks. After this, they created a **"stable environment calendar"** as part of the strategy.

A structured meeting-schedule ensures continuous risk tracking and resolution throughout the project as well as the test lifecycle.

Meeting Type	**Frequency**	**Objective**	**Attendees**
Daily Testing Meeting	Daily	Track the testing progress.	QA Team, Vendors
Weekly Status Meeting	Weekly	Review defect summary, track issues/ risks.	Project Manager, QA Team, Business Leads, Vendors
Ad-hoc Testing Meeting	As Needed	Address the critical defects.	Test Manager, Functional Leads, Vendors
Functional KT	As Needed	Conduct demos to the QA team.	Functional and QA Teams
Sprint Showcase	Per Sprint	Demonstrate test design and test execution (including automation).	QA, Business and Functional Teams

Table 10.6: *Test Strategy – Risk Mitigation Plan*

Test Project Estimation Techniques

Test estimation is a vital component of SAP S/4HANA project success, ensuring the right allocation of time, effort, and resources for thorough and high-quality testing. This section highlights leading estimation techniques for SAP test projects, complemented by real-world examples from customer implementations.

We use the 3-Point estimation method in this book to explain the following estimation techniques. What is this - "**3-Point estimation method**" about? The 3-point estimation method is a technique used in project management to estimate effort, duration, or cost more accurately. Instead of relying on a single value, it considers three estimates:

1. **Optimistic Estimate (O) –** The best-case scenario where everything goes smoothly.
2. **Pessimistic Estimate (P) –** The worst-case scenario with potential risks and challenges.
3. **Most Likely Estimate (Realistic) (M) –** The realistic estimate based on typical conditions.

Using these values, the final estimate is calculated using the PERT (Program Evaluation and Review Technique) formula:

$$E = \left(\frac{O + 4M + P}{6}\right)$$

where E is the expected estimate.

The following table highlights the key differences between traditional and 3-point estimation methods.

Aspect	Traditional Estimation	3-Point Estimation
Approach	Uses a single-point estimate (often based on expert judgment).	Uses probabilistic approach with three estimates.
Accuracy	Prone to underestimation or overestimation.	Provides balanced estimate considering risks.
Risk Consideration	Does not explicitly account for uncertainties.	Accounts for best, worst, and likely scenarios.
Decision-Making	May lead to unrealistic expectations.	Helps in risk-informed decision-making

***Table 10.7**: Three-point Estimation Methodology*

By incorporating uncertainty and risks, the 3-point estimation method provides a more realistic and data-driven approach to effort and cost estimation for SAP Testing projects.

Estimation Based on Test Volume

This approach estimates testing efforts based on the number of test cases, complexity, and execution efforts. It is useful for projects with well-defined test scenarios.

For example, a customer has about 1000 test cases to support their SAP S/4HANA upgrade. Here is how you would go about with the estimation.

- **Optimistic**: 1000 test cases @ 2 hours each = 2000 hours
- **Realistic**: 1000 test cases @ 3 hours each = 3000 hours
- **Pessimistic**: 1000 test cases @ 5 hours each = 5000 hours

$$E = \left(\frac{2000 + 4 * 3000 + 5000}{6}\right) = 3166\ hours$$

When to Use:

- When test cases are well-documented and structured.
- When test automation coverage is clear.
- For regression testing or large-scale functional testing.

Estimation Based on Timelines

This method aligns testing efforts with project timelines and business priorities - High-priority test cases are tested earlier, and low-priority cases may be tested later or dropped.

As an example, a manufacturing company prioritized finance and procurement modules, reducing testing efforts on low-risk processes.

Assume:

- **Optimistic**: 8 weeks (with zero defects)
- **Realistic**: 12 weeks (with moderate defects)
- **Pessimistic**: 18 weeks (with severe defects)

$$E = \left(\frac{8 + 4 * 12 + 18}{6}\right) = 12.67\ weeks$$

When to Use:

- When project timelines are tight.
- When risk-based testing is preferred.
- When testing resources are limited, and need prioritization.

Estimation Based on Percent-of-Development Effort

This approach uses historical data to estimate testing efforts as a percentage of development effort. Additionally, testing is estimated to consume about 30%-50% of the overall SAP project implementation effort, with approximately 30% of the IT budget allocated to testing activities.

Common Ratios (observed in a standard QA project):

- Unit Testing: 20-30% of the Development Effort.
- Integration Testing: 30-50% of the Development Effort.
- System Testing: 50-100% of the Development Effort.
- UAT: 10-30% of the Development Effort.

For example, a logistics company estimated testing efforts based on 40% of the development time for an SAP S/4HANA conversion project to ensure adequate testing coverage, while staying within the budget.

If development effort is 10,000 hours:

- **Optimistic**: 25% = 2,500 hours
- **Realistic**: 40% = 4,000 hours
- **Pessimistic**: 60% = 6,000 hours

$$E = \left(\frac{2500 + 4 * 4000 + 6000}{6}\right) = 4000\ hours$$

When to Use:

- When the historical project data is available.
- When there is a need for a high-level effort estimate early in the project.
- When management prefers estimates as a proportion of the development effort.

Estimation Based on Expert Judgement

Expert judgment leverages insights from the past SAP projects to determine the effort.

For example, a pharmaceutical firm migrating from ECC to S/4HANA wants an expert-based approach based on previous projects to ensure regulatory compliance in testing.

Assume, for a similar SAP S/4HANA project with 12,000 hours of testing effort:

- **Optimistic**: 10,000 hours
- **Realistic**: 12,000 hours
- **Pessimistic**: 15,000 hours

$$E = \left(\frac{1000 + 4 * 12000 + 15000}{6}\right) = 12{,}166.67\ hours$$

When to Use:

- When similar SAP S/4HANA projects have been completed.
- When industry benchmarks and SME knowledge are available.
- When formal estimation techniques are infeasible due to lack of test data.

As you may have noticed, choosing the right estimation technique depends on project complexity, data availability, and stakeholder expectations. The 3-point estimation method improves accuracy in all techniques, ensuring reliable SAP S/4HANA test planning.

Team and Capability

Testing is not just skills but mindset. In a global SAP rollout, business users in Germany were deeply engaged in UAT, while users in Asia treated it as "*extra work*." To fix this, the project ran "UAT *roadshows*," showcasing how defects found early impact the project and the users positively. This shifted the perception from burden to ownership.

A well-structured test team with the right blend of business expertise, SAP functional knowledge, automation skills, and risk management experience ensures that the solution is validated effectively, risks are mitigated early, and business continuity is maintained post-go-live.

Testing teams must address these complexities by bringing together:

- Functional experts who understand SAP processes and transactions.
- Automation engineers who reduce manual testing efforts.
- Business SMEs who validate real-world workflows.
- Integration and security specialists who ensure seamless data flows and system compliance.

Let us study a couple of SAP implementations to appreciate how teams and capabilities are managed.

Case Study 01: Global Consumer Goods Company

Project Scope and Challenges:

Company embarked on a multi-country SAP transformation, aiming to:

- Consolidate multiple ERP instances into a single global system.
- Standardize finance, procurement, and supply chain workflows.
- Ensure regulatory compliance across 100+ countries.

Key Challenges:

- The global scale of the program meant that business processes had regional variations.
- A high number of integrations with third-party logistics and tax systems.
- Significant data migration complexity from various legacy SAP and non-SAP systems.

Team and Capability Strategy:

The company structured its SAP Testing Organization into:

Team	Key Responsibilities
Global Test Governance Team	Defined the test strategy, tools, and reporting framework. Managed defect governance and escalations.
Regional Functional Test Teams	Validated SAP FI, MM, SD, PP, and TM processes in their specific regions. Conducted User Acceptance Testing (UAT).
Test Automation Team	Automated end-to-end procure-to-pay and order-to-cash flows, reducing manual efforts.
Data Validation Team	Ensured data accuracy and reconciliation post-migration. Used automated scripts for data consistency checks.
Performance and Security Testing Team	Assessed system scalability, and ensured compliance with GDPR and industry regulations.

Table 10.8: *SAP Testing Team Structure – Case Study #1*

Case Study 02: A Leading Automotive Manufacturer

Project Scope and Challenges:

This company implemented SAP S/4HANA to:

- Integrate manufacturing plants, dealerships, and supply chain networks.
- Enable real-time financial consolidation across global subsidiaries.
- Improve efficiency using SAP Fiori applications.

Key Challenges:

- Required heavy customization to align SAP with automotive manufacturing workflows.
- Needed to test SAP integrations with over 200+ suppliers and dealer networks.
- Complex regulatory requirements (for example, emissions reporting, and supplier compliance).

Team and Capability Strategy:

The company structured its SAP Testing Organization into Hub-and-spoke Model:

Team	Key Responsibilities
Central Test Governance Team	Defined the overall testing framework and ensured standardization across business units.

SAP Functional Testers	Verified core SAP functions (Manufacturing, Logistics, Finance) and Fiori apps.
Business Process Champions	Led UAT in manufacturing plants, ensuring real-world validation.
Test Automation Specialists	Automated end-to-end order management and inventory tracking.
Security & Compliance Testing Team	Validated data encryption, access controls, and GDPR compliance.

Table 10.9: *SAP Testing Team Structure – Case Study #2*

The business impact reported by the customers include:

- 95% of business users signed off on UAT ahead of schedule due to a structured engagement model.
- Automated regression tests reduced manual effort by 60%, allowing faster release cycles.
- Performance testing ensured that SAP could handle peak manufacturing loads without slowdowns.

The following list of skills has been curated from real-world SAP S/4HANA transformation programs - drawing on lessons learned from leading global enterprises, implementations led by top technology firms and system integrators (including Deloitte, PwC, Accenture, Infosys, and so on), and insights from seasoned SAP test leaders.

These capabilities represent what is consistently proven essential in complex transformation initiatives–ensuring high-quality outcomes, strong business alignment, and accelerated, sustainable delivery.

Skill Area	**Why It is Essential**
SAP S/4HANA Functional Knowledge	Understanding the business processes (e.g., Order-to-Cash, Procure-to-Pay, Record-to-Report) and how they are configured in S/4HANA is critical to writing and executing meaningful test cases.
End-to-End Business Process Understanding	Testers must understand how business transactions flow across modules (e.g., FI-MM, SD-FI) to validate true business continuity.
Test Case Design and Execution	Ability to create risk-based, traceable, and reusable test cases aligned with business requirements.
Defect Lifecycle Management	Proficiency in logging, categorizing, triaging, and retesting defects within structured tools (example, JIRA, Solution Manager, Cloud ALM, ADO).

Test Planning & Prioritization	Capability to contribute to test scope definition, effort estimation, and cycle planning.
Stakeholder Communication	Strong verbal and written communication to collaborate with functional consultants, developers, and business users.
UAT Readiness and Support	Familiarity with preparing users for UAT, coordinating walkthroughs, and capturing user feedback.
Basic SQL/Data Querying	Useful for validating data in backend systems or checking data migration accuracy.

Table 10.10: *SAP Testing Team Capability – Must-Have Skills*

While not mandatory for every role, the following highlighted skills significantly enhance efficiency, coverage, and scalability of the testing efforts:

Skill Area	**Why It Adds Value**
Test Automation	Ability to design and maintain automated test scripts help accelerate regression cycles, and improve coverage.
Fiori/UI5 Testing Experience	As S/4HANA introduces a new UX, familiarity with SAP Fiori test tools (for example, commercial or open source frameworks) is advantageous.
Integration Testing Experience	Experience validating interfaces (for example, EDI, API, and IDoc) with third-party systems is key in modern, hybrid landscapes.
Agile/DevOps Exposure	Understanding how testing fits into sprints, continuous testing, and CI/CD pipelines adds maturity to the test delivery model.
SAP Solution Manager / Focused Build / SAP Cloud ALM	Hands-on experience with these tools helps align test cases with change requests and accelerates traceability.
Data Migration Validation	Skills in comparing legacy data vs. S/4HANA data and supporting mock cutovers boost confidence in project readiness.
Performance & Security Testing	Knowledge of load testing tools (for example, LoadRunner, Neo Load, JMeter) and familiarity with compliance testing (for example, GDPR and SOX).
Industry-Specific Knowledge	Familiarity with domain-specific processes (for example, utilities, manufacturing, and life sciences) improves context-aware testing.

Table 10.11: *SAP Testing Team Capability – Good-to-Have Skills*

The following table highlights some important role-specific skills.

Role	Must-Have Skills	Good-to-Have Skills
Functional Testers	SAP module knowledge, process flows, and test execution.	Data validation, and integration test awareness.
Automation Engineers	Scripting, test framework knowledge, and regression automation.	CI/CD integration, Fiori.
Test Managers/ Leads	Test planning, defect governance, and stakeholder reporting	Risk-based testing, WBS and effort modeling.
Business Users (UAT)	Business process ownership, and UAT scenario execution.	Change impact awareness, basic test logging.
Integration/ Technical Testers	Middleware flow understanding, IDoc/ API testing.	Debugging/ log tracing, and Interface mapping
Data Migration Testers	Reconciliation, and mock cutover testing.	Transformation rule validation, data profiling.

Table 10.12: *SAP Testing Team Capability – Role-specific-skills*

Conclusion

A strong test strategy is the foundation for delivering a stable, high-quality SAP S/4HANA solution. In this chapter, we debunked common myths, outlined the key building blocks of an effective strategy, and explored practical ways to estimate efforts to build the right team.

Up next, we dive into Continuous Testing—where testing becomes part of every step, not just a final phase. You will also see how to accelerate delivery, scale automation, and keep quality embedded throughout your SAP transformation.

References

- https://community.sap.com/t5/enterprise-resource-planning-blogs-by-members/case-study-of-transition-to-sap-s-4hana/ba-p/13542099
- https://blog.sap-press.com/case-study-lessons-learned-from-a-tough-sap-s4hana-implementation
- https://www2.deloitte.com/us/en/pages/technology/articles/sap-case-studies.html
- https://www.slideshare.net/slideshow/unilever-149380450/149380450
- https://www.deloitte.com/de/de/services/risk-advisory/services/data-migration-sap-s-4hana

- https://community.sap.com/t5/enterprise-resource-planning-blogs-by-members/case-study-of-transition-to-sap-s-4hana/ba-p/13542099
- https://www.asug.com/insights/baillie-lumber-takes-on-heavy-lift-of-sap-s-4hana-implementation-part-2
- https://www.asug.com/insights/asug-pulse-of-the-sap-customer-research-sap-users-invest-in-automation-data-analytics-ai-to-accelerate-s-4hana-cloud-migrations
- https://www.asug.com/insights/tips-and-takeaways-for-architecting-electronic-data-interchange-edi-in-sap-s-4hana
- https://www.asug.com/events/ibm-migrates-to-sap-s-4hana-with-rise-using-its-rapid-move-methodology-in-18-months
- https://www.asug.com/events/sap-s-4hana-clean-core-implementation-enabling-efficiencies-for-future-operations
- https://www.asug.com/insights/how-yamaha-motor-drives-organizational-change-management-with-sap-signavio

CHAPTER 11
Continuous Testing

Introduction

The release and maintenance strategy of SAP S/4HANA provides organizations with a stable, predictable framework for managing continuous change. However, to fully realize its benefits, organizations must approach upgrades and updates strategically–not reactively. When upgrades are treated as operational afterthoughts, teams often grapple with technical debts, project delays, compliance risks, and business disruption.

Analyst perspectives reinforce this challenge: Gartner notes that enterprises treating ERP modernization as a series of one-off projects often "*fail to capture innovation at scale*", and instead accumulate costly backlog. Forrester highlights that proactive quality strategies in ERP programs reduce both unplanned downtime and compliance exposure by double-digit percentages. In short, reactive execution translates directly into lost business value, and higher operational risk.

To succeed, enterprises must embrace proactive quality management. This means embedding quality assurance from the outset, aligning program governance with SAP's product roadmap, and fostering a culture of **continuous testing**. By doing so, organizations can evolve their SAP landscape into a true innovation platform, driving business agility and resilience–release by release.

Continuous Testing in a SAP S/4HANA project is the automated, ongoing validation of software quality across the Software Development Lifecycle (SDLC), integrated tightly into DevOps or Agile delivery models. It ensures that a change - whether it is transport, configuration, or enhancement - is validated early, frequently, and comprehensively to reduce risks, increase speed, and maintain compliance even in complex SAP environments.

Structure

This chapter explores the key aspects of continuous testing for SAP S/4HANA, including:

- SAP S/4HANA Release Strategy
- Continuous Testing
- Common Myths
- Core Components of Continuous Testing
- Customer Story #1
- Customer Story #2
- Organizational Change Management for Continuous Testing

SAP S/4HANA Release Strategy

Understanding SAP's release strategy can often feel overwhelming, even for seasoned professionals. The abundance of SAP documentation, sometimes with overlapping or contradictory information, makes it challenging to form a clear, consistent view.

While writing this book, we have encountered exactly that. An information overload which often led to confusion. We have done our best to distill and clarify SAP's release strategy by carefully cross-referencing multiple official sources. However, it is important to note that SAP's release strategy is not static. It evolves almost every year in response to changing customer needs and cloud innovation cycles.

In 2023, SAP introduced a revised release strategy for both SAP S/4HANA Public Cloud and SAP S/4HANA Private Cloud. Here is a brief summary of what changed, and what testing teams need to know.

Release Cycle Overview

- Two major releases a year for SAP S/4HANA Public Cloud that include:
  - **Continuous Feature Delivery (CFD)**: New feature releases - monthly
  - Companies have a choice to activate CFDs when available initially. But these CFDs will automatically get installed in the next release.
- Biennial Base Releases for SAP S/4HANA (Private Cloud) include:
  - A new base release is introduced every two years.
  - Each base release receives mainstream maintenance for seven years.

- **Feature Pack Stacks (FPS)**:
  - Released every six months following a new base release.
  - Introduce non-disruptive, incremental features and enhancements.
- **Support Pack Stacks (SPS)**:
  - Once a subsequent base release is available, the previous release transitions to receiving SPS every six months.
  - SPS focuses solely on corrections, and does not include new functionalities.

Key Points: As a testing team, you are typically looking at 12 releases a year in the SAP S/4HANA public cloud and about 3 in the SAP S/4HANA Private Cloud. The following table provides a summary of the release timelines.

Aspect	SAP S/4HANA Public Cloud	SAP S/4HANA Private Cloud
Release Timelines	2 major releases with monthly CFDs	1 base release every 2 years, with 2 Feature Pack Stacks or 2 Support Pack Stacks every year
1-year view	12 releases/year	2-3 releases/year
3-year view	36 releases	9 - 12 releases

***Table 11.1:** SAP S/4HANA Release Strategy*

As we have explored many times already, in many organizations, SAP S/4HANA does not operate in isolation. When you combine its release cycles with those of other critical enterprise systems such as CRM, HRM, and Integration Platforms, you are typically looking at around 12 major releases per year, and up to 40 releases over a 3-year period. This creates a continuous demand for continuous end-to-end testing to ensure business process stability and integration resilience.

Here is what a typical enterprise release calendar might look like:

- **SAP BTP and SAP Fiori**: 2 releases/year
- **SAP SuccessFactors (HRM)**: 2 releases/year
- **Salesforce (CRM)**: 3 releases/year
- **Workday (HRM)**: 2 releases/year
- ServiceNow, Microsoft Dynamics 365, Oracle Cloud – typically 2 to 4 releases/year

Together, these release cycles underscore the importance of a sustainable test strategy, also known as continuous testing and automation, that can keep up with the pace of change across your digital core.

Pro Tip: *Without automation, how many manual test cycles can your team realistically run?* If a retailer uses SAP S/4HANA Public Cloud plus Salesforce and SuccessFactors, they may face 18+ *updates in a year.*

The following figure illustrates the phases of the SAP Activate methodology, and highlights critical points for testing in an SAP project lifecycle. To accelerate testing in a SAP S/4HANA implementation, companies adopt continuous testing as a strategy to embed validation into every phase of development, from initial configuration to post-deployment. This proactive approach enables early detection of defects and resolution, ensuring higher software quality, reducing risks, and supporting seamless business operations.

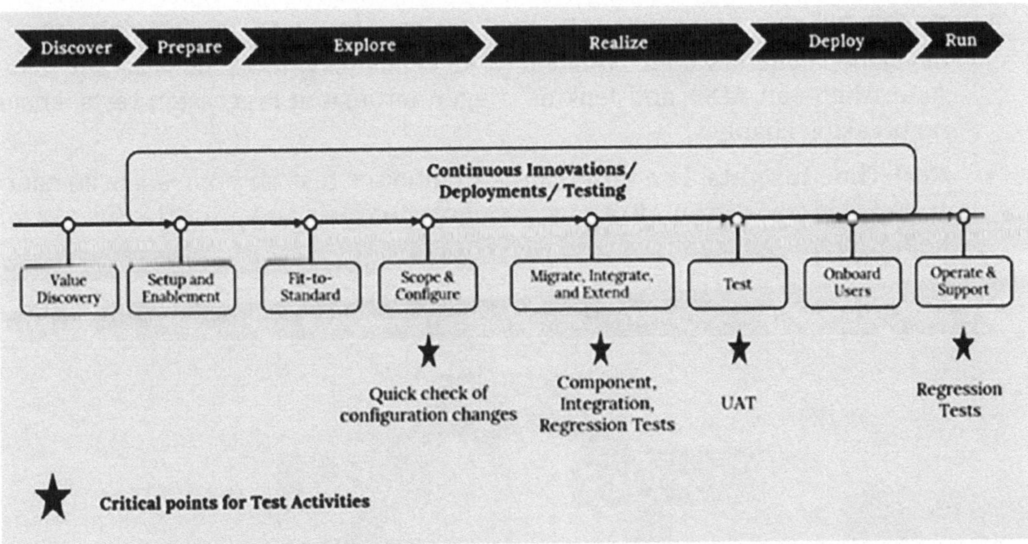

Figure 11.1: *SAP Activate Methodology with Critical Points for Testing*

Pro Tip: *Create a release-readiness matrix that maps critical processes (P2P, OTC, and RTR) against each vendor's release schedule. Align test automation coverage accordingly.*

Continuous Testing

Continuous Testing (CT) in SAP S/4HANA projects is the practice of iteratively validating configurations, custom code (for example, ABAP or Fiori apps), data migrations, and third-party integrations throughout the project lifecycle. Unlike traditional "*big bang*" testing at the end of development, CT embeds quality checks into every phase - from design to post-deployment monitoring. This ensures that risks are identified early, compliance is maintained, and business processes remain uninterrupted.

Core Principles

To succeed in SAP S/4HANA projects, customers adhere to these principles:

- **Early Collaboration:** Involves testers, developers, and business analysts during requirement-gathering. Also includes jointly defined test cases to align with business goals (for example, validating a new financial report's accuracy).
- **Test Automation Framework:** Develop or adopt a framework tailored to SAP's ecosystem. For example, use functional and performance testing tools to automate end-to-end business process validations (for example, order-to-cash).
- **CI/CD Pipeline Integration:** Embed testing into DevOps workflows. When a developer commits code to SAP's ABAP repository, tools such as SAP Cloud ALM, Microsoft ADO, and Jenkins trigger automated regression tests, ensure no breaking changes.
- **Real-Time Insights:** Use dashboards to monitor test outcomes. For instance, track failed transactions in a procurement workflow, and prioritize fixes before deployment.

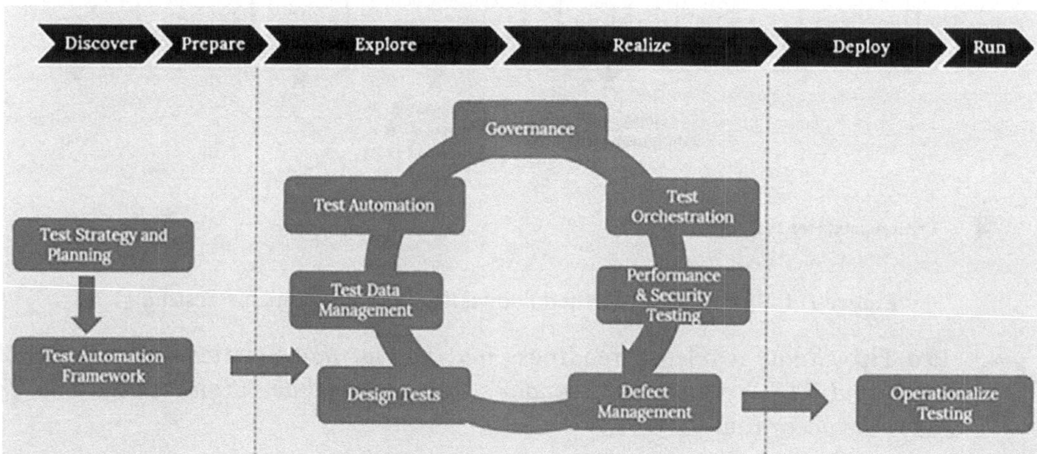

Figure 11.2: *Continuous Testing*

Let us explore a real case study of a retailer. A retailer needed to launch a "`Click and Collect`" (Online Order Fulfilment), requiring real-time stock sync between SAP and their eCommerce platform. Their Continuous Testing approach included test automation, performance testing, and automated test data management.

- **Integration Testing**: Automated scripts validated inventory updates across systems.
- **Performance Testing**: Simulated 10,000 users checking stock levels concurrently.

- **Outcome**: The module launched with a <1-second response time and zero stock mismatches.

As we have studied earlier, SAP S/4HANA projects frequently involve upgrades and customizations. Consider a scenario where a custom-built financial module is updated to align with new regulatory requirements. Continuous testing ensures that the update does not adversely impact the existing functionalities. Automated regression tests are run continuously to confirm that the upgrade maintains system stability, while meeting new business needs.

Common Myths

Continuous testing in SAP S/4HANA projects is an aspiration for many enterprise architects and program management teams. They recognize its potential to accelerate project timelines, reduce business risks, and enhance system reliability. By embedding automated testing across the software development lifecycle, they aim to achieve faster feedback loops, and ensure that business processes remain intact despite frequent system changes.

However, while the vision is clear at the leadership level, project teams often perceive continuous testing as complex and difficult to implement due to some misconceptions. These misconceptions often lead to ineffective test strategies, project delays, and production defects. Let us explore some of the most common myths, and debunk them with real-world insights.

Myth #1: Continuous Testing is Too Complex

Many believe that implementing continuous testing in SAP S/4HANA projects is too complex, requiring extensive automation, advanced tools, and dedicated technical teams. While continuous testing does involve automation, modern tools simplify the process by offering low-code/no-code solutions, AI-powered test generation, and built-in integrations with CI/CD pipelines. By adopting a step-by-step approach, organizations can progressively introduce automation, and scale it efficiently.

Myth #2: Continuous Testing is Only for Technical Teams

A widespread misconception is that continuous testing is solely the responsibility of technical teams. In reality, it requires collaboration between business users, functional consultants, and testers. Business process experts play a crucial role in defining test scenarios, validating automation results, and ensuring that critical workflows function correctly. Without their involvement, test coverage may miss essential business logic, leading to undetected defects.

Pro Tip: *Encourage "Business User Fridays" where functional business users spend 2 hours weekly reviewing automation scripts and validating the results.*

Myth #3: Our SAP Team Takes Care of All the Testing

Sometimes, it is assumed that their SAP teams handle all testing, eliminating the need for additional investment in test automation. However, SAP implementation partners often focus on configuration and deployment, while testing remains the customer's responsibility. Without a well-defined test strategy, organizations risk inadequate test coverage, leading to costly defects in production.

Myth #4: Complex Tooling and Integration Challenges

While tools offer automation capabilities, integrating them seamlessly into CI/CD pipelines and test data management processes requires expertise. Hence, some believe that traditional testing approaches such as manual testing and post-development validation, are sufficient for SAP S/4HANA projects. However, with frequent updates, cloud-based deployments, and evolving business processes, relying solely on traditional testing is risky. Continuous testing ensures early defect detection, faster feedback loops, and greater agility in managing SAP changes.

Myth #5: Perceived Effort versus Benefits

Project teams often prioritize go-live deadlines over automation investments, seeing testing as a one-time phase, rather than a continuous process. This mindset shift is critical to making continuous testing successful.

Ultimately, continuous testing in SAP S/4HANA projects is not just a technical challenge–it is an operational and cultural transformation. Overcoming these barriers requires structured best practices, better tooling adoption, and a shift in mindset from testing as a compliance necessity to testing as a business enabler.

Core Components of Continuous Testing

Continuous testing in SAP S/4HANA requires a well-integrated toolchain to enable a seamless continuous testing experience with robust automation, test data management, CI/CD, and efficient defect tracking. A robust tool stack for Continuous Testing includes:

Test Automation Framework

A robust test automation framework is crucial for accelerating test execution, and reducing manual efforts. In SAP S/4HANA projects, frameworks must support:

- **UI-based Testing**: Using tools such as SAP Fiori Test Automation Tool, Tricentis, Microfocus, Worksoft, and UiPath for automated validation of SAP Fiori applications.
- **API Testing**: Validating OData and SOAP-based services for seamless integration testing.
- **Business Process Testing**: Automating end-to-end business process validation with tools that integrate with SAP Solution Manager and SAP Cloud ALM.

Test Data Management (TDM)

Reliable and secure test data is critical for effective test execution. The key aspects of TDM include:

- **Test Data Automation**: Ensuring that the right test data is available at the right time.
- **Data Masking and Anonymization**: Ensuring compliance with data protection regulations.
- **Synthetic Data Generation**: Wherever possible, creating test data when real production-like data is unavailable.
- **Subset and Refresh Mechanisms**: Providing fresh, relevant test data, while optimizing storage and performance.

Test Environment Management

SAP S/4HANA projects require well-managed test environments that closely mimic production. The key components include:

- **Service Virtualization**: Simulating dependent SAP and non-SAP systems to enable early-stage testing.
- **Environment Monitoring**: Tracking test environment health and performance.

Test Orchestration and Execution

Orchestration tools streamline execution across different test types. These capabilities include:

- **CI/CD Integration**: Automating test execution within SAP DevOps pipelines (for example, integrating with SAP BTP, GitHub Actions, or Jenkins).

- **Parallel Execution**: Running multiple test cases across different environments for faster feedback.
- **AI-driven Execution Optimization**: Using AI-powered tools to prioritize high-impact test cases.

Defect and Test Management

An integrated defect and test management system is necessary for tracking test results and issues:

- **Test Case Management**: Using tools such as Jira, SAP Solution Manager, or ALM tools.
- **Defect Logging and Root Cause Analysis**: Ensuring seamless defect logging process from automation frameworks and quick resolution through effective root cause analysis processes.

Performance and Security Testing

Performance, Security vulnerabilities, and compliance gaps can impact business continuity. Continuous Testing components include:

- **SAST/DAST:** Static and dynamic security testing for SAP custom code.
- **Access Control Testing:** Ensuring that user roles and authorizations are correctly configured.
- **Regulatory Compliance Validation:** Automating compliance checks for GDPR, SOX, and industry-specific regulations.

Customer Story #1

A large mining company successfully transitioned from manual testing to a robust, continuous testing framework as part of their SAP S/4HANA upgrade from 1709 to 2210. Their journey underscores the importance of automation, iterative User Acceptance Testing (UAT), and leveraging SAP tools to improve efficiency and quality.

Background

During their initial SAP ECC to S/4HANA migration, the company heavily relied on manual testing, leading to inefficiencies, extended testing cycles, and a high risk of defects making their way into production. This experience highlighted several points:

- **Extended testing timelines**: Manual execution of over 10,000 UAT test cases was time-consuming and resource intensive.

- **Lack of repeatability**: Ensuring consistency in regression testing was difficult.
- Scalability issues: Increasing the test coverage for critical business processes was constrained by manual efforts.
- **Integration validation challenges**: The company's landscape included multiple integrations, making end-to-end testing complex.
- **Performance bottlenecks**: Testing under real-world load conditions was not feasible with a manual approach.

Determined to overcome these challenges, the company aimed to embed automation into their continuous testing strategy, ensuring a seamless SAP S/4HANA upgrade.

The Solution: Embracing Automation and Continuous Testing

The company's enterprise architecture team, alongside a leading system integrator, devised a plan to integrate test automation and iterative testing into their SAP upgrade program. Their strategy included:

- **Functional Test Automation**: Automating 50% of the most critical and time-consuming test cases using a code-less test automation tool integrated with SAP Solution Manager.
- **Performance Test Automation**: Simulating real-world transaction loads to ensure system stability and scalability.
- **Integration with SAP Solution Manager**: Leveraging Solution Manager's Test Suite for test execution, defect tracking, and reporting.
- **Iterative UAT Cycles**: Conducting frequent UAT iterations, validating standard functionality, reports, data, customizations, and integrations.
- **End-to-End Test Orchestration**: Ensuring business process continuity across SAP and non-SAP applications through automated workflows.

Architecture Overview

The following is a high-level architecture of the tools and technologies enabling continuous testing in this SAP upgrade:

- **SAP Solution Manager**: Centralized test execution and defect management.
- **Functional Test Automation Tools**: Script-less tools for automating business process validation.
- **Performance Testing Tools**: Load simulation to ensure system resilience.

- **CI/CD Pipelines**: Automated build and deployment processes integrating with testing frameworks.
- **Defect Management System**: Integration with Jira for defect tracking and resolution for non-SAP teams.
- **Test Data Management**: RPA tools used for creating data for testing needs.
- **Dashboard**: Microsoft PowerBI used for continuous monitoring of the project and testing needs.

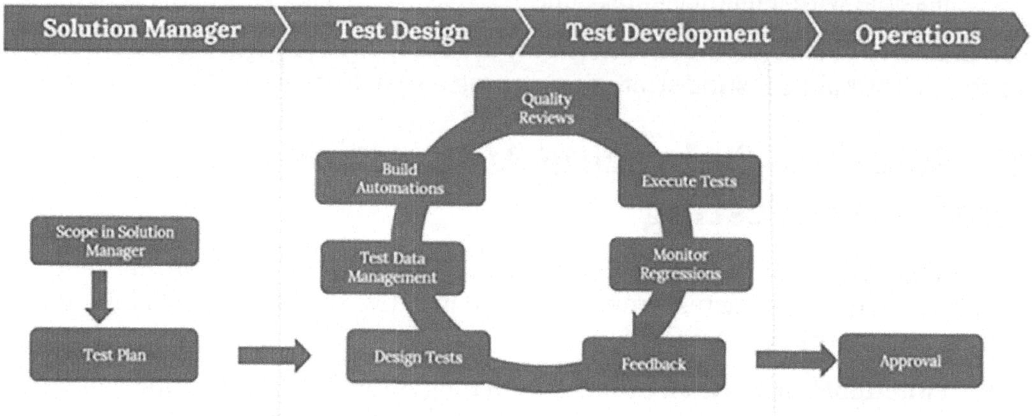

***Figure 11.3:** Case Study #1 – CT Architecture*

Challenges in the Continuous Testing Transition

For this company, transitioning from a traditional manual testing approach to continuous testing was not without challenges, and here are some of the key ones.

- **Skill Gaps**: Though codeless automation tools were chosen, testers still needed training on automation methodologies. Traditional QA teams often lacked SAP process expertise, requiring prolonged support from functional teams.
- **Test Data Management**: Ensuring accurate and consistent test data was complex. Business and functional SMEs had to provide extensive support for data preparation and management.
- **Tool Integration**: Seamless integration between automation tools, SAP Solution Manager, and CI/CD pipelines required technical expertise to ensure smooth execution and reporting.
- **Change Resistance**: Manual testing teams were initially hesitant to embrace automation due to concerns about job security, and the shift in required skill sets.

Results Reported

By adopting this approach, the mining company realized the following significant improvements in their testing process:

- **50% reduction in UAT effort**: Automation of critical test cases reduced manual effort.
- **Accelerated Testing Cycles**: Faster execution of UAT, regression and performance tests.
- **Enhanced Test Coverage**: Broader validation across business processes and integrations.

Best Practices

Based on their experience, the following best practices are recommended for enterprises embarking on a similar journey:

- **Start Small, Scale Gradually**: Begin with high-value test cases before expanding automation.
- **Invest in Training**: Upskill teams in automation frameworks and SAP testing tools.
- **Leverage SAP ALM Tools**: Utilize built-in test management capabilities for streamlined execution.
- **Adopt a Shift-Left Mindset**: Integrate testing earlier in the development cycle.
- **Optimize Test Data Management**: Use synthetic data and automation techniques for creating and managing data.
- **Foster a Culture of Continuous Improvement**: Encourage feedback loops and iterative enhancements.

The company has recently expanded Continuous Testing and Test Automation methodologies to the following programs as well: Microsoft CRM integration with SAP S/4HANA and Supply Chain Transformation.

Customer Story #2

A global food processing corporation with multiple business units across North America embarked on a large-scale SAP S/4HANA migration to streamline operations and unify business processes. Following significant acquisitions, the company found itself managing multiple legacy ERP systems, which created inefficiencies, inconsistencies, and high operational costs.

Background

Before transitioning to SAP S/4HANA, the company operated on a fragmented ERP landscape that included:

- **SAP ECC (Central Finance and Supply Chain Management)**: Used by the core business unit before acquisitions.
- **Oracle E-Business Suite (EBS)**: Used by one of the acquired companies for financials and procurement.
- **Microsoft Dynamics AX**: Supporting regional supply chain operations in select geographies.
- **JD Edwards EnterpriseOne**: Used for manufacturing and inventory management by another acquired entity.
- **Infor M3**: Primarily used for food safety compliance and regulatory reporting.

Each of these ERPs had different testing strategies, leading to silos, inefficiencies, and high maintenance costs.

Challenges

The decision to overhaul the QA strategy alongside the ERP transformation exposed critical pain points that threatened the success of the migration:

- **Risk of Fragmented Processes and Test Data Chaos:** Merging five ERPs–each with unique data models, workflows, and reporting logic–into a single SAP S/4HANA instance demanded flawless alignment of supply chain, financial, and manufacturing data. Legacy system disparities risked corrupted migrations, broken processes, and compliance gaps.
- **Lack of Standardized Testing Approach:** Each ERP operated in its own QA silo: Oracle EBS teams relied on Waterfall-driven scripts, Dynamics AX used Agile frameworks, and JD Edwards had no formal testing standards. This inconsistency created conflicting timelines, unrepeatable tests, and critical testing blind spots.
- **Testing Tools:** Over six commercial test automation tools and four test management tools were in use, yet a significant portion of testing remained manual and untraceable, and quality reviews were lacking.
- **High Total Cost of Ownership (TCO):** Duplicative tools, fragmented test environments, and redundant BU-specific QA teams inflated TCO by 40%. Delays from poor cross-team coordination further escalated risks of budget overruns and post-migration defects.

The Testing Strategic Solution

To address these challenges, the company viewed testing as part of its overall consolidation strategy:

- **Unified Test Automation Framework:** Consolidated all test automation initiatives under a single, enterprise-wide platform, replacing multiple legacy tools used across business units.
- **Standardized Test Processes:** Created a central test governance model to ensure that all business units followed the same test management, execution, reporting standards, and cross-BU alignment.
- **Shared Testing Resources:** Consolidated testing teams to operate as a centralized quality engineering function, reducing the need for redundant roles in each business unit.

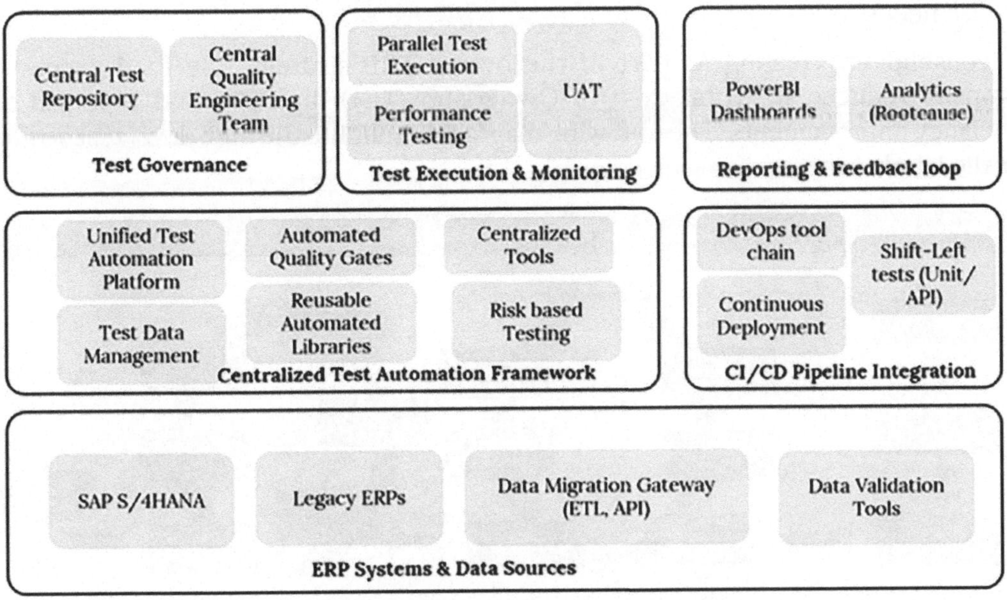

Figure 11.4: *Case Study #2 – System Strategy*

Continuous Testing Implementation

- **Test Coverage Optimization**: By leveraging test unification principles, QA teams have reviewed and migrated all business-critical tests into new test frameworks.
- **CI/CD Integration:** Integrated automated testing with DevOps pipelines to support continuous integration and delivery.

- **Shift-Left Testing Approach:** Focused on early-stage testing by embedding quality checks into development processes (for example, financial reconciliation, and supply chain integrations)
- **Risk-Based Testing:** Prioritized test execution based on business-critical processes, and areas with the highest likelihood of defects.
- **Automated Regression Testing:** Established a robust regression suite to validate new releases and configurations before deployment.
- **Business User Training:** Empowering business users with low-code/no-code test automation tools to enable citizen testing.
- **AI-Powered Test Automation:** Exploring AI-driven test case generation and self-healing automation frameworks.
- **Performance and Load Testing:** Implementing performance testing strategies using JMeter to ensure that the SAP S/4HANA environment meets business needs.

By consolidating testing as part of the overall ERP strategy, the food processing company reduced its Total Cost of Ownership (TCO) by 35%, and reported test efficiency improvements. The following diagram highlights the high-level test strategy for the whole program.

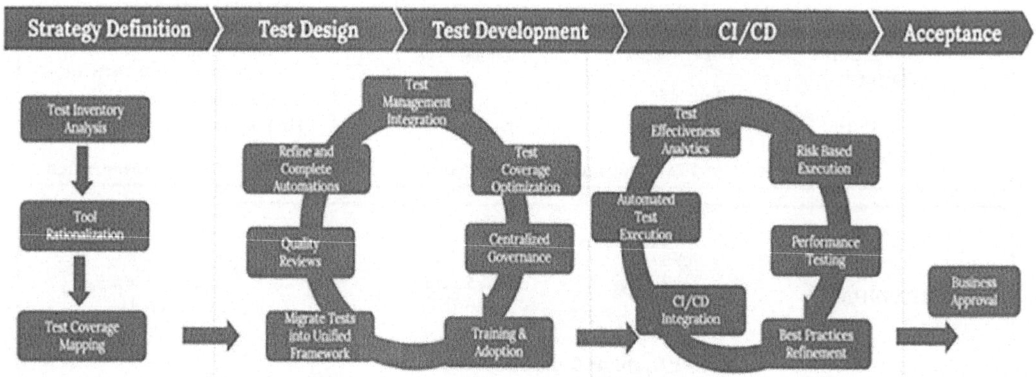

Figure 11.5: *Case Study #2 – Continuous Development and Testing Approach for Test Migrations*

Organizational Change Management for Continuous Testing

In traditional SAP projects, testing is typically reactive, manual, and limited to predefined project phases. Continuous testing, however, requires a shift in mindset—where testing becomes a proactive, automated, and integrated activity throughout the software delivery lifecycle. A global manufacturing company was transitioning its SAP S/4HANA testing team from predominantly manual testing to a more automated continuous testing approach. Despite selecting user-friendly, low-code automation tools, many testers were hesitant to embrace automation, fearing complexity, job displacement, or lack of technical skills. To overcome resistance and accelerate automation adoption, the QA leadership organized a week-long internal "*Automation Hackathon*" focused on empowering testers to create and showcase small but impactful automation wins.

This section explores the organizational challenges, and outlines best practices for embracing continuous testing through effective change management.

Key Challenges

Transitioning from traditional SAP testing to continuous testing often encounters resistance due to several factors:

- **Mindset Shift:** Teams accustomed to manual testing may resist automation, fearing complexity.
- **Skill Gaps:** Continuous testing requires expertise in automation, CI/CD, and SAP-specific tools.
- **Organization Siloes:** SAP functional teams, testing teams, and DevOps often work in isolation, slowing down test execution.
- **Tool Overload**: Organizations struggle to choose the right test automation and management tools.
- **Test Data and Environment Issues:** Reliable test data is crucial for automation, but many teams face challenges in maintaining up-to-date, production-like test data.
- **Lack of Executive Buy-in:** Without leadership support, continuous testing initiatives may be underfunded or deprioritized.

Understanding these challenges is the first step toward managing change effectively.

Best Practices

1. **Build Awareness and Secure Executive Buy-In**

   Sustained success with continuous testing starts at the top. Executive champions are essential for funding, prioritizing, and removing organizational roadblocks.

   - Faster SAP S/4HANA upgrades and rollouts.
   - Reduced business disruption due to proactive defect detection.
   - Higher test coverage with automation.
   - How to achieve executive buy-in.

a. Showcase case studies where continuous testing led to tangible business benefits (for example, reduced testing cycles and fewer production defects).

b. Align testing objectives with broader business goals such as agility, compliance, and risk reduction.

c. Present a roadmap demonstrating how continuous testing will integrate with the existing processes.

2. **Foster a Culture of Quality across Functions**

   Continuous testing must become a shared responsibility—not one owned solely by QA or test teams. Driving cross-functional engagement is the key.

   - **Best Practices:**

     a. Establish a "*Shift-Left*" testing culture where testing is considered at the requirement and design stages, not just before go-live.

     b. Create cross-functional teams that include testers, business analysts, and developers.

     c. Encourage business process owners to participate in UAT automation.

     d. Provide incentives for teams that successfully implement automation-driven testing.

Pro Tip: *Use gamification. For example, teams with the lowest defect leakage or highest automation coverage could be rewarded. This fosters healthy competition around quality.*

3. **Upskill and Reskill SAP Testing Teams**

   Upskilling is the cornerstone of adoption. Continuous testing relies on diverse competencies across automation, business logic, and system integration.

   - Provide hands-on training in SAP automation tools.
   - Provide workshops on SAP functional, and data management.
   - Educate teams on CI/CD, Agile, and DevOps concepts to align testing with modern development practices.
   - Offer certifications and encourage "*learning by doing*" through pilot projects.

4. **Address Test Data and Environment Management**

   Even a robust automation framework will fail without reliable, dynamic test data, and viable non-production systems.

   - Synthetic test data generation to simulate various business scenarios.

- Test data provisioning with anonymization to comply with data privacy regulations (for example, GDPR).
- Automated test environment setup for SAP landscapes using cloud-based environments or containers.

5. **Establish Metrics and Continuous Feedback Loops**

   Measuring what matters helps teams analyze, impact and drive continuous improvement.

   - **Defect leakage rate**: Number of defects found in production versus testing
   - **Test automation coverage**: Percentage of automated versus manual test cases.
   - **Time-to-test execution**: How fast tests run compared to traditional methods.
   - A feedback-driven approach ensures continuous improvement. Automated dashboards (SAP Solution Manager, SAP Cloud ALM) can provide visibility into test effectiveness.

Pro Tip: *Track not only coverage but also automation failure recovery time - how fast a failed script is fixed. This metric directly correlates with automation* ROI.

Conclusion

In this chapter, we explored how aligning testing strategies with SAP's release roadmap helps organizations manage change proactively, rather than reactively. We defined continuous testing as an automated, ongoing process built into a project that validates changes early, and this often reduces errors as well as speeds up delivery. We also addressed common misconceptions, shared success stories, and highlighted the real-world value of making testing a continuous, integrated part of your SAP program.

Importantly, we emphasized that tools alone are not enough. A successful shift to continuous testing requires organizational change - teams must embrace new mindsets, update skillsets, and break down silos to build a true culture of quality.

With continuous testing as the foundation, the next step is to implement the best practices that help build a sustainable, enterprise-wide Quality Assurance (QA) program for SAP S/4HANA. We will also explore that next.

References

- https://news.sap.com/2022/09/new-sap-s4hana-release-maintenance-strategy/
- https://podcast.opensap.info/inside-sap/2025/02/26/episode-118-upgrades-in-sap-s-4hana-cloud-private-edition/
- https://blog.sap-press.com/testing-sap-s4hana-cloud-implementations
- https://learning.sap.com/learning-journeys/implementing-sap-s-4hana-cloud-private-edition/navigating-release-upgrades_ae2d796c-bafd-4e04-8b41-562ebda9eb49
- https://www.sap.com/documents/2022/11/dcd7890b-517e-0010-bca6-c68f7e60039b.html
- https://help.sap.com/whats-new/5fc51e30e2744f168642e26e0c1d9be1?Version=2023&locale=en-US
- https://help.sap.com/docs/sap-cloud-for-customer/sap-cloud-for-customer-release-dates-and-timelines/release-schedule-and-dates-for-2024
- https://help.sap.com/docs/sap-cloud-for-customer/sap-cloud-for-customer-release-dates-and-timelines/release-schedule-and-dates-for-2025
- https://community.sap.com/t5/technology-blogs-by-members/difference-between-sap-s-4hana-public-vs-private-edition-rise-with-sap/ba-p/13546250
- https://help.sap.com/docs/sap-cloud-for-customer/sap-cloud-for-customer-release-dates-and-timelines/general-upgrade-information
- https://www.youtube.com/watch?v=P4RzUMLwi48

CHAPTER 12
Best Practices

Introduction

Industry-research reveal that up to 55–80% of SAP S/4HANA testing projects face major setbacks such as cost overruns, delays, or failing to meet business objectives within their first year. For example, a 2024 SAP customer study found only 36% of the project stayed on their original plan, while nearly half (48%) failed to scale up to their intended business goals. SAP projects are uniquely vulnerable because of their complexity, reliance on quality test data, and demanding integrations.

Following time-tested best practices in SAP testing are essential for making teams and processes more resilient. Reliable testing fuelled by effective automation, rigorous data management, and proactive governance help reduce risks, and accelerate upgrades.

Structure

This chapter delves into the best practices shared by successful SAP testing leaders, offering insights on building scalable and effective test programs. The aspects of testing covered in this chapter include:

- Test Environment
- Test Architecture
- Test Automation
- Automating Business Processes with Batch Jobs
- Defect Triaging
- Optimizing Total Cost of Ownership

Test Environment

Every SAP S/4HANA ecosystem is an integrated landscape that includes multiple SAP and non-SAP systems such as SAP ERP, SAP Business Technology Platform (BTP), SAP Ariba, Salesforce, and several third-party applications. A poorly planned test environment can lead to test failures, data inconsistencies, and delays in deployment cycles. This section outlines the best practices to establish a reliable, scalable, and high-quality test environment tailored to SAP S/4HANA landscapes.

Align Environments with the SAP Landscape Strategy:

- Ensure that the test environment aligns with SAP's 3-system landscape (Development, Quality, and Production) or 4-system landscape (Development, Sandbox, Quality, and Production) for better risk management.
- Set up additional sandboxes or innovation environments, if frequent Proof-of-Concepts (POCs) are needed.

Data Consistency across SAP and Non-SAP Systems:

- Use production-like test data to ensure realistic testing scenarios.
- Implement automated data refresh cycles from production to non-production environments, while ensuring data masking for security compliance.
- **Example:** For a supply chain scenario where SAP S/4HANA integrates with an external Warehouse Management System (WMS), ensure test data replication across both systems to prevent inconsistencies in inventory testing.

Stable and Isolated Test System Configurations:

- Ensure dedicated test systems for System Integration Testing (SIT), regression testing, and User Acceptance Testing (UAT) to avoid conflicts.
- Use client-independent configurations where possible to minimize the risk of test contamination.
- **Example:** In a SAP S/4HANA finance implementation, separate client configurations should be maintained to test different financial periods independently.

Service Virtualization or Mocking for External Dependencies:

- Use service virtualization tools to simulate unavailable SAP and non-SAP systems, reducing delays in test execution.
- **Example:** If a SAP S/4HANA system integrates with a third-party banking API that is not available in the test environment, simulate API responses to enable continuous testing.

Test Data Management and Anonymization:

- Implement test data provisioning automation to create reusable datasets across test cycles.
- Use data masking techniques to protect sensitive information in GDPR-compliant industries.
- Implement AI or Automation-based Solutions to enable Self-Provisioning of data for QA teams.

- **Example:** For SAP SuccessFactors payroll testing, anonymize employee salary data, while maintaining realistic data structures.

Automatic Outage Monitoring and Defect Notifications:

- Implement automated system/data availability monitoring to detect and report outages in real-time.
- Use event-driven notifications integrated with collaboration tools such as Microsoft Teams or Slack to alert stakeholders instantly.
- **Example:** If a SAP S/4HANA system goes down during integration testing with a third-party CRM, an automated alert should notify the test manager, and trigger defect logging in tools such as Jira or ServiceNow, saving significant troubleshooting time.

Test Architecture

With modern test architecture, industry data shows that automated SAP testing solutions reduce testing time by up to 45%, and integration defects by as much as 60%. This section highlights the five most essential best practices for SAP test architecture in S/4HANA environments. These imperatives enable robust automation, seamless team collaboration, and rigorous QA integration, driving sustainable value across the SAP lifecycle.

End-to-End Test Coverage across Integrated Systems

A fragmented testing approach can lead to defects in production due to overlooked integrations.

- Design an end-to-end testing strategy that covers all integrated systems, ensuring data consistency and process integrity.
- Use a combination of API testing, middleware validations, and UI-based automation to verify integration points.
- **Example:** In a project where SAP S/4HANA was integrated with Ariba and a legacy procurement system, automated API tests validated the flow of purchase requisitions that can potentially accelerate test cycles by over 70%, and reduce integration defects by 60%.

Automation-First Approach for Regression Testing

Frequent SAP updates and business process changes require a scalable test automation strategy to ensure continuous quality.

- Prioritize automating high-frequency test cases such as regression suites, master data validations, and high-volume transactions.

- Leverage SAP-certified automation tools to create resilient automated test scripts.
- **Example:** A manufacturing company automated 80% of their regression suite, cutting testing cycles from three weeks to three days, enabling faster SAP upgrade adoption.

Integrated Test Management with ALM Tools

Managing test cases, defects, and test execution results efficiently is critical to maintaining traceability and compliance in SAP S/4HANA projects.

- Use SAP Solution Manager or Cloud ALM to centralize test case design, execution tracking, and defect management.
- Implement test data management practices to maintain consistency across different environments.

Skilled Test Teams and Continuous Training

Capgemini's World Quality Report 2024 found that **66% of successful SAP testing programs train functional consultants on automation basics, enabling hybrid skill sets.**

- Invest in training for SAP functional and technical testers on tools such as test automation tools, and API testing frameworks.
- Promote collaboration between functional consultants, test architects, and automation engineers to enhance test case design.
- **Example:** An energy company adopted a Test Center of Excellence (TCoE) model, training business users and technical testers on automation, leading to a 30% reduction in the manual testing effort.

Seamless QA Integration into SAP Activate Methodology

Testing cannot be an afterthought, but a continuous process integrated into SAP Activate phases.

- **Align QA Activities with SAP Activate Phases:** Prepare (Test Strategy), Explore (Test Capability), Realize (System Integration Testing, UAT), Deploy (Cutover Testing), and Run (Regression Testing).

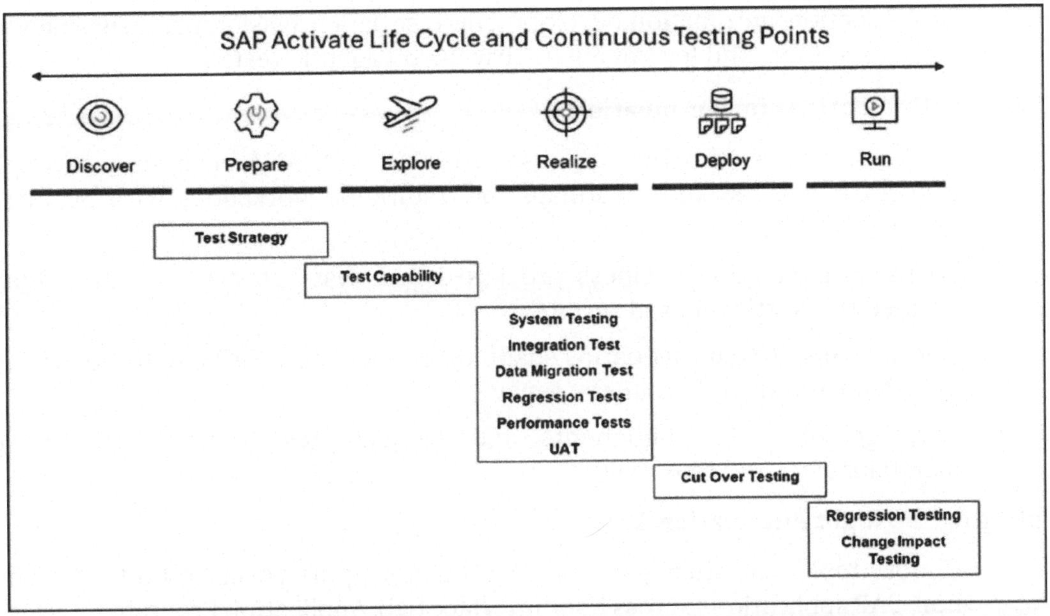

Figure 12.1: *SAP Activate and Continuous Quality Checkpoints*

- **Implement Shift-Left Testing** to identify defects early by involving QA in blueprinting, and configuration validation.
- **Example:** A logistics company embedded Test-driven Development (TDD) practices in their SAP business process implementation, identifying 40% of critical defects during the Realize phase, reducing go-live risks.

Adopting these best practices in SAP test architecture ensures reliable, high-quality SAP S/4HANA implementations, while minimizing defects and project delays. By integrating test automation, robust test management, skilled teams, and seamless QA integration, organizations can enhance the resilience and performance of their SAP landscapes. A well-defined SAP test architecture is the foundation for delivering business value, while ensuring system stability and compliance.

Test Automation

A recent industry research report from Data Insights shows that 28% of leading SAP organizations have already implemented automated testing tools for S/4HANA migrations or upgrades. Test automation is consistently cited among the most effective levers for reducing project risks and release timelines. Organizations adopting SAP's continuous release strategy must move beyond ad-hoc test automation efforts, and implement a well-thought-through test automation program that delivers sustainable outcomes.

This section outlines the best practices in SAP test automation, covering aspects such as tool selection, automation development, test data provisioning, maintenance, orchestrated execution, and leveraging AI-driven and agentic testing.

Strategic Foundations for Automation:

- Understand how your business uses the SAP S/4HANA ecosystem through process models, system heatmaps, or traditional workshops with business users.
- Focus on high-value business process-driven test automation, rather than isolated transaction-based scripts.
- Prioritize end-to-end scenarios spanning SAP and non-SAP integrations such as order-to-cash and procure-to-pay.
- Leverage reusable components and modular test design to improve maintainability and reusability.

Selecting the Right Automation Tools:

- Choose tools that offer deep SAP S/4HANA support covering both SAP, and non-SAP applications across User Interface (UI), Application Program Interface (API), and Database layers.
- Ensure compatibility with Fiori applications, SAP GUI, SAP Web, Web Services, and API-based integrations.
- Evaluate AI-powered tools for self-healing automation and autonomous test execution.
- If a significant portion of your automated tests cover SAP Web applications, evaluate the effectiveness of your automation tools on SAP Fiori applications, particularly in handling Smart List Boxes and Lazy Loading objects.

Test Development Best Practices across SAP Applications:

- **SAP Fiori:** Automate dynamic smart controls, pop-ups, and filter elements efficiently with dynamic (AI-based) locators.
- **SAP GUI:** Handle modal windows, ALV grids, Menu bar, Toolbar, and Status bar controls with screen-independent selectors so that they can be reused across all test cases.
- **SAP Web:** Automate dynamic SAP web elements with support for dynamic elements and lazy-loaded components. Use context time outs and hard-coded waits to handle application response.
- **SuccessFactors:** Automate transactions efficiently with reusable modules, while managing complex object types such as dropdowns, list boxes, and search-based selection fields. For example, create reusable components for personal information, advertising details, work calendar details, and so on.

- **Recommendations:** Avoid reliance on custom testing frameworks for SAP applications as their maintenance costs significantly increase over time, making them unsustainable beyond a few release cycles.

Pro Tip: *Do not automate what changes every sprint. Instead, automate high-value processes with stable business impact.*

Automation of Data Provisioning:

- Establish synthetic test data generation where it is feasible to create realistic business scenarios.
- Utilize data masking techniques to comply with GDPR, and other regulatory requirements.
- **Example:** Automating the creation of vendor master data with variations in tax codes and payment terms to support regression testing.

Efficient Test Maintenance:

- Implement self-healing mechanisms (predictive and cognitive) to reduce maintenance efforts when UI or APIs change.
- Maintain a central test repository with versioning for tracking test script changes.
- Use dynamic locators and AI-based test object recognition to reduce script failures.
- **Example:** Using AI-based locators to automatically adapt test scripts when SAP Fiori UI changes.
- Decouple Object (Object Repository) and Data (Test Data Management) from automated tests improve design, and reduce maintenance significantly.

Orchestrated Execution across SAP and Non-SAP Systems:

- Implement CI/CD pipelines integrating SAP test automation with DevOps tools (for example, Jenkins, Azure DevOps, and so on).
- Execute cross-system test orchestration, covering SAP, Salesforce, and legacy applications.
- Schedule test runs with data-driven triggers to optimize execution efficiency.
- **Example:** Running automated payroll verification tests by orchestrating test data in the SAP SuccessFactors, SAP S/4HANA, and external banking systems.

Leveraging AI and Agentic Testing:

- Use AI-based capabilities available in SAP, and test automation tools to accelerate test activities such as design tests for nearly 100% coverage, and build automations for standard functionalities.

- Identify test failures caused by dynamic UI changes.
- Implement agentic test execution where bots intelligently select and run relevant test cases based on business risk analysis.
- **Example:** Using AI-powered impact analysis to determine which test cases need execution after an SAP S/4HANA upgrade.

Performance Testing Best Practices:

- Design realistic load scenarios based on actual user behavior and transaction volumes. Use process models or heat maps to gain insights into realistic load scenarios.
- Use performance tools with SAP-specific plugins to simulate SAP GUI, Fiori, and web-based transactions.
- Include end-to-end performance validation covering SAP S/4HANA, middleware, and integrated third-party systems.
- Continuously monitor and benchmark performance to detect performance degradation over multiple release cycles.
- **Example:** Conduct stress testing on a SAP S/4HANA procurement system to validate system behavior under peak demand conditions.

Pro Tip: *Pair automated regression with manual exploratory SAP testing. Automation accelerates coverage, but human testers uncover contextual business issues, where automation will not do so.*

Automating Business Processes with Batch Jobs

Batch jobs are critical components in every SAP landscape, playing a pivotal role in automating and executing business processes efficiently in production environments. Testing these business processes in conjunction with the batch jobs in Pre-Prod environments is necessary to ensure accurate operation, and minimize business disruption.

Pro Tip: *Always validate downstream process completion after a batch job executes. For example, when testing payroll jobs in SAP HCM running nightly, validate net salary postings in FI/CO to ensure that financial integration has not broken downstream.*

Understanding SAP Batch Jobs

A batch job in SAP is a scheduled background process designed to execute specific tasks without requiring user intervention. These jobs are particularly useful for handling large volumes of data processing, automating routine tasks, and optimizing system performance during off-peak hours. SAP's Background Processing System efficiently manages batch jobs, ensuring operational continuity, and resource optimization.

For example, let us consider a SAP business process as shown in the following figure where a couple of activities rely on batch jobs to complete before proceeding further.

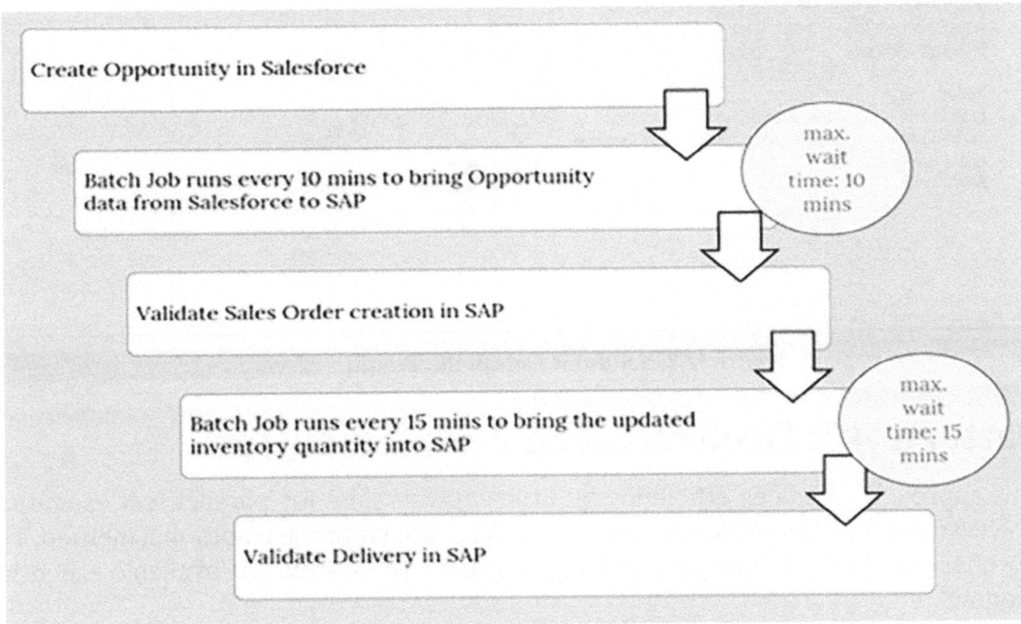

Figure 12.2: *A Simple Business Process with Batch Jobs*

To ensure accurate and efficient test automation for such a process, we commonly see three design patterns. For explaining these patterns in simple terms, let us consider a typical scenario where the automated tests for Create Opportunity, Sales Order, and Delivery processes, each require approximately 10 minutes to execute completely.

Pattern #1: Traditional (Manual Test Replica)

This method employs hard-coded wait times, pausing test execution until the batch job completes. It mimics manual testing but is inefficient due to its reliance on fixed time intervals.

- **Total Turnaround Time**: ***55 minutes*** (10 mins + 10 mins + 10 min + 15 mins + 10 mins)

- **Challenges:**
  - If batch job schedules change, test execution efficiency is negatively impacted.
  - Inflexible and inefficient.

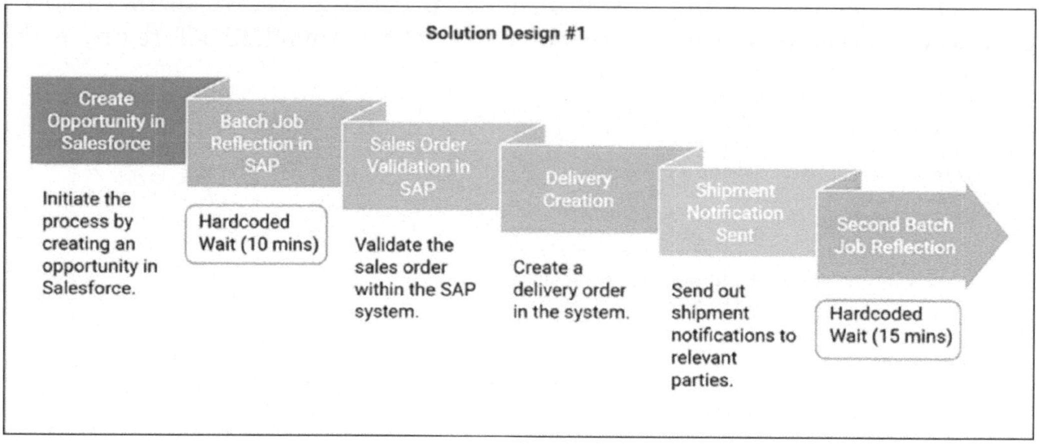

Figure 12.3: *Solutions Design the Traditional Way*

Pattern #2: Orchestrated Test Execution

This approach enhances efficiency by utilizing wait time for parallel test execution. However, it still requires 55 minutes to complete, similar to the traditional method. The key challenge lies in identifying and aligning test cases within the available execution window.

- Total Turnaround Time: **55 *minutes***
- **Advantages**: While the test execution waits for the batch job to complete, the orchestration engine can reuse the computing resources to execute another test case.
- **Challenges**:
  - Requires test cases that fit within execution windows.
  - Dependency on test orchestration and coordination.

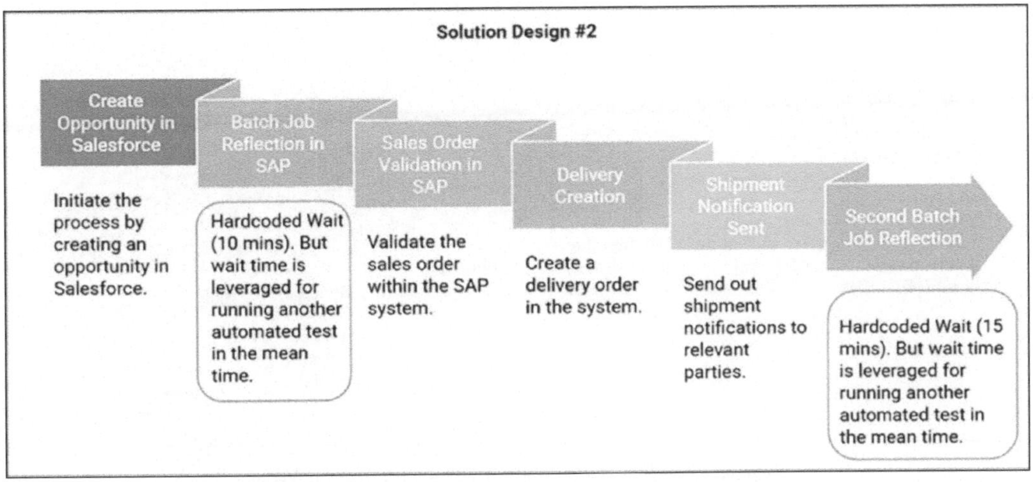

Figure 12.4: *Solutions Design the Orchestrated Execution Way*

Pattern #3: Optimized (On-Demand Batch Execution)

This solution eliminates predefined scheduling dependencies by triggering batch jobs on demand. Automating batch execution significantly reduces testing time, and increases efficiency.

- Total Turnaround Time: **30 minutes** (*25 minutes faster than other approaches*)
- **Advantages**:
    - Highly efficient and scalable.
    - Adaptable to changes in batch intervals.
    - Less maintenance effort compared to scheduled batch testing.
- **How to Achieve It:**
    - Use the following T-codes or Fiori apps to automate the execution of batch jobs: SM36, SM37, SM50, SM66, Schedule Background Job, and Monitor Jobs.

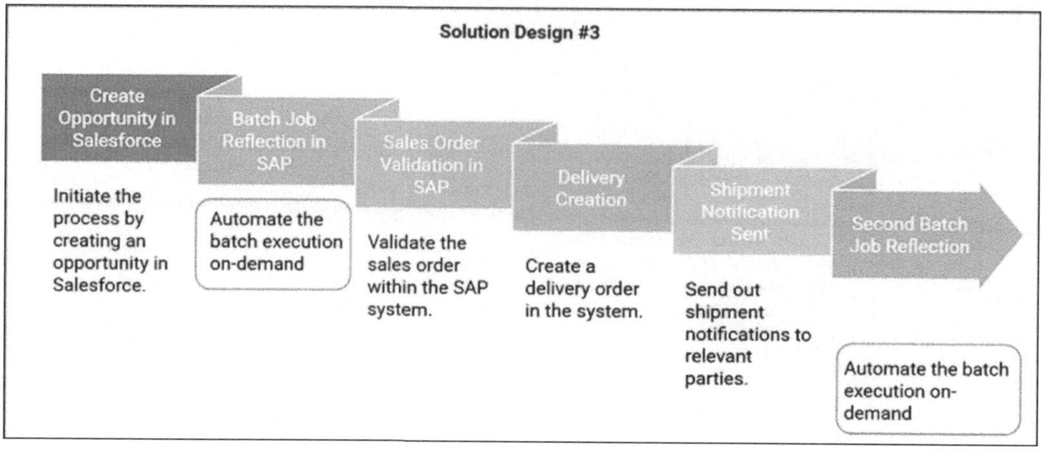

Figure 12.5: *Solutions Design the Optimized Way*

Comparative Analysis:

Design Approach	Turnaround Time	Efficiency	Scalability	Flexibility
Traditional (Hardcoded Wait)	55 mins	Low	Low	Low
Orchestrated Execution	55 mins	Medium	Medium	Medium
Optimized (On-Demand)	30 mins	High	High	High

Table 12.1: *Batch Job Test Design and Comparison*

The choice of test automation design depends on the specific business needs, team expertise, and the complexity of the SAP environment. The Optimized "*on-demand batch execution*" solution provides the best combination of efficiency, flexibility, and future-proofing for dynamic SAP landscapes. While it requires advanced SAP knowledge, it significantly reduces test execution time, and ensures greater adaptability to batch job schedule changes.

Businesses aiming for scalable and efficient test automation should prioritize the on-demand approach to achieving optimal results, while maintaining seamless SAP operations.

Defect Triaging

Defect triaging is crucial to the success of any testing project. Industry research highlights that organizations with mature triaging processes achieve up to 40% faster defect resolution, and 30% fewer escaped defects reaching production compared to those without systematic triaging approaches. In the context of large-scale SAP transformations, these improvements are essential for controlling project costs, and minimizing disruption.

The Impact of Effective Triaging: A Case Study

During a recent global SAP S/4HANA implementation, a persistent issue emerged where sales order and delivery data were mismatched between SAP and a third-party CRM system. Initial analysis pointed to an interface problem.

However, through meticulous log analysis during the triaging process, QA experts uncovered something unexpected - a data truncation issue within an ABAP routine. This discovery not only solved the immediate problem but also improved the entire data flow between systems. This case demonstrates the power of thorough defect triaging.

Five Proven Techniques for Effective Defect Triaging

1. **System Log Analysis**
    - **Utilize System Logs**: SAP provides powerful diagnostic tools such as ST22 (for dump analysis) and SM21 (for system logs) that can reveal the root cause of issues.
    - **Leverage Monitoring Tools**: Industry leaders implement SAP Cloud ALM, Solution Manager, or external monitoring tools to capture the runtime data. Research has documented instances where these tools identified memory leaks in Finance module batch jobs that would have been impossible to spot otherwise.
2. **Cross-Module Validation**
    - **Collaborate across Domains**: Successful QA teams engage functional consultants to validate process flows across modules. Studies show that in complex implementations, what appears as a defect in one module is often caused by configuration issues in another. In one documented case, a defect in Order-to-Cash was traced to incorrect tax code mapping in the Finance module - a discovery only possible through cross-module validation.
3. **Effective Test Case Design**
    - **Test Design Techniques**: Leading testing teams use boundary value analysis and equivalence partitioning to identify edge cases. For example, when testing the Sales and Distribution module, effective testing includes checking pricing scenarios at both minimum ($0.01) and maximum ($10,000.00) allowed values.
    - **Include Negative Testing**: Research confirms that tests deliberately pushing systems beyond normal parameters consistently uncover hidden vulnerabilities that would otherwise reach production.

4. **End-to-End Business Process Testing**

    - **Create Comprehensive Scenarios**: Enterprise testing frameworks now routinely develop test cases that reflect complete business processes. A properly designed Order-to-Cash test should flow from sales order creation through inventory checks to final billing.
    - **Track Integration Points**: Data analysis from multiple SAP implementations confirms that integration points between modules represent the highest concentration of defects. Successful testing strategies emphasize these handoff points.

5. **Leverage Test Automation Insights**

    - **Implement Repetition:** Industry research validates that executing the same process repeatedly reveals intermittent issues. In a documented production planning scenario, automation identified a timing issue in job scheduling that only occurred under specific conditions - an issue manual testing had repeatedly missed.

Pro Tip: *Encourage triaging sessions to always ask - what module could have caused this defect instead of where it appeared? This mindset prevents siloed* Root Cause Analysis (RCA), *and often accelerates resolution timelines by weeks.*

Optimizing Total Cost of Ownership

As organizations embrace SAP's continuous release model, the Total Cost of Ownership (TCO) of testing becomes a critical factor influencing project success. A comprehensive TCO optimization approach encompasses test automation, tool consolidation, AI-driven testing, and robust test data management. Each of these aspects are vital in reducing costs, accelerating delivery, and maintaining software resilience.

Leveraging Test Automation for Cost Efficiency

Manual testing is time-consuming, resource-intensive, and prone to inefficiencies. With SAP S/4HANA's continuous release cycles, manual regression testing becomes unsustainable, leading to increased risk, prolonged test cycles, and high maintenance costs.

- Embrace automated regression and end-to-end testing methodology to accelerate feedback loops.
- Use orchestrated test runs by enabling agile delivery and continuous integration.

- Automation enables early identification of defects, and significantly lowers the cost of late-stage fixes, reducing technical debt.

Consolidating Test Automation Tools

Even with automation in place, organizations often struggle with tool sprawl, using multiple test frameworks across business units. This fragmented approach leads to inefficiencies, higher maintenance efforts, and increased costs.

- A unified test platform can eliminate redundant expenses in licensing and infrastructure costs.
- Standardizing on a selective toolset fosters deeper expertise and higher productivity within test teams.
- A consolidated toolchain enables smooth execution of UI, API, and performance tests, reducing complexity in SAP landscapes.

For example, an enterprise using separate tools for UI, API, and performance testing can achieve significant cost and efficiency gains by migrating to an integrated automation suite.

Implementing AI-Powered Testing Tools

AI-powered test automation introduces a paradigm shift by leveraging AI-driven autonomous agents to intelligently adapt to system changes, and proactively automate risk mitigation. This approach reduces test maintenance overhead, while enhancing test effectiveness.

- Code-less, AI-powered tools empower manual testers and business users to actively contribute to testing and automation.
- AI-driven scripts dynamically adjust to UI and workflow changes, minimizing failures due to SAP Fiori and backend updates.
- AI solutions can prioritize test cases based on business risk, ensuring critical functions are validated first.
- Advanced analytics detect defect patterns, preventing recurring issues in SAP upgrades.
- Reduced Resource Dependence: Intelligent automation minimizes manual intervention in script execution and monitoring.

Agentic automation is particularly valuable for enterprises undergoing cloud migrations or ERP consolidations, where evolving business processes necessitate adaptive and resilient testing strategies.

Enhancing Test Data Management (TDM)

Poor test data takes way over 30% of the test execution cycle time in SAP landscapes. Test Data Management (TDM) strategy is crucial for ensuring high-quality, consistent, and compliant data availability for testing.

- Automate test data generation and masking to streamline test setup.
- Set up TDM strategies to help comply with data privacy regulations such as GDPR.
- Simulate production-like test data without exposing sensitive information.
- Regularly update the test data to reflect real-world scenarios.
- Maintain a unified data management system to reduce duplication and inconsistencies.

Implementing Risk-Based Testing

It is almost impossible to test every possible business logic and configuration in SAP. However, mitigating high-value risks is achievable. This is where Risk-Based Testing comes in handy. By focusing on the most critical and high-risk areas of a SAP S/4HANA implementation, this technique ensures efficient resource utilization, while maintaining quality.

- Use process usage heatmaps based on historical usage, defect data and business process impact analysis to prioritize test cases.
- **Adopt Test Impact Analysis**: Leverage AI to determine the most relevant tests based on recent system changes.
- **Continuously Update Risk Assessments**: Align testing priorities with the evolving business and technical risks.

Pro Tip: *To get buy-in from business leaders, track the cost of escaped defects. On average, a SAP defect fixed post-production costs 7-10x more than one caught in SIT (Gartner 2023). Use this to justify upfront investment in robust testing.*

Conclusion

This chapter provided a definitive exploration of best practices that transform SAP S/4HANA testing from a challenge to a strategic advantage. Drawing upon proven methodologies and real-world insights from leading SAP testing teams and industry forums, it underscored how a comprehensive, architected testing approach accelerates deployment velocities, mitigates risk exposure, and ensures superior system quality and user experience. The concepts outlined here form the foundation of resilient SAP test strategies that can scale with the evolving business demands and technological complexity.

The next chapter transitions from high-level best practices to the practical realities of an actual SAP-Activate based implementation. It will systematically traverse each phase of the SAP Activate methodology such as Prepare, Explore, Realize, Deploy, and Run - illuminating how manual and automated testing, performance validation, integration testing, and data migration are orchestrated seamlessly within this framework.

References

- Inside SAP S/4HANA Customer Stories: https://podcast.opensap.info/inside-sap/
- World Quality Reports: https://www.capgemini.com/insights/research-library/world-quality-report-2024-25/
- SAP ASUG Presentations: https://www.asug.com/content-collections
- SAP Webcasts: https://support.sap.com/en/alm/sap cloud-alm/sap-cloud-alm-technical-deep-dive-webinars.html

CHAPTER 13
Navigating a Realtime SAP Test Project

Introduction

Navigating a real-time SAP S/4HANA migration project is an intricate endeavor that demands meticulous planning, cross-functional collaboration, and unwavering focus on quality engineering. This chapter offers a comprehensive day-to-day view of how SAP implementation teams and testing teams synchronize their efforts, from initial blueprinting to go-live.

According to industry experts, organizations with a testing team that possesses strong SAP domain knowledge and project awareness can achieve up to **90% better software quality outcomes.** This is primarily because such teams understand the nuances of SAP's evolving ecosystem, and can proactively manage risks related to data migration, process disruptions, and integration challenges.

This chapter took shape amid the complexity of distilling a multifaceted SAP S/4HANA migration into digestible guidance, reflecting the real-world intricacies and critical dependencies that define successful transformations today. Its lessons aim to elevate the quality mindset, and provide a strategic blueprint to help SAP testing teams be not only gatekeepers of quality but true enablers of transformation excellence.

Structure

This chapter provides an in-depth exploration of the SAP project lifecycle using an Order-to-Cash (O2C) process transformation, with a strong focus on testing across various project phases. We will examine:

- Project Context
- Discover Phase
- Prepare Phase
- Explore Phase

- Realize Phase
- Deploy Phase
- Run Phase

Project Context

This section uses a fictional case study to illustrate a typical O2C transformation. While the scenario is fictional, it reflects real-world challenges and solutions.

Company Profile

PrecisionCore Industrial Systems (PCI) is a global leader in precision-engineered industrial equipment, with a presence in over 30 countries and manufacturing hubs across North America, Europe, and Asia. With over 20,000 employees and annual revenues exceeding $5 billion, PCI serves clients in the automotive, energy, and heavy machinery sectors. Its portfolio includes hydraulic systems, automation components, and custom assembly solutions used by Fortune 500 manufacturers worldwide.

Traditional Business Model

For over four decades, PCI relied on a regionally operated business model. Sales, fulfillment, and finance operations were decentralized, with each geography using its own systems - ranging from SAP ECC to legacy homegrown tools that handle customer orders, credit assessments, delivery tracking, and invoicing. While this model allowed for regional autonomy, it led to fragmentation in the Order-to-Cash (O2C) process, inconsistent customer experiences, and limited visibility into working capital and receivables.

New Business Strategy

Facing global competition, volatile supply chains, and increasing demands for digital services, PCI has adopted a new global operating model anchored on operational efficiency and customer centricity. The strategy prioritizes:

- Harmonized global processes to reduce cost and complexity.
- Faster lead-to-cash cycles to unlock working capital.
- Real-time insights to empower business decisions.
- Automation-first approach to eliminate repetitive, manual tasks.
- Unified customer experience across regions.

To enable this strategy, PCI launched "*Project Vantage*" - a multi-year digital transformation program to standardize and modernize its core O2C processes using SAP S/4HANA as the digital foundation.

Why O2C Transformation Mattered

PCI Industrial Systems faced mounting inefficiencies in its Order-to-Cash (O2C) process. Its fragmented IT landscape - spanning SAP ERP and multiple third-party systems for credit checks, order fulfillment, and invoicing - was driving up costs and slowing operations. Rising customer expectations and stricter regulations prompted a bold decision: To modernize the entire O2C process through SAP S/4HANA Private Cloud.

Led by the CFO and CIO, the company launched a transformation program to unify operations, enhance financial visibility, automate manual tasks, and accelerate fulfillment. SAP S/4HANA, with its powerful capabilities in credit management, logistics, and real-time finance, was selected after a comprehensive evaluation.

Over 18–24 months, the company undertook a phased implementation - standardizing processes, migrating systems, and enabling automation. SAP EWM and TM were also adopted to streamline warehouse and transportation operations.

The transformation was orchestrated using SAP Activate. A **Global System Integrator (GSI), Advisora Consulting Group (ASG),** defined the roadmap and led implementation and testing, while **SAP as an OEM (Original Equipment Manufacturer) provided architectural and strategic guidance.** The enterprise architecture team worked closely with business stakeholders to shape the target solution and integration strategy. Meanwhile, the in-house business team played a hands-on role in driving iterative User Acceptance Testing (UAT), ensuring that the solution aligned with real-world scenarios.

The following figure highlights the as-is process for reference.

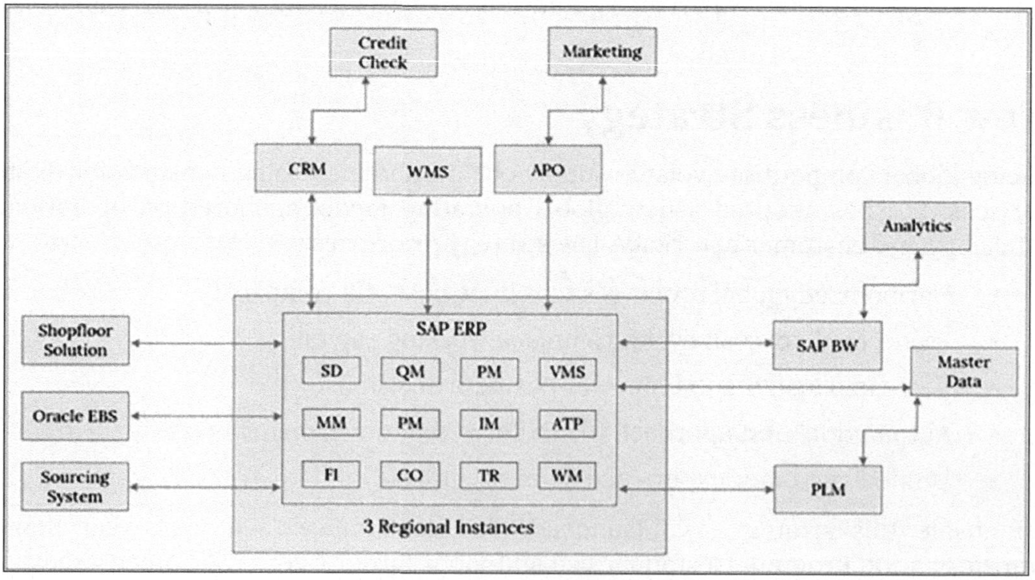

Figure 13.1: *As-Is Landscape of PCI*

Project Methodology

Key stakeholders unanimously aligned on SAP Activate as the delivery framework - combining SAP Best Practices with guided configuration for a focused and disciplined execution. In the following sections, we will dissect this transformation story phase by phase, examining the project implementation using Activate Methodology in action through the lens of this O2C modernization. Here is a diagram that highlights the key implementation tasks and testing activities, as part of the Activate Methodology for reference.

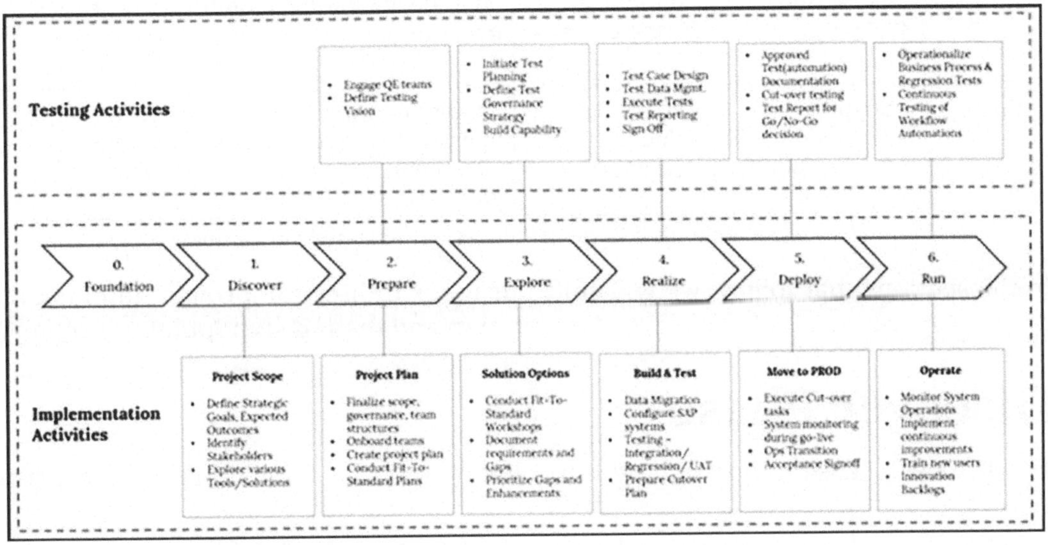

Figure 13.2: *Project Implementation Cycle with Key Activities*

Executive Engagement

Phase	CIO Key Focus	CFO Key Focus	SAP's Strategic Involvement (Architecture and Guidance)
Discover	Architecture, Strategy	Business Case, ROI	Provides reference architectures, validates solution fit, advises on integration landscape and value realization roadmap
Prepare	Governance, Resource Planning	Scope Refinement, Risk Management	Reviews system landscape design, sizing recommendations, and ensures alignment with SAP best practices and Activate methodology

Explore	Solution Design Governance	Financial Process Design	Guides fit-to-standard workshops, reviews integration strategy, and advises on data model and extensibility design
Realize	Cutover Readiness, Technical Risks	Financial Validation, UAT	Provides quality assurance reviews, integration guidance, performance optimization input, and validates technical implementation
Deploy	Go/No-Go, Vendor Oversight	Business Continuity, Financial Risks	Supports go-live readiness checks, advises on issue mitigation, monitors system performance and stability post-cutover
Run	Support Transition, Optimization	KPI Tracking, Value Realization	Enables continuous improvement through upgrade planning, innovation roadmap alignment, and architecture evolution guidance

Table 13.1: *Roles and Responsibilities – Executive Perspective*

In the sections that follow, we will shift our focus to how the project unfolds over the next 18–24 months from an implementation and testing standpoint.

Discover Phase

The Discover Phase is particularly critical as it sets the foundation for the entire project.

Objectives of the Discover Phase

The Discover Phase aims to:

- Understand the business requirements and pain points
- Identify transformation opportunities
- Develop the business case
- Plan the implementation approach
- Establish project governance
- Define the scope and roadmap

The following diagram shows a high-level business and technology architecture at the business process level.

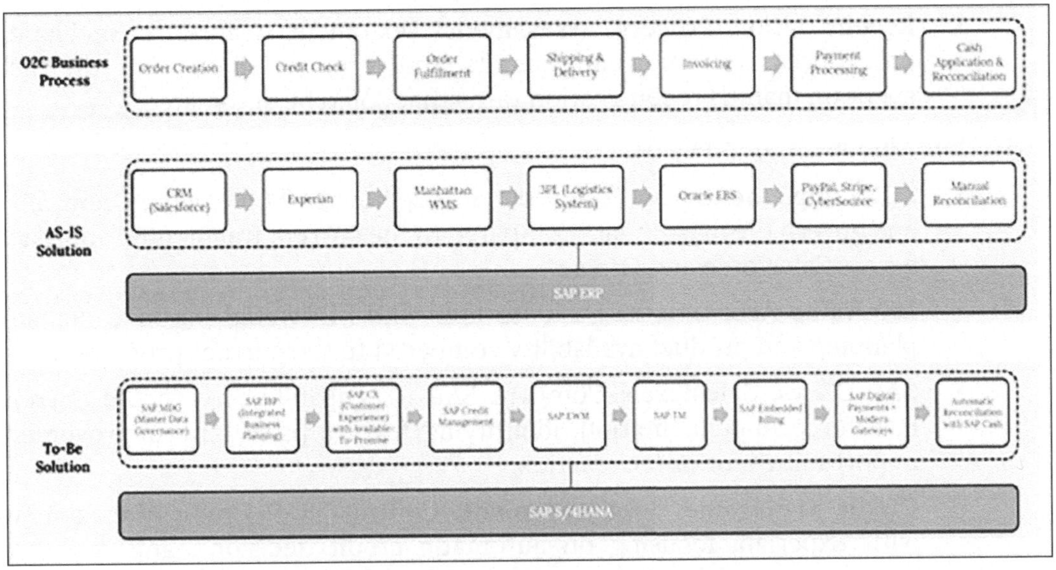

Figure 13.3: O2C Process - *High-level Architecture*

Key Activities

1. **Business Process Assessment (Determining As-Is State)**
    - **Current CRM Analysis**: Evaluate how Salesforce CRM handles customer master data, quotations, and order creation. Identify the limitations in data flow between Salesforce and downstream systems.
    - **Credit Management Review:** Assess Experian implementation, examining credit check workflows, approval hierarchies, and integration points. Identify manual touchpoints and delays in credit approval processes.
    - **Warehouse Operations Assessment:** Analyze Manhattan WMS functionality, picking processes, and inventory management capabilities. Document the pain points in order fulfillment that affect delivery reliability.
    - **Logistics Evaluation:** Review 3PL logistics system integration, shipment tracking, and delivery scheduling. Identify the visibility gaps and communication breakdowns in the shipping process.
    - **ERP System Analysis:** Examine Oracle EBS functionality for order processing, invoicing, and financial posting. Document data synchronization issues between systems.
    - **Payment Processing Review:** Evaluate the current payment gateway integrations (PayPal, Stripe, or CyberSource) and identify reconciliation challenges.

- **Reconciliation Process Assessment**: Document manual reconciliation procedures, resource requirements, and error rates. Calculate the time spent on manual reconciliation tasks that could be automated.

2. **Solution Fit/Gap Analysis**
   - **MDG Implementation Potential:** Analyze how SAP MDG would centralize and govern the master data compared to the current fragmented approach across Salesforce and Oracle.
   - **IBP Value Assessment:** Evaluate how SAP IBP would improve demand planning and product availability compared to the current processes.
   - **SAP CX vs. Salesforce:** Compare SAP CX capabilities with the current Salesforce implementation, identifying feature parity and improvement opportunities for order creation.
   - **Credit Management Enhancement:** Contrast SAP Credit Management with Experian, focusing on automatic credit decisions, and real-time availability.
   - **Warehouse Management Comparison:** Analyze SAP EWM functionality against Manhattan WMS, with focus on real-time inventory visibility, and integration benefits.
   - **Transportation Management Evaluation:** Compare SAP TM capabilities with the current 3PL systems, highlighting opportunities for shipment optimization and cost reduction.
   - **Billing Process Enhancement**: Evaluate how SAP Embedded Billing improves upon the current Oracle EBS invoicing process, reducing time to invoice and error rates.
   - **Payment Processing Modernization:** Assess SAP Digital Payments against current payment providers, identifying improvements in payment processing time, and customer experience.
   - **Reconciliation Automation Benefits**: Compare automatic reconciliation capabilities in SAP Cash versus the current manual reconciliation processes, quantifying time savings, and accuracy improvements.

3. **Technical Assessment**
   - **Integration Analysis:** Map the current integrations between Salesforce, Experian, Manhattan WMS, 3PL systems, Oracle EBS, and payment processors. Document data exchange methods, formats, and failure points.
   - **Data Migration Complexity:** Assess the data volume, quality, and structure in the existing systems. Identify transformation requirements for customer, product, pricing, and transaction data.

- **Infrastructure Requirements:** Evaluate the current hardware/cloud resources against SAP S/4HANA requirements. Determine sizing based on transaction volumes in the current O2C process.
- **Security Model Assessment:** Review the current security roles and authorizations across multiple systems. Map to future S/4HANA security concept.
- **Interface Redesign:** Identify all the external systems that must connect to the new S/4HANA landscape. Determine API and middleware requirements.

4. **Implementation of Strategy Development**
   - **Phasing Strategy:** Determine whether to implement SAP MDG and IBP first as foundation before core O2C processes, or implement the entire solution simultaneously.
   - **Cutover Planning:** Develop strategies for transitioning from each legacy system to S/4HANA components with minimal business disruption.
   - **Resource Allocation:** Identify skill requirements based on the current system expertise (Salesforce, Oracle, and Manhattan) and the required SAP skills.
   - **Risk Analysis**: Document specific risks related to each system transition, with detailed mitigation approaches for high-impact areas like payment processing and credit checks.
   - **Change Impact Assessment**: Evaluate how each department will be affected by transition from current tools to SAP, especially for everyday users of Salesforce and Oracle.

5. **Business Case Development**
   - **Order Cycle Time Reduction:** Calculate the current end-to-end cycle times from order creation to cash application, identifying bottlenecks in manual credit checks and reconciliation processes.
   - **Cash Flow Improvement:** Estimate DSO (Days Sales Outstanding) reduction through integrated processes and automated reconciliation versus the current manual approach.
   - **FTE Efficiency Gain:** Quantify staff time currently spent on manual activities across the fragmented systems that could be redeployed after automation.

- **Error Rate Reduction:** Document the current error rates in manual processes, especially in reconciliation, and project improvements with automated processes.
- **IT Cost Consolidation:** Calculate the current maintenance and license costs across all systems (Salesforce, Experian, Manhattan, Oracle, and Payment processors) versus future SAP landscape costs.

The Discover phase concludes with a formal decision to proceed with the project based on the approved business case. This triggers the start of the Prepare phase, where detailed planning begins.

Prepare Phase

This second phase of SAP Activate methodology serves as the formal project initiation phase where detailed planning occurs, project teams are established, and the implementation foundation is created. This phase is crucial for setting up the project for success.

Objectives of the Prepare Phase

The primary objectives of the Prepare phase include:

- Mobilizing the project team with clear roles and responsibilities.
- Establishing the project governance structure.
- Creating detailed project plans and schedules.
- Setting up the project environment, including development systems.
- Defining project standards and procedures.
- Initiating change management activities.
- Finalizing project scope and implementation strategy.

The following diagram illustrates the technical architecture created in this phase.

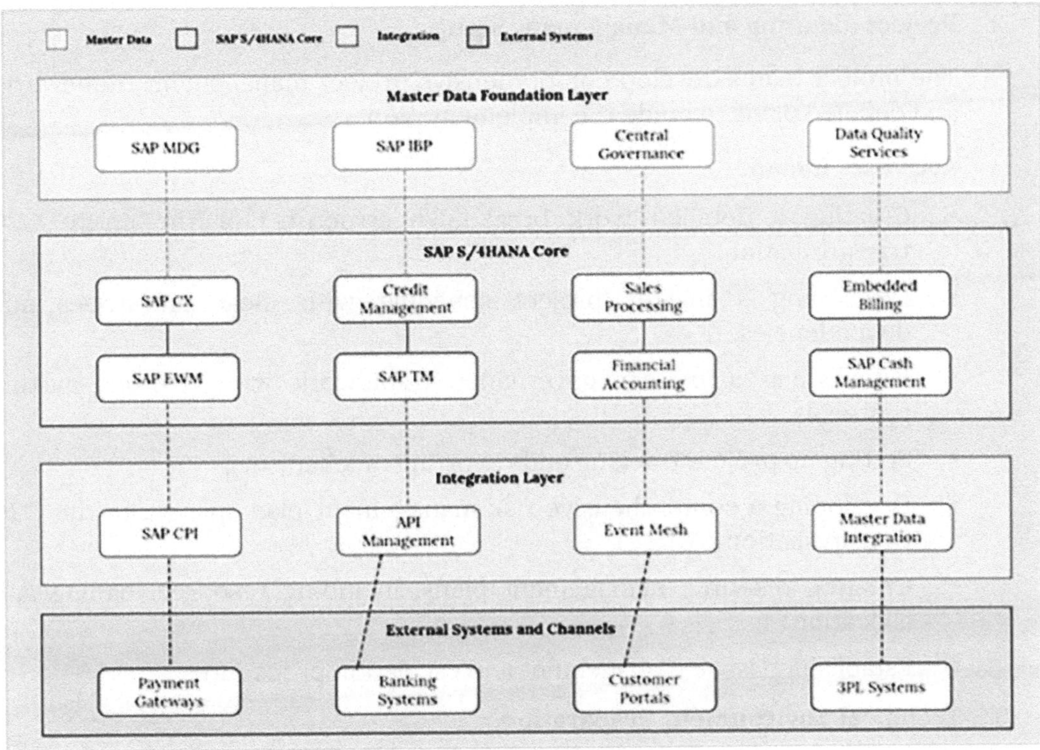

Figure 13.4: *High-level Technical Architecture*

Key Activities

The ASG's project teams will lead the following key activities during the Prepare phase:

1. **Project Team Mobilization and Onboarding**

   ASG assembles and on boards the project team, ensuring that all necessary roles are filled with qualified resources.

   Activities Include:

   - Defining the project team structure with dedicated tracks for each O2C component (MDG, IBP, CX, Credit Management, EWM, TM, Billing, and Cash Application).
   - Conducting knowledge transfer on the existing systems (Salesforce, Experian, Manhattan WMS, and Oracle EBS) to the implementation team members.
   - Evaluating team skills and arranging SAP-specific training where needed.
   - Creating a detailed RACI matrix for all project activities.

2. **Project Planning and Management Setup**

   The project teams develop comprehensive project management frameworks and detailed plans to guide the implementation.

   Activities Include:

   - Creating a detailed work breakdown structure for the entire O2C transformation.
   - Developing a master project schedule with clear milestones and dependencies.
   - Establishing a project governance framework with decision-making protocols.
   - Setting up project tracking and reporting mechanisms.
   - Developing a comprehensive risk management plan specific to the O2C transformation.
   - Creating resource management plans, including resource loading and allocation.
   - Establishing issue management and escalation procedures.

3. **Technical Environment Preparation**

   The project teams lead the setup of the technical landscape required for the implementation.

   Activities include:

   - Designing the system landscape architecture for all environments (DEV, QA, PRE-PROD, and PROD).
   - Planning and executing the provisioning of development systems for SAP MDG, IBP, SAP S/4HANA.
   - Configuring development tools and transport management systems.
   - Setting up source control and code management tools.
   - Establishing system connectivity between SAP components with legacy systems.
   - Implementing initial security frameworks and authentication mechanisms.
   - Creating system backup and recovery procedures.

4. **Standards and Procedures Definition**

   The project teams establish the standards and procedures to ensure consistency throughout the implementation.

Activities Include:

- Defining development standards and conventions for all customization work.
- Creating documentation standards and templates.
- Establishing testing methodologies and standards.
- Defining configuration management procedures.
- Creating change control processes.
- Establishing quality assurance standards, and review procedures.
- Defining approval workflows for deliverables.

5. **Project Scope Refinement**

   The project teams refine the project scope based on additional information gathered since the Discover phase.

   Activities Include:

   - Conducting detailed fit-gap workshops for each O2C component.
   - Refining the solution scope document with precise boundaries.
   - Creating a backlog of requirements for each functional area.
   - Documenting business scenarios and process variants to be implemented.
   - Finalizing the integration scope with detailed interface specifications.
   - Developing a data migration strategy with detailed scope.
   - Refining custom development requirements.

6. **Change Management Initiation**

   The project teams start change management activities to prepare the organization for the transformation.

   Activities Include:

   - Conducting detailed impact assessments for all stakeholder groups.
   - Developing a comprehensive stakeholder engagement plan.
   - Creating an initial communication plan for the project.
   - Performing organizational readiness assessments.
   - Developing a change network of change agents throughout the organization.
   - Creating a preliminary training strategy.
   - Establishing change metrics and monitoring mechanisms.

7. **Define Vision for Testing**

   The QA team starts to align testing functions to the key implementation activities.

   Activities Include:

   - **Master Test Strategy Development**: Define high-level scope, approach, and success criteria.
   - **Test Governance Methodology**: Establish roles, responsibilities, and processes for test management.
   - **Test Environment Planning**: Plan the system landscapes.
   - **Preliminary Test Data Strategy**: Define high-level approach for test data creation, masking, refreshes, and data ownership.
   - **Resource Planning**: Identify skill gaps, and plan upskilling for test automation and business process testing.

The following table highlights the Test Environment Planning Matrix that is defined during this Phase.

Environment	Purpose	Refresh Frequency	Data Strategy
DEV	Unit testing, initial configuration testing	As needed	Subset of anonymized data
QA	Integration testing, functional testing	Sprint-based	Representative anonymized dataset
PRE-PROD	UAT, performance testing, security testing	Milestone-based	Full production-like dataset
PROD	Production validation, hyper care	N/A	Production data

Table 13.2: *Test Environment Planning Matrix*

The following table highlights the communication plan to engage stakeholders at the right time for completing the key testing activities.

Stakeholder Group	Communication Needs	Frequency	Channel
Executive Sponsors	Testing status summary, risk exposure	Bi-weekly	Executive dashboard
Business Process Owners	Detailed testing progress, defect status	Weekly	Status report, meetings
Project Management	Comprehensive test metrics, blockers	Daily	Project dashboard, stand-up

Development Team	Defect details, fix verification status	Daily	Defect management system
End Users	UAT preparation, testing involvement	As needed	Training sessions, communications

Table 13.3: *Stakeholder Communication Plan*

Pro Tip: *Introduce the concept of "shift-left testing" during these phases, encouraging early involvement of test teams in fit-gap analysis to mitigate defects early.*

At the conclusion of the Prepare phase, the project undergoes a formal quality gate review to ensure that all required activities have been completed, and the deliverables meet the quality standards. Upon successful completion of this review, the project transitions to the Explore phase, where the team will work with business stakeholders to validate business requirements, configure the system based on best practices, and conduct fit-gap workshops to identify custom requirements.

The thoroughness of the Prepare phase directly impacts the success of subsequent phases, as it establishes the foundation upon which the entire implementation will be built.

Explore Phase

This phase focuses on validating business requirements, configuring the system based on SAP best practices, conducting fit-gap analysis, and creating the blueprint for the solution. For the Order-to-Cash (O2C) transformation from legacy systems (Salesforce, Experian, Manhattan WMS, and Oracle EBS) to an integrated SAP S/4HANA solution, the Explore phase brings the conceptual design to life through prototyping and iterative configuration.

Objectives of the Explore Phase

The primary objectives of the Explore Phase include:

- Validating business requirements through workshops and prototyping.
- Configuring the system based on SAP best practices.
- Conducting detailed fit-gap analysis for all O2C processes.
- Creating the solution blueprint for all components.
- Defining integration requirements in detail.
- Planning data migration and conversion.
- Establishing testing strategy and test plan.

The following conceptual design and prototype has been created primarily during the "*System Configuration and Prototyping*" activity of the Explore phase.

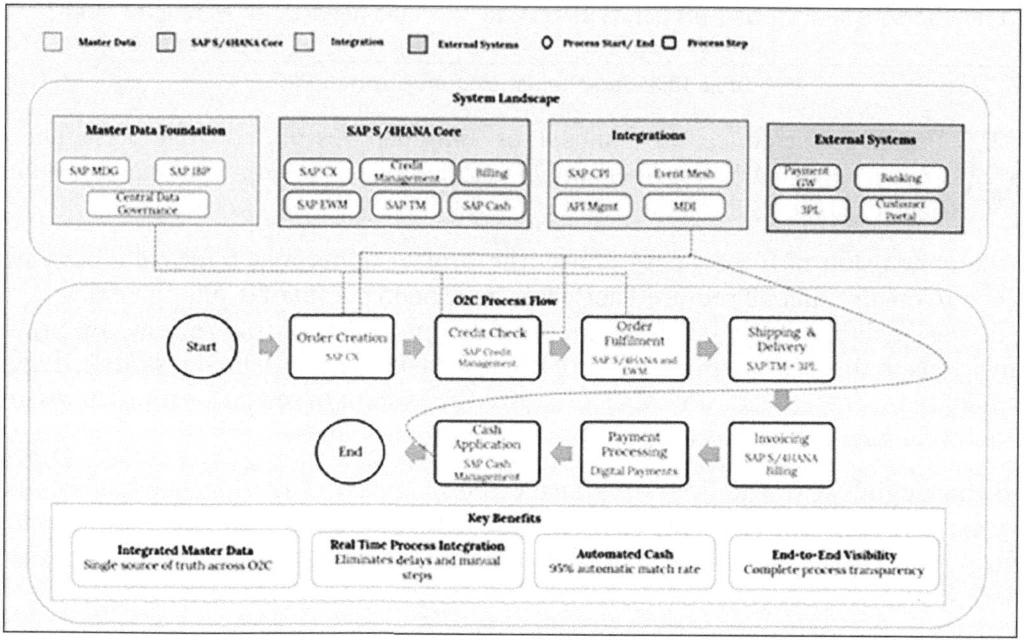

Figure 13.5: *Conceptual Design and Prototype*

Key Activities

The project teams will lead the following key activities during the Explore phase:

1. **Business Process Exploration and Validation**

   The project teams facilitate workshops with business stakeholders to validate requirements and processes against SAP best practices.

   Activities Include:

   - Conducting fit-to-standard workshops for each O2C component (MDG, IBP, CX, Credit Management, EWM, TM, Billing, and Cash Application).
   - Demonstrating SAP best practice processes as alternatives to the current Salesforce, Experian, Manhattan WMS, and Oracle EBS processes.
   - Documenting process decisions, and configuration requirements.
   - Creating process flows for all O2C scenarios in the target solution.
   - Identifying process gaps requiring configuration or development.
   - Validating process integration points across the O2C flow.
   - Documenting business rules and decision points for each process.

2. **System Configuration and Prototyping**

   The project teams configure the system based on best practices and validated requirements to create working prototypes.

   Activities Include:

   - Activating SAP Best Practices packages for O2C processes.
   - Configuring organizational structures to match the client's organization.
   - Setting up master data structures that will be managed in SAP MDG.
   - Configuring customer credit management processes to replace Experian functionality.
   - Setting up warehouse management processes to replace Manhattan WMS functionality.
   - Creating working prototypes of end-to-end O2C processes.
   - Demonstrating prototype capabilities to business stakeholders for validation.

3. **Fit-Gap Analysis and Solution Design**

   The project teams conduct detailed fit-gap analysis and design solutions for identified gaps.

   Activities Include:

   - Analyzing gaps between standard functionality and business requirements.
   - Evaluating alternatives for addressing gaps (configuration, extension, and process adaptation).
   - Designing solutions for high-priority gaps.
   - Creating functional specifications for required extensions.
   - Designing workarounds for non-critical gaps.
   - Prioritizing gaps based on business impact.
   - Creating a backlog of enhancement requirements.
   - Developing the overall solution design document.

4. **Integration Design and Planning**

   The project teams design integration solutions for all components within the O2C process with external systems.

   Activities Include:

   - Designing integration between SAP components (SAP MDG to SAP S/4HANA, SAP IBP to SAP S/4HANA, SAP S/4HANA to SAP CX)

- Planning integration with the remaining external systems.
- Creating interface design specifications.
- Defining integration architecture using SAP CPI/PO.
- Designing real-time vs. batch integration processes.
- Planning for migration from point-to-point integrations to SAP integration platforms.
- Conducting integration workshops with technical teams.

5. **Data Migration Strategy and Planning**

   The project teams develop detailed plans for migrating data from legacy systems to the SAP landscape.

   Activities Include:

   - Creating data migration strategy for all O2C data entities.
   - Mapping data structures between source systems, and target SAP systems.
   - Defining data transformation rules, and cleansing approaches.
   - Designing data extraction methods from Salesforce, Oracle, and other legacy systems.
   - Planning data validation and reconciliation procedures.
   - Creating data migration schedules and cutover strategies.

6. **Testing Strategy Development**

   Description: The QA team develops comprehensive testing strategies for all aspects of the solution.

   Activities Include:

   - Creating the master test strategy document.
   - Developing test plans for each O2C component.
   - Creating test scenarios and test cases for key business processes.
   - Designing integration test plans.
   - Planning user acceptance testing approach.
   - Establishing test data management procedures.
   - Setting up test automation frameworks where applicable.
   - Defining defect management processes.

The following diagram highlights the strategy for the test data.

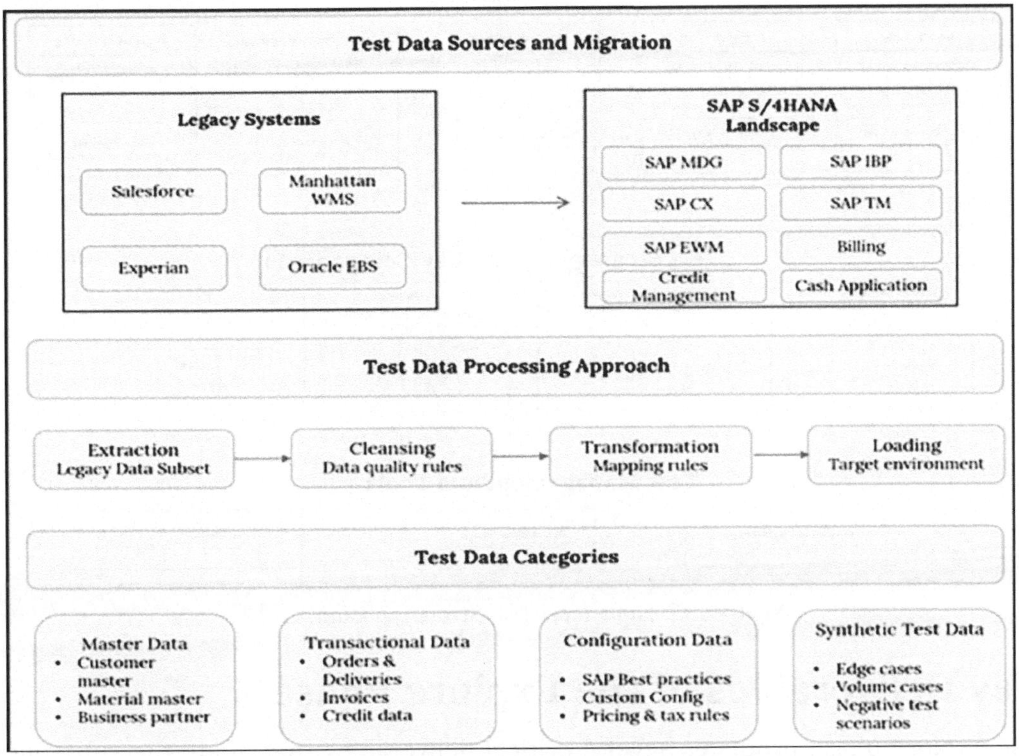

Figure 13.6: *Test Data Strategy Visualization*

7. **Change Management Refinement**

   The project teams refine the change management approach based on the detailed understanding of process changes.

   Activities Include:

   - Updating impact assessments with detailed process change information.
   - Refining the stakeholder engagement strategy.
   - Developing detailed communication plans for specific stakeholder groups.
   - Creating change agent network engagement plans.
   - Designing training curriculum based on the identified role changes.
   - Developing organizational readiness assessment criteria.
   - Creating an end-user adoption measurement approach.

The following diagram shows a high-level test framework for this O2C process transformation.

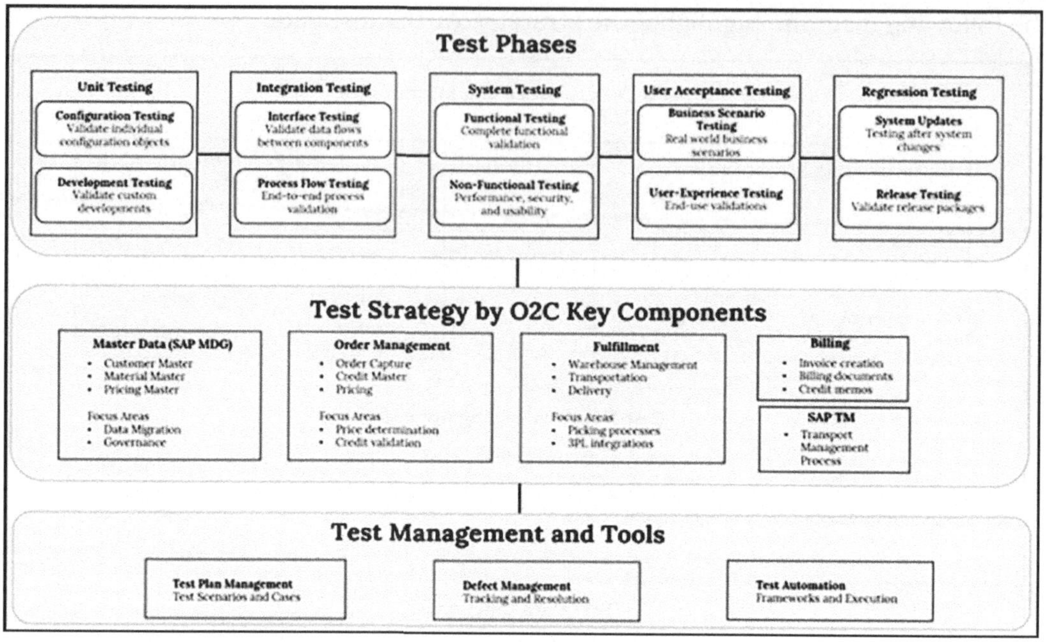

Figure 13.7: *High-level Test Strategy Visualization*

Key Deliverables of the Explore Phase

The Explore phase produces several critical deliverables that guide the subsequent Realize phase:

- **Business Process Master List (BPML)**: Comprehensive inventory of all O2C business processes (or variants) to be implemented, with configuration requirements.
- **Solution Design Document**: Detailed design of the entire solution, including process flows, configuration decisions, and gap resolutions.
- **Configuration Baseline**: Initial configuration of the system based on the best practices and validated requirements
- **Gap List and Resolution Approach**: Documented gaps between standard functionality and requirements, with planned resolution approaches.
- **Integration Design Document**: Detailed design of all integration points, including interface specifications.
- **Data Migration Strategy and Plan**: Comprehensive approach for migrating data from legacy systems to SAP.
- **Testing Strategy and Test Data**: Master test strategy, detailed test plans, Testing Tools selection, Test Environment, and Test Data Management methodology.

- **Change Impact Assessment**: Detailed analysis of organizational impacts of the transformation.
- **Training Needs**: Assessment of training requirements based on role changes.
- **Functional Specifications**: Technical specifications for the required custom developments and extensions.

Pro Tip: Plan to *automate test data creation, and masking early to ensure secure yet realistic test cycles.*

The Explore phase is critical as it provides the detailed blueprint that will guide all implementation activities in the Realize phase, ensuring that the solution addresses the business requirements, while leveraging SAP best practices.

At the conclusion of the Explore phase, the project undergoes a formal quality gate review to ensure that all the required activities have been completed, and deliverables meet the quality standards.

Realize Phase

This phase focuses on building, configuring, testing, and validating the solution based on the design approved in the Explore phase. For the O2C transformation from legacy systems (Salesforce, Experian, Manhattan WMS, and Oracle EBS) to an integrated SAP S/4HANA solution, the Realize phase represents the transition from design to execution, where the solution is built, validated, and prepared for deployment.

Objectives of the Realize Phase

The primary objectives of the Realize phase include:

- Implementing the full scope of the solution through configuration and development.
- Executing integration points between all components.
- Migrating data from legacy systems to SAP.
- Conducting comprehensive testing at all levels.
- Validating the solution against business requirements.
- Training the key users, and preparing end-user training materials.
- Finalizing cutover planning, and organizational readiness.
- Preparing for the Deploy phase.

Key Activities

The project teams will lead the following key activities during the Realize phase:

1. **Solution Configuration and Development**

   The project teams implement the complete solution through configuration and development activities based on the solution design.

   Activities Include:

   - **Master Data Configuration**: Configuring SAP MDG and master data structures to replace Salesforce and Oracle EBS master data management, including customer master data fields, material master data structures, and pricing condition tables.
   - **Order Management Configuration**: Implementing SAP CX and SAP S/4HANA sales processes to replace Salesforce functionality, including sales document types, item categories, and schedule line determination.
   - **Credit Management Implementation**: Configuring SAP Credit Management to replace Experian, including credit rules, scoring procedures, and approval workflows.
   - **Warehouse Management Setup**: Configuring SAP EWM to replace Manhattan WMS, including warehouse structures, storage bin management, and picking strategies.
   - **Transportation Management Configuration**: Setting up SAP TM to replace 3PL systems, including carrier determination, route management, and freight cost calculation.
   - **Billing and Payment Configuration**: Implementing SAP embedded billing and payment processing to replace Oracle EBS, including billing types, pricing procedures, and payment methods.
   - **Cash Application Development**: Configuring SAP Cash Management with automated matching rules to replace manual reconciliation processes, including matching algorithms and exception handling.
   - **Custom Development**: Building enhancements and extensions for identified gaps, including custom workflows, reports, interfaces, conversions, enhancements, and forms (WRICEF objects).

2. **Integration Implementation**

   The project teams build and configure all integration points within the SAP landscape, with external systems.

Activities Include:

- **Internal Integration Configuration**: Setting up integration between SAP components (SAP MDG to SAP S/4HANA, SAP CX to Credit Management, SAP S/4HANA to EWM and TM) to enable seamless process flow that eliminates current manual steps between Salesforce, Experian, and Oracle.
- **External System Integration**: Implementing interfaces with the remaining external systems (payment gateways, 3PL systems, and banking systems) using SAP CPI/PO to replace the current point-to-point integrations.
- **API Development**: Building APIs for real-time integration scenarios, particularly for customer portals and mobile applications that currently interact with Salesforce and Oracle.
- **Event-Based Integration**: Configuring event-based integration using SAP Event Mesh for real-time process flows, replacing batch processes between the current systems.
- **Integration Testing**: Validating integration points through comprehensive testing, including error handling and exception scenarios.
- **Integration Monitoring**: Setting up monitoring for all integration points to ensure visibility and traceability across the end-to-end process.

3. **Data Migration Execution**

The project teams execute the data migration strategy to move the relevant data from legacy systems to SAP.

Activities Include:

- **Data Extraction**: Extracting data from Salesforce, Experian, Manhattan WMS, and Oracle EBS using appropriate extraction methods.
- **Data Transformation**: Transforming data to match the SAP data structures, including data cleansing, enrichment, and mapping.
- **Data Validation**: Validating the transformed data against business rules to ensure data quality and integrity.
- **Data Load**: Loading data into SAP systems according to the data migration strategy.
- **Reconciliation**: Reconciling the migrated data to ensure completeness and accuracy.
- **Migration Validation**: Conducting validation tests to ensure that the migrated data supports business processes correctly.

- **Delta Migration Planning**: Finalizing plans for delta migrations during cutover, particularly for transaction data from Oracle EBS.

4. **Test Environment Management**

The QA teams establish comprehensive test environment management processes to support the testing strategy.

Activities Include:

- **Environment Provisioning**: Setting up and configuring the required test environments (DEV, QA, and PRE-PROD) with appropriate system parameters and client settings.
- **Environment Scheduling**: Establishing processes for scheduling and allocating test environment resources to different testing activities.
- **Client Strategy Implementation**: Implementing the client strategy across environments to support various testing needs:
    - Development clients for configuration and unit testing.
    - Integration testing clients with the controlled data.
    - UAT clients with business-realistic data.
    - Performance testing clients with volume data.
- **Transport Management**: Establishing processes for managing (primarily, the testing) transports between environments, including approval workflows and validation procedures.
- **Environment Refresh Procedures**: Developing procedures for refreshing test environments from production or other sources, including data masking and post-refresh activities.
- **Environment Monitoring**: Implementing monitoring for test environments to ensure availability and performance.
- **Sandbox Environments**: Setting up sandbox environments for exploratory testing, and proof of concepts.
- **Test Data Reset Capabilities**: Implementing mechanisms to reset the test data to baseline states between test cycles.

5. **Testing**

The QA teams lead the execution of comprehensive testing activities to validate that the configured solution meets both the technical and business requirements. Testing spans multiple layers, each focused on mitigating risk, and ensuring solution readiness for production.

Core Activities Include:

- **Test Design and Planning:**
  - Design end-to-end test scenarios and scripts based on the Business Process Master List (BPML) and solution design.
  - Ensure that test cases cover both standard SAP flows and gap areas from Fit-Gap models, including edge cases and negative testing.
  - Test data design ensuring coverage of master and transactional data critical to O2C, including credit limits, delivery blocks, invoicing, and reconciliation.
- **Perform Test Execution Activities across Testing Phases:**
  - **Unit Testing**: Validate individual configuration elements and custom developments (WRICEF objects) to ensure that they perform as designed in isolation.
  - **Integration Testing**: Testing integration points between all components to ensure a seamless data flow across the O2C process.
  - **System Testing**: Conducting end-to-end process testing to validate the complete O2C flow from order creation to cash application.
  - **Performance Testing**: Testing system performance under various load conditions to ensure responsiveness and scalability.
  - **Regression Testing**: Conducting regression testing after fixes and changes to ensure solution stability.
  - **Security Testing**: Validating security configurations and authorizations to ensure proper access control.
- **Test Automation:**
  - Identify complex, high-volume or repetitive test cases for automation -typically regression, integration, and UAT test packs.
  - Implement test automation using tools.
  - Manage automated test life cycle with ALM, CI/CD, and Defect management tools.
- **Quality Reviews and Governance:**
  - Conduct test case peer reviews to ensure alignment with business requirements and test design standards.
  - Schedule formal quality gates at the end of each test phase (for example, unit, integration, system test exit, and so on).
  - Use predefined entry and exit criteria to validate test phase readiness and completion.

- **Defect Lifecycle:**

  Establish a structured defect management process using tools such as JIRA or SAP Cloud ALM, and maintain daily defect triage calls to drive resolution and improve turnaround:

  - Defect logging with severity and priority tagging.
  - Root cause analysis.
  - Assignment to responsible teams (functional/configuration/development).
  - Retesting and closure.

- **User Sign-Off and Test Completion:**
  - Generate test summary reports for each phase, including test coverage, pass/fail metrics, defect trends, and unresolved risks.
  - Conduct formal test sign-off workshops with business stakeholders and IT leads.
  - Gain approval to proceed to UAT and/or next phase of deployment, based on test completion and quality metrics.

6. **User Acceptance Testing**

   User Acceptance Testing (UAT) is a pivotal step where PCI's business users validate that the system meets real-world expectations.

   Activities Include:

   - **Business Scenario Definition and Test Case Finalization**
     - Collaborate with business process owners to define realistic, end-to-end O2C scenarios (for example, credit-approved sales order, expedited shipping, partial delivery, and returns).
     - Finalize UAT test cases that reflect daily operational complexity, and exception handling.
   - **UAT Environment and Data Preparation**
     - Set up a stable and isolated UAT environment that mirrors production (data volumes, master data, roles, and so on).
     - Load clean, representative test data–customer master, sales orders, pricing, inventory, and financial documents.
   - **Business User Training and Onboarding**
     - Conduct UAT training sessions for business users, focused on navigating the new SAP interfaces, workflows, and exception paths.
     - Provide role-based guides and walk-throughs for O2C test scenarios.

- **UAT Execution and Defect Management**
  - Facilitate execution of test cases by business users with support from QA and functional teams.
  - Log, track, and resolve defects using agreed tools (for example, SAP CloudALM), with clear severity and business impact classification.
- **User Sign-Off and Exit Criteria Validation**
  - Obtain formal sign-off from key business stakeholders once acceptance criteria are met.
  - Ensure all critical O2C flows (including integrations, credit checks, billing, and reconciliation) are validated and traceable to signed-off requirements.

7. **Documentation and Knowledge Transfer**

   The ASG's project teams create comprehensive documentation, and conduct knowledge transfer to the key users.

   Activities Include:

   - **Configuration Documentation**: Documenting all configuration decisions and settings for future reference and support.
   - **Technical Documentation**: Creating technical documentation for custom developments, interfaces, and enhancements.
   - **User Guides**: Developing user guides for key business processes in the new solution.
   - **Testing Guides**: Creating a comprehensive repository of test documents – strategy, planning, and test reports.
   - **Knowledge Transfer Sessions**: Conducting knowledge transfer sessions for the key users and IT support staff.
   - **Training Material Development**: Creating training materials for end-user training.
   - **Process Documentation**: Updating business process documentation to reflect the implemented solution.

8. **Cutover Planning and Organizational Readiness**

   The ASG's project teams finalize cutover plans, and assesses organizational readiness for go-live.

   Activities Include:

   - **Cutover Strategy Refinement**: Finalizing the cutover strategy based on technical and business considerations.

- **Cutover Plan Development**: Creating detailed cutover plans with task sequences, timings, and responsibilities.
- **Mock Cutover Execution**: Conducting mock cutover exercises to validate the cutover plan.
- **Rollback Planning**: Developing rollback procedures in case of cutover issues.
- **Organizational Readiness Assessment**: Evaluating organizational readiness for the new solution.
- **Go-Live Support Planning**: Developing plans for go-live support and hyper care.
- **Business Continuity Planning**: Ensuring business continuity during and after cutover.

Key Testing Deliverables of the Realize Phase

The testing activities in the Realize phase produce several critical deliverables that ensure solution quality and readiness:

1. **Test Strategy and Planning Deliverables**
    - **Master Test Plan**: Comprehensive plan covering all testing phases, approaches, and methodologies.
    - **Test Phase Plans**: Detailed plans for each testing phase (unit, integration, system, and UAT).
    - **Test Environment Plan**: Documentation of test environment requirements and setup.
    - **Test Data Management Plan**: Strategy for creating and managing test data across environments.
    - **Test Automation Strategy**: Approach for automated testing across the O2C process flow.
2. **Test Execution Deliverables**
    - **Test Scripts/Cases**: Detailed test cases for all O2C process variants and scenarios.
    - **Automated Test Scripts**: Automation scripts for regression, UAT, Performance, and high-value test cases.
    - **Test Execution Logs**: Documentation of all test execution activities and results.
    - **Defect Logs**: Comprehensive logs of all identified defects with classification and status.

- **Test Summary Reports**: Regular reports summarizing test execution progress and results.

For reference, here is a simple Integration Testing Report covering the O2C process variants, integration points, and summary on the volume of test cases.

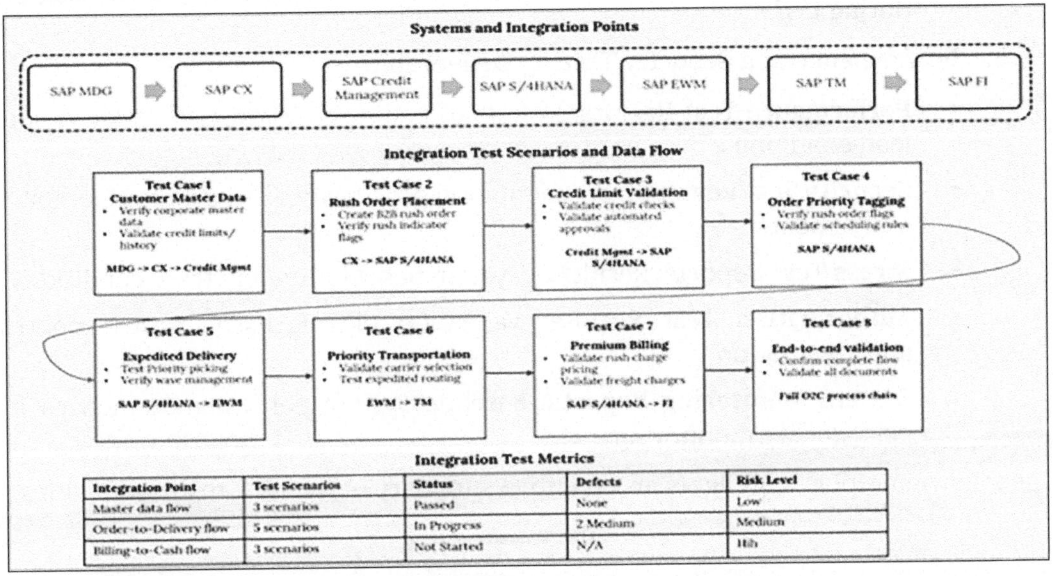

Figure 13.8: *Integration Test Plan and Execution – B2B Rush Order Example*

3. **Integration Testing Deliverables**
   - **Integration Test Plan**: Detailed plan for testing all integration points in the O2C process.
   - **Interface Test Scenarios**: Specific test scenarios for each interface in the O2C flow.
   - **End-to-End Process Test Results**: Results of complete O2C process flow testing.
   - **Interface Error Handling Test Results**: Documentation of error handling test results.
   - **Integration Performance Test Results**: Results of performance testing for key interfaces.
4. **User Acceptance Testing Deliverables**
   - **UAT Plan**: Detailed plan for user acceptance testing.
   - **Business Scenario Test Cases**: Test cases based on real-world business scenarios.

- **UAT Execution Results**: Documentation of UAT execution and results.
- **User Sign-off Documents**: Formal sign-off from business users on UAT results.
- **UAT Issue Resolution Documentation**: Documentation of issue resolution during UAT.

5. **Performance and Security Testing Deliverables**
   - **Performance Test Results**: Results of system performance under various load conditions.
   - **Security Test Results**: Documentation of security testing and vulnerability assessments.
   - **Stress Test Reports**: Results of system behavior under stress conditions.
   - **Authorization Test Results**: Validation of role-based access control implementation.
   - **System Monitoring Reports**: Baseline system performance metrics for post-go-live monitoring.

The following report highlights an executive summary of the O2C testing activities.

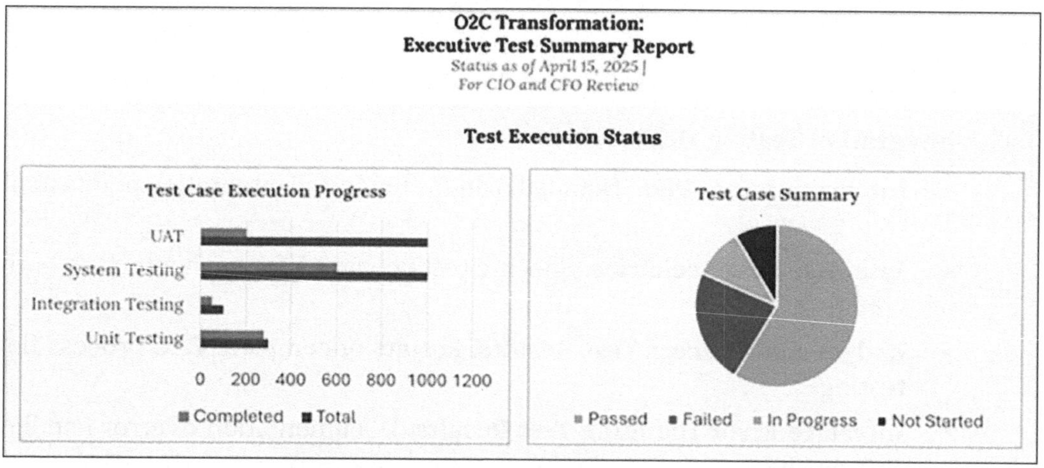

Figure 13.9: *Executive Test Summary Report*

6. **Test Management and Reporting Deliverables**
   - **Test Coverage Matrix**: Documentation of the requirements coverage through testing.
   - **Traceability Matrix**: Mapping of test cases to business requirements.
   - **Test Metrics Dashboard**: Visual representation of the key test metrics and KPIs.

- **Defect Trend Analysis**: Analysis of the defect trends throughout the testing lifecycle.
- **Executive Test Summary Reports**: Concise reports for executive stakeholders highlighting the key metrics, risks, and readiness assessment.

The Realize phase is the most execution-intensive phase of the project, where the solution design from the Explore phase is brought to life through configuration, development, testing, and validation. The thoroughness and quality of activities in this phase directly impact the success of the deployment, and the ultimate realization of business benefits from the transformation.

Deploy Phase

This phase focuses on the final preparations for go-live, cutover activities, and transition to production. For the Order-to-Cash (O2C) transformation from legacy systems (Salesforce, Experian, Manhattan WMS, and Oracle EBS) to an integrated SAP S/4HANA solution, the Deploy phase represents the culmination of all the previous efforts, where the solution is moved to production, and becomes operational.

Objectives of the Deploy Phase

The primary objectives of the Deploy phase include:

- Finalizing all the preparations for go-live.
- Executing the cutover plan.
- Migrating data to the production environment.
- Validating the production environment.
- Activating the production solution.
- Providing post-go-live support.
- Executing cut-over test cases.
- Transitioning to ongoing operations and maintenance.
- Completing the handover to the support organization.

Key Activities

The project teams will lead the following key activities during the Deploy phase:

1. **Cutover Preparation and Execution**

   The project teams lead the preparation and execution of the cutover plan to transition from legacy systems to the new SAP solution.

Activities Include:

- **Cutover Readiness Assessment**: Conducting a final assessment of readiness for cutover across technical, functional, and organizational dimensions to ensure that all systems (SAP MDG, CX, SAP S/4HANA, EWM, and TM) are ready to replace the legacy systems (Salesforce, Experian, Manhattan WMS, and Oracle EBS).
- **Cutover Plan Finalization**: Finalizing the detailed cutover plan with precise scheduling, including the timing for legacy system freezes, and SAP system activations.
- **Legacy System Freeze**: Coordinating the freezing of legacy systems according to the cutover plan, ensuring that all in-flight transactions are properly handled.
- **Production Environment Preparation**: Finalizing the production environment configuration, including system parameters, job scheduling, and user access.
- **Production Data Migration**: Executing the production data migration, including master data and open transactions from the legacy systems.
- **System Validation**: Validating the production system after data migration, to ensure data integrity and system functionality.
- **Go/No-Go Decision Support**: Providing information and recommendations for the go/no-go decision based on cutover progress and validation results.
- **Production Activation**: Activating the production system for end users after receiving go-live approval.
- **Cutover Issue Management**: Managing issues that arise during cutover, implementing contingency plans as needed.

2. **Post-Go-Live Support**

   The project teams provide intensive support immediately after go-live to ensure system stability, and address any issues.

   Activities Include:

   - **Hyper care Setup**: Establishing the hyper care support structure with appropriate resources, tools, and processes.
   - **Issue Management**: Implementing a robust issue management process to quickly identify, prioritize, and resolve issues.
   - **24/7 Support Coverage**: Providing round-the-clock support during the initial post-go-live period to address critical issues immediately.
   - **Performance Monitoring**: Continuously monitoring system performance to identify and address any bottlenecks or issues.

- **Business Process Monitoring**: Monitoring key business processes to ensure that they are functioning as expected, particularly those that replace the current manual processes like reconciliation.
- **Critical Business Process Support**: Providing specialized support for critical business processes, especially during key business events such as month-end closing.
- **Daily Status Reporting**: Producing daily status reports on system performance, issues, and resolutions.
- **Hyper care Exit Assessment**: Assessing readiness to exit hyper care based on predefined criteria, and transition to normal support.

3. **Knowledge Transfer and Support Organization Enablement**

   The project implementation teams ensure that the support organization is fully enabled to take over system support after the hyper care period.

   Activities Include:

   - **Knowledge Transfer Sessions**: Conducting comprehensive knowledge transfer sessions for support teams on system components, configurations, and customizations.
   - **Support Documentation Finalization**: Finalizing all support documentation, including system administration guides, troubleshooting guides, and standard operating procedures.
   - **Support Tools Setup**: Setting up support tools for monitoring, issue tracking, and knowledge management.
   - **Support Process Implementation**: Implementing support processes aligned with the organization's IT service management framework.
   - **Transition Planning**: Planning the transition from project team to support organization, including resource allocation and responsibilities.
   - **Support Handover**: Formally handing over support responsibilities to the permanent support organization.

4. **Project Closure**

   The project implementation team leads the formal closure of the project, ensuring that all the deliverables are complete and accepted.

   Activities Include:

   - Deliverable Verification: Verifying that all the project deliverables have been completed and accepted.
   - Documentation Finalization: Finalizing all the project documentation, and ensuring it is properly archived and accessible.

- Project Team Demobilization: Planning and executing the demobilization of the project team.
- Project Closure Meeting: Conducting the formal project closure meeting with the key stakeholders.
- Transition to Operations: Ensuring a smooth transition from project mode to operational mode.

Key Testing Deliverables in the Deploy Phase

The testing activities in the Deploy phase are focused on validating the production environment, and ensuring business readiness. The key testing deliverables include:

1. **Production Validation Test Plan and Results**

   A comprehensive plan for validating the production environment after deployment, with detailed test cases and results documentation.

   Key Components:

   - Production environment validation criteria
   - Critical business process validation test cases
   - System integration validation tests
   - Production validation test execution results
   - Issue log and resolution status

2. **Cutover Testing Checklist and Results**

   A checklist of testing activities needs to be performed during each stage of the cutover process, with the documentation of results.

   Key Components:

   - Pre-cutover testing requirements
   - Data migration validation tests
   - Post-migration system validation tests

3. **Performance and Volume Testing Results**

   Results of the final performance and volume testing in the production environment needs to be recorded under expected business load conditions.

   Key Components:

   - Performance test scenarios and expected results
   - Volume testing approach and data sets
   - System response time measurements

- Transaction throughput analysis
- Batch processing performance results
- System resource utilization metrics

4. **Business Continuity Testing Results**

   Documentation of business continuity testing to ensure that the organization can maintain operations in case of system issues.

   Key Components:

   - Business continuity test scenarios
   - Disaster recovery testing approach and results
   - System failover testing results
   - Backup and recovery testing results
   - Issue documentation and resolution approach

The following diagram provides an example report of cutover testing.

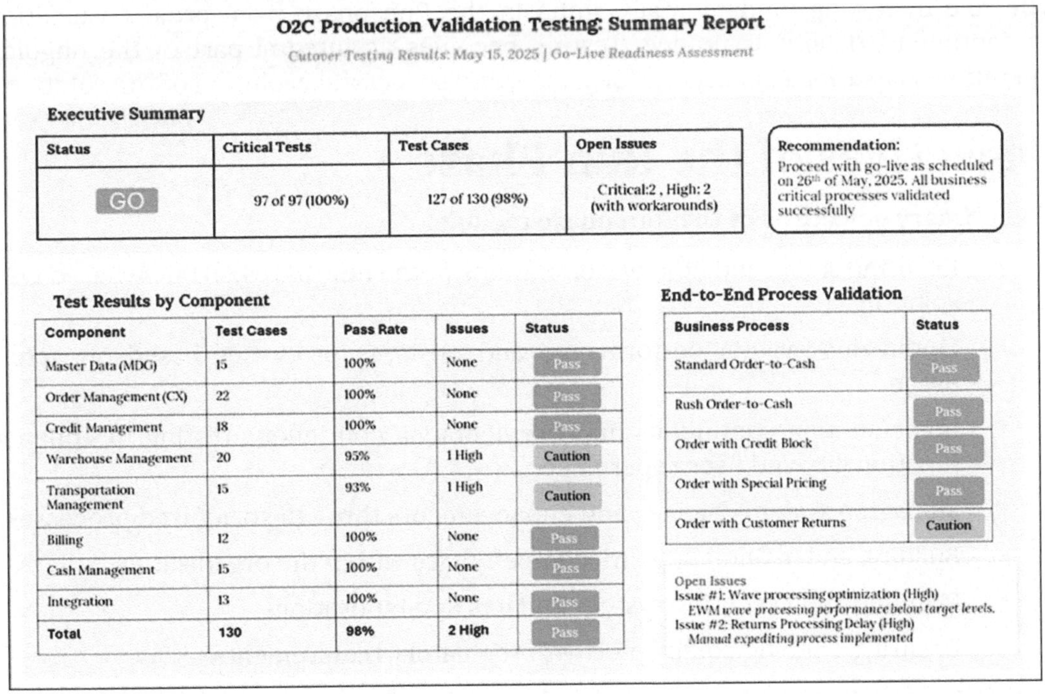

O2C Production Validation Testing: Summary Report

Cutover Testing Results: May 15, 2025 | Go-Live Readiness Assessment

Executive Summary

Status	Critical Tests	Test Cases	Open Issues
GO	97 of 97 (100%)	127 of 130 (98%)	Critical:2 , High: 2 (with workarounds)

Recommendation: Proceed with go-live as scheduled on 26th of May, 2025. All business critical processes validated successfully

Test Results by Component

Component	Test Cases	Pass Rate	Issues	Status
Master Data (MDG)	15	100%	None	Pass
Order Management (CX)	22	100%	None	Pass
Credit Management	18	100%	None	Pass
Warehouse Management	20	95%	1 High	Caution
Transportation Management	15	93%	1 High	Caution
Billing	12	100%	None	Pass
Cash Management	15	100%	None	Pass
Integration	13	100%	None	Pass
Total	**130**	**98%**	**2 High**	Pass

End-to-End Process Validation

Business Process	Status
Standard Order-to-Cash	Pass
Rush Order-to-Cash	Pass
Order with Credit Block	Pass
Order with Special Pricing	Pass
Order with Customer Returns	Caution

Open Issues
Issue #1: Wave processing optimization (High)
EWM wave processing performance below target levels.
Issue #2: Returns Processing Delay (High)
Manual expediting process implemented

***Figure 13.10:** Cutover Testing Report (aka Production Validation Testing)*

Pro Tip: *Establish a robust hyper care support process with clearly defined issue management processes to sustain go-live momentum.*

The Deploy phase represents the culmination of the transformation journey, where the new integrated O2C solution replaces the fragmented legacy landscape, and begins delivering business value. The thoroughness of preparations, attention to detail during cutover, and quality of post-go-live support directly impact the initial success of the implementation, and set the foundation for long-term value realization.

Run Phase

This phase focuses on the ongoing operations, support, optimization, and continuous improvement of the implemented solution. For the Order-to-Cash (O2C) transformation from legacy systems (Salesforce, Experian, Manhattan WMS, and Oracle EBS) to an integrated SAP S/4HANA solution, the Run phase represents the long-term value realization and evolution of the new system landscape.

The role of testing fundamentally shifts in the Run phase from project validation to continuous quality assurance. Testing becomes an integral part of the ongoing operations, ensuring stability, performance, and successful evolution of the solution.

Objectives of the Run Phase

The primary objectives of the Run phase include:

- Ensuring stable and efficient operations of the new SAP S/4HANA-based O2C solution.
- Optimizing system performance and business processes based on actual usage.
- Implementing continuous improvements via continuous testing to enhance functionality and user experience.
- Managing system changes and enhancements through structured processes.
- Building and maintaining SAP competencies within the organization.
- Planning and executing system updates and innovations.
- Ensuring ongoing compliance with regulatory requirements.

The following diagram highlights the foundation for continuous improvement – continuous testing.

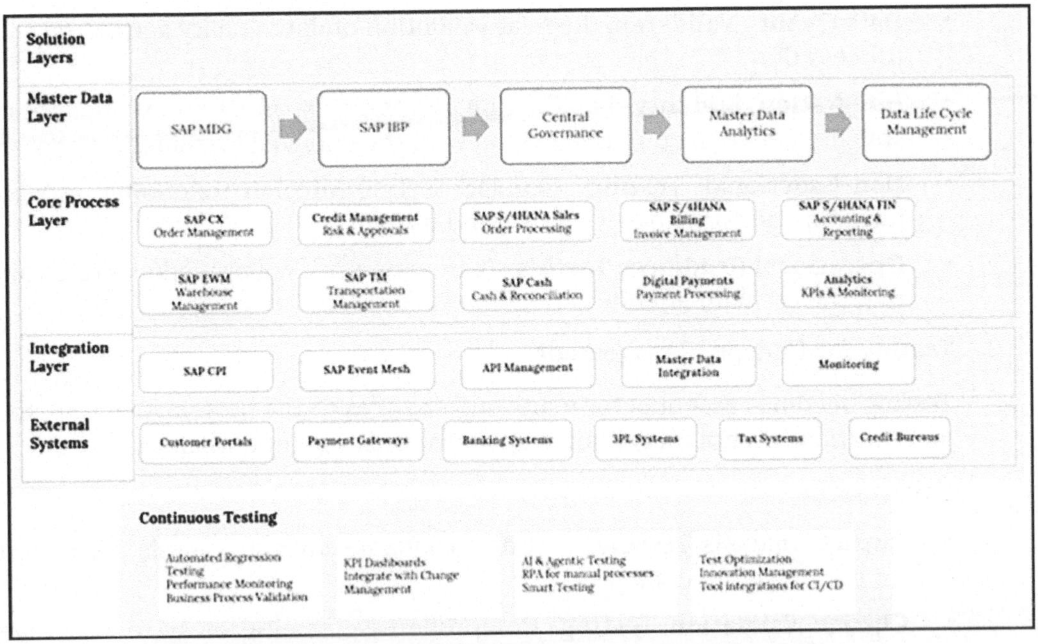

***Figure 13.11**: Solution Architecture for Continuous Testing Framework*

Testing in the Run Phase: Continuous Quality Assurance

The role of testing fundamentally shifts in the Run phase from project validation to continuous quality assurance. Testing becomes an integral part of ongoing operations, ensuring stability, performance, and successful evolution of the solution.

1. **Testing Mindset for Operational Excellence**

   Adopting a testing mindset becomes critical for operational excellence in the Run phase, focusing on proactive quality management, rather than reactive issue resolution.

   Key Aspects:

   - **Preventive Testing Approach**: Implementing preventive testing routines to identify potential issues before they impact business operations.
   - **Performance Monitoring**: Continuous monitoring and testing of system performance under varying business conditions.
   - **Business Process Validation**: Regular validation of critical business processes to ensure that they continue to function as expected.
   - **User Experience Testing**: Ongoing evaluation of user experience to identify friction points and improvement opportunities.

- **Data Quality Validation**: Regular validation of data quality across the O2C process flow.
- **Integration Stability Verification**: Periodic verification of integration stability between components and with the external systems.
- **Non-Functional Testing**: Regular testing of non-functional aspects, including performance, security, and usability.
- **Operational Readiness Testing**: Testing operational procedures to ensure that they remain effective.

2. **Testing for Change Management**

   Testing becomes essential for managing changes to the system, ensuring that modifications do not negatively impact the existing functionality.

   Key Aspects:

   - **Impact Analysis Testing**: Testing to validate impact analysis predictions for the proposed changes.
   - **Change Validation Testing**: Comprehensive testing of system changes before production implementation.
   - **Regression Testing**: Automated and manual regression testing to verify that changes do not break the existing functionality.
   - **Integration Testing for Changes**: Testing the impact of changes on the integration points.
   - **Performance Testing for Changes**: Verifying that changes do not negatively impact the system performance.
   - **User Acceptance Testing**: Business validation of changes before implementation.
   - **Post-Implementation Verification**: Testing to verify that changes are working correctly after implementation.
   - **Change Rollback Testing**: Testing rollback procedures for high-risk changes.

3. **Testing for Continuous Improvement**

   Testing provides the foundation for continuous improvement initiatives, validating enhancement ideas, and measuring their impact.

   Key Aspects:

   - **Improvement Hypothesis Testing**: Testing hypotheses about potential improvements before full implementation.
   - **Prototype Testing**: Testing prototypes of new features and enhancements.

- **A/B Testing**: Comparative testing of the alternative approaches to process improvements.
- **Business Value Testing**: Testing to verify the business value of improvements.
- **User Adoption Testing**: Testing user adoption and satisfaction with improvements.
- **Process Efficiency Testing**: Measuring the impact of improvements on process efficiency.
- **Automated Process Testing**: Implementing automated testing for improved business processes.
- **Benchmark Testing**: Regular benchmark testing against performance targets.

4. **Testing for Innovation and Updates**

   Testing enables safe adoption of innovations, updates, and new features in the SAP landscape.

   Key Aspects:

   - **Update Impact Testing**: Testing the impact of SAP updates before production implementation.
   - **Feature Adoption Testing**: Testing new features before enabling them for business use.
   - **Compatibility Testing**: Testing the compatibility of innovations with existing customizations.
   - **Security Patch Testing**: Testing security patches before implementation.
   - **Innovation Pilot Testing**: Controlled testing of innovations with the selected business users.
   - **Performance Impact Testing**: Testing the performance impact of updates and new features.
   - **Integration Stability Testing**: Verifying that updates do not disrupt integration points.
   - **Full Regression Testing**: Comprehensive regression testing for the major updates.

The following diagram shows the KPIs and the summary test program in a maintenance phase of SAP S/4HANA project.

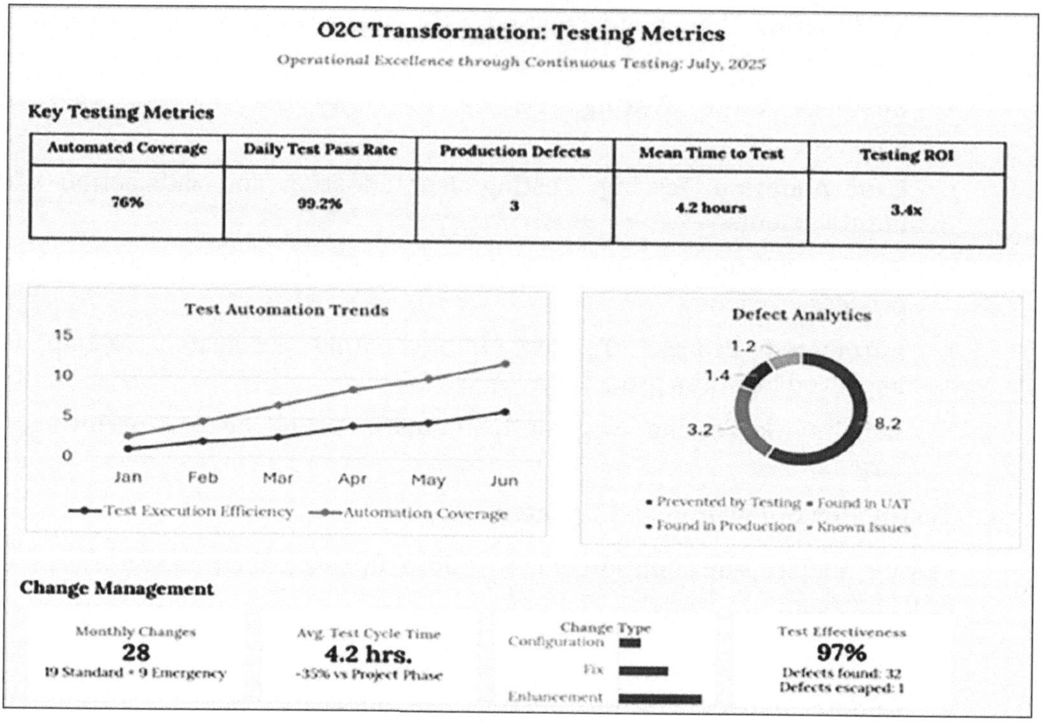

Figure 13.12: *Continuous Testing Dashboard*

The Continuous Testing Framework

To support the diverse testing needs in the Run phase, a comprehensive testing framework is created by QA leadership and stakeholders with the following components:

- **Test Automation Infrastructure**: Investment in test automation to enable efficient and frequent testing.
- **Continuous Integration/Continuous Deployment**: Integration of testing into CI/CD pipelines for system changes.
- **Test Environment Management**: Proper management of test environments to support various testing needs.
- **Test Data Management**: Processes for maintaining quality test data that represent production scenarios.
- **Risk-Based Testing Approach**: Methodology for prioritizing testing based on business risk.
- **Testing Center of Excellence**: Centralized expertise for testing best practices and standards.
- **Business Process Testing Capability**: Capability to efficiently test end-to-end business processes.

- **Testing Metrics and Reporting**: Framework for measuring testing effectiveness, and reporting results.
- **Testing Tools and Technology**: Appropriate tools for various testing needs, including automation, performance, and security.
- **Testing Skills and Competencies**: Development of testing skills within the organization.

Pro Tip: *Adopt a risk-based testing approach for the ongoing changes, focusing efforts on areas of the highest business impact.*

Conclusion

This chapter examined a live SAP S/4HANA implementation following the SAP Activate methodology, focused on an Order-to-Cash business transformation. It demonstrated how enterprises can successfully transition from fragmented legacy systems to a unified, and fully integrated SAP S/4HANA landscape.

Industry research consistently shows that when testing teams possess a deep understanding of the broader SAP S/4HANA project ecosystem, quality outcomes improve by over 90%. This stems from the team's holistic awareness of business processes, technical dependencies, and integration points, enabling proactive risk identification and mitigation throughout the delivery lifecycle.

The upcoming chapter will delve into the business case for SAP testing projects, focusing on how organizations can rigorously quantify the value delivered by their testing initiatives. Drawing on industry-standard ROI methodologies, we will demonstrate that a robust and strategically aligned testing approach not only mitigates operational risks but also acts as a vital enabler of transformation success.

References

- (Book) Enterprise Architecture with SAP
- (Book) SAP S/4HANA Architecture
- (Podcast) Inside SAP S/4HANA
- SAP Activate Course: https://learning.sap.com/learning-journeys/discovering-sap-activate-implementation-tools-and-methodology
- https://learning.sap.com/learning-journeys/exploring-business-and-solution-transformation-tools-and-methodology/demonstrating-usage-examples-for-sap-activate
- https://learning.sap.com/learning-journeys/explore-sap-cloud-erp/utilizing-sap-activate-implementation-methodology-and-sap-cloud-alm

CHAPTER 14
Business Case and Case Studies

Introduction

Organizations undertaking SAP S/4HANA implementations or migrations face significant challenges when justifying the software testing investments to stakeholders. According to a recent industry research, organizations with inadequate testing experience average cost overruns of 23% on major ERP implementations, and extend hyper care periods by an average of 4.2 months. McKinsey's 2023 survey found that projects with mature testing strategies were 3.5 times more likely to meet the business objectives, and deliver on time.

> *"Testing is not just about finding defects – it is about providing business confidence, and accelerating digital transformation. Organizations that view testing as strategic, rather than tactical consistently outperform their peers in major SAP implementations."* – SAP Executive Board Member (2023).

Despite these compelling statistics, testing is often underfunded, leading to increased risks, delays, and cost overruns. A well-structured business case for SAP testing is essential to secure buy-in from stakeholders, justify the necessary resources, and demonstrate testing's role as a business enabler, rather than merely a technical necessity.

This chapter aims to establish a clear understanding of what constitutes an effective business case in the context of SAP S/4HANA testing, and provides a methodical framework for creating a compelling case that resonates with decision-makers. By mastering the art of business case development, Quality Engineering leaders and professionals can secure the appropriate budget and resources necessary to execute comprehensive Quality Programs that make a sustainable impact on SAP S/4HANA projects.

Structure

In this chapter, we explore how to articulate testing value in business terms, quantify both tangible and intangible benefits with the following structure.

- Business Case Framework
- Core components of a business case
- Executive Business Case
- Discovery Methodology
- Common Objections and Counter-Arguments
- Calculating Test Automation ROI
- Case Study: Large-Scale SAP S/4HANA Maintenance Project
- Case Study: SAP S/4HANA 1809 to 2310 Upgrade Testing Project

Business Case Framework

A successful business case for SAP testing combines tangible financial benefits with critical risk mitigation elements to present a comprehensive value proposition. The framework below illustrates how these components intersect to create a compelling narrative for stakeholders. To interpret the diagram, start by focusing on the **Core Business Case** at the center, then trace the inputs feeding into it, and the stakeholders influencing its direction.

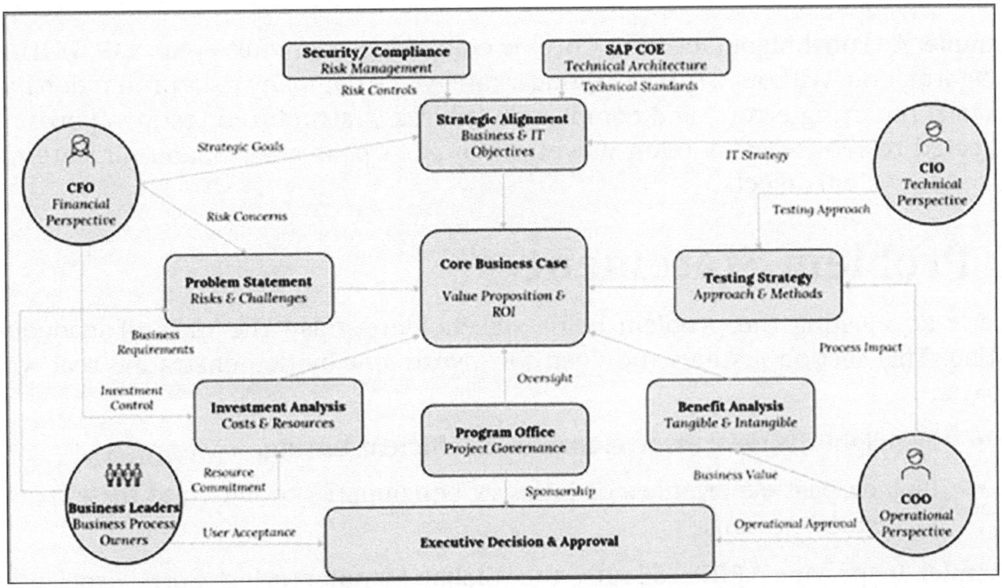

Figure 14.1: *Business Case Framework*

This process and framework diagram may look overwhelming, but do not worry. You will not need to create this kind of comprehensive business case for every SAP project. In most projects, you will simply need to present your testing business case focused on the key aspects such as risks, testing approach, and ROI. The subsequent sections will help you build such a business case quickly, and they also cover a couple of examples.

Core Components of a Business Case

To build a compelling business case, it should be structured around the following 8 core components:

1. Executive Summary

An executive summary provides a high-level overview of the need for focused SAP testing methodology, setting the stage for decision-makers. This section distills the essence of the business case, ensuring that stakeholders quickly grasp its importance.

- A concise statement highlighting the importance of SAP testing.
- Key objectives and expected benefits.
- Alignment with the overall SAP S/4HANA program goals.

Key Takeaway: The executive summary should be concise yet powerful, focusing on business impact, rather than technical details. It should be written last but appear first in your document.

Example: A Global Manufacturing Corp. is embarking on a multi-year SAP S/4HANA transformation. Without a robust testing strategy, the company risks production halts, financial reporting errors, and compliance failures. A structured testing approach is projected to reduce production downtime by 30% post-go-live, and mitigate risks related to system defects.

2. Problem Statement

Clearly articulating the problem helps stakeholders grasp the risks of inadequate testing. This section justifies the need for investment by demonstrating real-world impacts.

- Highlight the risks associated with insufficient testing.
- Include past experiences or industry benchmarks to illustrate the impact of inadequate testing.

Example: In previous ERP rollouts, the Global Manufacturing Corp. experienced untested defects in its supply chain management module, leading to a 15% increase in order fulfillment delays. The company also faced financial reporting discrepancies due to unverified integrations with third-party systems. A lack of automated testing resulted in an extended stabilization period, impacting business operations and customer satisfaction.

Pro Tip: *Use metrics and tangible past incidents to strengthen the problem statement section, making it relatable to decision-makers.*

3. Scope of SAP Testing

A well-defined scope ensures clarity on what will be tested, reducing ambiguity and ensuring comprehensive coverage.

- Coverage of functional, integration, performance, security, and User Acceptance Testing (UAT).
- Scope for automated vs. manual testing.
- Testing of custom developments and third-party integrations.

  Example: The company prioritized testing across functional, integration, performance, and security testing. The key focus areas included finance, supply chain, and procurement, with a goal of 70% of regression testing. This approach ensured critical business processes were safeguarded, while accelerating release cycles.

Pro Tip: *Incorporate AI tools and risk-based prioritization techniques to align scope with business impact, reducing unnecessary testing load.*

4. Value Proposition

It demonstrates the tangible benefits of SAP testing, such as cost savings and risk reduction.

> **Example:** Implementing a structured testing strategy was projected to reduce post-go-live defects by 40%, shorten testing cycles by 30% through automation, and enhance compliance. These improvements would lead to estimated savings of $3 million by preventing production disruptions, and minimizing manual effort.

5. Proposed Testing Strategy

It outlines the approach to executing testing efficiently and effectively.

> **Example:** The Global Manufacturing Corp. is adopting an enterprise test automation platform to manage testing across SAP S/4HANA, and its integrated applications. By embracing shift-left testing and leveraging business process

models, the company aims to detect defects earlier and prioritize testing in business-critical areas - maximizing defect detection where it matters most.

6. Key Metrics and KPIs

This establishes success criteria to measure the effectiveness of SAP testing.

Example: The company set key performance indicators, including reducing defect leakage to below 5%, achieving 90% test coverage for critical business processes, cutting test execution time by 40%, and securing a 95% user acceptance rate before go-live.

Pro Tip: *Leverage KPIs that can track the progress from past to future such as defect leakage rate, test coverage %, average defect resolution time, and percentage of automated test cases.*

7. Investment and ROI Analysis

It provides a financial assessment of testing investments, and expected returns.

Example: The business case justified a $2 million investment in test automation and resources, with an expected 300% ROI over three years due to reduce defect resolution costs, faster go-live, and minimized business disruptions.

8. Stakeholder Engagement and Approval Plan

It ensures alignment with the key decision-makers to secure funding and support.

The company typically engages the CIO, SAP program management function, finance controllers, and business process owners in structured workshops, presenting a cost-benefit analysis.

Through a comprehensive review of the business case, backed by a clear demonstration of financial and operational benefits, stakeholders successfully secure executive sponsorship, and obtain approval for the necessary funding to drive the SAP testing initiative forward.

Executive Business Case Example

Here is an example - a business case prepared by a Quality COE team.

Executive Summary

Organizations implementing SAP S/4HANA face a critical business risk: 65% of the failed implementations can be traced to inadequate testing. Our current ECC

6.0 environment supports 12 countries, 3,000+ users, and $2.5B in annual revenue processed through SAP. A testing program that ensures successful transition to SAP S/4HANA is not optional – it is imperative.

Problem Statement

- **Business Disruption**: Each hour of system downtime costs approximately $75,000.
- **Resource Drain**: Production defects cost 7x more to fix than those caught in testing.
- **Competitive Disadvantage**: System issues directly impact customer satisfaction scores.
- **Compliance Risk**: System errors could result in regulatory penalties up to $500,000.

Investment and Returns

Investment: $1.2M	**Returns: $10.85M (3-year)**
✓ Testing resources	✓ Risk mitigation: $8.5M
✓ Testing tools	✓ Reduced support costs: $400K
✓ Environment setup	✓ Faster implementation: $600K
✓ Test automation	✓ Productivity gains: $1.35M

Table 14.1: *Investment Returns*

ROI: 804% over 3 years with payback period of just 3.5 months after go-live.

Key Success Metrics

- 95% critical business process coverage.
- 35% reduction in hyper care resource needs.
- 20% reduction in implementation timeline.

Implementation Approach

Phase	**Timeline**	**Key Deliverables**
Preparation	Month 1-3	Test strategy, scenarios, and data
Execution	Month 4-14	Comprehensive test cycles across all modules
Go-Live	Month 14-18	Support, knowledge transfer and optimization

Table 14.2: *Implementation Approach*

Strategic Alignment

- **Digital Transformation**: Ensures reliable foundation for future initiatives.
- **Operational Excellence**: Validates critical business processes end-to-end.
- **Risk Mitigation**: Protects revenue streams and business continuity.
- **Cost Optimization**: Reduces long-term support and maintenance costs.

Executive Decision

To secure $1.2M investment for the SAP S/4HANA Testing Program to protect $15M+ SAP S/4HANA implementation investment, and ensure business continuity during this mission-critical transition.

In the next sections, let us explore how to create such a template by using comprehensive discovery methodology backed by strong data points.

Discovery Methodology

Enterprises operate in highly structured business and technology ecosystems, with unique processes, integrations, and regulatory requirements. A testing strategy that works for one company may be irrelevant for another due to differences in industry, organizational maturity, and technology stack.

You cannot base a business case on isolated case studies from different companies - a thorough study of the customer's specific environment is essential. The foundation of a strong business case is deep discovery, achieved through structured methodologies, data-driven assessments, and stakeholder engagements. By conducting interviews, workshops, and system assessments, we gather critical data points that reveal current inefficiencies, business risks, and opportunities for improvement.

For instance, an organization migrating from SAP ECC 6.0 to SAP S/4HANA may currently rely on manual testing but lack traceability and risk coverage. Their fragmented approach might not support new Fiori apps, embedded analytics, or cloud-based integrations. Without an understanding of these gaps, any testing proposal would be misaligned with business priorities, and fail to secure executive buy-in.

The following methodology ensures a structured approach to uncovering the key insights, and building a strong, evidence-based business case.

1. **Stakeholder Engagement and Interviews**

    a. Identify key stakeholders from IT, business, and compliance teams.

    b. Conduct structured interviews to understand challenges, pain points, and priorities.

2. **Current Testing Landscape Analysis**
    a. Review the existing test plans, tools, automation coverage, and test execution processes.
    b. Identify manual dependencies, lack of traceability, and compliance gaps.
3. **Business and IT Alignment Checks**
    a. Assess if testing is aligned with the SAP S/4HANA transformation goals.
    b. Identify areas where testing could impact business continuity.
4. **Risk and Impact Assessment**
    a. Analyze historical defect trends and production issues.
    b. Evaluate the risk of business process failures due to inadequate testing.
5. **Future Testing State Definition**
    a. Define the desired testing approach, including automation, shift-left testing, and AI-driven optimizations.

The following table provides critical questions that you can use to uncover the data points across the preceding five areas mentioned.

Aspect	Question
Current Testing State	• What testing tools are currently being used? • What percentage of testing is manual vs. automated? • How are test cases documented, and is there a test management system? • How do you track defects and test execution progress? • Are testing efforts aligned with business processes or just IT-driven? • What level of test coverage do you have for critical SAP processes? • How often are tests executed during development cycles? • Do you have a defined test strategy for regression testing? • What are the biggest pain points in the current testing approach? • How long does a typical testing cycle take, from planning to execution?

Understanding Business Drivers for SAP S/4HANA Project	• What is the key driver for SAP S/4HANA migration–compliance, performance, innovation, or cost reduction? • What are the core modules and integrations that must be tested? • Are there business-critical processes that cannot afford downtime? • What are the expected benefits of moving to SAP S/4HANA from a business perspective? • Are you planning a greenfield, brownfield, or hybrid migration? • How does testing fit into the overall SAP S/4HANA implementation roadmap? • Have previous ERP transformations resulted in post-go-live defects or delays? • How will business users be involved in user acceptance testing (UAT)? • What are the main risks identified for SAP S/4HANA migration? • Do you have compliance or audit requirements that influence testing?
Current Testing Processes and Gaps	• Do existing test cases cover Fiori apps, embedded analytics, and new SAP S/4HANA features? • Have test automation tools been evaluated for SAP S/4HANA compatibility? • How is performance testing handled today? • Are integrations with third-party systems included in the test strategy? • Do you have enough historical test data to compare results pre- and post-migration? • Have you faced challenges in test data availability? • How frequently are security vulnerabilities tested in SAP? • Are you using real-world business scenarios for testing, or is testing done in silos? • Are business users confident in the current testing process? • Have previous upgrades or patches caused unexpected system failures?

Definition of To-Be Testing State	• What improvements would you like to see in SAP testing? • Do you plan to increase test automation coverage? • Would a shift-left approach (early testing) be beneficial for your project? • Do you require testing support from SAP partners or vendors? • Would business process heatmaps help prioritize testing? • What are the key KPIs that should be tracked to measure testing effectiveness? • What level of risk is acceptable for production releases? • How do you plan to handle SAP updates and patches post go-live? • Are you considering AI-driven testing optimizations? • What is your vision for test governance and compliance?
Financial and ROI Considerations	• How much is currently spent on SAP testing (resources, tools, time)? • How much does production downtime cost your business? • Have defects in production led to regulatory fines or business losses? • What cost reductions could be achieved through automation? • How much time is lost in inefficient manual testing cycles? • Could reducing test cycle times improve overall SAP project timelines? • Are there unquantified risks that could become costly later? • Would a strong testing strategy help secure executive buy-in? • What investment would be reasonable for achieving SAP S/4HANA testing excellence? • What is the expected savings from reducing defects, avoiding rework, and improving efficiency?
Team Structure	• Who owns testing? (Internal IT, SAP implementation partner, or business users) • How testing is managed across the implementation lifecycle • What happens post-go-live–whether testing will be continuous or handed off • Future rollouts and how testing will scale

Table 14.3: *Discovery Questionnaire*

Calculating Test Automation ROI

While organizations universally recognize the critical role of Quality Engineering in SAP implementations, automation often remains an afterthought in budget allocation. The majority of funding is directed toward SAP software licenses and implementation teams, leaving testing - especially automation - with only a fraction of the resources it truly needs.

This oversight is not due to a lack of awareness but rather competing priorities. As a result, manual testing continues to dominate, reinforcing the perception of testing as a cost center, rather than a value-driven function. However, organizations that embed test automation from the beginning of their SAP projects unlock efficiencies, reduce risks, and accelerate time-to-value.

In this section, we will explore how to strategically position test automation as a business enabler by quantifying its ROI in SAP S/4HANA projects. By presenting a compelling business case, you can shift testing from an underfunded necessity to a strategic investment that delivers measurable impact.

Understanding the Basics

The ROI compares what you gain from an investment versus what you spend. For test automation, the formula is:

$$ROI = \frac{(Benefits - Costs)}{Costs} x\ 100\%$$

A positive percentage means your investment is profitable. For example, an ROI of 200% means you gained twice, what you invested.

How to Calculate

It is important to note that you do not need to measure and present all the aspects related to tangible and intangible benefits for your ROI calculation. The most compelling business case will focus on just a few Key Performance Indicators (KPIs) that:

- Align with your organization's current pain points.
- Resonate with your specific stakeholders.
- Are measurable in your current environment

First, let us explore some *of the common aspects of costs and benefits to include.*

- **One-time Costs**
    - **Tool licenses**: The upfront cost of purchasing automation tools.
    - **Training**: Getting your team up to speed on the tools.
    - **Initial setup**: Configuring environments and integrations.
- **Ongoing Costs**
    - **License maintenance**: Annual or monthly subscription fees.
    - **Script maintenance**: Time spent updating test scripts when S/4HANA changes.
    - **Infrastructure**: Cloud or hardware resources to run automated tests.
    - **Personnel**: Staff dedicated to maintaining and running automated tests.
- **Calculating Test Automation Costs**

<table>
<tr><th>Aspect</th><th>Cost</th><th>Total</th></tr>
<tr><td>Licenses</td><td>$ 250,000</td><td rowspan="3">One-time costs
$350,000</td></tr>
<tr><td>Training</td><td>$ 40,000</td></tr>
<tr><td>Setup</td><td>$ 60,000</td></tr>
<tr><td>Annual Maintenance</td><td>$50,000</td><td rowspan="3">Ongoing costs
$220,000</td></tr>
<tr><td>Personnel</td><td>$150,000 (you may want to waive off the personnel if it is of type Business-As-Usual)</td></tr>
<tr><td>Infrastructure</td><td>$ 20,000</td></tr>
</table>

Table 14.4: *Testing Costs*

- **Calculating Test Automation Benefits**

    Now, let us look at the benefits:

    Quantifiable Benefits

    - **Reduced testing time**: Hours saved by automating manual tests.
    - **Earlier defect detection**: Savings from finding bugs sooner.
    - **Increased test coverage**: Value of testing more scenarios.
    - **Reduced business disruption**: Value of fewer production issues.

    Productivity Benefits

    - **Faster releases**: Value of delivering features sooner.
    - **Resource reallocation**: Value of freeing up testers for more strategic work.
    - **Consistent quality**: Value of more reliable testing results.

- **Calculating Test Automation Benefits**

  For a team of 20 testers working on SAP S/4HANA testing:

  - *Manual testing costs: 20 testers * $60 x 40 hours/week x 4 weeks/cycle x 4 cycles/year = $768,000/ year*
  - *Automated testing costs: 6 testers * $60 x 40 hours/ week x 1 week/cycle x 4 cycles/year = $57,600/ year*
  - *Annual savings: $768,000 - $57,600 = $ 710,400*
  - ***Simple ROI calculation for Year1***

    First-year costs: $350,000 (one-time) + $220,000 (annual) = $570,000

    First-year benefits: $710,400

    First-year ROI: ($710,400 - $570,000) / $570,000 × 100% = 24.6%
  - ***Calculating multi-year ROI***

    Two-year costs: $350,000 (one-time) + $220,000 × 2 (annual) = $790,000

    Two-year benefits: $710,400 × 2 = $1,420,800

    Two-year ROI: ($1,420,800 - $790,000) / $790,000 × 100% = 79.8%

Common Objections and Counter-Arguments

Even the strongest business case will encounter resistance. Preparing for common objections in advance demonstrates thoroughness and builds credibility with stakeholders. The following table outlines the typical objections and effective counter-arguments:

Objection	**Counter-Argument**	**Supporting Data**
"We've always done manual testing successfully."	Manual testing scales poorly for S/4HANA complexity and does not provide consistent results. Automation delivers higher consistency, and allows for frequent regression testing.	Industry data shows manual testing misses 35-45% of defects in complex SAP environments, while automated approaches catch 85-90% of issues.
"Our implementation partner will handle testing."	Implementation partners focus primarily on technical testing, rather than business process validation. They lack deep knowledge of your specific business processes and industry nuances.	In a 2023 survey, 78% of organizations relying solely on partner testing reported critical business disruptions in the first 3 months post-go-live.

"We don't have budget for a robust testing program."	The cost of proper testing is minimal compared to the cost of fixing defects in production. Consider it as insurance, rather than expense.	SAP customers report production defects cost 5-7x more to fix than those caught in testing. A $1M testing investment typically prevents $3-5M in remediation costs.
"We can accelerate implementation by reducing testing."	Cutting testing does not save time– it shifts time to hyper care and problem resolution when issues are more expensive to fix.	Companies that cut testing scope reported 40% longer hyper care periods and a 25% increase in overall implementation timeline due to rework.
"Our SAP landscape uses standard SAP processes."	SAP S/4HANA introduces quarterly changes to data models and business processes that impact even seemingly simple landscapes.	Organizations consistently underestimate SAP S/4HANA testing complexity, with 70% reporting they would increase testing scope if they could repeat their implementation.
"We do not have resources to support extensive testing."	Modern testing approaches require fewer resources through automation and risk-based prioritization.	Risk-based testing approaches can reduce testing effort by 40-60%, while maintaining coverage of business-critical processes.
"Our timeline does not allow for comprehensive testing."	Testing can be executed in parallel with other activities, and automated testing accelerates timelines.	Organizations with mature testing automation report 30-40% reduction in the overall test execution time.

Table 14.5: *Business Case – Common Objections*

Key Takeaway: Do not avoid difficult conversations. Instead, prepare with data-driven counter-arguments that address concerns directly, and demonstrate your thorough understanding of both the technical and business aspects of SAP Quality Engineering.

One CFO remarked, 'We *never realized testing was a business enabler until the last upgrade meltdown*' - after which testing budget doubled and system stability improved.

Case Studies

Let us now examine how these business case principles translate to practice through two comprehensive case studies - one for a maintenance testing program, and another for an upgrade testing project. Each case study aims to highlight different aspects of a successful SAP testing business case.

Study 1: Large-Scale SAP S/4HANA Maintenance Testing Program

Company Profile

- **Company**: Global Manufacturing Corporation (Anonymized)
- **Industry**: Industrial Manufacturing
- **Revenue**: $5.2 Billion
- **Employees**: 24,000 worldwide
- **SAP Landscape**: Global SAP S/4HANA 2021 implementation across 12 countries

Project Background

Global Manufacturing Corporation (GMC) operates a complex SAP S/4HANA landscape supporting critical business processes across procurement, manufacturing, supply chain, sales, finance, and HR. The company implements quarterly maintenance cycles to address bugs, implement enhancements, and apply SAP notes and patches. Each maintenance cycle impacts multiple modules and requires comprehensive testing to ensure business continuity.

Testing Challenges

- **Scale**: Managing 10,000 test cases across system, integration, and regression testing.
- **Resource Constraints**: Limited availability of business testers.
- **Global Impact**: Changes affecting users across 12 countries and multiple time zones.
- **Complex Integration**: 18 third-party system integrations requiring validation.
- **Regulatory Compliance**: Industry-specific compliance requirements in multiple regions.
- **Testing Window**: Compressed 3-week testing timeline before each quarterly release.

The following diagram highlights the key components of a test framework of this case study.

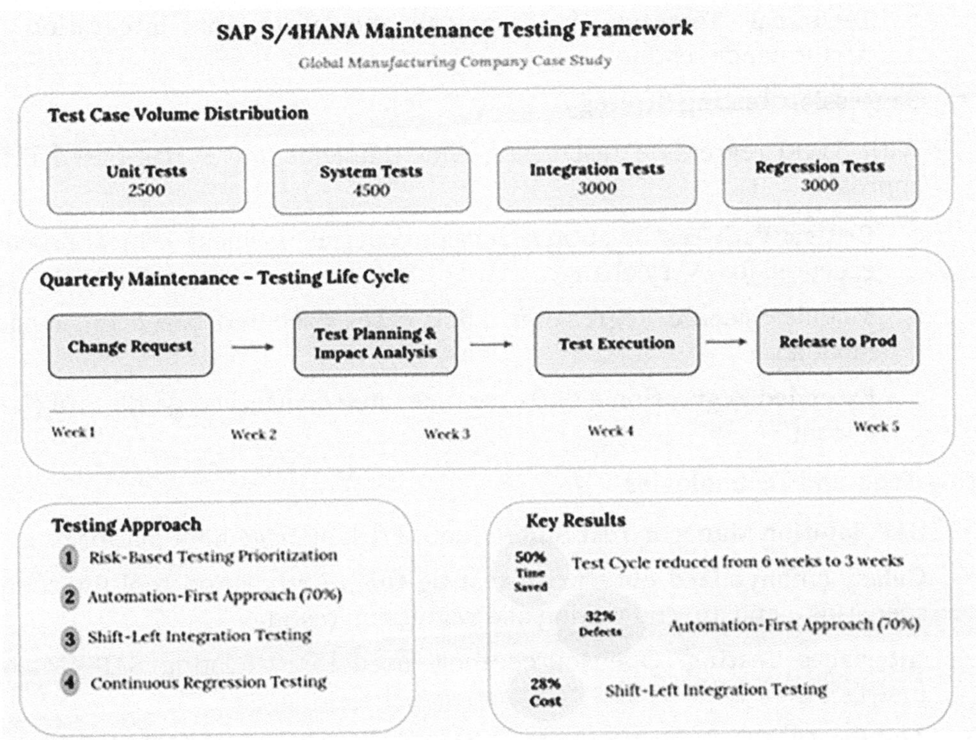

Figure 14.2: *Testing Framework*

Testing Approach

- **Test Strategy Overview**

  GMC implemented a multi-layered testing approach for their maintenance projects:

Testing Layer	Description	Test Cases	Automation
Unit Testing	Component-level testing by developers	2,500	95%
System Testing	Functional validation of individual modules	4,500	70%
Integration Testing	End-to-end process validation	3,000	40%
Regression Testing	Verification of existing functionality	3,000	85%

Table 14.6: *Test Volumes*

- **Test Management Structure**
  - **Central Testing CoE**: Core team of 15 automation specialists and test managers.
  - **Module SMEs**: 24 subject matter experts across business domains.
  - **Business Testers**: 120 part-time business users for UAT validation.

- **Technical Testers**: 18 technical specialists for integration and performance testing.

- **Regression Testing Strategy**

  With 3,000 regression test cases, GMC implemented a risk-based testing approach:

  - **Critical Path Testing**: 500 scenarios covering business-critical processes executed for every change.
  - **Module-Specific Regression**: 1,500 cases executed based on impacted modules.
  - **Extended Regression**: 1,000 cases executed quarterly regardless of change impact.

Testing Tools and Technologies

- **SAP Solution Manager Test Suite**: Central test management platform.
- **Galaxy (anonymized enterprise testing tool)**: Automation tool for complex scenarios – end-to-end testing and regression testing.
- **Interfaces Testing**: Opensource tools used for validating SAP S/4HANA interfaces.
- **Jenkins**: CI/CD orchestration for automated testing.
- **JIRA**: Defect management integrated with SAP Solution Manager.
- **Custom Dashboards**: Real-time testing metrics and KPIs.

Implementation Approach

- **Phase 1**: Test Repository Optimization

  GMC began with a comprehensive review of their test case repository:

  - **Test Case Audit**: Eliminated 3,200 redundant or obsolete test cases.
  - **Test Case Consolidation**: Merged similar scenarios, reducing count by 15%.
  - **Risk Classification**: Applied risk-based classification to all test cases.
  - **Automation Assessment**: Evaluated all manual tests for automation potential.
  - **Documentation Standardization**: Implemented consistent test case documentation.

- **Phase 2: Automation Framework Enhancement**

  To handle the scale efficiently, GMC substantially enhanced their automation capabilities:

  - **Framework Modernization**: Updated to the latest SAP TAF version compatible with SAP S/4HANA 2021.
  - **Script Refactoring**: Implemented modular design pattern for test scripts.
  - **Data Management**: Created centralized test data management system.
  - **Environment Management**: Implemented parallel test execution capabilities.
  - **Self-Healing Mechanisms**: Added intelligent recovery for failed automation steps.

- **Phase 3: Execution Strategy Implementation**

  GMC implemented a carefully structured execution approach for their 10,000 test cases:

  - **Parallel Execution Streams**: Multiple concurrent testing tracks by module.
  - **Shifted-Left Testing**: Integration of automated tests into development pipeline.
  - **Continuous Testing**: Daily execution of the core regression tests.
  - **Defect Triage**: Daily defect review and prioritization meetings.

Results and Benefits

GMC's structured approach delivered significant benefits such as:

- **Testing Efficiency**: Reduced testing cycle from 6 weeks to 3 weeks.
- **Defect Detection**: 32% increase in defects detected before production.
- **Resource Optimization**: 45% reduction in manual testing efforts.
- **Maintenance Cost**: 28% reduction in the overall maintenance testing costs.

Key Success Factors

- **Executive Sponsorship**: Strong support from CIO and business leaders.
- **Test Automation Investment**: Dedicated resources for automation development.
- **Business Engagement**: Early and continuous business user involvement.
- **Metrics-Driven Approach**: Clear KPIs and continuous measurement.
- **Knowledge Management**: Comprehensive documentation and training.

Lessons Learned

- **Start with Test Case Optimization**: Reducing test case redundancy was a critical first step.
- **Automate Strategically**: Focus automation on business-critical, high-execution-frequency tests first.

- **Data Management is Critical**: Test data preparation was initially underestimated.
- **Balance Coverage and Efficiency**: 100% test coverage is not always necessary or cost-effective.

Practical Takeaway: Begin any test improvement initiative with a thorough audit of the existing test assets. GMC eliminated over 3,000 redundant test cases before implementing automation, which significantly reduced the automation development effort, while maintaining comprehensive coverage.

Pro Tip: *Emphasize periodic test case audits to prune obsolete scripts, which reduces maintenance overhead, and accelerates automation.*

Study 2: SAP S/4HANA 1809 to 2310 Upgrade Testing Project

Company Profile

- **Company**: Financial Services International (FSI) (Anonymized)
- **Industry**: Banking and Financial Services
- **Revenue**: $3.5 Billion
- **Employees**: 11,000 worldwide
- **SAP Landscape**: SAP S/4HANA 2018 with Banking Industry Solution

Project Background

Financial Services International (FSI) implemented SAP S/4HANA 2018 four years earlier to support their core financial operations. With SAP's announced end of mainstream maintenance for their version, FSI initiated a project to upgrade to S/4HANA 2310. The company engaged a Global System Integrator (GSI) to perform the technical upgrade, while maintaining responsibility for User Acceptance Testing (UAT) internally.

Project Scope

Upgrade Components	Testing Scope
• Core SAP S/4HANA platform upgrade from 1809 to 2310 • Banking industry solution upgrade • SAP Fiori front-end server upgrade • Integration adapters for 22 connected systems • Custom code remediation (approximately 15,000 objects)	• GSI responsible for: Technical validation, integration testing, and security testing. • FSI responsible for: User acceptance testing (UAT), and regulatory compliance validation.

Table 14.7: *Project Scope*

Testing Challenges

- **Technical vs. Business Focus**: Balancing technical upgrade testing (performed by the implementation team) with business process validation (owned by the FSI).
- **Functional Changes**: New features and functionality changes between versions.
- **User Experience**: Significant UX changes in newer Fiori interfaces.
- **Custom Solutions**: Heavy customization requiring extensive remediation and testing.
- **Regulatory Validation**: Financial industry regulatory requirements.
- **Timeline Pressure**: Fixed 12-week window for full UAT execution.

UAT Testing Strategy

FSI defined clear objectives for their UAT program:

- Validate all business-critical processes work correctly post-upgrade.
- Ensure that regulatory compliance requirements are met.
- Verify user experience changes are acceptable.
- Confirm that the performance meets business requirements.
- Validate all interfaces with external systems.
- Ensure business continuity during and after cutover.

UAT Scope Definition

FSI implemented a risk-based approach to define UAT scope:

Process Criticality	Description	Test Coverage
Critical (P1)	Core financial processes	100%
High (P2)	Important daily operations	85%
Medium (P3)	Regular business processes	60%
Low (P4)	Occasional processes	30%

Table 14.8: *Risk-based Approach for UAT Design*

This resulted in 1,450 test cases across business areas:

- **Financial Core**: 480 test cases
- **Banking Operations**: 320 test cases
- **Treasury**: 280 test cases
- **Reporting and Analytics**: 220 test cases

- **Interfaces and Integration**: 150 test cases

Collaboration Framework

FSI established a clear framework for collaboration with the GSI:

- **Testing Phases Sequence**:

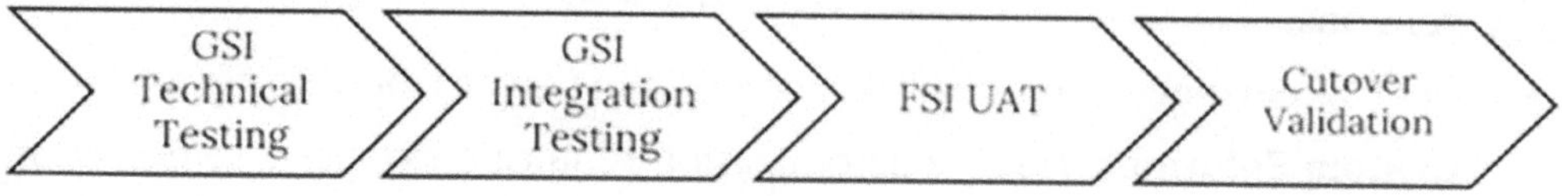

***Figure* 14.3:** *Testing Phases*

- **Handover Requirements:**
    - GSI to provide completed test results for all technical tests.
    - Detailed documentation of configuration changes.
    - Impact analysis of functional changes.
    - Zero P1/P2 defects before UAT commencement.
- **Defect Management Process**:
    - Shared JIRA-based defect management system.
    - Daily defect triage meetings with both teams.
    - Clear severity classification criteria.
    - Defined SLAs for defect resolution by priority.
- **Knowledge Transfer**:
    - GSI-led training on new functionality before UAT.
    - Technical documentation of all changes.
    - Sandbox environment for early user familiarization.

Results and Outcomes

The UAT program delivered significant value:

- 1,450 test cases executed with 98.5% pass rate.
- 142 defects identified, with 28 critical/high severities.
- 100% of critical/high defects resolved before go-live.
- All core business processes validated.
- Compliance requirements confirmed.
- 15% efficiency improvement in key transaction processing.
- No critical issues during cutover.

- 30% reduction in post-implementation support tickets compared to industry average.

UAT Implementation Approach

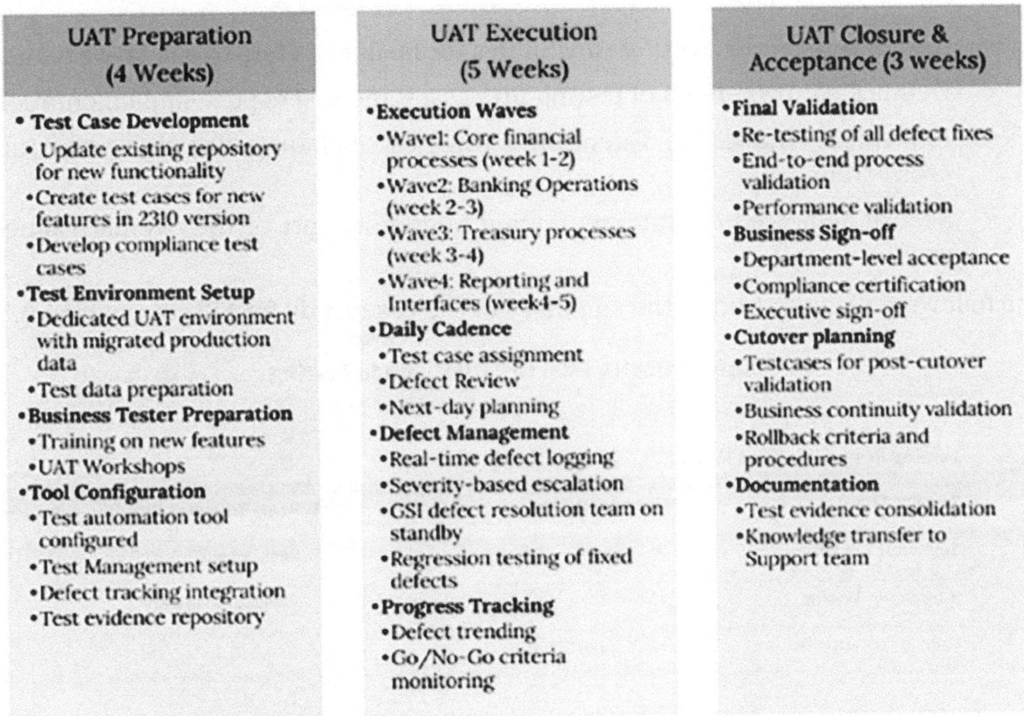

Figure 14.4: *UAT Implementation Approach*

Key Success Factors

- **Clear Responsibility Matrix**: Distinct separation between GSI and internal testing scope.
- **Business Engagement**: Early and continuous business stakeholder involvement.
- **Risk-Based Approach**: Focus on business-critical processes and compliance.
- **Structured Collaboration**: Well-defined processes for working with GSI partner.
- **Executive Support**: Visible leadership commitment to testing quality.

Transitioning from Project to Operational Testing

Following the successful S/4HANA upgrade, FSI recognized that maintaining testing excellence would require a structured approach beyond the project phase.

The organization strategically integrated testing into their ongoing SAP operations with five key objectives:

- Establish a Testing Center of Excellence (TCoE) that spans both project and operational phases.
- Create self-service testing capabilities for business users to validate changes.
- Define clear ownership of testing processes and assets post-implementation.
- Implement knowledge retention strategies, including documentation and cross-training.
- Secure dedicated operational testing budget as part of the overall business case.

The following diagram shows the summary of the case study for FSI (anonymized).

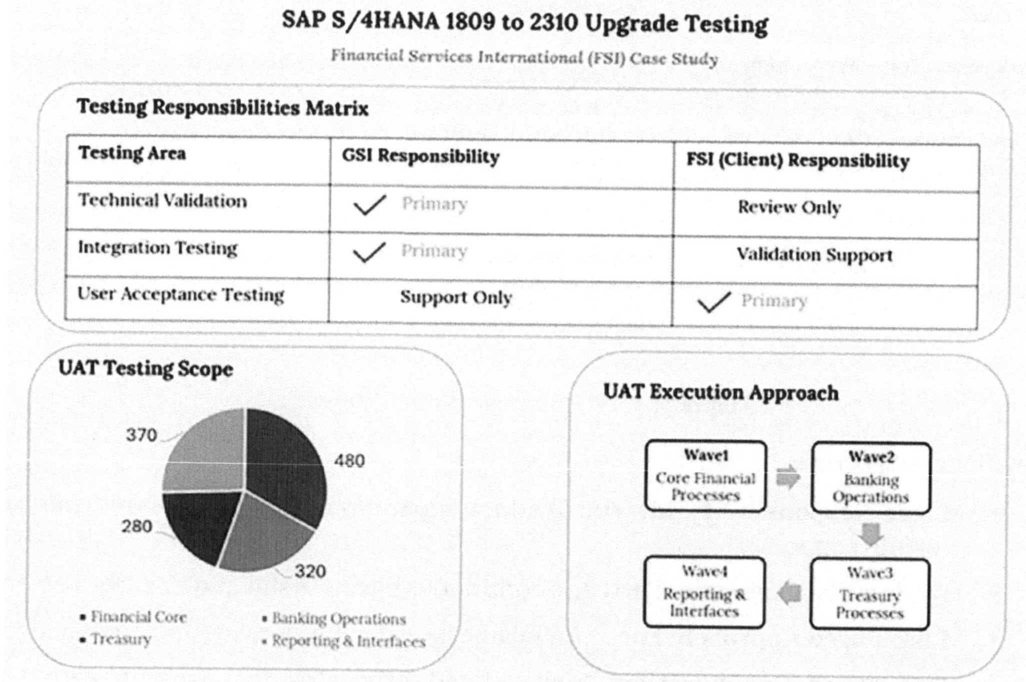

Figure 14.5: *FSI Case Study*

This case study demonstrates how a well-structured UAT approach can ensure business continuity during a major SAP S/4HANA version upgrade, while maintaining clear separation of responsibilities between the internal team and the implementation partner.

Pro Tip: *Value of clear roles and collaboration frameworks between internal teams and system integrators avoids scope confusion.*

Conclusion

Securing stakeholder buy-in for SAP S/4HANA testing demands more than just cost justification. It requires a compelling business case that clearly communicates testing's strategic value.

Thus, this chapter explored the common hurdles organizations face, from limited resources to the persistent view of testing as a cost center. It introduced a structured framework to help professionals craft persuasive business cases that resonate with executive decision-makers. Real-world case studies brought these concepts to life, showcasing proven strategies for gaining investment in large-scale SAP initiatives.

The next chapter explores the importance of AI and Agentic test strategies for SAP Testing projects.

References

- https://www.sap.com/india/about/customer-stories.html
- https://www.sap.com/india/events/sapphire/orlando.html
- https://podcast.opensap.info/inside-sap/
- https://www.sap.com/india/events/teched.html

Chapter 15
SAP and AI

Introduction

SAP is clearly undergoing a transformative shift by embedding Artificial Intelligence (AI) across its product suite, including SAP S/4HANA. SAP Sapphire 2025 marked a decisive pivot toward an AI-first enterprise platform, positioning SAP not just as an ERP platform, but as an orchestrator of intelligent business operations. According to Gartner, by 2026 nearly 80% of enterprises will use generative AI APIs or deploy generative AI-enabled applications in.

These AI-driven features bring immense potential - contextual recommendations, predictive insights, and automated decisions across procure-to-pay, order-to-cash, and finance transformation journeys. Yet they also redefine the scope of quality assurance.

Consider an enterprise using an AI-powered procurement recommendation engine in SAP S/4HANA. Unlike fixed rules, recommendations vary by user role, previous transactions, and external market data, making static test scripts ineffective. QE teams must develop adaptive validation techniques that combine automated tests with ongoing business feedback loops.

Structure

This chapter explores how *AI-driven and agentic testing approaches* provide the necessary framework to test what was once untestable, such as: Autonomous decision-making, dynamic recommendations, and intelligent automation within SAP S/4HANA.

In this chapter, we will cover the following topics:

- The AI Journey of SAP
- AI-Powered Testing
- AI-Infused Application's Testing
- Current State of AI Testing Tools
- Building SAP AI Skills for QA Teams

The AI Journey of SAP

SAP's AI journey began in earnest with the launch of SAP HANA in 2010. More than just an in-memory database, HANA's architecture was a strategic bet on the convergence of massive computational power and real-time analytics to unlock unprecedented business intelligence. This breakthrough laid the groundwork for intelligent enterprise systems.

By 2015, with SAP S/4HANA, AI capabilities were integrated directly into core business processes. The platform enabled real-time analytics and on-the-fly computations. For example, SAP S/4HANA can perform on-the-fly target cost calculations for manufacturing orders during goods receipt, allowing businesses to instantly analyze production costs without waiting for period-end closing. This capability provides immediate, data-driven cost insights to operational teams, enabling faster response and decision-making.

The 2017 introduction of SAP Leonardo marked SAP's first comprehensive AI platform strategy, named after Leonardo da Vinci to evoke innovation across disciplines. SAP Leonardo combined machine learning, IoT, blockchain, and advanced analytics into a single framework. It offered pre-built AI services accessible via APIs, allowing developers to embed AI functions like image recognition and text analysis without deep data science expertise. For example, in manufacturing, SAP Leonardo has been used for automated defect detection by analyzing images of production lines, significantly reducing faulty products, and improving quality control.

By 2020, SAP evolved from AI-powered insights to AI-driven actions. SAP AI Business Services began autonomously executing business tasks within defined parameters such as providing AI-assisted financial insights or intelligent document processing. This demonstrated AI's ability not only to understand context but also to act within it.

At SAP Sapphire 2025, the company unveiled what may be the most significant transformation in SAP applications: A comprehensive ecosystem of autonomous AI agents that can collaborate across business functions and even organizational boundaries. The three key highlights of AI at SAP Sapphire 2025 include:

- **Joule AI**: Now an omnipresent AI assistant embedded deeply within SAP applications. Joule acts like a digital copilot, helping users to complete tasks faster and smarter by providing contextual recommendations and insights within workflows.
- **Agentic AI:** It represents a step beyond assistants, agentic AI systems autonomously manage workflows, make decisions, and handle exceptions across SAP systems. It takes over routine and complex tasks without constant human intervention, except in truly exceptional cases.

- **Cloud-first Approach:** Innovations primarily roll out on cloud platforms such as SAP BTP and RISE, while on-premises landscapes see these features at a slower pace.

Challenges

Despite the compelling vision, SAP's AI transformation faces significant challenges that will determine its ultimate success. Technical complexity remains substantial—integrating AI capabilities across decades of accumulated business logic and data structures requires careful orchestration to avoid unintended consequences.

More fundamentally, the transition to AI-augmented business processes requires organizational change that extends far beyond technology implementation. Employees must learn to work alongside intelligent agents, managers must develop new approaches to oversight and accountability, and organizations should establish governance frameworks for autonomous systems.

Trust represents perhaps the greatest challenge. While SAP emphasizes "*human-in-the-loop*" approaches and transparent AI operations, the effectiveness of autonomous agents ultimately depends on users' willingness to delegate critical business decisions to artificial intelligence.

Opportunities

Just as ERP systems transformed organizational efficiency in the 1990s and cloud computing enabled global scalability in the mid-2000s, intelligent agents could define competitive advantage in the 2030s.

The future belongs to companies that embrace autonomous AI—not only will they accelerate beyond their peers, but they will redefine what is possible in their industries. Real-time optimization across global supply chains, instant adaptation to market changes, and personalized customer experiences at a massive scale become possible when intelligent agents can coordinate seamlessly across all business functions.

For SAP, this transformation represents both an enormous opportunity and an existential necessity. As cloud-native competitors build AI-first business applications, traditional enterprise software providers must demonstrate that their decades of business process expertise can be successfully augmented with cutting-edge AI capabilities.

The early indicators are promising. With over 130 AI-powered scenarios currently available and plans to expand to 400 by the end of this year, SAP is demonstrating the breadth and depth of AI integration possible when artificial intelligence is treated as core infrastructure, rather than supplementary functionality.

SAP's shift toward agentic AI creates unprecedented opportunities and responsibilities for Quality Assurance teams. Traditional QA focused on testing predetermined user journeys and system responses. With autonomous AI agents that can reason, learn, and make independent decisions, QA teams must evolve to become guardians of intelligent system behavior.

AI-Powered Testing

AI-powered testing symbolizes a fundamental leap forward in SAP quality management. AI-powered testing can transform how QE teams validate SAP S/4HANA implementations, migrations, and upgrades. Generative AI (Gen AI) and agentic approaches are no longer futuristic concepts. They are now operational tools that accelerate test creation, execution, and maintenance, while reducing risks and improving quality outcomes.

AI-powered testing, where generative AI models and agentic autonomous agents act as intelligent assistants throughout the test life cycle. These AI engines can automatically generate comprehensive test cases from business process models, mining millions of possible variants from SAP data sources. This drastically cuts the time and human effort needed for test design and data preparation.

Agentic AI agents go further by autonomously prioritizing test scenarios based on risk and usage analytics, executing tests, analyzing outcomes, and dynamically adjusting future test plans. They continuously learn from system changes, optimizing coverage and eliminating redundant tests to maximize business impact.

Examples of AI in practice include platforms like UiPath Test Cloud, INT4, Tricentis, Worksoft, OpenText, and KTern.AI, which leverage agentic AI to automate SAP interface validations, regression suites, and defect identification. They deliver measurable cycle time reductions and quality gains.

The World Quality Report 2024 confirms this shift, highlighting that over 70% of enterprises now embed AI in their testing lifecycle, with AI-driven automation rising to nearly 45% penetration in SAP environments. This trend signals AI's role in reshaping not just testing but the entire quality engineering function for SAP.

While AI-powered testing seems optimistic, human expertise remains vital for compliance and nuanced business validations. AI-powered autonomous testing agents take over repetitive, error-prone tasks, enabling teams to focus on strategy, innovation, and risk mitigation. This synergy will define next-generation SAP S/4HANA quality engineering, carving a path to faster innovation adoption and sustainable operational excellence. To summarize, investing in AI-driven testing is no longer a "*nice-to-have*" but a business imperative.

Here is a detailed comparison table that clearly contrasts traditional SAP S/4HANA testing with AI-powered testing across several key aspects, highlighting the benefits of AI-powered testing such as improved test coverage, fewer errors, and faster execution.

Aspect	Traditional SAP Testing	AI-Powered SAP Testing	Benefits of AI-Powered Testing
Test Case Generation	Manual creation based on requirements and doc	Automated from business process models using Gen AI	Saves time, reduces human error, generates more comprehensive cases
Test Data Preparation	Manual or semi-automated, labor-intensive	AI mines realistic test data from SAP tables	Covers diverse scenarios and variants for higher quality
Change Adaptation	Manual script updates prone to delays and gaps	Autonomous self-healing scripts through agentic AI	Faster adaptation to process or configuration changes
Risk Prioritization	Based on tester experience and static analysis	AI-driven dynamic risk-based prioritization	Focuses testing on high-impact areas improving defect detection
Test Execution Speed	Sequential runs, often slow	Parallel, autonomous execution by AI agents	Accelerates testing cycles, supporting rapid releases
Maintenance Overhead	High due to manual updates and redundancies in test library	Automated optimization removes redundant tests. Lean test library.	Reduces effort and cost, ensures up-to-date test suites
Error-Prone Tasks	Manual scripts susceptible to human errors	Automated scripts with AI validation and correction	Reduces defects caused by testing errors, increasing reliability
Test Coverage	Limited by manual resources and time	Expanded coverage through AI's exhaustive scenario mining	Ensures business and compliance coverage across global variants
Defect Identification	Reactive, often post-execution	Predictive analytics identify issues earlier	Earlier defect detection reduces rework and project risk
Resource Requirement	High dependency on skilled SAP testers	Enables testers to focus on strategy and complex reviews	Alleviates skill shortages, improves productivity

Cycle Time	Weeks to months for major regression runs	Days due to continuous AI-powered automation	Speeds up SAP releases and business agility
Example Tools Used	Manual scripting tools, traditional automation	UiPath Test Cloud, KTern.AI, SAP AI Foundation	Proven enterprise platforms with AI-driven capabilities

Table 15.1: *Differences between Traditional Testing and AI-Powered Testing*

In a major SAP S/4HANA Greenfield transformation, agentic AI tools enabled functional consultants to independently validate outbound EDI interfaces without relying on integration specialists. By loading thousands of real historical EDI messages, consultants used natural language chat to select relevant test cases and recreate authentic business documents inside SAP. The AI then compared newly generated outbound messages to historical originals, instantly identifying discrepancies caused by configuration changes. This autonomous, end-to-end process removed dependencies, sped up test cycles, and ensured consistent partner communications throughout the SAP migration, empowering business teams with faster, higher-quality validation.

AI Infused Application's Testing

Unlike conventional SAP testing that focuses on deterministic business logic, and predefined workflows, AI application's testing must account for probabilistic outcomes and dynamic learning capabilities. Traditional SAP testing validates whether a purchase order approval workflow follows exact business rules, but AI testing must also evaluate whether an intelligent document processing system can accurately extract data from invoices with varying formats, languages, and quality levels, while maintaining acceptable confidence thresholds.

For instance, an AI-powered invoice processing tool may encounter a new invoice layout or handwritten notes. QA must validate that despite these changes, the system accurately extracts critical fields like vendor name, amounts, and dates, and correctly flags low-confidence cases for manual review. This continuous learning nature creates an ongoing QA responsibility to ensure AI outputs remain aligned with business objectives.

Software Quality teams must develop frameworks for continuous testing that detect when AI agents begin making decisions that are technically correct but misaligned with business intent. For example, an AI might approve invoices with minor discrepancies, if it learns from past overrides, potentially exposing the business to risk. This situation requires a governance model where QA teams work closely with business stakeholders to define not only what AI systems should do but how they should evolve over time. Quality assurance thus transforms into quality governance.

Differences between AI-Infused Application's Testing and Traditional Testing

The core difference lies in what is being tested. Traditional SAP applications follow explicit programming logic where the same input consistently produces the same output, making test case design straightforward and results predictable. AI applications, however, involve machine learning models that make predictions or decisions based on patterns learned from training data, introducing inherent variability and uncertainty. This means test cases must evaluate model performance across diverse scenarios, edge cases, and data distributions rather than simply verifying functional requirements. Additionally, AI applications require continuous monitoring and revalidation as models may drift over time, or when exposed to new data patterns, unlike traditional applications that remain stable once deployed. The following table summarizes it very well.

Aspect	Traditional Testing	AI Application's Testing
Focus	Functional validation of business rules	Model accuracy and performance validation
Test Objectives	Verify deterministic input-output relationships	Evaluate probabilistic predictions and confidence levels
Success Criteria	Binary pass/fail based on exact matches	Statistical metrics (accuracy, precision, recall)
Data Requirements	Predefined test data with known outcomes	Diverse datasets including edge cases and real-world variations
Test Environment	Static test scenarios	Dynamic scenarios with varying data quality and formats

Table 15.2: *Differences between Traditional Testing and AI-Applications Testing*

Case Study

Consider a real-world example of testing an AI-powered invoice processing system integrated with SAP S/4HANA Finance. The following tables highlight the key differences between traditional testing methodology and modern AI testing methodologies across different testing types.

Key differences in Functional Testing:

Traditional Test Cases	AI-Enhanced Test Cases
TC001: *Valid Invoice Entry*	**TC001: *Document Recognition Accuracy***
Verify that the invoice with standard format (vendor name, amount, date, PO number) is correctly processed into SAP	Validate AI model accurately extracts vendor name, amount, date, and PO number from invoices with 95%+ confidence across 10 different invoice templates

Expected Result: Invoice data populates exactly in the accounting document	*Expected Result:* Extraction accuracy ≥95%, confidence score ≥0.85 for all key fields
TC002: Tax Calculation	**TC002: Multi-format Invoice Processing**
Verify tax calculation for invoice amount $1,000 with 10% tax rate equals $100	Validate AI processes invoices in PDF, image (JPEG/PNG), and scanned formats with consistent accuracy rates
Expected Result: Tax amount = $100.00 exactly	*Expected Result:* Accuracy variance <5% across all formats, processing time <10 seconds per document

Table 15.3: *Key Differences between Traditional Testing Methodology and Modern AI Testing Methodology in Functional Testing*

Key Differences in Data Validation Testing:

Traditional Test Cases	**AI-Enhanced Test Cases**
TC003: *Mandatory Field Validation*	**TC003: *Confidence Threshold Testing***
Verify system rejects the invoice when the vendor name field is empty	Test the AI model's behavior when the confidence score falls below a threshold (for example, <0.7) for extracted fields.
Expected Result: Error message "Vendor name is required"	*Expected Result:* Invoice flagged for manual review, human-in-the-loop workflow triggered.
TC004: *Data Format Validation*	**TC004: *Edge Case Handling***
Verify invoice date format validation (MM/DD/YYYY)	Validate AI handles corrupted images, rotated documents, handwritten notes, and multi-language invoices.
Expected Result: Invalid date formats rejected with a specific error	*Expected Result:* System maintains >80% accuracy on edge cases, properly escalates unclear documents.

Table 15.4: *Key Differences in Data Validation Testing*

Key Differences in Business Process Testing:

Traditional Test Cases	**AI-Enhanced Test Cases**
TC005: *Approval Workflow*	**TC005: *Intelligent Routing***
Verify invoice >$5,000 triggers manager approval workflow	Test AI-based routing system assigns invoices to appropriate approvers based on vendor, amount, and department patterns.
Expected Result: Workflow status = "*Pending Manager Approval*"	*Expected Result:* 95%+ routing accuracy, average processing time reduction of 40%.

TC006: Duplicate Detection	**TC006: Fuzzy Duplicate Detection**
Verify system rejects invoices with the same invoice number from the same vendor	Validate AI identifies potential duplicates even with minor variations in vendor names, amounts, or formats.
Expected Result: Error "*Duplicate invoice number detected*"	*Expected Result*: Duplicate detection rate >98%, false positive rate <2%.

Table 15.5: *Key Differences in Business Process Logic Testing*

Key differences in Performance Testing:

Traditional Test Cases	AI-Enhanced Test Cases
TC007: System Load	**TC007: Model Performance Under Load**
Process 1000 invoices simultaneously, verify system response time <5 seconds	Test AI model processing 1000+ invoices concurrently while maintaining accuracy and response time
Expected Result: All invoices processed within 5 seconds	*Expected Result*: Accuracy degradation <3%, average processing time <8 seconds per invoice
TC008: Database Performance	**TC008: Model Inference Optimization**
Verify invoice data retrieval from the database within 2 seconds	Validate optimized AI model inference time and resource utilization during peak loads
Expected Result: `Query response time ≤2 seconds`	*Expected Result*: Inference time <3 seconds, CPU usage <70%, memory usage <4GB

Table 15.6: *Key Differences in Performance Testing*

Key differences in Error Handling and Recovery Testing:

Traditional Test Cases	AI-Enhanced Test Cases
TC009: System Error Recovery	**TC009: Model Failure Graceful Degradation**
Verify system recovery when database connection fails during invoice processing	Test system behavior when the AI model fails or returns low confidence scores
Expected Result: Transaction rolled back, error logged, user notified	*Expected Result*: Fallback to manual processing, admin notification, audit trail maintained
TC010: Invalid Input Handling	TC010: Adversarial Input Testing
Test system response to invoice with negative amount (-$500)	Validate AI model robustness against intentionally misleading or corrupted invoice data

Expected Result: Business rule validation error displayed	*Expected Result*: Model maintains stability, flags suspicious patterns, prevents data poisoning

Table 15.7: *Key Differences in Error Handling and Recovery Testing*

Key differences in Security and Compliance Testing:

Traditional Test Cases	AI-Enhanced Test Cases
TC011: User Authorization	***TC011: AI Model Bias Testing***
Verify that only authorized users can approve invoices >$10,000	Test AI model for bias in vendor treatment, currency handling, or approval recommendations
Expected Result: Unauthorized access denied	*Expected Result*: No statistical bias detected across vendor categories, fair treatment validation
TC012: Audit Trail	***TC012: AI Decision Explainability***
Verify all invoice changes are logged with user ID and timestamp	Validate AI provides explainable decisions for invoice processing and can generate audit reports
Expected Result: Complete audit log maintained	*Expected Result*: Decision rationale available, model prediction explanations generated, compliance reports accessible

Table 15.8: *Key Differences in Security and Compliance Testing*

Key differences in Testing Metrics (Key Performance Indicators):

Traditional Metrics	AI-Specific Metrics
Pass/Fail Rate	Accuracy, Precision, Recall, F1-Score
Response Time	Inference Time, Model Latency
System Uptime	Model Availability, Confidence Distribution
Transaction Throughput	Prediction Throughput, Batch Processing Rate
Error Count	False Positive/Negative Rates, Confusion Matrix
Authorization Rules	Data Quality Scores
	Explainability Index, Bias Metrics

Table 15.9: *Key Differences in Metrics or Key Performance Indicators*

Current State of AI Testing Tools

The AI testing market is at the same stage that web application testing was in the early 2000s - full of potential but lacking mature solutions barring a very few. According to a recent market analysis, the global AI-enabled testing market is projected to grow at a compound annual growth rate (CAGR) of 20.9%, reaching over $3.8 billion by 2032. Organizations and professionals who recognize this opportunity and invest early in AI testing capabilities will benefit from first-mover advantages, establishing themselves as market leaders before this space becomes saturated.

Emerging Innovations Areas

Historically, QE technology has evolved hand-in-hand with software development trends: from manual scripting to record-and-playback tools, from GUI checks to API automation, and from waterfall to continuous integration pipelines. Similar evolutionary forces are driving innovation in AI-powered application testing, especially for SAP enterprise environments. Key emerging trends include:

- **AI-Driven Automated Test Generation and Maintenance:** Future testing platforms are leveraging AI to autonomously create and maintain comprehensive test suites that cover edge cases, adversarial inputs, and bias scenarios. For example, testing tools use machine learning to generate adaptive test cases that self-heal when UI or API changes occur, dramatically reducing flaky tests and maintenance overhead.
- **Intelligent Test Orchestration:** Advanced AI-driven test orchestrators monitor model performance and business KPIs to dynamically adjust test parameters and prioritize high-risk scenarios. This approach enables continuous quality assurance for AI models and workflows, ensuring alignment with evolving business goals. A practical instance is continuous validation pipelines that automatically expand testing around areas where AI confidence scores drop, preventing erroneous business decisions.
- **SAP-Native AI Testing:** Specialized solutions tailored for SAP environments will emerge, offering pre-configured test templates for common AI use cases such as intelligent document processing, predictive analytics, and automated decision-making.
- **Continuous AI Quality Assurance:** Continuous AI quality assurance tools will provide real-time detection of AI drift or degradation and trigger corrective interventions. This ensures model reliability over time without manual oversight. For example, AI can flag when an autonomous decision-maker starts deviating from compliance thresholds and automatically roll back changes or escalate issues.

Building SAP AI Skills for QA Teams

As organizations increasingly integrate artificial intelligence into their SAP landscapes, Quality Engineering (QE) teams face an unprecedented opportunity to transform their roles and capabilities. This section highlights key enablers for QE professionals to position themselves as valuable assets in the evolving enterprise technology ecosystem.

SAP AI Landscape Overview

Before diving into skill development, QE teams must understand the comprehensive SAP AI ecosystem.

Component	Purpose	QA Relevance
Joule Copilot	AI assistant across all SAP applications	Testing conversational AI, natural language processing, contextual responses
SAP AI Foundation	Development platform for custom AI solutions	Validating AI model deployment, performance testing, API testing
SAP AI Core	ML lifecycle management service	Model testing, MLOps validation, pipeline testing
SAP AI Services	Pre-built AI capabilities (document extraction, recommendations)	Functional testing of AI services, accuracy validation
Generative AI Hub	Access to multiple LLMs through a unified interface	Testing prompt engineering, model
SAP Joule Studio and Knowledge Graph	Development platform to build, extend, and run custom AI solutions and agents at scale	Testing the AI-powered tasks and agents.
UiPath Agents and Maestro **(SAP SOLEX *partner for Agentic Automation*)**	Development platform to build, customize, and orchestrate agents across SAP and non-SAP ecosystems of applications.	Testing the orchestrated end-to-end agentic workflows.

Table 15.10: *Core SAP AI Components*

Getting Started with SAP AI

This section provides a practical approach for QA teams to start exploring AI-enabled SAP applications without getting overwhelmed by the complexity. The following are AI resources offered by SAP for free in their SAP Learning (https://learning.sap.com):

- **Exploring the SAP Business AI Portfolio**

  Duration: 4-6 hours | Level: Beginner | Focus: Overview of SAP AI capabilities

- **Learning SAP AI Core Service on SAP BTP**

  Duration: 8-12 hours | Level: Intermediate | Focus: Hands-on AI model development

- **Generative AI at SAP**

  Duration: 2-3 hours| Level: Beginner | Focus: Understanding generative AI in SAP context

The following are community channels facilitated by SAP for AI topics (https://community.sap.com):

- **AI/ML Community Forum**: Peer discussions and expert insights
- **Blog Series**: "*Generative AI with SAP*" - comprehensive tutorial series

  https://community.sap.com/t5/technology-blog-posts-by-sap/generative-ai-with-sap-part-1-introduction-to-sap-business-ai/ba-p/13792501

- **Code Samples**: Reusable AI testing scripts and examples. https://github.com/orgs/SAP-samples/repositories

Conclusion

This chapter explored how AI is rapidly transforming SAP applications, and why testing AI-driven features differs fundamentally from traditional testing approaches. Unlike conventional testing of fixed workflows and deterministic logic, AI testing involves handling dynamic, probabilistic outcomes, and continuous learning systems.

Given today's limited but rapidly evolving AI testing solutions, there is a significant opportunity for technology innovators and service providers to create specialized tools aligned with SAP's AI strategy. For QA professionals, developing AI testing skills represents a valuable growth path with the potential for high impact, as these skills are increasingly sought in the market.

While AI technology and testing methodologies can initially seem complex, starting with foundational principles makes this transition manageable. Embracing AI testing empowers teams to enhance quality assurance effectiveness and future-proof their testing capabilities in an increasingly intelligent enterprise landscape.

References

- https://www.sap.com/estonia/events/sapphire/innovation-guide.html
- https://www.sap.com/events/sapphire/virtual.html
- https://learning.sap.com/courses/positioning-sap-spend-management-solutions/unlocking-better-insights-by-combining-sap-spend-management-with-sap-business-data-cloud
- https://www.cio.com/article/3990312/sap-goes-all-in-on-agentic-ai-at-sap-sapphire.html
- https://blogs.infosys.com/quality-engineering/erp-package-testing/how-gen-ai-can-change-sap-s-4hana-testing-and-qa.html
- https://community.sap.com/t5/enterprise-resource-planning-blog-posts-by-members/agentic-ai-testing-for-greenfield-s-4hana-outbound-interfaces-part-1/ba-p/14232427
- https://community.sap.com/t5/enterprise-resource-planning-blog-posts-by-members/int4-suite-agents-empowers-functional-consultants-to-test-integrated-sap-s/ba-p/14234100

Index

E

F

H

I

Q

R

S

T

U

V

W